Understanding and Working with Shame

This book discusses the pivotal role of shame in a wide range of mental disorders and as a driving force in societal polarization and escalating conflicts between nations and population groups.

Exploring the phenomenology of one of the most vulnerable and painful of human emotions, shame, Jørgensen dives deep into its many facets and the ways in which it manifests in mental illnesses and everyday life. Delving into an in-depth discussion of the differentiation between the moral and ethical feelings of guilt and shame, he presses the need to distinguish between constructive and destructive feelings of shame. He examines how shame permeates societal and cultural expectations, on both individual and collective levels. Solution-centric in its approach, the author not only discusses the destructive feelings of shame particularly common among individuals with more severe mental disorders, but also offers specific advice to therapists on how to deal with it.

The book will be an essential read for psychoanalysts, psychotherapists, philosophers, and anyone wanting to understand the power of shame in our lives.

Carsten René Jørgensen is a professor of clinical psychology at Aarhus University, Department of Psychology, trained in group analytic psychotherapy and (since 2001) attached to the Clinic for Personality Disorders, Aarhus University Hospital, Skejby.

Understanding and Working with Shame

Psychotherapeutic, Cultural and Philosophical Perspectives

Carsten René Jørgensen

Routledge
Taylor & Francis Group

LONDON AND NEW YORK

Designed cover image: Sad or depressed woman sitting cornered surrounded by pointing hands. Credit: rudall30. Getty Images

First published in English 2025
by Routledge
4 Park Square, Milton Park, Abingdon, Oxon OX14 4RN

and by Routledge
605 Third Avenue, New York, NY 10158

Routledge is an imprint of the Taylor & Francis Group, an informa business

First published in Danish by Hans Reitzels Forlag 2023

British Library Cataloguing-in-Publication Data
A catalogue record for this book is available from the British Library

ISBN: 978-1-032-86071-8 (hbk)
ISBN: 978-1-032-83602-7 (pbk)
ISBN: 978-1-003-52117-4 (ebk)

DOI: 10.4324/9781003521174

Typeset in Optima LT Std
by Newgen Publishing UK

To Vibeke, Mathilde and Johanne

I am grateful to the many who showed me the profound trust of sharing some of their innermost thoughts and experiences while engaging in psychotherapeutic treatment with me or by participating in the interviews I carried out in connection with various research projects. For obvious reasons, they will remain anonymous. Your contributions were indispensable, and without them, the book would not have been possible. Thank you!

Contents

1 Introduction

Everybody experiences shame and has at times been overwhelmed by painful feelings of shame, to varying degrees. Nevertheless, it is a feeling that most of us try to hide and which we are reluctant to talk about. Paradoxically, the less prepared we are to acknowledge and talk about our shame, the more likely it is to torment and control us (Brown et al., 2011, p. 360). Thus, I am almost ashamed to admit that I have only recently – after more than 30 years of working with psychopathology and psychotherapy – fully realized how central the feeling of shame is in human psychology and, not least, in the difficulties many people with severe mental disorders struggle with on a daily basis.

But what sort of feeling is shame? How is shame experienced? Are feelings of shame always negative and destructive, or might they also serve a constructive function for us as individuals and for our social communities? It will be obvious to most people that shame can contribute to the repression and restriction of human freedom, but might some forms of shame be a key condition for freedom and our capacity for social functioning in human communities? Might shame contribute to our understanding of current dysfunctions in modern society, including escalating internal division and polarization as well as escalating intercultural conflicts? And might shame exacerbate psychological vulnerabilities and lead to the development of mental illness? Might shame even be a central component of certain mental disorders? These are some of the key questions that I will address in this book.

Among other consequences, shame is associated with a general feeling of being wrong, inferior or inadequate, either (1) because the person is not living up to prevailing ideas about an exciting, perfect life and self – ideas that many people go to great lengths to try to realize, even if they seem unrealistic for most people – or (2) because the person is unable or unwilling to live up to certain normative ideas about what they are supposed to be like and act in order to be accepted as a good, normal, decent person in a given social group, culture or subculture. Shame is a fundamental aspect of being human, and we can trace this feeling far back in cultural history. The Bible describes how shame was introduced into human life when Adam and Eve ignored the divine prohibition against eating from the Tree of Life and were

DOI: 10.4324/9781003521174-1

banished from the Garden of Eden. Many ancient Greek philosophers also addressed the feeling of shame (see Chapter 2). The groundbreaking English evolutionary scientist Charles Darwin also studied shame as a peculiar and uniquely human feeling.

In connection with in-depth analyses of interview material from a qualitative study of severe identity disturbances in persons with borderline personality disorders (Jørgensen & Bøye, 2022) I was struck by the key role of shame in the psychological pain that they, and many other people with psychological difficulties, experience: shame because they see themselves as fundamentally inadequate or wrong, defective, unwanted and unlovable; or, in some cases, a feeling of not being seen and treated as a person but as an inferior being, an animal or an inanimate object that is not attributed any value or met with respect. This latter experience is a severe and unambiguously destructive form of shame.

However, shame is much other and more than this, and we need a much more nuanced and dimensional understanding of shame than the concept that has prevailed so far; an understanding capable of capturing how shame can be constructive and necessary for our social functioning as well as severely destructive to our psychological development and well-being. Thus, viewing shame exclusively as a negative and scandalous feeling that we should do everything to eliminate in all its manifestations would be an unsophisticated and simplistic understanding. The core goal of this book is to present a psychological study of the feeling of shame that takes an in-depth view, examining the deep roots of shame in basic human sociality – shame as an intersubjective affect – as well as a broad view, exploring the full scope of the feeling. Shame is addressed as a dimensional phenomenon ranging from brief, constructive shame to chronic and severely destructive shame that is closely associated with painful subjective experiences and mental illness.

As discussed in the following chapters (see, especially, Section 3.1), the particular human capacity for shame is significant for our ability to sense, respect and defend our own and others' personal integrity, inner space and boundaries of intimacy. This capacity is also crucial to our capacity for self-reflection and, not least, our ability to view ourselves from outside, from someone else's perspective, and to regulate our behaviour in ways that enable us to function in interpersonal relations and be part of well-functioning social communities. On the other hand, shame can also be a deeply destructive feeling that renders us susceptible to developing a variety of mental disorders, self-destructive behaviour, abuse and relational difficulties, just as it may be a contributing factor in painful loneliness.

Destructive shame may also prevent people from seeking help and sharing their difficulties with others, because it comes with a strong inherent urge to retreat and avoid interpersonal contact. Destructive shame in particular can be described as anti-therapeutic, in the sense that it undermines a person's tendency to seek, engage in and benefit from psychotherapeutic treatment. This is especially pronounced if the person encounters a therapist who is not attentive to or capable of addressing their shame when it is manifested in the therapeutic relationship and in the psychotherapeutic space. This book presents my understanding of shame in its many variations and how we might approach and help to dampen and heal shame in psychotherapeutic work. In a sense, shame remains a rather unexplored feeling in both theoretical and, especially, empirical terms. However, I will attempt to include existing empirical studies wherever they are relevant, and my discussion is based on existing psychological theory, philosophy, sociology, anthropology and cultural analyses.

1.1 Shame in contemporary culture

Once we begin to explore the topic of shame, it seems to be a ubiquitous feeling that plays an increasingly important role in the public space. At the same time, however, it seems unclear exactly what shame is and whether everyone means the same thing when they speak of shame. Many young people, not least young women from religious and patriarchal or authoritarian environments, have articulated how they struggle with and try to escape feelings of shame which they feel restrict their ability to live out their freedom and sexuality (see, e.g., Al-Mersal, 2022; Röst, 2021; Slimani, 2018). The Norwegian TV series *Skam* (Shame), which attracted considerable international attention for its groundbreaking presentation of everyday life among a group of teenagers, has addressed some of the emotional challenges related to being young today in the borderland between physical reality and life on social media, between the real and the digital self.

We are living in a late modern culture, where positive thinking is seen as the answer to a wide variety of psychological difficulties, and where the urge to appear 'happy' and 'successful' seems almost as natural and necessary as breathing to many, especially young people, under the motto that 'you can do anything you put your mind to'. 'Happiness' is perceived as a manifestation and result of a successful life (Schreiber, 2022, p. 41). Anyone who is not happy, or able to appear happy, is weak, has made bad choices and is at risk of being marginalized. In a culture where anything, allegedly, is possible and where everyone has ample and equal opportunities to be happy, it is shameful not to be happy, to be unable or unwilling to appear successful. It is shameful for a person to be sad or preoccupied with real difficulties in life, perhaps because they were subjected to experiences that were beyond their control and which are not easily remedied by positive thinking or attempts at reframing negative incidents as 'excellent opportunities for growth'. To the extent that we learn to focus exclusively on positive feelings and stories about ourselves, while heavier and more challenging (some might say 'negative') feelings, including shame, are repressed and seen as taboo, we risk losing (or failing to develop) our capacity for embracing, articulating and detoxifying these feelings, psychological pain and human suffering in general. When we are struck by these emotions – as we inevitably are, because they are inescapable aspects of being human – we may find ourselves completely naked, unprepared and defenceless. Thus, we need to develop our ability to embrace, address and cope with shame and other challenging human emotions.

'Cancel culture', which is becoming increasingly widespread, especially on social media, singles out and seeks to socially eradicate persons whose thinking or lifestyles differ from our own, or from those of a dominant and vocal social group, by labelling them immoral. This trend may be seen as a manifestation of a widespread urge to shame and exclude what we do not like or do not want to tolerate. Body activists fight the stigmatization and shaming of bodies that do not meet narrowly defined beauty ideals and ideas about what constitutes a 'normal', 'healthy' body, just as a growing number of other minority and identity groups struggle to be accepted on equal terms with others and escape the feelings of shame that come from being seen as deviant or inferior. In addition, there is growing focus on the key role that more destructive and chronic shame, in particular, may play in a wide range of mental disorders (see Chapter 5). In light of the many different contexts in which shame appears as an important reference in descriptions of life and behaviour in modern society, we need a nuanced understanding of shame and its many different manifestations, which include dramatically different degrees of intensity and appear in many different areas of people's individual and social lives.

The global attention stirred up by the drawings of the prophet Muhammad in the Danish newspaper *Jyllands-Posten* many years ago illustrates how a conflict can escalate out of control when we are unable or unwilling to understand each other across (sub)cultures and thus activate feelings of shame. With reference to the principle of freedom of speech, *Jyllands-Posten* insisted that everyone should be prepared to endure taunts and ridicule. Because taunts and ridicule typically trigger feelings of shame, this insistence on freedom of speech was also, in practice, an insistence that Muslims had to be prepared to endure shame. In the wake of the national crisis that the drawings sparked, there were intense debates about how we can strike the right balance between the inviolability of freedom of speech and Danish laws prohibiting acts or statements of blasphemy and racism. However, another topic in the debate was how we can establish respectful interactions based on mutual acknowledgement of each other's boundaries without undue respect for religious dogma and institutions.

It is worth considering whether we also need to reflect on how and why some people find insults to their honour to be so shameful and intimidating that they react with intense anger, aggression and violence – even though this cannot in itself tell us how we should act in similar situations in the future. There is no simple or standard answer to how we can strike the right balance between these concerns. However, we do need to address and consider as many relevant aspects as possible, including the dynamic psychological connections between affronts to a person's sense of honour and pride, shame and escalating aggression and violence. This is a further reason why it is important to examine the phenomenology and psychology of shame more closely.

Feelings of shame are often hidden or masked, even to ourselves, and when they do come to the surface, we have an almost instinctive urge to push them away and hide them, both from others and from ourselves (see Section 4.3). Shame is an unwanted feeling that shuns light and attention. This is both because feelings of shame are painful and because exposing our shame to others is in itself shameful and makes us feel small, vulnerable and weak. That is why shame often operates unseen, in the sense that it often controls our experiences and behaviour unbeknownst to us. On the other hand, if we dare to look our shame in the eye and examine what it is about, we can achieve a better understanding of ourselves and our culture. In order to detoxify destructive feelings of shame and dismantle their negative impact on our life and actions, we need to shine a light on them instead of allowing them to hide in the dark, out of sight. To the best of our ability, we should air them out in an open dialogue with others.

This is arguably what happens when the LGBTQ+ environment organizes Pride parades, challenging the obviously antiquated idea that people should be ashamed to be homosexual, for example, and instead celebrating and taking pride in diverse forms of sexuality and gender identities. As more and more people come forward, in part in extension of the MeToo movement, to speak about being abused or humiliated by individuals in positions of power (or about being guilty of abuse themselves) – experiences that are often associated with profound shame – this, too, should be seen as a positive development, as it makes it less likely that shame is allowed to remain hidden in the dark, where it can ruin people's lives. The positive impact of course requires that the growing openness unfolds in ways that do not primarily result in new abuse, escalating shame and spirals of victimization but instead lead to new insights and initiate the necessary ongoing dialogue about how we should perceive and treat each other as human beings, with mutual empathy and respect.

The growing prominence of feelings of shame in contemporary society may, to some extent, be due to an internal conflict in modern Western culture that mainly affects adolescents and young adults whose identity development is still ongoing. On the one hand, modern Western culture provides an unprecedented degree of freedom to be whoever you are and wish to be. On the other hand, it also rests, to a high degree, on a fairly narrow – and largely tacit – notion of normality, which means that large sectors of modern meritocratic societies (see Section 6.1) are not, in practice, particularly welcoming to diversity. This affects individuals who do not conform to the prevailing high performance standards in education, at work and in the competition to be the most interesting and attractive date, friend, partner or network connection on various social platforms. This internal conflict or systemic dysfunction means that if someone does not live up to prevailing performance requirements, this mainly falls back on individuals, who perceive themself as inadequate, inferior or defective because they have failed to realize their assigned 'freedom' in certain appropriate ways; an experience that is closely associated with shame.

1.2 Different understandings of shame

Although we can find references to shame dating all the way back to ancient Greek philosophy (Aristotle, ca. 350 BCE/2020), it is not until the 1970s that shame becomes a significant theme, initially mainly in psychoanalysis and subsequently in academic psychology (see Chapter 2). In recent decades in particular, the interest in shame has spread to many other disciplines, including sociology (Scheff & Retzinger, 1991; Neckel, 1991, 2009), history (Frevert, 2017/2020, 2020/2023), philosophy (Scheler, 1957/1913); Sartre, 1943/2018; Zahavi, 2013, 2014) and areas of clinical psychology (Retzinger, 1991; Tiedemann, 2010). In psychoanalysis, the main contributors to our understanding of the psychology of shame are Helen Lewis (1971), Leon Wurmser (1981b, 2019), Günther Seidler (1995/2000) and, more indirectly, Heinz Kohut (1971) (cf. Morrison, 1989). Both psychoanalysis and clinical psychology focus mainly on destructive shame and its negative consequences.

Affect theory (Tomkins, 1963; Nathanson, 1992) has also addressed the topic of shame but often with an overly one-sided focus on the technical aspects of specific affective mechanisms. Furthermore, early affect theory in particular conflated feelings of shame and guilt (Tomkins, 1963). When Erving Goffman, one of the principal figures of sociology, writes about the human urge to manage others' impression of ourselves (impression management) in order to avoid embarrassment, this could arguably be seen to contain a major component of shame, even though Goffman does not actually use this term. Similarly, it could be argued that stigmatization, which is another key social phenomenon that Goffman (1963) addresses in his work, is closely associated with shame (see Section 6.1). Thus, shame is relevant well beyond the boundaries of psychology, even if the term is not always explicitly used or when it is used somewhat vaguely.

1.3 Shame poisons people and relationships

Shame can poison and destroy relationships and be a contributing cause of painful loneliness. Destructive feelings of shame act as a wall that divides and creates distance between people. They block our capacity for intimacy and interpersonal trust and our ability to feel at ease and acknowledged in social communities. When we are overwhelmed by destructive shame, we can come to feel that we have dropped out of or been excluded from the social order and are losing our place in the world and in the human community. Over time, destructive shame can erode and hamper the development of a mature and well-functioning identity. If someone perceives themselves as inherently wrong or inferior, letting others in and allowing them to see who the person really is can be associated with considerable fear of rejection and abandonment. If someone is convinced that there is something inherently wrong with them, and that they are essentially inadequate, it is difficult to let friends, a partner, family and therapists in and to engage in deeper emotional and psychological contact. While such contact is crucial for avoiding feelings of loneliness, it also increases the person's vulnerability, including vulnerability to shame, if others dislike, disparage or even despise or ridicule what they see when the person shows their true self.

Thus, someone who is tormented by shame might feel the need to do everything in their power to keep others from discovering how defective and inadequate they really are. The first solution that comes to mind is often to keep others at bay, preventing them from getting too close and hiding behind various masks or facades. In this way, they seek to give the appearance of being perfect, carefree and happy or of having no need for positive attention and approval, even though they are in fact lonely and feel completely alone with shameful self-perceptions and self-aspects that have to be hidden from view. Many young people, in particular, struggle with shame because they feel wrong or inadequate in their persistent efforts to realize a vision of the perfect life that most of us know, deep down, is unrealistic. To deal with the many indications of stress and psychological pain that this leads to, we all need to get better at acknowledging that we are all 'just' human, vulnerable, with faults and deficits. We also need to develop our capacity for containing, recognizing and decoding feelings of shame, especially destructive shame, to reduce the power they hold over us. One of the primary conditions of this is to achieve a deeper, more nuanced understanding of shame.

1.4 Shame and human vulnerability

The deeper we delve into the psychology of shame, the clearer it becomes how widespread this feeling is and how crucial it is to key aspects of human psychology and behaviour. Feelings of shame are associated with awareness of our own vulnerability. We come face to face with this vulnerability when we are confronted with others' gaze at and assessment of our ways of being and acting in the world. The uniquely human capacity for feeling shame is crucial to our ability to enter into well-functioning relationships and social communities and our ability to read and respect each other's boundaries and personal integrity. It makes us pause, self-reflect and perhaps adjust our behaviour in situations where we might be compromising ourselves or violating the boundaries of others. That is the function of constructive shame. On the other hand, feelings of shame are also a key driver of some of the darker sides of human life, including the development of psychological disorders as well as anger, hate, violence and other forms of aggression in interpersonal interactions, which are often related to unbearably shameful experiences of inferiority and perceived loss of or threats to our own honour and dignity.

In these cases, the shame is clearly destructive and a possible vulnerability factor for psychological suffering, mental illness and human destructiveness.

Everyone is familiar with shame as an unpleasant feeling that can suddenly overwhelm us when we least expect it. We have all had the experience of saying or doing something embarrassing or ridiculous in a social setting where we felt we were the object of disapproval, laughter and friendly – or not so friendly – ribbing. In these situations, we feel the pang of shame and the discomfort of feeling wrong and worrying that our place and standing in a social group might be at risk. We blush, lower our gaze and lose the ability to think clearly, and everything suddenly seems to confirm how wrong, inferior and ridiculous or even despicable we are, in our own and others' eyes. Most of us have experienced being rejected or passed over by others and know how this can make us feel inadequate, inferior and wrong. These experiences are closely associated with shame. In these situations, we might react by retreating. We decide not to put ourselves forward the next time round, or, to some extent, avoid putting ourselves in social situations where we risk being passed over or let down by others (see Table 1.1). We do this because we are afraid of experiencing the same painful feeling of shame and resulting defensive reactions, which might limit our social life and thus our psychological well-being, in some cases severely, in other cases less severely and temporarily but still psychologically painful.

Most of us have, to some degree, had the experience of failing to live up to our family's implicit or explicit expectations or, in certain situations, failing to fill the role we have, for various reasons, chosen or been assigned in the family. When that happens, we might encounter reactions from others in our family that make us shameful. We may be struck with emotional anguish over being wrong because we fail to be and act the way we have learned we should in order to be deserving of others' love and approval – anguish that is often driven by shame. Similarly, feeling different from others and not quite fitting in, either in our family or in our social group, can be a double-edged sword associated with ambivalence and, possibly, shame. On the one hand, we might feel that being different is proof of our individuality, independence and unique identity. On the other hand, being different and standing out from the group might also make us feel wrong, inadequate and inferior in relation to others and the prevailing expectations and standards of normality in our family or the social group we are and wish to be a part of.

The shame-related challenges that come from feeling wrong and inadequate may be further exacerbated by religious beliefs. Deeply religious people may be shameful because they perceive themselves as being sinful and failing to live up to – sometimes superhuman – requirements of how, for example, a good Christian or Muslim is supposed to live and act. Furthermore, shame has historically been closely associated with human sexuality, especially female sexuality, as strict religious beliefs and rules can heighten the challenges of debilitating shame. Sadly, this remains a significant problem in certain (sub)cultures, while it seems to be gradually disappearing in other, modern (sub)cultures.

Danish journalist Souha Al-Mersal (2022, p. 36) has painted a powerful picture of how she sees Muslim women being held down by a culture with a strong component of shame: that they 'have to live in submissiveness for life'. They are told that boys have unlimited possibilities, because boys have no shame, while girls have all the shame: 'They tell us that our bodies, hair and voices are associated with shame, they tell us we need to adapt'.

From a related perspective, in her novel *The Last One*, French-Algerian writer Fatima Daas (2021) describes how living as a lesbian woman in a Muslim community makes her feel deeply torn between different identities and between her own individuality and her concern for the community around her, especially her own family. This internal conflict leads to identity issues and shame. She writes (Daas, 2021, pp. 38–40) that she feels like a sinner and a bad Muslim, that God doesn't love her like she loves him and will abandon her, because she is a lesbian.

Daas also describes how her urge to be herself, speak her mind and show her emotions clashes with her desire not to bring shame on her parents for failing to live up to the religious rules (ibid., p. 178): 'What will our families think when they find out that …'. She will bring shame upon her family and soil its reputation. She feels like a bad Muslim, a sinner and a liar, and she is afraid she might end up in Hell because she is a lesbian, does not live up to the community's (faith-based) expectations and is doing all the 'wrong' things.

People who have been subjected to physical or sexual abuse or other traumatic experiences (for example, acts of war or serious accidents) may find that these experiences caused a painful fracture in or irreparable harm to their sense of identity and self-perception. They may also struggle to understand and share this experience with others, and they may be unable to see how they can ever repair the damage that the traumatic experiences inflicted on the self. Their traumatic experiences may leave them feeling inherently wrong, defective, broken or different from other ('normal') people in a negative and painful way. Feeling a painful undercurrent of alienation and detachment from others, they do not feel that they are on the same wavelength as or in authentic contact with others because the traumatic events have changed them and put up a wall between the self and others. The bridge to others has fallen down (Kaufman, 1985).

All of these consequences may be driven by shame about what happened to them and their subsequent feelings of being defective or 'damaged goods'. Being the victim of sexual abuse can scar a soul for life, and the victim may fear that others will be able to see these scars and will therefore see the self as defective and irreparably damaged. In this light, it is understandable that the person might want to hide the perceived scar or stigma, even though they may never be able to fully erase all the scars from the abuse or avoid being reminded of them, for example when they are close to others or otherwise find themselves in situations that activate memories of the abuse, and the related shame overwhelms the self.

1.5 Shame manifested in the form of anger and aggression

We may also react with anger and aggression when we sense the feeling of shame coming on (see Table 1.1). This can be expressed in many – mainly destructive – ways. For example, we might feel the urge to mock, disparage, ridicule or attack the 'other' or 'others' we feel have somehow rejected us or otherwise put us in a shameful situation. In some cases, this can develop into a more general urge to attack, mock and disparage others. This is especially common on social media but also occurs in more extreme forms, for example in the behaviour of so-called 'incels': men who react to perceived, general rejection from women by attacking and even killing more or less randomly chosen women, typically younger women (see Section 6.2). Related psychological dynamics may be at play in connection with school shootings and other forms of random mass killings. More generally, escalating spirals of shame and anger can develop into blind, uncontrolled and unreflective rage that consumes the person until they act with no thought for the consequences for themselves or others. Driven by shame, anger and perhaps other strong affects that the killer does not understand or is unable to achieve the necessary reflective distance from, they (almost always a man) have no way to stop this self-perpetuating spiral before it becomes a serious threat to both the person themselves and the targets of their unbridled hate.

Turning again to aggression and anger as a more general reaction to and strategy for dealing with destructive shame, one of the immediate perceived psychological 'advantages' of 'going on the offensive' instead of withdrawing

Table 1.1 Two main categories of specific expressions of feelings of shame: internalizing and externalizing manifestations of shame

Primary direction of manifestations and reactions	Internalizing, inward	Externalizing, outward
Initial and visible manifestations	Withdrawal, hiding, becoming invisible; being passive, receptive, defensive	Aggression, anger; active behaviour, being on the offensive
Subsequent visible manifestations	Social isolation (loneliness), rumination over own faults and deficits	Blames, despises and attacks others, who are seen as being the cause of perceived injustices against the self
Clearly destructive manifestations	Self-hatred, self-contempt, self-harm (masochism)	Hate, violence against others (sadism)

when affected by shame may be that this means abandoning a passive, defensive and inward position in favour of a more active, assertive and outward approach. Initially, and superficially, this avoids the self-contempt, self-pity and sadness that often accompany destructive feelings of shame. Instead of despising and disparaging themselves – and experiencing others' contempt – the person hates others. To the extent that the person manages to escape the painful acknowledgement of their own shame, this may also serve to protect their self-esteem, which, at the very least, is jeopardized when they are struck by shame over being exposed, passed over, rejected (feeling ignored, insignificant and inferior in the eyes of others) or are otherwise put into a humiliating situation.

Generally, shame-driven anger and aggressive behaviour can be seen as attempts to stabilize fragile self-esteem, which may be severely jeopardized if the self is overwhelmed by shame. Similarly, aggressive behaviour and hate directed at others may be attempts at reclaiming or defending the person's own honour and self-respect and, possibly, diverting their own and others' attention from their own shame. The internalizing and inward manifestations described above should basically be seen as the most immediate and 'natural' human expression of shame (cf. the urge to hide, disappear and so forth as part of the 'nature' of shame), while the more outward expressions in the form of aggressive attacks on others should be understood more as reactions to – and attempts at escaping – shame.

Inward and outward manifestations of shame are not necessarily mutually exclusive, just as shame and guilt may, of course, also coexist. Some people mainly manifest shame as reactions directed at their own self, while others are much more likely to try to handle shame through various forms of outward behaviour. These reaction forms may be described as, respectively, internalizing and externalizing reaction modes, just as we speak of predominantly internalizing or externalizing forms of psychopathology (Costa & McCrae, 1992; Blatt, 2008). Destructive feelings of shame and their role as the driving force of psychopathology are most obviously evident in internalizing types of pathology, such as eating disorders, depression, certain forms of anxiety and certain personality disorders. On the other hand, for example, ADHD, psychopathy and dissocial personality disorder are pathological conditions with primarily externalizing concrete manifestations, in which shame appears to play a much lesser role; in psychopathy, all manifestations of shame are remarkably absent (see Chapter 5).

A wide range of factors can influence whether feelings of shame are primarily manifested as internalizing or externalizing behaviours in an individual. Temperamental factors, attachment style, psychological defence structure (predominantly inward or outward defensive reactions), gender-specific cultural and subcultural norms of socially acceptable behaviour, specific factors in the individual's childhood family environment and socialization and, not least, basic personality features must all be assumed to have a significant influence on the manifestation of shame in a person's ways of being and acting. For example, we should expect that someone who is generally hostile, impulsive, externalizing and has a low degree of conscientiousness in their interpersonal interactions (cf. the personality features of agreeableness and conscientiousness) will be much more likely to try to prevent feelings of shame from occurring by blaming or attacking others in various ways. On the other hand, in individuals who are generally more introvert, internalizing and have a high level of conscientiousness and empathy, we would expect shame to be mainly manifested as more internalizing behaviour (self-harm, social isolation and so forth). Thus, we should expect considerable individual variation in the tendency to react with either shame or guilt in various situations, depending on socialization, history, personality and embeddedness in a specific culture (for a precise differentiation between shame and guilt, see Section 4.4). However, this remains an understudied area.

Shame is, thus, a potentially extraordinarily painful, at times unbearable and highly toxic feeling that can break a person down from inside and be a contributing cause of mental illness as well as physical and psychological violence against others, acts of war and destructive societal polarization. This is especially true if we fail to recognize and deal with destructive feelings of shame and instead, more or less deliberately, allow them to control our ways of being and acting in the world. Destructive feelings of shame can be a vulnerability factor in the development of psychological difficulties, a secondary consequence of mental illness or a key element in the phenomenology of certain mental disorders, that is, the specific manifestation of a mental disorder in the individual's subjective experience (see Chapter 5).

1.6 Shame as a moral and ethical feeling

> The thing that moves us to pride or shame is not the mere mechanical reflection of ourselves, but an imputed sentiment, the imagined effect of this reflection upon another's mind.
>
> (Cooley, 1902, p. 152)

Shame and guilt can be considered moral and ethical feelings, in the sense that they are closely associated with human existence, as we are inherently social beings with a fundamental need for positive attention and recognition from others. The main distinction between the two moral and ethical feelings is that we typically feel guilt over specific acts, which we may be able to atone or seek forgiveness for and thus dampen or escape our feeling of guilt, while shame – destructive shame in particular – is associated with a much more fundamental and inescapable feeling of being wrong and inadequate (see Section 4.4).

As social beings who need well-functioning relationships and embeddedness in social communities to survive, we need to be able to function in social settings. In interactions with others, we have to be and act in ways that make others want to connect and engage with us in interpersonal relationships.

Among other issues, morality and ethics are about how people are supposed to be and act in interactions with others and in the world overall, including what it takes for an individual to be recognized as a decent and socially accepted person and to be able to function as an equal member of social communities.

Feelings of shame and guilt signal that the ways in which we are and act are socially, morally or ethically unacceptable or, at least, out of step with outside expectations – and that our relationships with important others may therefore be jeopardized. In that sense, shame and guilt are associated with the human ability to live in accordance with the moral and ethical rules that are necessary for a high degree of interpersonal trust and well-functioning human communities. Shame and guilt confront us with our basic social and relational way of being; they are emotions that spring from our awareness of how we are always already embedded in relationships with others and in social communities that are crucial for our self-perception and behaviour in the world (Zahavi, 2014, p. 234). Perhaps the most fundamental function of these two feelings is to halt – and, in a sense, act as an inner punishment for – dissocial behaviour that might harm others and our relationships and communities.

Feelings of shame may signal that our bond with others and, thus, our social existence are under threat: that our distance to others is too small or too great, which implies a risk of overexposure of the self and puts our own and others' boundaries of intimacy at risk. Alternatively, the self may be invisible, overlooked and at risk of being socially marginalized and isolated. Either of these situations may present a threat to our inner psychological balances, identity and existence. The feeling of shame is also associated with our general interest, as social beings, in how we appear to and are perceived by others (Rinofner-Kreidl, 2009, p. 152), and also maintains important functions in relation to our ability to decode signals from others telling us that we have overstepped their boundaries of intimacy or that others perceive us as being wrong and that we might therefore be wise to modify our behaviour.

In connection with the constructive functions of feelings of shame, several scholars have described how constructive shame can be an important resource of ethical behaviour in the workplace and in organizations in general. Here, it can promote harmonious internal relationships, the capacity for cooperation and a tendency to act in ways that are approved by others (Murphy & Kiffin-Petersen, 2017), for example by making us feel shame when we overstep others' boundaries of intimacy, act in asocial ways or consistently flout widely accepted social norms of collegial behaviour. On the other hand, it has also been pointed out that an organizational culture characterized by aggressive shaming may increase the risk of unethical behaviour, and that employees with a strong tendency to react with shame are more likely to act in unconstructive ways towards others in the organization. Thus, organizations may need strategies for handling shame in a constructive way (Murphy & Kiffin-Petersen, 2017, p. 662f.).

In order to function in civilized and complex communities and interact without violating each other's boundaries and thus contributing to destructive and escalating conflicts, we all need, to some degree, to repress inner drives, individual needs and primitive forces. What we call culture is based, in part, on the repression of the more primitive or animal aspects of human nature by deflecting and channelling them into more mature and constructive directions in a way that, ideally, supports the realization of overriding, long-term individual and social goals. In relation to this point, Freud speaks of the sublimation of human drives and the more primitive and regressive elements of the human psyche as the result of the successful socialization of individuals to function in complex human cultures and communities. Constructive shame plays an important role in this process by serving as a warning signal that we are about to overstep (or have already overstepped) one or more of the red lines and taboos that, for various reasons, are necessary for the capacity of a (sub)culture to provide a stable setting for human life and interactions, and that we therefore need to pause and act differently.

In this context, I am not addressing whether the red lines and taboos of a given culture are reasonable or well-founded, or which perspectives or considerations might be relevant for determining this. My point is simply that when we are affected by (constructive and, to some extent, destructive) shame, this has a great deal to do with the violation and overstepping of these red lines and taboos in contemporary culture. Moreover, it is important to consider the sociocultural context of shame. Thus, in some areas there may be significant cultural differences in the perception of what is shameful and thus a potential source of destructive shame. For example, there are substantial cultural differences in whether and to what extent nudity, certain forms of sexuality and violations of individual or family honour are perceived as socially unacceptable and may lead to shame or shaming.

In a tongue-in-cheek suggestion, the American philosopher Aaron James (2012, p. 35) has proposed that a good test of whether a person is an actual asshole (or, we might say, sociopath) would be to see how the person reacts to the notion of being considered an asshole by others. According to James, an actual asshole feels no shame at the thought of being regarded as such, and certainly does not feel any urge to pause and subject their own behaviour to critical reflection. Thus, a shameless disinterest in and remarkable indifference to others' perception of the self may be an indication that the person really is an asshole and incapable of social functioning. Based on this amusing, yet not entirely unfounded idea, James (2016) subsequently wrote an entire book about why the 45th US President Donald Trump is an asshole: someone who appears extraordinarily shameless in his urge to be the centre of attention, promote himself and overstep other people's boundaries of shame (see Section 6.2). Finally, it is also worth noting how shame and excrement are linked in this description of shameless and otherwise off-putting individuals as 'assholes'. A similar connection is at play when we try to humiliate and shame others by describing their words or actions as 'bullshit' (Schafer, 1997, p. 96).

1.7 A driving force of submission as well as rebellion

The uniquely human capacity for shame also has a potential down-side: feelings of shame can become the driving force of excessive submis-sion, adaptation and conformity, as they can help maintain a social order that involves unnecessary restrictions on the freedom and psychological well-being of large groups of the population (Büttner, 2020, p. 32; Neckel, 1991). On the other hand, the same feelings of shame also hold the potential to become a basis and a driving force of rebellion against unfair treatment and unreasonable living conditions, if they are translated into anger directed at the actual causes of humiliating and degrading treatment (Büttner, 2020, p. 19; Neckel, 1991). Feelings of shame can become a driving force of the struggle for greater social justice and quality if we are able to join forces and direct our anger over perceived shameful injustice at the underlying causes: the structural aspects of society that are the real cause of social inequity and dys-function and not, for example, migrants or other maligned minority groups or a vaguely defined social elite.

In this regard, it is remarkable that the growing socioeconomic and cul-tural disparities of modern society do not spark more anger, rage and rebellion than they do; instead, they primarily give rise to feelings of inferiority, resigna-tion and shameful withdrawal in most of the people who are hardest hit by the real-life consequences of growing inequality, especially among people with limited education living in precarious situations. It is also worth considering whether the populist parties and protest movements that are increasingly gaining ground in modern Western societies are not drawing some of their impetus for protests and rebellion from perceived shame, translated into anger, among parts of the population. In extension of this point, it could be argued that feelings of shame should be included, more generally, in our understanding of the emotional motivation behind certain political and social phenomena (see Chapter 6). Finally, feelings of shame have an interesting capacity to manifest social norms and conventions that are not necessarily explicit and conscious in our awareness but which are exposed when we feel shame for accidentally overstepping prevailing notions of normality (the socially expected and desirable), for example with regard to people's expres-sion of their gender or sexuality or how power is managed in relationships and organizations.

The feeling of shame as a moral and ethical reaction may also be manifested in other contexts and in slightly different forms. Social and healthcare workers who, for various reasons, are under pressure to treat citizens, clients and patients in ways that they find professionally unsatisfactory, even unconscion-able, may experience shame as a result. Over time, they may react either by developing a more cynical approach to their job as a means of survival, or they might experience burnout and have to leave their profession, unless their working conditions improve. The main causes of this unfortunate develop-ment are usually a lack of the time and resources required to do a professional job and provide the service that the individual citizen or patient needs and is entitled to.

In relation to this, as citizens of a welfare society, we might feel shameful over the language some political leaders use to refer to migrants, people with mental illness or other marginalized citizens or how they seem to think these groups should be treated – and how we, as a society, subject vulnerable citizens to humiliating treatment without sufficient respect for their human dignity. Similarly, we might be struck with shame when we witness how people are humiliated and dehumanized in war zones, in connection with humanitarian disasters or, closer to home, in nursing homes or other institutions for the weakest members of society, who are unable to defend themselves if they are subjected to humiliating and dehumanizing treatment. An artistic example of how we can experience shame over humiliating and degrading treatment of animals is the American artist Diana Thater's (1998) video installation *The Best Animals Are the Flat Animals*, which consists of short sequences of animals being put into humiliating situations and appearing vulnerable and scared and, to some degree, being ridiculed. The video clips can be difficult to watch without feeling shame that 'we' (humankind) treat animals in this way. As several writers have pointed out, by 'playing' with what might trigger shame in the observer, art can help enhance our awareness of the feeling of shame and its many possible manifestations (Alphen, 2020).

1.8 Shame, individual freedom and community

Shame is a feeling that is very much about balance: the balance between different considerations and between the individual and the social community. These balances are viewed and handled very differently in different (sub) cultures and have historically varied over time. On the one hand, shame helps regulate human behaviour by inhibiting behaviour that might lead to the unnecessary exposure of the self or unnecessary transgressions against others and behaviour that violates prevailing norms, ideals and notions of what is socially acceptable. The latter concern in particular can defend and protect social communities. On the other hand, shame can also restrict human freedom and our possibilities of expression and development to a degree that may seem unreasonable and which can undermine human well-being and even contribute to the development of mental illness. In these cases, the concern for the prevailing norms and for a community that might be borderline totalitarian may be given too much weight, at the cost of individual freedom and autonomy. A key aspect of conflicts between different models of society and worldviews is the way in which the unavoidable conflicts between these partially opposing considerations are approached. This underlying cultural framework for when and why people experience shame and the variation between (sub)cultures and societies will not be explored in any depth in this context (see Jørgensen, 2020); it is simply mentioned here in order to contextualize the discussion of shame in the present book.

The fight for liberation from prevailing cultural norms and expectations in relation to, for example, gender, sexuality and religious dogma is often also a fight against shame; shame that is triggered in the individual when norms are challenged or which is manifested in the form of others' (imagined or actual) disapproval, disparagement or shaming of someone who fails to comply with prevailing norms or live up to external expectations of 'normal' and socially acceptable behaviour. In some (sub)cultures, this may be the consequence for homosexuals or for women who are perceived as being too sexually 'active', 'aggressive' or 'demanding'. In other (sub)cultures, it may happen to men who act in ways that are perceived as manifestations of 'toxic masculinity' or, conversely, are considered insufficiently masculine (acting as a 'sissy' or a 'pussy') or to women who prefer to stay at home with the children while the husband goes into the world as the breadwinner. Failure to identify with one of two binary genders can in itself be associated with considerable shame or the risk of shaming. In a deeply religious culture, failing to comply with certain religious ideas and rules can be associated with great shame, while this is not the case in more secularized or atheist societies. In these latter societies, on the other hand, overly dogmatic (fundamentalist) and unquestioning religious observance and practices may be perceived as shameful.

Depending on the particular (sub)culture we live in, there can be considerable variation in the individual behaviours that cause social shaming and shame. For example, many modern people perceive it as shameful to be lonely, old, overweight or profoundly dependent on help from others or being unable to control certain bodily functions (defecation, facial expressions and so forth). Many men today still find it very shameful to be impotent, appear vulnerable or cry in front of others, to be inferior in competitions with others or to have a neglected and unfit body (Lietzmann, 2007, p. 221). Similarly, many women find it shameful to be unable to bear children or to be sexually promiscuous and too outwardly impulsive and aggressive. Although some might claim that modern culture is shameless rather than characterized by shame, there is no indication that shame is a less central feeling in modern Western society compared to earlier or other contemporary cultures; in fact, quite on the contrary. To some extent, however, shame is manifested in new ways. Certain forms of shame, including shame related to one's own body and sexuality and to food and diet, might be more common among women than among men, but generally, there do not appear to be major gender-based differences in the occurrence of shame (Else-Quest et al., 2012). However, gender-specific norms and expectations might mean that the specific causes of perceived shame vary between men, women and people who do not have a binary gender identity.

1.9 Shame and human self-perception in late modernity

A high degree of self-insight and self-control are common aspects of human self-perception in late modernity. We perceive ourselves as being clearly delimited and autonomous, with a high degree of sovereignty, fairly independent of what others think of us and with a high level of agency in our lives. In this light, it is not surprising that shame remains a taboo and a fairly unpopular feeling that most of us would prefer to be without. Thus, feelings of shame are not easy to reconcile with modern human beings' established self-image as independent, clearly delimited and autonomous individuals. When the feeling of shame suddenly arises and overwhelms us, it mercilessly reveals the somewhat illusory, perhaps even grandiose aspects of our self-perception. When we are overwhelmed by shame we are suddenly paralysed and confused. We lose our initiative and feel exposed, vulnerable and inferior. The feeling of shame reveals that we might not be as clearly delimited from and independent of others and their opinion of us as we might think. Our ability to function as mature, autonomous individuals is challenged and undermined and might collapse for a shorter or longer period of time. We feel exposed, subjected to other people's approval or disapproval. And we are confronted with the fact that, as a minimum, there are parts of ourselves and our bodies, feelings and reactions that we do not necessarily have as much control of as we might think or want.

The feeling of shame confronts us with alien parts of ourselves, our personal history and drives and emotions that we ordinarily deny and repress, although most of us are well aware of them or at least suspect they exist. In this context, it is also worth noting that the primary purpose of the socialization of children and young people in late modern Western societies seems to be to develop persons with a high degree of self-determination, agency, independence and autonomy. The feeling of shame and its persistent role in human life represents something very different: an element of other-determination and an anxiety-inducing risk of suddenly feeling powerless, vulnerable and at the mercy of others.

Thus, it might be claimed that we should include the development of a better ability to recognize, contain and deal with feelings of shame in the socialization of coming generations with the aim of preventing feelings of shame from accumulating and transforming into intense and harmful destructive shame and thus keep such feelings from controlling human behaviour. To achieve this, we need to stop repressing feelings of shame and treating them as taboo and instead consider them as a natural and unavoidable part of being human; a part that we must be able talk about if we wish to develop our resilience to destructive shame – regardless of how painful and challenging this may be in the moment. On the other hand, it does not in any way imply that explicit and toxic shaming is a helpful element in the socialization of children and young people. As developmental psychologist Erik Erikson (1963, p. 253) points out, too much shaming 'does not lead to genuine propriety but to a secret determination to try to get away with things, unseen – if, indeed, it does not result in defiant shamelessness'. Using 'the naughty corner' or trying to reprimand children or young people with a 'you ought to be ashamed of yourself' appear primitive, almost in themselves shameful and obviously out of step with modern Western culture.

On the contrary, we should primarily rely on affirmation and other, more positive and self-esteem-building strategies that promote the development of autonomy and creativity while minimizing the tendency to react with destructive shame, although this will not make feelings of shame, as such, go away. When a child's or young person's behaviour needs to be corrected, this should be done with a clear focus on specific undesirable actions and with clear instructions about alternative paths of action, not by shaming the self and person. Naturally, this leads us into the borderland between feelings of shame and guilt (see Section 4.4).

When we experience shame, we are confronted with certain fundamental questions relating to what it means to be human and extending into the core of our identity and self-esteem, which might be challenged and destabilized if we are overwhelmed by destructive shame. These are questions such as: Who am I really? How do others see, perceive and judge me – and how does that relate to my own thoughts about who I am and who I want to be? Am I worth loving, or am I all wrong? Am I part of a human community where I feel at home and free to be myself, or do I feel homeless, no matter where and who I am? And do I have to put on a mask or construct a facade in the hope of being accepted as good enough by others, even though that would mean I am not or cannot truly be myself? Shame is also associated with the social status and recognition of the self, in the sense that it can be shameful not to feel approved by others and to find that one's social status or position in a social community is low or tenuous.

1.10 Chapter overview

Chapter 2 opens with an introduction to the cultural history and etymology of the concept of shame. As described, there is no professional consensus definition and delimitation of shame, just as shame has also been addressed in several different professional fields without necessarily being clearly defined, let alone referring to the same set of affects and phenomena.

Chapter 3 provides a fairly extensive description of the phenomenology of feelings of shame and outlines how we can distinguish between constructive and destructive forms of shame. The chapter discusses how the feeling of shame may be fleeting and situational or, conversely, reflect a more characterologically based tendency to experience shame in certain contexts. It also describes how shame may be a more or less chronic, very painful and debilitating state. As part of the description of the phenomenology of shame, the chapter paints of picture of the typical manifestations of shame in our subjective experiences, thoughts (cognitions), bodily sensations, behaviour and ways of being in interpersonal relationships.

Chapter 4 suggests some distinctions between different forms and degrees of shame. It also discusses how shame is rooted in basic elements of human existence, extended between our animal-physical being and our uniquely human subjectivity. This discussion draws in part on the works of Jean-Paul

Sartre and Max Scheler. The feeling of shame is described as the affect of the eye or the human gaze, as eye contact can both be the path to deep emotional and psychological closeness and a cause of shame; this is why breaking eye contact is typically one of our first reactions when we want to avoid or escape shame. Furthermore, the chapter discusses specific ways to distinguish between the two related social affects of shame and guilt. This discussion draws on empirical studies of the differences between shame and guilt and also addresses the considerable difficulties in trying to study shame based on questionnaires and quantitative research methods. Finally, the chapter describes typical reactions to and strategies for defending against shame, including the tendency to withdraw from contact with others, anger directed at the self or others, perfectionism and exaggerated pride.

Chapter 5 describes the central role of destructive shame in a range of mental disorders, including eating disorders, posttraumatic disorder (PTSD), various types of self-harm and substance abuse, identity disturbances, depression and more severe personality disorders, especially borderline, narcissistic and evasive personality disorders. It also points out that shame can be a consequence of mental illness, since being mentally ill, seeking help and having to disclose one's challenges to others can in itself be associated with shame.

Chapter 6 discusses some key connections between prevailing trends in late modern societies and the prevalence of shame, especially among more disadvantaged groups: people who, for various reasons, struggle to succeed in modern societies organized around mutual competition and a tacit but widespread expectation for everyone to strive to optimize themselves (and their 'worth' in the marketplace of attractive identities), as expressed in the common perception of late modern societies as individualistic and meritocratic competition societies. People who do not have the same possibilities as more privileged groups of being seen and recognized as valuable members of society (and attractive partners, friends, social media contacts and so forth) are at increased risk of experiencing destructive shame. Being recognized as a valuable member of a social community counteracts feelings of shame. Conversely, feeling socially marginalized and having a tenuous social position can exacerbate the risk of destructive shame.

The chapter also discusses the possible role of the explosive growth of social media in accelerating the prevalence of painful shame, especially among young people, as social media increase their tendency to constantly compare themselves with others and rate themselves and their life in relation to constructed images of the perfect self and life. Finally, it touches on the role of – mostly unacknowledged – feelings of shame in certain population groups as a strong emotional driver of escalating polarization and internal conflicts in modern Western societies (see also Jørgensen, 2020). This includes the growth of violent movements of people, most of them men, who feel that their (historical and, in their opinion, rightful) social status and position in society are under threat. These feelings of shame can also be exploited by populist leaders for the political mobilization of people who feel overlooked and humiliated by a distant and dismissive political and economic elite.

In extension of this discussion, the chapter further discusses how the shame that often accompanies perceived humiliation and the loss of social status can be turned into anger directed at specific groups. This transformation is often orchestrated by leaders who manage to give their followers the sense that they are seen and that they matter, which can ward off painful feelings of shame, and who are able to craft a story about how they can achieve new greatness and pride, as individuals and as a social group, if they join these leaders and their movements. Adolf Hitler and Donald Trump are briefly discussed as examples of political leaders with the ability to exploit a widespread sense of shame among certain groups as a driver of political mobilization behind themselves and their political projects. Hitler's Nazi Germany is also a prime example of the potentially disastrous consequences of allowing unacknowledged and unprocessed shame to drive the development of society.

In closing, Chapter 7 outlines how psychotherapists can approach destructive shame, which seems to play a central role for a much larger share of patients than I, at least, was aware of until I began to focus more directly on shame in my patients in the therapeutic space. The main point and organizing principle of this chapter is that we need to understand the feeling of shame, register it and stay with (remain in contact with) our patients when they are overwhelmed by destructive shame. Not least, as therapists, we need to be able to contain the shame and look it in the eye if we are to help our patients develop their capacity for containing and managing painful destructive shame and its psychological consequences in the form of disorders related to each patient's identity and interpersonal interactions.

This is not intended to suggest that we should develop a new, special therapeutic model or method for treating shame or shame-based mental disorders, in a time when there is a general tendency to develop specific standardized techniques for the treatment of ever more narrowly defined mental disorders. My main point is, rather, that we should focus more on the role of shame in our psychotherapeutic work in general – and in particular when destructive shame is a key aspect of the emotional dynamic behind the patient's presented and immediately observable difficulties. Besides, we should continue to base our treatment on an understanding of the common therapeutic factors and the main elements of the psychotherapeutic stance (see Jørgensen, 2019). Similarly, having a firm theoretical foundation and practical training in one of the main therapeutic traditions is an indispensable condition of qualified psychotherapeutic treatment. This applies to psychotherapeutic work with shame, as it does to largely all other mental disorders and difficulties. To me, modern psychoanalysis clearly offers the best and most nuanced foundation for providing psychotherapy, but I fully acknowledge that others will have a different view and that, for example, different variants of cognitive behavioural therapy may provide a better basis for their work for a variety of personal and professional reasons.

2 Historical developments in our understanding of shame

Feelings of shame are mentioned repeatedly in the Bible, especially in the Old Testament. The Book of Genesis says about Adam and Eve that 'the man and his wife were both naked and were not ashamed' (*The Holy Bible: English Standard Version*, 2001, Genesis 2:25). Not until the Fall and the banishment from Eden does man become (self-)aware, an independent subject capable of knowing good and evil and of feeling shame. The moment we eat from the tree of knowledge and turn our back on the childish naivety and absence of (self-)reflection that characterize life in Paradise, shame enters our life as a painful reality. The serpent in the Garden of Eden says to Eve,

> 'God knows that when you eat of it your eyes will be opened, and you will be like God, knowing good and evil.' So when the woman saw that the tree was good for food, and that it was a delight to the eyes, and that the tree was to be desired to make one wise, she took of its fruit and ate, and she also gave some to her husband who was with her, and he ate. Then the eyes of both were opened, and they knew that they were naked. And they sewed fig leaves together and made themselves loincloths.
> (*The Holy Bible: English Standard Version*, Genesis 3:5–7)

Thus, by violating God's directive, Adam and Eve act as independent subjects.

This ancient biblical scene associates the process of becoming human, or the emergence of human independent volition and subjectivity, with the advent of shame as an aspect of the human condition. Shame is further associated with seeing and being seen. As Adam's and Eve's eyes are opened, they see each other and become self-aware and aware of how they appear to each other and to God. They both realize that the other can see their body and self; they feel shame for being naked and feel the urge to cover themselves and hide – reactions that are all fundamental elements of the human experience of shame. We may also read this as a story about how the feeling of shame arises the very moment when human intersubjectivity is born – the moment when Adam and Eve see each other and become aware that they are both objects of each other's (and God's) judging and potentially judgmental gaze.

DOI: 10.4324/9781003521174-2

And they heard the sound of the LORD God walking in the garden in the cool of the day, and the man and his wife hid themselves ... But the LORD God called to the man and said to him, 'Where are you?' And he said, 'I heard the sound of you in the garden, and I was afraid, because I was naked, and I hid myself.'

(*The Holy Bible: English Standard Version*, Genesis:8–10)

Here, Adam reveals that he is aware of and shameful for being naked. This tells God that Adam has eaten from the tree of knowledge and has become self-aware and aware of how he appears to others. Adam is ashamed in the presence of God as an external moral authority (Küchenhoff, 2018).

He [God] said, 'Who told you that you were naked? Have you eaten of the tree of which I commanded you not to eat?' The man said, 'The woman whom you gave to be with me, she gave me fruit of the tree, and I ate.' Then the LORD God said to the woman, 'What is this that you have done?' The woman said, 'The serpent deceived me, and I ate.'

(*The Holy Bible: English Standard Version*, Genesis 3:10–13)

This describes some of the classical defensive strategies against feelings of shame and guilt. The passage illustrates how we may struggle to take responsibility for our actions and instead try to escape feelings of shame and guilt by assigning blame to others. In particular, Adam's somewhat pathetic attempt at making Eve responsible for his own act of eating of the fruit from the tree of knowledge does not come across as heroic or mature but mostly as shameful. Or, perhaps, as an example of universal human imperfection. It is also worth noting that although God punishes the pair for the transgression, he does not explicitly shame them or break off all ties with the sinners, which we have to assume would have led to profoundly destructive shame in both Adam and Eve. In the biblical story, shame, so to speak, arises in the individual through the other's revealing or disapproving perception of the self (Marks, 2021, p. 67).

The biblical story of the banishment from the Garden of Eden may also be seen to represent the belief that, before the Fall and original sin, human beings lived in a sort of innocent natural state, free of guilt and shame, in part because they had no awareness of self or of how others perceived them (Piers & Singer, 1953, p. 8). Humanity had not experienced or manifested the freedom of rejecting external prohibitions or directives. In addition to freedom, guilt and shame thus becoming part of human life in one fell swoop (Greiner, 2014, p. 94f.), shame is also portrayed as a manifestation of a particular human sensitivity to a large gap between how we wish to appear or be seen by others and how we experience or fear that others actually see and judge us (which may give us the urge to cover up or hide). This discrepancy can destabilize our self-image and self-esteem and give rise to self-criticism or even self-hatred. If we had not developed this uniquely human self-awareness and sensitivity to how we are perceived by others, we would not feel shame. When we interpret the biblical myth of the Fall as a story about how human self-awareness arises when the first humans eat of the fruit from the tree of knowledge, the story offers significant insights about the foundations of shame.

The biblical story of Adam and Eve's sons, Cain and Abel, also contains elements that can be understood as manifestations of shame and provide insight into our cultural perceptions of the possible manifestations and consequences of shame. Thus, Cain's slaying of his brother can be interpreted as a result of the shame Cain feels when he sees God rejecting his offering and accepting Abel's (Bastian & Hilgers, 1990):

> In the course of time Cain brought to the LORD an offering of the fruit of the ground, and Abel also brought of the firstborn of his flock and of their fat portions. And the LORD had regard for Abel and his offering, but for Cain and his offering he had no regard. So Cain was very angry, and his face fell.
>
> (*The Holy Bible: English Standard Version*, 2001, Genesis 4:3–5)

Because God rejects his offerings, Cain does not feel respected and recognized by God, which makes him both angry and shameful. He hangs his head as he walks away. He feels insignificant and neglected by God, and this experience causes toxic and destructive shame in Cain. In addition, we may also imagine that Cain is jealous of his brother over the attention he receives from God – a feeling that may also be a relational manifestation of or associated with shame (see Section 4.3).

Over time, shame can grow into anger. It can become the driver of hate and violence directed at others and may even lead to murder, as when Cain kills his brother – perhaps also in an attempt to acquire some form of significance, respect and recognition in the eyes of God and others, in addition to acting out his urge for revenge (cf. Gilligan, 2003, p. 1156). Alternatively, we might see Cain's fratricide as a desperate attempt to recover from his loss of face or as an attack on 'the other' (Abel), who has witnessed Cain's unbearable shame. Finally, by slaying his brother, we could say that Cain moves from being a passive object of vague and diffuse shame, which he feels powerless to change, to a more active position with a higher degree of agency, in which we must expect that he feels guilt over killing his brother (Bastian & Hilgers, 1990, p. 1106). With the murder, he goes from being a passive, powerless victim of (imposed) shame to being an active perpetrator who feels guilt over his own concrete act. He escapes his perceived impotence and claims a form of power. From outside, this power may be viewed as indicative of a new and perhaps even deeper impotence and desperation. In the biblical story, God places a mark on Cain after he has slain his brother (Genesis 4:15) to protect him from blood vengeance. Interestingly, today, the term 'mark of Cain' is often used to mean a mark of sin and shame, a stigmatizing sign of disgrace;

rather than protecting the person who carries this mark, it is associated with the risk of expulsion from human communities.

In his psychological masterpiece *Notes from Underground*, the Russian author Fyodor Dostoyevsky portrays a deeply abused and humiliated human being who is filled with shame, hate and contempt for himself and the people around him. This male protagonist is shown tender care and attention by Liza, a prostitute. Incapable of receiving this, instead, he turns his pervasive and shame-fuelled self-contempt into intense contempt for Liza: 'I was angry with myself, but, of course, it was she who would have to pay for it. A horrible spite against her suddenly surged up in my heart … "She is the cause of it all," I thought' (Dostoyevsky, 1864/1996, chapter IX).

Dostoyevsky's protagonist attempts to overcome the humiliation, inferiority and shame he has experienced by subjugating and humiliating Liza: 'I had to avenge the insult on someone to get back my own again … I had been humiliated, so I wanted to humiliate; I had been treated like a rag, so I wanted to show my power' (ibid.). Both Dostoyevsky's novella and the biblical story of Cain's fratricide illustrate how shame as a result of perceived humiliation can break a person down and cause them to engage in violence, humiliation of others or even murder in a desperate attempt at getting satisfaction and escaping the unbearable feeling of shame. Dostoyevsky's 'underground man', in particular, also exemplifies how people might sometimes try to deal with the painful state of passivity and paralysis that accompanies shame by attacking and humiliating others, thereby claiming a more active position with greater agency. In an attempt to deal with lack of respect from others and the accompanying shame, they might humiliate, shame, threaten or intimidate others, instilling a fear that may be perceived as sign of a (perverted) form of respect (Gilligan, 2003) (see Section 6.2).

2.1 The etymology of the concept of shame

The etymological roots of the word 'shame' are found in the Proto-Germanic terms 'skamo'/'skem', which in turn have their roots in the Proto-Indo-European word 'kam'/'kem', which roughly translates as covering, veiling or hiding (Tiedemann, 2010, p. 23). According to *Dansk Etymologisk Ordbog* [Danish Etymological Dictionary] (Nielsen, 1989, p. 370), the basic meaning of shame is also associated with shortening and degrading and related to disfiguring, injuring, harming, violating, offending, vanquishing and depriving of esteem (ibid.) – all aspects that are meaningfully related to our current perception of the concept of shame.

Some languages have two or more closely related words for 'shame'. For example, German has both 'Scham', which captures the feeling of shame, and 'Schande', which refers, among other acts, to scandalizing, scandalous behaviour, loss of dignity and something or someone being a disgrace as well as to dishonouring or putting oneself to shame through one's acts or way of being in the world. If something is a 'Schande', it is scandalous, a disgrace and a dishonour, while the verb 'schanden' (shaming, dishonouring, disgracing) is related to violating, defiling or corrupting. Similarly, French has 'pudeur' and 'honte', which distinguish between the shame effect in itself ('honte') and reactions or ways of being ('pudeur') aimed at preventing shame from arising and overwhelming the self (Lansky, 1994, p. 436). In Danish, these ways of being and characteristics are associated with modesty, chastity, humility, restraint and bashfulness, which in their milder forms can be viewed as manifestations of what might be called constructive shame (see later): a form of shame that relates to human virtues and serves a positive purpose for social behaviour and communities without necessarily standing in opposition to healthy self-assertion, pride and a balanced sense of self-esteem based on actual characteristics and achievements.

Danish has the fine but rarely used words 'skæmme' and 'skænde', the former meaning to disfigure, degrade or make to look bad, the latter to disgrace, defile, violate, damage, scold or bring shame on someone or something, whether persons or revered objects (Nielsen, 1989, p. 384f.). In Greek, the word for shame ('aidos') is closely related to human sexual organs ('aidoia'), illustrating the deeply rooted historical connection between shame and – especially female – sexuality in Christian Western culture (cf. Nussbaum, 2004, p. 182). Similarly, the Danish term for the lip-shaped folds of the female vulva is 'skamlæber' (literally: 'shame lips'), just as the Danish term for the pubic bone is 'skambenet' (literally: the 'shame bone').

It is a disgrace when someone behaves in a way that is inappropriate or dishonourable in their own or others' eyes (or, perhaps, in the eyes of God). In that sense, we may disgrace or degrade ourselves through our actions. I may feel shame about myself, my being and my acting in the world, and I may be shamed by others for being who I am, which may contribute to my feelings of shame, in part because I see others' disapproving gaze at my person, my self and my acting in the world. When we defile people or valuable objects, we mistreat them, disrespecting their dignity, honour and integrity. We may also be dishonoured and disgraced by others, who consider our actions or character shameful, scandalous, unworthy or highly inappropriate. In the historical *Ordbog Over det Danske Sprog* [Dictionary of the Danish Language], shame is associated with being improper, inappropriate, dishonourable or ridiculous. In addition, the word 'skam' (shame) refers to a 'feeling (of discomfort) evoked by something that is improper, inappropriate, dishonourable'. In more concrete terms, the word 'skam' is associated with baring one's body and, not least, one's sexual organs, losing a fight or competition, appearing deeply inferior, failing to achieve a goal or having one's expectations utterly disappointed. Finally, the dictionary mentions the decapitation of a person as close to the ultimate form of shaming or putting an enemy's shame on display; a method that is still applied today by the most barbaric religious fighters. Historically, decapitation was also a widespread method of execution in our part of the world. A somewhat related practice was the creation of a monument of infamy to traitors as a way of publicly shaming, dishonouring and expressing contempt for a bad and despicable person.

From the late Middle Ages to the end of the nineteenth century, the pillory was used as punishment for various undesirable acts, a method that relies on shaming and activating the sinner's feelings of shame through public exposure and humiliation. The pillory would be placed in a busy public location, such as the village square or in front of the local church, and the guilty person would be locked into this wooden frame in a humiliating position, exposed to public scorn, contempt and shaming. Thus, being pilloried involved dual humiliation and shaming by locking the person into a position that is humiliating and which underscored their powerlessness and inferiority and by doing so in a public place, where the person was exposed to others' contempt and disapproving gaze. This further illustrates the central role of the gaze and the exposure to real or imagined others' eyes and judgment in the feeling of shame. In modern usage, 'to be pilloried' refers more generally to situations of public exposure and shaming, often on social media or in other mass media. A 'shitstorm' on social media may be seen as a modern form of pillorying, as faceless and anonymous detractors pelt the unfortunate recipient with metaphorical 'shit'.

Finally, shame and defiling are included in a number of concepts, such as the old Danish 'skandbillede' (from German 'Schandbild'), an image that derides, caricatures and presents someone in an obscene and contemptible way, and in contemporary terms, such as 'flight shame', shame over using airline travel because of its heavy carbon footprint, the related but broader 'climate shame' relating to actions that exacerbate the climate crisis, and 'meat shame' stemming from eating meat. In another area, 'slut shaming' describes how young women (and, to some extent, homosexual men) might be shamed if they fail to live up to prevailing ideas about how women (or homosexual men) are 'supposed to' appear, act and deal with their sexuality. This is especially pronounced on social media. Similarly, individuals who are perceived, by some, as overweight, thus failing to live up to prevailing body ideals, may be subjected to 'fat shaming'.

2.2 The legacy of Aristotle

In Greek philosophy, Aristotle in particular addressed what we must now regard as a somewhat narrow and rather peculiar notion of shame, which he associated closely with human honour and strength of character. Aristotle (ca. 350 BCE/2020, p. 101) viewed shame as a feeling stemming from the fear that others will think badly of us, related to our ordinary fear of frightening things and the loss of honour, dignity and social status, which may pose an existential threat to us as social beings. In one of his principal works, *Rhetoric*, Aristotle explored shame and shamelessness, examining 'the things that cause these feelings, and the persons before whom, and the states of mind under which, they are felt' (Aristotle, ca. 350 BCE/2013, p. 98). In this treatise, shame is defined as 'pain or disturbance in regard to bad things, whether present, past, or future, which seem likely to involve us in discredit; and shamelessness as contempt or indifference in regard to these same bad things' (ibid.). Thus, Aristotle linked shame with having a bad or weak character, in the sense that experiencing shame is a reflection of poor judgment, lack of self-control and/or violation of elevated values. This is especially true when shame is experienced by adults.

According to Aristotle, bad acts that cause shame are

> in the first place, those due to moral badness. Such are throwing away one's shield or taking to flight; for these bad things are due to cowardice … . Also, having carnal intercourse with forbidden persons, at wrong times, or in wrong places; for these things are due to licentiousness.
>
> (ibid.)

Among other manifestations of poor character that cause shame and do damage to the person's honour and reputation, he mentioned greed and meanness and, in money matters, 'giving less help than you might, or none at all, or accepting help from those worse off than yourself' (ibid.). 'We are moreover ashamed of having done to us, having had done, or being about to have done to us acts that involve us in dishonour and reproach; as when we surrender our persons, or lend ourselves to vile deeds' (ibid., p. 99). Generally, shame is associated with notions of what it means to be a decent human being and a person of character; thus, shame arises when someone fails to live up to these ideas about what it takes to be a sufficiently good human being.

Aristotle explicitly denied that experiencing, or having the capacity to experience, shame is a virtue; he considered shame a feeling, not a desirable character trait (virtue). According to Aristotle, experiencing shame reflects a lack of human virtues and desirable character traits. Again, we should remember that Aristotle operated with a very narrow and, by modern standards, fairly primitive and rigid concept of shame; unlike modern concepts of shame, for example, he did not allow for a possible distinction between constructive and destructive or toxic shame. More on this point later. Aristotle (ca. 350 BCE/2020, p. 101) argued that shame is only appropriate for young people, who, as he saw it, are governed mostly by their feelings and apt to make mistakes, and shame might help to regulate their behaviour. With this, he introduced the idea that shame can contribute to necessary self-regulation. By contrast, in Aristotle's analysis, older, more mature individuals should not experience shame, since they ought not to act in a way that gives them cause to feel shame. This represents the notion of the stoic, a person with such a high degree of moral and ethical awareness and rational self-control that they are able to eschew shameful acts. 'Shame in fact is not the emotion of a good man' (ibid.); only bad people should feel shame.

According to Aristotle (ibid.), it is thus absurd to think that feeling ashamed after doing something shameful makes someone a decent person. In his opinion, a decent person would never commit such shameful acts in the first place – and although he clearly had a negative view of shamelessness, that does not mean that feeling shame over shameful and disgraceful behaviour is good. Thus, he rejects the idea that shame generally (with the possible exception of young people) serves any positive or constructive purpose in human life. Shame is, so to speak, a superfluous feeling for good and mature individuals or an indication that the person is failing to live up to prevailing norms for decent human beings. Still, he did associate shame with the moral virtues, an area in which – as in all aspects of human life – it is crucial to strike the right balance. Thus, Aristotle believed that excessive shame-proneness leads to excessive caution and bashfulness, while insufficient shame-proneness, on the other hand, may lead to shameless behaviour.

By contrast, in his classical dialogue *Protagoras* (Plato, ca. 380 BCE/1956, p. 20f.) the slightly older Greek philosopher Plato views shame ('aidos') as key to prevent people from acting in ways that disrespect others and thus as crucial for the human ability to establish and live in well-functioning social communities. Without the feeling of shame acting as an emotional brake when we are about to deal unjustly with others, we cannot live in social communities. He even believed that individuals who are incapable of feeling or acquiring the ability to feel shame (and a sense of justice) should be put to death in order to protect the social community. Arguably, the apparent disparity between the perceptions of shame in Aristotle and Plato reflects that they are in fact speaking of two different kinds of shame: an anticipatory, preventive form of shame (Plato) and a retrospective or reactive form (Aristotle); a form of shame (associated with fear) that keeps people from acting in ways that are disrespectful of others and a form of shame that only arises after a disrespectful or dissocial act (Meyer-Drawe, 2009, p. 40f.).

According to Aristotle (ca. 350 BCE/2013, p. 102), we are more likely to feel shame when we are seen by others, and we 'feel more shame about a thing if it is done openly, before all men's eyes … "shame dwells in the eyes"' (ibid.). Several later leading theorists in the field have similarly associated shame with the outside gaze at the self (Sartre, 1943/2018; Wurmser, 2019). However, it makes a difference who the observers are:

> the people before whom we feel shame are those whose opinion of us matters to us. Such persons are: those who admire us, those whom we admire, those by whom we wish to be admired, those with whom we are competing, and those whose opinion of us we respect.
>
> (Aristotle, ca. 350 BCE/2013, p. 100)

'And, generally, we feel no shame before those upon whose opinions we quite look down as untrustworthy (no one feels shame before small children or animals)', as Aristotle (ibid., p. 101) put it. His point is that our own and others' social status affect our experience of shame. Even though the other's gaze, observation and judgment of the self influences our experience of shame, our understanding of shame should consider the relationship between the self and the specific other and, not least, between our own and the other's social status. This is part of the reason why, for example, the aristocracy could behave with little restraint, in ways that would normally have been shameful if they had been observed by others, when their servants were the only ones present to witness their behaviour. Since servants were not generally viewed as equals and had much lower social status than the aristocracy, their (judging) gaze was not considered significant and was thus unlikely to cause shame.

2.3 Early psychoanalysis and psychology

For the first many decades after its emergence as a scientific discipline in the late twentieth century, psychology did not address the issue of shame. Classical psychoanalysis as practised by Freud and his immediate successors applies what is, at best, a very primitive concept of shame that clearly does not distinguish between shame and guilt and which attributes shame to rather speculative notions of an intrinsically exhibitionistic drive, an urge to self-exposure and to observe others (voyeurism), which supposedly is a cause of shame. Moreover, shame (primarily constructive shame, bashfulness) is described as a predominantly female affect that, according to Freud (1933/1963, p. 132), is related to the female urge to conceal her (defective, compared to the man's) sexual organs. It should be noted that as early as 1932, psychoanalyst Sándor Ferenczi (1985, p. 163) views shame as a 'typically male invention', which is used to impose certain moral rules on others, especially women; Ferenczi also associates shame with being alone and unloved (ibid., p. 164).

Freud's early attempts at grasping potentially unique aspects of female psychology were obviously misguided, but before condemning him for considering shame a primarily female affect, we should remember that from the Middle Ages, shame had been regarded as a primarily feminine virtue, which was both expected from and appreciated in women and was associated with passivity, self-sacrifice, a high degree of self-control, humility and chastity, among other qualities (Frevert, 2017/2020, p. 42). For example, the great Russian author Lev Tolstoy's principal work, *Anna Karenina*, can be read as an exemplary illustration of this phenomenon (Tolstoy, 1878/2002). We also often appear to forget that well into the twentieth century, Europeans too were preoccupied with the honour of the self, and women in particular were socialized to believed that a woman without shame was a woman without honour (Frevert, 2013, p. 20) and to view shame as a particularly feminine virtue.

The tendency of early psychoanalysis to ignore the topic of shame may be explained, to some extent, by the organization of the therapy room in classical psychoanalysis, where the patient is lying on a couch while the therapist is seated behind – and thus unseen by – the patient. As mentioned earlier, the feeling of shame is closely associated with the other's gaze at the self and is especially activated by eye contact. Such eye contact was largely impossible in the physical layout of the therapeutic space in classical psycho-analysis, and we can assume that this diminished the occurrence of shame in the analyst (Tiedemann, 2010, p. 69). However, this is unlikely to be the only reason why shame received such limited attention in early psychoanalysis, just as the organization of the psychoanalytical space did not offer nearly the same degree of protection for the patient. Thus, the psychoanalyst could freely observe the patient, who might also become preoccupied with, per-haps even overwhelmed by, shameful (projective) thoughts about what the psychoanalyst might think about them. Besides, some of the ground rules of classical psychoanalytic treatment, including the expectation that the patient share all their thoughts, associations, dreams and so forth with the analyst without censoring them, more than suggest that there was little focus on – not to mention understanding of – the psychology of shame. This problem is by no means isolated to classical psychoanalysis but reflects a general lack of understanding of shame during Freud's time (however, see Scheler, 1957).

Psychoanalyst Otto Fenichel (1945) was one of the first to mention shame as a trigger of defence mechanisms, although he did not distinguish between shame and guilt and did not go beyond a fairly rudimentary concept of shame. However, although the feeling of shame was largely ignored or mis-understood in early psychoanalysis, the main credit for 'discovering' the sig-nificance of shame and putting it on the agenda, from the 1950s, belongs to several psychoanalysts. Nevertheless, the understanding of shame in modern psychoanalysis should still be regarded as a work in progress, with some of the most important contributions coming from intersubjective psychoanalysis and further developments of Kohut's self psychology (Morrison, 1989). The founder of self psychology, Heinz Kohut (1971), made a key contribution to the early understanding of the significance of feelings of shame in psy-chopathology, particularly to our understanding of the relationship between shame and narcissistic issues in a broad sense, and also pointed out pos-sible connections between deficiencies in early (self–object) relationships and the development of destructive shame. However, his more fundamental understanding of the feeling of shame in itself remains limited, in part because he relies on a primitive Freudian drive-based understanding, which views shame as being grounded in an intrinsically human exhibitionistic drive (an urge to self-exposure and to be seen by others); when this drive is blocked or goes unrealized, it becomes a source of shame (cf. Morrison & Stolorow, 1997, p. 73f.).

In their 1953 book *Shame and Guilt: A Psychoanalytic and Cultural Study*, psychoanalysts Gerhart Piers and Milton Singer were among the first to dis-tinguish between guilt and shame, based on the ego's position in relation to the superego and the ego ideal. In their analysis, guilt can be attributed to an inner conflict between ego and superego, or the individual's conscience, while shame was attributed to an excessive distance or even a gulf between ego and ego ideal, or the person's ideals and expectations of themselves. These ideals are, to some degree, a result of the individual's internalization of external expectations and ideals, as is, to some extent, the superego. The ego ideal may also be regarded as an inner mental representation replacing the ego's originally perceived (primary narcissistic) perfection, which will always include a gulf between the ego ideal and the real ego, which the individual will seek to abolish (Chasseguet-Smirgel, 1985, pp. 4–5). Since the gulf can never be fully abolished, however, everyone experiences varying degrees of shame due to perceived imperfections and inability to live up to their own inner (internalized) standards and to realize their own perceived potentials.

Piers and Singer (1953) also relate shame to an inherent human fear of abandonment, which can be seen, in part, as a precursor of the idea of a close relationship between shame and intense efforts to avoid being abandoned and alone, which is especially pronounced in people with borderline personality disorder (see Section 5.3). It also anticipates the idea of shame as a social affect that helps to prevent us from acting in ways that would lead to a loss of social status and to social marginalization and expulsion from social communities (Gilbert, 2007). Piers and Singer's introduction of this distinction between guilt and shame in 1953 marked a significant step forward in our understanding of shame and its underlying dynamic psychological processes. By now, however, it should be viewed as representing an overly narrow one-person psychology that fails to capture the intersubjective character of feelings of shames. In her 1958 book *On Shame and the Search for Identity*, sociologist Helen Lynd examines the relationship between shame and identity formation, albeit in very general terms. In the 1960s, Silvan Tomkins (1963), whom many regard as one of the founders of modern affect theory, described the affect of shame but without sufficiently clarifying the distinction between shame and guilt. Tomkins de facto, and apparently quite deliberately, conflated guilt and shame, which constitutes a significant problem for his affect theory, which was otherwise groundbreaking for its time. He viewed shame as one of nine innate human affects along with anger-rage, fear-terror, disgust, dissmell, surprise-startle, distress-anguish, interest-excitement and enjoyment-joy. He argued that shame is associated with the reduction or complete blocking of positive affects such as enjoyment-joy and interest-excitement, and that the activation of shame will halt the exploration powered by these positive affects (ibid., p. 123).

The two main milestones in the development of a modern understanding of the psychology of shame are Helen Lewis's book *Shame and Guilt in Neurosis* (1971) and Leon Wurmser's principal work *The Mask of Shame* (1981b). Based on in-depth analyses of psychotherapy sessions, Lewis quite convincingly argued that feelings of shame play a much greater role in clinical psychotherapy than previously assumed and that, for many patients, shame is one of the most significant affects. This applies in particular to patients with more severe mental disorders, who struggle with destructive feelings of shame. A key point in this context is that when therapists overlook or misinterpret difficult feelings of shame in the therapeutic space, this can exacerbate the patient's condition. It may also increase the risk of premature termination of treatment, in part because the patient does not feel seen, let alone understood, by the therapist with regard to an important area (the patient's perceived shame) or because the patient finds the therapist incapable of containing and dealing with the patient's shame.

Lewis also argued that shame is often manifested as 'by-passed' shame; a diffuse sense that others look at and talk about the self accompanied by significantly heightened attention to what others think of the self and a vague sense of discomfort. However, this happens without a clear and conscious affective experience of shame, which is thus bypassed, denied, repressed or turned into anger directed at 'the other' who is observing and judging the self (Lewis, 1971, p. 38f.). Lewis also describes how shame can sometimes operate 'underneath' guilty ideation, which may prevent us from becoming aware of the feeling of shame (ibid., p. 196f.).

Wurmser identified several subcategories of shame (see Section 4.2). Based on the ego psychology school of psychoanalysis (Hartmann, 1939/1958, 1964/1972), he associated shame with inner psychological conflicts. A main focus in his work is how shame may relate to the ego being caught in the middle between high ego ideals, the superego, the inadequacies of the real ego and external demands. He also examined how shame can hide behind multiple masks, based on the activation of psychological defence mechanisms in an attempt to escape feelings of shame, which can be so painful that they are very difficult to deal with. Wurmser further described how aggression directed at the self (self-harm, masochism) or others (rage, violence) may be masked manifestations of unbearable shame. Finally, Wurmser examined the different psychological functions that the feeling of shame can serve in an individual, for example as a defence of personal boundaries and integrity. Unfortunately, his theory must be considered mainly monadic in nature and based on one-person psychology (see Jørgensen, 2019, p. 123ff.) in its focus on the individual, while Wurmser only managed to limited degree to develop a nuanced understanding of the need to consider the relational and cultural embeddedness of shame.

2.4 Shame cultures and guilt cultures

Historically, several writers have argued that it is possible to distinguish between cultures and somehow rank their relative levels of civilization or modernity based on the relative significance they place on shame versus guilt (Benedict, 1946; Elias, 1939). This proposed classification has some connection with the traditional distinction between predominantly collectivist cultures (for example, China or Japan) and individualistic ones (for example, the United States). Roughly put, the idea is that members of shame cultures (including cultures in China and Southeast Asia) are very likely to modify their behaviour based on how it is judged by most other members of their culture and social communities, mainly in order to avoid becoming the target of disapproval or contempt from others. Thus, individuals incorporate others' gaze at and judgment of the self in order to protect their own reputation and social status. It is viewed as essential to live up to one's obligations to the community – and similarly shameful to fail to do so (cf. Benedict, 1946, p. 222ff.). These cultures may also be described as honour-based: cultures that place a high priority on respect for and defence of the honour of both individuals and social groups (Gilligan, 2011, p. 111f.). If an individual violates social norms and expectations, this will result in overwhelming shame that will destabilize the individual's person, self and integrity. However, as long as the faults and deficits of the self are not discovered, 'exposed' or known by others, the person will not necessarily experience shame; feelings of shame are regarded as a reaction to others' perceptions or criticism, ridicule and rejection of the self. This paints a picture of a largely other-directed, group-oriented, socially conformist person with a low level of independence. In this context, people's actions are not primarily regulated by inner psychological processes but by external social sanctions, including shaming. The ability to feel shame is perceived as a virtue, a sign of honour and dignity.

Guilt cultures (which are found mainly in Protestant communities in parts of Europe and the United States), on the other hand, place a much higher emphasis on individuals evaluating and regulating their behaviour based on intrinsic standards for correct and acceptable behaviour (cf. the superego, the conscience). This intrinsic standard may be perceived, to some degree, as part of human (innate) nature or as the internalization of the community's and important others' norms and values. When feelings of guilt arise, they may overwhelm and torment the self relatively independently of whether the self's missteps or transgressions are 'found out' or noticed by others. The deciding factor is the individual's own conscience, inner evaluation and potential condemnation of themselves, and condemnation primarily gives rise to feelings of guilt or a troubled conscience (not shame). Guilt-based cultures place a strong emphasis on developing the individual members' conscience and common moral standards (superego and ego ideals). Unacceptable acts are primarily acts that harm, violate or otherwise negatively affect other individuals.

When an individual's actions violates the person's own inner norms, values and ideals, this may give rise to guilt but, importantly, only in relation to the person's own specific acts. Unlike shame, this does not involve all-encompassing condemnation and destabilization of the self as a whole. Compared to people in shame-based cultures, people in guilt cultures are perceived as having much more autonomy and independent agency. Furthermore, members of guilt-based cultures will, to varying degrees, be able to temper and escape perceived guilt by confessing, apologizing, atoning and accepting the potential punishment for socially unacceptable acts. By contrast, shame-based cultures do not offer similar ways to move on from perceived or imposed shame; here, there is no relief in acknowledging faults and deficits, on the contrary (cf. Benedict, 1946, p. 222f.).

Today, the general consensus is that this simplistic, almost dichotomous categorization of cultures, which also includes ranking these cultures' relative levels of civilization, is unfounded and reflects a profoundly ethnocentric worldview from an early modern Western perspective (Römer, 2017, p. 314f.), which categorizes Asian and other cultures as shame-based and thus backwards. To some extent, it might be meaningful to describe certain cultures and subcultures as placing a greater emphasis on honour, not just of individuals but also of the family and the social community, than other cultures. At first glance (but only at first glance), these cultures and subcultures may also appear to rely more on shame and shaming as instruments of social control than cultures that place a stronger emphasis on guilt and on the use of guilt as a means of social control (cf. Fessler, 2007, p. 186). However, that does not justify this broad reduction of complex cultures and subcultures to simplistic categories of either shame- or guilt-based.

Shame is also a highly significant affect in late modern Western societies. However, to some extent, it could be argued that it had 'gone underground' and has begun to resurface in recent decades, as it has, in a sense, become a prominent public topic, albeit not always with the ideal degree of depth and nuance (cf., for example, the important distinction between constructive and destructive shame). Disagreements about the possible existence of shame- and guilt-based cultures, which are not always fruitful, may also stem, in part, from a lack of conceptual clarity, since shame and guilt have not always been sufficiently precisely defined or delimited. Moreover, there has not necessarily been a clear understanding of how shame and guilt, especially in their more destructive forms, may fuse together and thus become difficult to discern in practice.

2.5 Professional challenges and points of disagreement

One of the main problems resulting from the growing interest in the phenomenon of shame is that many of the numerous writers and others who address this topic in the public and professional debate fail to define to what they mean by the term. When anthropologists, philosophers, sociologists, social and personality psychologists and psychoanalysts mention shame, they do not appear to be referring to the same phenomenon, even though they use the same term. This is not an uncommon phenomenon in psychology but also applies, for example, to the study of human identity and identity problems (see Jørgensen, 2008, 2020).

One consequence of this is that many writers, especially of the older generation, conflate feelings of shame and guilt, to some degree, just as most writers still fail to draw a sufficiently clear distinction between what we might call healthy, constructive or adaptive shame and destructive, clearly maladaptive and, in many cases, pathological shame (see Section 3.1). Thus, they do not distinguish between shame stemming from 'ordinary' bashfulness, physical or sexual exposure, violations of taboos, breaches of social conventions and so forth and shame that may potentially undermine and harm a person's mental health.

Furthermore, since both shame and guilt may be related to and activated by violations of moral norms, values and ideals, they may in practice occur simultaneously, in which case they might seem to fuse into one. When this happens, the reaction is likely to be interpreted solely as guilt, in part because guilt carries less psychological pain and is easier to manage. That is because feelings of guilt can be traced to concrete acts, which it is possible to change, while it is much more difficult to cope with and escape deep feelings of shame. These challenges continue to affect some of the empirical studies of shame and guilt, in part because most of the widely used tools for operationalizing and measuring shame and guilt (see Section 4.5) are based on imprecise definitions and a superficial understanding of the two phenomena. Unfortunately, psychologists and other scholars are more preoccupied with figuring out how to operationalize, measure and quantify shame and other affects using relatively simple questionnaires and rating scales than with fully grasping the substance, core and phenomenology of these affects (cf. Lindsay-Hartz, 1984, p. 689).

Another challenge for empirical studies and psychotherapeutic practice directed at shame is the difficulty, in practice, of discerning destructive shame from pathological guilt – a form of guilt characterized by enduring rumination on the self's faults and deficits as well as obviously unrealistic ideas about the scope of the self's influence on and thus responsibility for negative events. This challenge is further exacerbated when quantitative empirical studies seek to discern shame and guilt based on simple self-report questionnaires that are far from capable of producing a sufficiently nuanced distinction between the two affects. Moreover, shame is often non-verbal, difficult to put into words and associated with a powerful urge to conceal, deny or divert one's own and others' attention from a feeling that is profoundly painful and difficult to contain and acknowledge. Finally, the characteristic tendency to withdraw from contact that accompanies feelings of shame makes it even more difficult to talk to people about their shame, which is an important condition for exploring and improving our understanding of shame (see Jørgensen & Bøye, 2024).

There seems to exist a widespread professional consensus that shame is, generally, an unpleasant feeling that is largely uniquely human and thus separates us from the animals. On the other hand, there continues to be professional disagreement about a number of fundamental questions related to how we should understand shame, including the following:

- Should shame be viewed as a purely destructive affect, or can we also speak of a constructive variant of shame that, among other functions, helps people defend their integrity, honour and dignity and which may also play a key role for people's social functioning and for establishing and maintaining thriving human communities? Might constructive shame have a civilizing effect on people's behaviour and ability to self-regulate in accordance with prevailing norms, values and ideals without causing individually or socially destructive conformity, including instilling dominant ideologies and discourses in individuals (subjects) to an excessive degree?

The general point of view in the present book is that we need to distinguish between constructive and destructive variants of shame and that shame is thus, like so many other aspects of human life, a matter of balance. Constructive shame serves certain clearly positive functions for social communities and people's ability to contribute to the establishment and development of these communities. Situational constructive shame that does not overwhelm the self can help regulate interpersonal behaviour and motivate individuals to act in accordance with the norms and values of the social community and thus preserve their positive attachment to the community and prevent social marginalization or expulsion. Furthermore, constructive shame can be a motivating force for positive changes of the self: 'That is not what I am like, that is not how I wish to be, I need to change my attitude and behaviour.' As the Danish educational philosopher Lars-Henrik Schmidt (2006, p. 136) explained, constructive shame can animate self-correction, which is a necessary condition for any socialization. Naturally, parents cannot be expected to show up with well-behaved children on the first day of school. However, it might be necessary to ask, 'Has your child developed a sense of shame?' (ibid., p. 138), since this is one of the conditions for the ability of the school and its teachers to change the individual students' relationship with themselves. This is not, however, the sort of shame that could be described as 'existential shame, the shame of being alive, surviving, being present, present at the cost of others' (ibid., p. 138).

The Swedish psychoanalyst Else-Britt Kjellqvist (1996, p. 7f.) speaks of 'red' and 'white' shame: while red shame helps us protect what is most private and intimate, white shame is destructive, paralysing and an ally of death. As a destructive power, white shame invades what is private and intimate. The concept of constructive shame refers mostly to less severe and more fleeting forms of shame and their instrumentally practical value for individual self-regulation. It is a form of shame that supports our ability to function in social relationships and communities and to act in accordance with the prevailing social order in thriving interpersonal communities, not the inner subjective experience of shame that is generally negative and associated with discomfort (cf. Rinofner-Kreidl, 2009, p. 156).

- Is the feeling of shame an unavoidable consequence of human self-awareness, self-reflection and ability to observe and judge ourselves from another's point of view, which implies that it will never be possible to eliminate the feeling of shame from human life?

As discussed in Chapter 4, there are strong arguments in support of the notion that shame is inextricably related to basic elements of human psychology.

Thus, it is not possible to imagine a normally functioning human being who does not experience shame. Severely dissocial individuals or people with dementia have little or no sense of shame, but this is precisely an indication of their severely disturbed state. Moreover, there is nothing to suggest that shame is associated especially with certain cultures or historical periods (Paul, 2011, p. 201) or with certain types of socialization practices. However, the scope and intensity of feelings of shame and the specific behaviours, acts and incidents that might activate feelings of shame will vary across cultures and time.

- Is it possible to distinguish clearly between feelings of shame and guilt, and if so, how do we go about it?

Section 4.4 proposes some specific criteria for distinguishing between shame and guilt, although it is important to bear in mind that both shame and guilt should be viewed as dimensional affects of varying severity. Furthermore, it may be particularly difficult to distinguish clearly between severely pathological versions of the two affects. Also, the two affects may be dynamically linked and may also mutually maintain and reinforce each other. In general, key aspects of the two affects are so markedly different that in most cases, it will be fairly unproblematic to differentiate fairly accurately between them.

- To what extent can we understand shame solely by focusing on processes within the individual, such as biologically derived primary and secondary affects or disparities between an individual's ego ideals and their real self?

This book takes the point of view that such a one-person psychology approach (Jørgensen, 2019, p. 123ff.) to the fundamentally social affect of shame will inevitably lack complexity and can never provide a sufficiently nuanced understanding of its complexity and its embeddedness in social interactions. This does not deny the contribution of modern affect theory to our understanding of shame, just as our understanding of shame should consider how an overly wide gulf between an individual's ideal and real selves or between the individual's desired appearance and their actual self-perception (cf. human self-awareness and self-reflection) can contribute to painful feelings of shame. In this context, however, it should be noted that a person's ego ideal is always socially determined, as it is, to some degree, a result of internalized expectations and demands held by important others and the wider community. Thus, the ego ideal cannot be understood solely through a focus on the individual's inner psychological processes.

- Since shame is fairly obviously associated with the destabilization of self-esteem, how are shame and narcissism related?

There is no clear-cut answer to this, in part because it depends on how we define shame, including, especially, whether we are speaking solely of more severe and destructive shame – which presumably involves a close relationship with narcissistic disorders – and whether we are speaking of narcissism in a broader, more general sense or whether we are applying a somewhat narrower concept of narcissism that is closely related to narcissistic personality disorder. See Section 5.4 for a slightly more in-depth discussion of this issue.

We have now looked at some aspects of the linguistic meaning of shame and examined how shame, as an important element of Christian cultural history, has been understood by ancient Greek philosophers and in early psychoanalysis and academic psychology. We have also discussed how shame and guilt have been used in attempts to understand cultural differences. Furthermore, we have briefly outlined some of the professional points of disagreement about the concept of shame. The next chapter will examine the phenomenology of shame, including what characterizes shame and how we can distinguish between constructive and destructive feelings of shame.

3 The phenomenology of shame
How is shame experienced?

As we now delve deeper into the phenomenology of shame – its manifestations in subjective experiences – we should bear in mind that all the elements in its description do not apply equally to all forms of shame. Brief and less severe experiences of shame, which may be difficult to distinguish clearly from, for example, normal feelings of awkwardness, bashfulness or embarrassment over specific acts in concrete situations or a general sense of shyness, will not be accompanied to a similar degree by the subjective experiences described in the following. The primary focus in the present context will be on deeper, clearly destructive and potentially pathological manifestations of shame that give rise to painful psychological states and subjective experiences and which can be related to more enduring character traits in individuals and to pervasive and problematic patterns in their interpersonal relationships. This primary focus is applied here because those are the types of shame that might poison and undermine people's lives and relationships and which will therefore be a topic of psychotherapeutic practice and other forms of psychological interventions.

For a number of reasons, some people are more likely to be overwhelmed by shame in various situations, just as shame in some people can manifest as a persistent painful emotional mood, while others rarely experience shame and then typically just as a brief feeling related to a concrete situation, for example inadvertently overstepping someone else's boundaries of intimacy, or finding themselves in 'awkward' situations, for example when standing close to strangers on crowded public transport, in a lift or in a busy public space. Often, we can regulate this situational shame by lowering our gaze and avoiding eye contact, taking up as little room as possible (in order to avoid physical contact) and, in a sense, being partially 'absent' at an emotional and mental level. Alternatively, we may disarm and detoxify the feeling of shame by politely apologizing for inadvertent violations of the other's boundaries of intimacy or by sharing the humorous aspect of the 'awkward' situation. Other examples of slightly awkward situations characterized by brief situational shame include inadvertently witnessing other people's personal arguments, intimate conversations or

DOI: 10.4324/9781003521174-3

shared intimacy, or opening the door to an unlocked toilet and finding that someone is already in there.

3.1 The spectrum of shame: Constructive versus destructive shame

A deeper, more nuanced understanding of the nature of shame will need to include the dimension of time and a spectrum of shame, ranging from light, brief shame, which typically dissipates after a few minutes, to more enduring or near chronic and psychologically destructive shame. To develop a sufficiently nuanced understanding of shame, we need to include at least three dimensions: (1) scope (what parts and how much of the self and, potentially, the self's social group the shame applies to), (2) intensity and (3) duration (see Table 3.1). It might be debated whether the light and brief feelings of shame, which can be difficult to distinguish from 'ordinary' bashfulness or introversion, should be labelled differently. In the present context, however, we will apply a broad, dimensional understanding of shame with a primary focus on the more pervasive and psychologically interfering shame.

From a more semantic point of view, and considering the many terms that exist for different aspects or versions of shame, we might see shame as the common core of a family of closely related terms for emotional states, from brief moments of embarrassment in a concrete situation to loss of face due to the exposure of a moral flaw to severely destructive, deep-rooted, chronic and pathological shame in individuals with severe mental illness. The subjective experience of shame is always negative, albeit to varying degrees. Most people do not find shame to be a pleasant or desirable feeling that they would want to invite or voluntarily evoke. We can distinguish between at least three degrees and categories of shame.

Brief situational shame

Brief situational shame is typically predominantly constructive and has no negative impact on the individual's general psychological well-being and balance beyond the concrete situation that activated it. In this case, shame protects the 'private' sphere and the boundary between private and public space. It protects the core of our identity and our boundaries of intimacy, physical boundaries and personal integrity. In this sense, constructive shame is important to our personality development and psychosocial functioning. We can view brief constructive shame as a shield that protects our own and others' humanity and decency. It reflects respect for self and others and for the degree of discretion and regard for our own and others' honour or self-respect that is necessary for interpersonal relationships and communities to function and thrive (Wurmser, 2015, p. 1618). Situational shame may, for example, be activated if someone suddenly realizes that they are the only person in a social situation who is not appropriately dressed or that no one else in the group they are in finds the sexist joke they are in the middle of telling the least bit funny but instead considers it embarrassing and tone-deaf. Fairly trivial missteps or indications that the person is imperfect – like everyone else – can cause brief and fleeting feelings of shame in the moment, for example when someone discovers that they went out with toothpaste on their shirt or that their trousers have a split seam in the crotch, which someone else has clearly noticed. When this happens, we typically take steps to 'fix' the situation in order to avert potential humiliation or ridicule – with varying degrees of success.

Brief shame also includes non-pathological shyness, demureness, introversion and bashfulness, which may cause a person to react faster and more strongly to situations that activate their shame. In these cases, the shame is not associated with (notions of) others' enduring negative perceptions of or general contempt for the self (see below) but rather with a particular sensitivity to how one appears and ought to behave. It will also involve extraordinary sensitivity to how others perceive and react to the self, which may be a strength but also a potential stress factor for the person. Situational shame is primarily associated with discomfort (or ambivalence) related to being the focus of others' attention and judgment. This is true even when the attention is positive, for example in situations where the self is the subject of praise and explicit recognition. Praise can also give rise to situational shame if it comes from the 'wrong' source, is based on values and ideals the person does not share or is perceived either as intimidating or as inauthentic or hypocritical (Hell, 2018, p. 62). An example of the latter would be a mother praising her daughter for being psychologically resilient and good at looking after herself, when this is obviously not the case or might in fact represent wishful thinking on the part of the mother and an attempt at avoiding expectations of supporting her daughter when she is most vulnerable and in need of her mother's help.

Situational shame can briefly affect our self-esteem but does not in itself lead to pervasive destabilization of our self-esteem or to toxic self-disparagement. Unease, shyness and the feeling that a specific behaviour or situation is embarrassing and awkward will typically be associated with varying degrees of brief situational shame. Brief, situational and constructive shame is typically experienced by people who generally have a high level of psychological functioning, a well-developed and mature personality and a generally well-developed capacity for self-regulation and affect regulation. All well-functioning individuals will occasionally experience passing shame, even if some modern people are not consciously aware of this and tend to simply experience shame-inducing situations as 'awkward' or vaguely uncomfortable without actually decoding and understanding their perceived shame. Constructive shame enables self-reflection, allows us to see ourselves from outside and supports mature and nuanced considerations of how we appear and behave in interactions with others – am I too domineering, am I taking up too much room, am I overstepping other people's boundaries, or am I violating community norms and rules to a degree that puts me at risk of being sanctioned or even marginalized or ostracized if I do not change?

Shame-proneness

A characterologically rooted tendency to react with, often excessive, feelings of shame across a wide range of different situations may reflect a clearly heightened sensitivity to shame or an unconscious reaction pattern of frequently activated shame affects. Such a reaction pattern will often – but not always – have a negative impact on psychological functioning and well-being without, in itself, leading to severe mental illness. This is the case, for example, if someone is overwhelmed by shame every time they are about to establish more intimate emotional contact with someone else or need to talk about themselves and their feelings and dreams or otherwise become the centre of more personal attention from others. For example, social phobia and other anxiety or compulsive disorders (OCDs) may be associated with characterologically heightened shame-proneness.

Similarly, individuals who find that certain characteristics of their body, person or being in the world are inferior or wrong may be more likely to react with shame when these characteristics are somehow exposed or become the object of attention from others. For example, some people may be sensitive about body issues, perhaps because their body does not live up to prevailing body or health ideals, or about their sexual orientation and preferences or gender identity because some people judge it as 'deviant' or wrong. Finally, a person may also be particularly prone to shame in relation to their ways of being and acting in social contexts because they think that they always talk too much and are too domineering or, conversely, are too quiet and invisible.

Chronic shame

In the case of more or less pervasive, destructive and *chronic shame*, the person has a dominant self-image of being inherently wrong, defective, despicable, useless, unimportant, unlovable and subject to ridicule. Like a painful psychological undercurrent, this self-image influences all interpersonal interactions and most or all everyday situations. This category involves more or less permanent and destructive shame with potentially severe negative consequences for individual psychological functioning and well-being, which can also be a significant contributing factor in the development of sometimes severe mental illness. It also occurs as unmentalized shame, which is subjectively experienced as a signal of imminent risk of destruction of the self and as shame that cannot be regulated (dampened) by the normal human capacity for detached reflection on painful subjective experiences and mental states (Fonagy, 2021, p. 117). This chronic feeling of shame often results in significant destabilization of the person's self-esteem, identity, fundamental trust in the world and ability to engage in interpersonal relationships. In this form, shame may be a fundamental trait, a painful core element of the individual's general self-perception and being in the world (Tignor & Colvin, 2017, p. 342).

Severe chronic shame may also be a consequence of mental illness and related difficulties with living up to prevailing performance ideals and expectations of certain forms of appearance and behaviour in social contexts. Perceiving oneself as 'abnormal', mentally ill, 'mad', 'crazy' and unable to live up to prevailing ideas about a good or just a 'normal' life can in itself be severely shameful to some. Chronic, pervasive and destructive shame typically occurs in people with different types of moderate or severe personality pathology, identity disturbances and a deficient capacity for affect regulation rooted in early maladaptive experiences (see Chapter 5). People with severe personality disorders can also sometimes struggle to distinguish clearly between feelings of shame and guilt, which to some degree fuse into one, replace each other or are activated in defence against each other (cf. Benecke & Peham, 2007, p. 25ff.).

Table 3.1 outlines what I consider the basic characteristics of *constructive shame* (or sense of shame) and *destructive shame*, including more specific ways of distinguishing between these two basic categories of shame.

Constructive shame protects communities and individual boundaries of intimacy. As we will examine in more depth later, the German philosopher Max Scheler (1957) proposed an understanding of shame that may be read as a defence of the constructive functions of light and passing shame in human life, especially for our capacity for social interactions and for establishing well-functioning communities (see Section 4.1). Briefly put, Scheler offered a distinction between having a sense of shame and being shameful or overwhelmed by destructive shame. The sense of shame is related to tact, discretion, respect for the boundaries of self and other, sense of own and others' boundaries of intimacy and the ability to strike the right balance between closeness and distance to others across different situations. Moreover, a sense of shame is understood as a delicate sense of how the self appears in the eyes of others – a social 'radar' capable of detecting signs of threats to the self's social bonds with others and thus helping to preserve these vitally important interpersonal connections. All of these are elements of sensitivity to and efforts to protect individuals' 'private' space and important values and ideals. This is constructive shame.

Destructive shame, on the other hand, is shame that is too comprehensive, too toxic, too frequent and too intense for the self to be contained and managed in a productive way that supports the self's navigation in the world. This form of shame undermines human well-being, psychological freedom and the ability to lead a normal and well-functioning life. When its intensity and frequency overwhelm the self, destructive shame can activate various strategies to defend the self that often compromise the self's psychosocial functioning and contribute to the development of mental illness.

A meta-analysis of empirical studies with a focus on possible connections between shame, guilt and prosocial behaviour lends some support to this point (Tignor & Colvin, 2017). The analysis found some associations between a general tendency to experience shame (shame as a character trait) and less prosocial behaviour (primarily higher levels of hostility). Conversely, a small positive correlation was found between a tendency to experience guilt and prosocial behaviour. Thus, roughly speaking, the more (maladaptive) shame and the less guilt a person experiences, the less social (empathic, helpful,

Table 3.1 Basic elements of constructive shame (sense of shame) and destructive shame

	Constructive shame (sense of shame)	Destructive shame
Intensity	Low to moderate.	Moderate to high.
Duration	Brief, situational – typically balanced to match the concrete situation in which it was activated.	Potentially persistent, sometimes chronic – often appearing without any evident specific occasion/trigger.
Scope	Typically with a main focus on a particular aspect of the self; elements of the self's ways of being and acting in the moment/ the specific situation.	The whole self, its overall being and existence.
Cognitive and behavioural consequences	Risk of temporary and limited decline in nuanced perception of self and others – typically motivates self-improvement and context-sensitive social behaviour, correction of own being and behaviour.	Potentially enduring compromised capacity for nuanced perception of self and others. May cause anger/aggression directed at both self and others.
Emotional consequences	Brief, emotionally painful experience. Possibly brief negative impact on self-esteem, while the fundamental capacity for defending one's self-esteem is preserved.	The self is flooded with emotional pain. Risk of more persistent destabilization of self-esteem and the development of massive self-criticism, self-hatred.
Impact on relationship with self	Leads to delimited and nuanced critical self-reflection and a desire for self-improvement. Basic empathy and forgiving and accepting compassion with self are preserved.	May lead to more pervasive and unnuanced attacks on own self. Potential collapse of basic empathy and forgiving and accepting compassion with the self. Severe threat to own identity, increased risk of developing severe identity disturbance.
Impact on psychological well-being	Brief stress with no negative impact on well-being otherwise – is part of normal psychological functioning and holds potential for improving the self's social functioning.	Potentially severe impact, may increase the risk of developing mental illness and may be a symptom of mental illness. May inhibit/block the capacity for empathy and intimate contact with others.

forgiving, altruistic, compassionate and so forth) the person will typically be in their interactions with others. However, a major problem of this meta-analysis is that the underlying empirical studies draw no distinction, or draw too vague a distinction, between constructive and destructive shame (the same applies to feelings of guilt; see Section 4.4). This makes it difficult to determine whether the identified negative correlation between higher levels of shame and less prosocial behaviour includes both what we have described as destructive shame and constructive shame – which weakens earlier arguments for the positive functions of constructive shame. In order to resolve this, we need more and better empirical studies that distinguish clearly between constructive and destructive shame (see Table 3.1).

In small, brief doses that do not overwhelm and destabilize the self, shame and a sense of shame can thus help define the boundaries of the self, improve self-awareness (Tiedemann, 2010, p. 42) and enhance our ability to sense, read and respect others' boundaries of intimacy. Conversely, more enduring and destructive shame can undermine our basic trust in the world and the inner calm that is a condition for psychological well-being and development. Destructive shame may disturb the development of safe attachment relationships and destabilize people's self-esteem and identity, just as it may inhibit the self's capacity for rational and nuanced thinking. Over time, persistent or recurrent episodes of destructive shame will undermine our ability to mentalize (cf. dramatically diminished cognitive functioning in a self that is overwhelmed by shame), including the ability to mentalize and thus detoxify and understand the shame that is overwhelming the self. When this happens, the person may experience a painful sense of inner emptiness, social isolation and alienation from self and others; the person's inner life and emotions may shut down in an attempt to escape the unbearable shame (Nathanson, 1994, p. 804).

We all need to be able to regulate how much of our inner psychological life and private space we wish to share with the people around us. We need boundaries and strategies to prevent overexposure and invasion of our private and intimate space, and we need for others to respect these boundaries. In relation to this, constructive shame serves as a social radar that alerts us when our own or others' boundaries of intimacy, core values and taboos are at risk of violation (cf. Lansky, 1994, p. 437). We need boundaries that define private versus public space. If these boundaries of intimacy collapse, or if they are overstepped and violated by others, the result may be intense experiences of humiliation and shame (Pines, 1995; Lietzmann, 2007, p. 201). Some of the most extreme examples of this are seen in individuals who have been subjected to sexual abuse, rape or torture. Conversely, this shame-based mechanism for regulating social behaviour is defective in shameless and dissocial individuals who perpetrate these egregious violations of personal boundaries.

Constructive shame and the sense of shame thus represent human sensitivity to own and others' personal boundaries and emotions. Reacting with shame when someone's boundaries of intimacy or private space are violated reflects basic human moral and social sensitivity (Rinofner-Kreidl, 2012, p. 173). With Aristotle (see Section 2.2), we can say that constructive shame ('aidos') protects us from violating or revealing what is forbidden, taboo or secret and enables us to handle these issues with an appropriate degree of reverence and respect. Aristotle described shame feelings as a human value, while violating the feeling of shame by acting shamelessly without any sense of shame was considered a sin to be punished by the gods (cf. Neckel, 1991, p. 19).

Thus, the sense of shame has both an inward and an outward orientation. Inwardly, it alerts us when our own self and private space is at risk of being violated or overexposed and lets us know that we might need to tone down our self-exposure or withdraw completely or partially from a social situation. Similarly, we may react if we find that core norms, values and ideals are being violated. Outwardly, the sense of shame is associated with human empathy and helps to sensitize us, as social beings, to others' feelings, boundaries and integrity; as such, it also promotes society's social cohesion (Tiedemann, 2010, p. 43). It lets us know when others' boundaries of intimacy, private space and core values are being exposed or violated and that we need to retreat slightly in our contact with the other or, alternatively, help the other defend and uphold their boundaries, values and private space.

The sense of shame is immensely valuable to our social sensitivity and may be activated in any social situation or interpersonal interaction, from brief contacts in the public space to intimate contacts with close or important others or the contact between patient and therapist in the psychotherapeutic space. It may also be activated in connection with exposure of our own or others' selves on social media, where it can help us protect our own and others' boundaries of intimacy and personal integrity – provided we have learned to listen to and read this inner social radar. Unfortunately, the human sense of shame appears to be less effective on social media, where the relational contact is typically much more distant and faceless, and where more authentic contact, including actual eye contact, is not an option (see Section 6.1).

However, the sense of shame is not a purely inner phenomenon that can be isolated to clearly delineated individuals; it is a sense that awakens, is activated and may be an important non-verbal element in interpersonal contact and interactions. Generally, when an individual's sense of shame and constructive shame are activated – whether due to a threat to their own or others' boundaries of intimacy – the individual will non-verbally signal the need to proceed with caution in the interpersonal interaction. For the individual, shame not only plays a role in regulating the self's behaviour in interpersonal interactions, including by inhibiting excessive curiosity and enthusiasm (two basic affects) or anger, which may lead to the violation of others' boundaries of intimacy. It can also dampen more narcissistically organized people's grandiosity and help correct their illusory self-perception (cf. Hilgers, 2013, p. 16), provided they do not have a severe personality disorder, which might limit or disable their capacity for shame. This can help protect both their own and the other's self from being overwhelmed by mere destructive shame as a result of their shameless behaviour in interpersonal interactions.

The uniquely human sense of shame helps protect people's dignity, honour, reputation, social status and personal integrity. Furthermore, it helps us to avoid acting in ways that would be embarrassing, degrading or offensive to others and thus risk contempt and social marginalization or exclusion (Marks & Mönnich-Marks, 2008, p. 1019); a fate that in most cultures over time would befall people who behave shamelessly, violate taboos and overstep other people's boundaries without empathy or any sense of shame. Our sense of shame and the activation of constructive shame may thus provide direction for our behaviour in interpersonal interactions. In this sense, it can be regarded as a civilizing force (cf. Tiedemann, 2010, p. 15).

Our sense of shame and capacity for empathy will normally make us feel ashamed if we treat others as dehumanized objects or witness others doing so. This may occur, for example, when we see primitive pornographic material (far from all pornography is primitive, just as the definition of 'pornography' will vary), in which a concrete person is degraded and being treated as a mute, passive object for the satisfaction of others' needs. In this case, we may feel shame when we see the concrete person who is being subjected to this treatment and become aware that, through our gaze, we have viewed another human being as a sexualized object, bereft of individuality. When this person then 'reclaims' their status as a human subject, or when 'our eyes are opened to' the fact that the actors involved in the pornography are human subjects, deserving of respect and dignity, we may become shameful over having reduced another person to a subjectless object for our own objectifying and sexualizing gaze (Janin, 2015, p. 1612f.; see also Nussbaum, 2011). Furthermore, we may also experience shame on behalf of the pornographic actors.

Naturally, this raises more complicated questions about whether the pornographic actors are consenting adults playing a role they have voluntarily chosen and so forth; these questions will not be explored further in the present context. In extension of this topic, it is remarkable how sex workers often seek to protect themselves against shameful invasion of their private space by taking steps to create distance between the innermost and most intimate aspects of themselves and their work as prostitutes, for example by staging themselves and their body in the social role of a prostitute, including using not their own name but an alias that often explicitly signals their specific social identity as a sex worker (cf. Lietzmann, 2007, p. 142).

Before we lose ourselves in a celebration of the positive impact of shame, we should remember that its potentially constructive functions apply only to the intrinsic human potential for developing a sense of shame and activating constructive shame. They do not apply to destructive shame, which can both erode the individual and have a destructive impact on social communities, if it becomes widespread and leads to aggression and escalating social conflicts.

Social conflicts and polarization may be driven and continually escalated by self-perpetuating spirals of shame, in which abuse of others activates feelings of shame. In trying to cope with this, those affected by shame may then turn to aggressive attacks on and abuse of others, who are then also subjected to shame and similarly defend themselves through aggressive attacks on selected others in a continually self-perpetuating process (see Section 6.2).

These spirals of shame may also be an emotional driver behind escalating acts of war, with mutual abuse and humiliation activating a thirst for vengeance as the positions of victim and perpetrator continually alternate. Societies that fail to contain and feel shame for the abuse they suffer and inflict may become permeated by destructive shame and a tendency to use violence and abuse others, as violence and even acts of war (including war crimes, such as torture, systematic sexual abuse, extreme humiliation and so forth) are lauded as heroic. This cycle is driven by a powerful (typically unacknowledged) need to escape unbearable destructive shame. Activation of destructive shame anxiety may also contribute to the oppression of others and to exaggerated conformity and adaptation to the demands and expectations of authority figures that severely hamper psychological well-being and development.

Thus, constructive shame and the sense of shame enhance individuals' social integration and also help protect communities and their members against shameless, transgressive and abusive behaviour from individuals and representatives of the system. As this inevitably implies certain restrictions on individual behaviour and self-realization, highly individualistic (sub) cultures and political groups (for example, libertarians) may consider shame unacceptable and scandalous. In these contexts, shame is seen exclusively as an instrument for repressing individual autonomy and enforcing conformity and submission to the norms and rules of a perceived dictatorial community.

In such a (sub)culture, any form of shame is associated exclusively with forced submission, inferiority and powerlessness of the individual and surrender to a dictatorial external power that restricts individual freedom. Shame is seen solely as the result of repressive socialization practices or outrageous limitations on personal freedom by the government and social institutions. There is no appreciation of the potential of some forms of shame and the sense of shame to promote constructive and de facto indispensable functions for autonomous human beings, for example by enabling a social order that is necessary for creating a safe environment for autonomous human beings and their ability to live in freedom. On the other hand, it is equally obvious that shame and shaming may be instrumentalized by those in power as an instrument of social control and the maintenance of a social order and balance of power that is destructive for the general population and which helps to maintain their own position of power (cf. Rinofner-Kreidl, 2012). Shame is thus potentially a very impactful affect that should generally be regarded as a double-edged sword with the power to strengthen and weaken human beings, freedom and social communities.

3.2 The aetiology of destructive shame

The feeling of shame is a fundamental part of being human, a self-reflective subject and a social being, which means that others' perception of the self is highly significant for our self-perception and self-esteem. That is why we should not pathologize all forms of shame, let alone make them the object of psychotherapeutic treatment. On the other hand, it is equally clear that intense, chronic and severely destructive feelings of shame are harmful to people's life, identity and well-being (see Chapter 5). Thus, clinical psychology should primarily deal with pathological feelings of shame and help develop therapists' ability to identify and heal pathological feelings of shame in the therapeutic space (see Chapter 7).

Chronic and destructive feelings of shame may develop for an infinite number of reasons and in interactions involving a wide range of factors, both in the individual person's life and relationships and in the wider contemporary culture, including in certain (religious, authoritarian and so forth) subcultures. However, the main search for causes should always focus on interpersonal relationships, especially (attachment) relationships with important others during childhood and youth (parents, siblings, classmates), perhaps supplemented with a focus on interactions between the individual and elements of contemporary culture, including certain body and performance ideals or religious views of human nature and sexuality that place tight restrictions on individual life and possibilities and may lead to moral condemnation or even threats of social exclusion if people fail to comply with certain rules for a morally appropriate life. In this context, it is important to be mindful of the existence of gender-specific norms and beliefs about how people ought to be and act. Due to these norms, the risk of developing destructive shame is often lower among heterosexual men, who have historically held the most powerful position in most cultures and who for this reason alone have had the lowest risk of being shamed. On the other hand, this should not make us blind to the fact that heterosexual men too can be tormented by destructive shame.

Although destructive shame is associated with significant psychological pain and may be a contributing factor to a wide range of mental disorders (see Chapter 5), it is not in itself a mental disorder. Hence, it is not meaningful to develop independent theories about its aetiology (specific causes). In order to understand the psychological basis of severely destructive feelings of shame, we need to view them in combination with other aspects of human psychology and with more specific mental disorders that often have destructive shame as a core component. Thus, it is not meaningful to speak of an independent or specific 'aetiology of destructive feelings of shame'.

Fundamentally, however, it is clear that early relationships with important others that are characterized by a lack of recognition of the self as an independent and valuable subject and a childhood environment characterized by a lack of loving and empathic mirroring of the self will increase the risk of developing chronic and destructive shame considerably. This is especially true if the child or young person has not had access to other relationships and social settings that might compensate or make up for these deficits in the family, perhaps due to the parents' psychological or social difficulties and limited capacities. Destructive shame may also involve the child's shame because of their parents and the situation in the family home. The German writer Helene Hegemann has described the shame she felt as a child because of her dysfunctional family:

> The basic feeling throughout my childhood was shame. From the age of three, I was constantly entangled in various lies to make sure the rest of the world did not know what was going on at home. I was worried about the truth coming out, because that would have meant I would be sent to a children's home.
>
> (Hegemann, quoted in Michaelsen, 2022, p. 30)

In this context, we need to consider the issue of intergenerational transmission and refrain from moralistic attacks on parents who might have struggled to provide adequate parenting because they were themselves struggling with destructive shame due to their own upbringing and family background.

All human beings have a fundamental need to be seen, heard and recognized as individuals of equal worth by important others. We all have a need to feel loved and lovable and to feel that we are valued and important members of social communities. People who have not had these experiences in life, or only to a very limited degree, often tend to develop deeply negative self-perceptions and ideas about how they are seen and (not) valued by others. These negative perceptions may be more or less conscious (or subconscious) and associated with destructive feelings of shame. Thus, a shameful feeling of being inherently wrong, defective, inferior and, hence, unlovable, will typically have deep roots in earlier relationships with important others (parents, siblings, teachers, romantic partners and so forth). This also applies in cases where it could be argued that elements of contemporary culture or a particular subculture influenced the emergence of shame, since cultural demands and expectations will always be open to individual interpretation and are most strongly expressed in relationships with important others. How these important others express and represent cultural norms and expectations in concrete acts towards and specific ways of being in the contact with the self play a key role for their influence on the development, self-expression and well-being of the self.

Someone who is convinced that others find them inferior, despicable, insignificant or unlikable will generally find it very difficult to establish the degree of trust in and openness towards others that are indispensable for more profound, positive relationships with others. It will be tremendously difficult or impossible for such a person to engage in close emotional and psychological contact with others and to perceive themselves as being appreciated or even loved for who they are, which is necessary for developing more positive self-perceptions and healing the destructive shame that is associated with a deeply negative self-image. Instead, the person will be subject to self-perpetuating vicious cycles that prevent them from having the corrective emotional experiences of feeling seen, heard and appreciated for who they are in interactions with others that they need in order to dampen and heal the shame. Over and over, the person has experiences that affirm their existing negative self-perceptions and their beliefs about others' negative perceptions of them.

Alternatively, the person may repeatedly find that the front they have put up to hide their shameful self is, to some extent, perceived by others as desired and expected; meanwhile, the 'true self', or the parts of the self that are kept out sight for fear of being mocked, humiliated or shamed, has to remain in the dark, concealed from others, at the risk of quietly perishing, unseen and without the contact with others that is necessary for all parts of the self to remain vital and alive. Not only do destructive feelings of shame spring from dysfunctional relationships and the lack of deeper, intersubjective contact. Destructive shame may also be maintained or even heightened in dysfunctional relationships or due to the absence of any deeper and positive emotional and psychological contact with others that would allow for new emotional experience and, thus, corrections of established negative self-perceptions and beliefs about how others view the self.

3.3 The internal saboteur

As discussed earlier, in principle, there is no upper limit to the range of interpersonal and inner psychological processes that may lead to the development of chronic and destructive shame in a person. In the present context, the focus will be on a general discussion of intersubjective and inner psychological processes that might interact and contribute to the development of destructive shame. This discussion will be inspired by the work of one of the founders of psychoanalytical object relations theory, William Ronald Fairbairn (1952; see also Greenberg & Mitchell, 1983, p. 151ff.).

When someone has repeated experiences of not being seen, let alone appreciated for who they are, but instead feels humiliated and encounters indifference or contempt from important others, the person will, over time, internalize these recurring patterns in interpersonal relationships. These internalized interaction patterns may also be based on a fundamental experience of having to be someone else (hiding behind a mask, developing a false self) in order to have a chance of being seen, loved or merely accepted and allowed to exist by important others. Through internalization, key elements of emotionally painful experiences from early attachment relationships become key elements of the child's and, later, the adult's inner life, internal object relationships and fundamental perceptions of self and others. The child internalizes experiences from interpersonal interactions in which their self was overlooked, humiliated, degraded or met with condemnation. Gradually, the child begins to perceive and treat themselves in the same humiliating and degrading manner that important others did. The child, or the child's self, attacks, degrades and humiliates themselves or aspects of themselves and perhaps others (including therapists) who invite closer emotional and psychological contact or give the ego loving attention.

Based on Fairbairn (1952, p. 101ff.), we can say that the child – and, later, the young person and adult – develops a bad internal object: an internal saboteur that repeatedly attacks the self from within and which may become a driver of chronic and inescapable destructive shame, self-contempt and self-shaming. The bad internal object, the internal saboteur, is the accumulated effect or consequence of countless negative experiences from interpersonal interactions as well as any specific traumatic experiences (abuse, severe neglect and so forth). The internal saboteur may also emerge as the accumulated result of early relationships marked by a general absence of emotional and psychological contact and the absence of love and empathic care. The internal saboteur consistently makes the child and, later, the adult feel wrong, defective, unwanted, repulsive, inferior and generally unlovable. A person who contains such an internal saboteur (judge or executioner) will feel constantly monitored and judged (persecuted) by a profoundly critical and judgmental imagined other – the object of a gaze that the person cannot hide from or escape. This judging other lurks everywhere, threatening to influence, pollute or destroy any chance of positive and genuine contact with real others. Unlike a strict superego, the internal saboteur is not related to (internalized) moral constructs, which means it may contain socially maladaptive elements. The internal saboteur is exclusively destructive and a key driver of destructive shame.

The internal saboteur is related to Anna Freud's (1936/1993, p. 110) description of the psychological defence mechanism of 'identifying with the aggressor' (see also Ferenczi, 1933/1988, p. 202f.), as the ego identifies with the other who attacks the self. Internalizing the other's (external) criticism and humiliation allows the self to move from a passive to a more active position and also, in a sense, to gain control of painful or traumatic experiences (see also Vaillant, 1993, p. 49ff.). If the aggression is not directed at the person's self (cf. internalizing destructive shame) but at others, in a sense, the self can escape the unbearable shame by externalizing it (transferring it to others). In these cases, the self identifies even more closely with the aggressor and begins to attack others the way the self was previously attacked by them. The cost of this may include wrecked relationships and difficulties with engaging in closer contact with others. When Freud and Ferenczi wrote about psychological defence mechanisms for dealing with relational traumas and aggression directed at the self, the field generally drew no distinction between identification and introjection. Today, we would say that the self introjects the traumatizing other or the other's attack into the self and thus develops an inner authority that represents the other and attacks the self from within, similar to Fairbairn's concept of the internal saboteur (cf. Hirsch, 2022, p. 60f.).

To understand the dynamic psychological and relational background of the development of the internal saboteur, we need to imagine the child or young person as the more or less helpless object of dysfunctional relationships with parents and other significant persons. As the child is dependent on their parents, in an attempt to preserve the relationship with parents and important others and to survive psychologically in these relationships, the child will perceive themselves as wrong and defective (bad) while seeking to construct and maintain an image of the parents and important others as good (Greenberg & Mitchell, 1983, p. 170). The child cannot survive without their parents and other significant persons, almost regardless of how stressful the contact with them might be for the child's development and self-esteem.

Rather than leaving (which is practically impossible) or withdrawing from psychological and emotional contact with them (which would cause significant psychological pain), the child establishes a relational constellation in which the child perceives themselves as wrong and defective – which is associated with painful shame (possibly also irrational and destructive guilt) – while attempting to maintain a perception of mum and dad as good and caring. Such a fundamentally masochistically structured relationship, which also contains a certain 'understanding' of the 'problems' in the child's relationships and family, is less painful than having to acknowledge that mum and dad are 'bad' or indifferent to the child (cf. Greenberg & Mitchell, 1983, p. 173): 'I have good and loving parents who always want what's best for me' (idealizing the parents and viewing the childhood family context as idyllic). 'I am stupid and a burden on others, I feel sorry for my parents having to deal with someone like me' (self-devaluation and self-denigration). This dynamic may later become actualized and re-enacted in relation to romantic partners, friends and therapists. For example, the therapist may be idealized as exceedingly competent, understanding and caring, while the patient perceives themselves as a difficult, annoying, overly demanding and generally 'bad' patient, who talks too much or not enough and whom the therapist must surely be tired of and want to get rid of as soon as possible.

3.4 The subjective experience of shame

Shame is typically described as an all-encompassing and overwhelming affect that arises as an emotional and cognitive shock when we suddenly see ourselves from outside, through others' eyes, and see ourselves as wrong, inadequate, ridiculous or even repulsive. Situational shame, in particular, is characterized by suddenness. It catches us by surprise and is generally accompanied by subjective experiences and immediate reactions involving large parts of our emotional, cognitive, bodily, behavioural and relational being in the world. It is a feeling everybody knows and which we recognize when we encounter it, in ourselves or others. Nevertheless, it is also a feeling that most people have difficulty accessing and discussing with others, in part because it is characterized by an intense and acute urge to hide ourselves and the feeling and to escape from the situation that caused it. 'You do not talk about shame, nor do you show your shame, you try to hide it and keep it secret' (Marks, 2021, p. 14). Hence, it is often confused with or concealed behind other affects, such as guilt, anxiety, anger and rage – and behind various forms of intimidating behaviour, including arrogance, callousness, contempt, extreme subservience or grandiosity in interpersonal interactions, which may be either reactions to or defences against shame.

Shame is associated with a painful feeling that others are watching, evaluating, judging and, not least, condemning the self, including regarding the self with disapproval, contempt or disgust. This makes us feel transformed into and viewed as objects of others' critically observing and evaluating gaze and contributes to the aforementioned urge to break off or avoid contact with others and to avoid social situations in general. In his short story *The Metamorphosis*, which can be read as an allegory of destructive shame, Franz Kafka (1915/1971, p. 39) describes that as the story's protagonist, Gregor Samsa, 'awoke one morning from uneasy dreams he found himself transformed in his bed into a gigantic insect'. In the story, Gregor Samsa is then excluded from his family and other communities. Others find him disgusting, and he has to hide under a sofa to prevent others from being overwhelmed by his revolting and repulsive form. This whole experience is driven by intense shame due to his failure to live up to others' expectations, his negligence at work and the knowledge that his parents will now face blame because of their lazy son.

At one point, when his mother sees him lying on the floor, she is overwhelmed by disgust:

> in the same moment as he found himself on the floor, rocking with repressed eagerness to move, not far from his mother, indeed just in front of her, she who had seemed so completely crushed, sprang all at once to her feet, her arms and fingers outspread, cried: 'Help, for God's sake, help!'
>
> (Kafka, 1915/1971, p. 103)

His sister, too, is frightened and overcome with disgust at the sight of him. One day, as Gregor has ventured out from his hiding place underneath the sofa, his sister unexpectedly enters the room:

> she jumped back as if in alarm and banged the door shut; a stranger might have well thought that he had been lying in wait for her there meaning to bite her. … This made him realize how repulsive the sight of him still was to her, and that it was bound to go on being repulsive, and what an effort it must cost her not to run away even from the sight of the small portion of his body that stuck out from under the sofa.
>
> (Kafka, 1915/1971, p. 113)

Kafka's story paints a compelling and tragicomic picture of the self's feeling of being revolting, met with disgust, excluded from the human community and needing to hide – a feeling related to the deepest, most toxic and most destructive feeling of shame.

With almost unbearable precision and empathy, Danish writer Tove Ditlevsen has described how the self can be overwhelmed by shame and try to defend against this shame by turning it into contempt for others. In her autobiography, she describes a meeting that she and her mother have with the principal of the primary school where she is about to enrol. Tove's mother proudly explains that her daughter can already read and write without mistakes. Contrary to their expectations, the principal is not pleased to hear this, as it does not appear to fit into the school's established systems.

> The woman gives me a look as if I were something she had found under a rock. 'That's too bad,' she says coldly. 'We have our own method for teaching that to children, you know.' The blush of shame floods my cheeks, as always when I've been the cause of my mother suffering insult. Gone is my pride, destroyed is my short-lived joy at being unique. My mother moves a little bit away from me and says faintly, 'She learned it by herself, it's not our fault.'
>
> (Ditlevsen, 1967, 1971/2020, p. 15)

Instead of the mother supporting and defending her daughter or insisting what a great accomplishment it is that the girl has taught herself to read and write, Tove finds that her mother lets her down. She feels ashamed over her mother's weakness and inability or unwillingness to stand up for her. This shame quickly turns into contempt for her mother:

> As we stand there in front of the witch, I also notice that my mother's hands smell of dish soap. I despise that smell, and as we leave the school again in utter silence, my heart fills with the chaos of anger, sorrow, and compassion that my mother will always awaken in me from that moment on, throughout my life.
>
> (Ditlevsen, 1967, 1971/2020, p. 15)

Precisely because the affected person expects to be met with disapproval and contempt, it is difficult for them to share their feeling of shame with others. This may further cause the person to withdraw from others and to feel isolated and abandoned, a feeling many people struggle to contain and deal with on their own. As French writer Annie Ernaux (1997/2023, p. 64) so aptly put it: 'The worst thing about shame is that we imagine we are the only ones to experience it', and that, unlike most other feelings, shame is not a feeling we want to share with others in expectation of being met with empathy. Moreover, shame is always associated with subjectively perceived defects of the self – the person's body, abilities, competencies, needs, emotions, self-control and general ability to live up to one's own and others' expectations.

Shame is a reaction to a person revealing through their actions, being and appearance, either generally or in a specific situation, that they are not who they pretend to be or would like to be, that they are inadequate, failing to live up to their own and others' expectations, norms, values and ideals. In addition, it could be argued that the shame is inextricably related to an acknowledgement of the self's inherent vulnerability, fragility and dependence on others – and thus related to being human. But more on this point later. Feelings of shame are also manifested at many different levels of human psychology and existence: emotionally, physically and bodily and in our relationships and behaviour.

Emotionally

Shame is, to some degree, associated with a diffuse sense of being wrong, abnormal, stupid, defective, ugly, inadequate, helpless, deeply unattractive, miserable, humiliated, a loser, disgusting, ridiculous or repulsive. In extension of these feelings, we feel that we are making a fool of ourselves, screwing up and violating social norms and conventions for the proper behaviour for someone of our age, position and social status. These missteps reflect on and expose us as defective, incompetent, laughable, scandalized or generally inadequate; 'I am wrong in comparison to everyone else', as one middle-aged woman who was tormented by chronic shame put it. In many cases, shame is accompanied by fear of rejection, abandonment, exclusion from a social group or even of no longer being (or never having been) worthy of being included in the human community. A fear of complete and total loss of love. A feeling of being excluded, not belonging to or part of any community. Moreover, pathological shame, in particular, may be accompanied by a sense that the person actually deserves to be excluded and abandoned, because they are defective and do not meet their own or others' minimal expectations of what a person ought to be like and, furthermore, do not know how a person is supposed to be, let alone what they might do in order to earn a place in the social community.

   This involves a deep emotional sense of being unlovable and worthless and of being excluded from social communities because of this worthlessness – even though this feeling may not necessarily be conscious in the sense of being accompanied by similarly conscious notions that the person would be able to express explicitly. In its more destructive forms, the feeling of shame may include a feeling of having no right to exist; a feeling that the person's emotions, needs, ideas and dependency of others are illegitimate. The self may have a sense of both internal and external homelessness; a sense of not belonging, not being able to fully be themselves or feeling safe and 'at home' anywhere in the world. In some contexts, this phenomenon is described as 'primordial shame' and is often associated with problems or deficiencies in early relationships (Tiedemann, 2010, p. 134f.), where non-verbal communication, facial expressions and interactions based on eye contact are of crucial significance. This is associated with preverbal contact – or an intense absence of contact and deathly silence signalling coldness, contempt and rejection rather than empathic warmth, love, interest and a desire for contact. Shame trumps and appears to stifle all other affects, especially positive affects such as joy, pleasure, engagement, interest and curiosity, just as it blocks the self's desire and makes it impossible to be free, spontaneous and creative in one's engagement with the world.

Cognitively

When feelings of shame are activated, the person will typically be overwhelmed by confusion and negative self-perceptions to some degree. The person becomes extraordinarily self-conscious about how they appear in others' eyes and convinced that others look down upon or even despise the self. The person's perception of the way others perceive the self is dominated by intensely negative views, often to a degree where these have to be under-stood as negative distortions of others' perceptions of the self. In the moment, shame causes some degree of disorganization of the self, and the person may get the sense that everything is about the self's honour, dignity, social status and interpersonal bonds, which are perceived as jeopardized or lost – a form of tunnel vision where everything seems to be about the self, who is exposed and the object of everyone's disapproving gaze and negative attention. This leads to a profoundly narrowed field of attention with potentially severe nega-tive consequences for the person's cognitive functioning as long as shame continues to dominate their psychological and affective system.

However, it is far from given that the person is aware of being flooded by shame, whether in the moment or more persistently. In the person's conscious-ness, the shame may be manifested as a more diffuse subjective experience of feeling 'like a fool', exposed, awkward or embarrassed. Shame typically has fairly limited cognitive 'content' in the sense that the individual may not necessarily be aware that what has overwhelmed the self is feelings of shame. Furthermore, it may be difficult to understand or adequately verbalize what sort of emotional experience or sensation it is that has disorganized the self, or why. Shame is often a 'tacit' feeling that leads to significantly diminished cognitive functioning. Also, it is not always possible to draw a clear distinction between feelings of shame and intense self-criticism bordering on self-hatred and a generally negative self-image and global self-perceptions dominated by devaluation and degradation of the self.

Shame can lead to a state of near panic, in which the capacity for rational and nuanced thinking collapses; a feeling of the mind 'going blank'. The person becomes unable to think clearly and seems absorbed by the feeling of shame in the moment, as all attention turns to the self and, not least, to the ways in which the self is wrong, inadequate and powerless. A young woman struggling with chronic underlying shame said, 'I am insignificant, I am a failure, I am never going to amount to anything, I am just a pathetic addict'. The ability to rise above the current situation collapses, and it feels as if time stands still (Lindsay-Hartz, 1984, p. 694), or as if the person is swallowed up by an all-encompassing present moment, with the subjective feeling that the current overwhelming shame is going to last forever (Rinofner-Kreidl, 2009, p. 164).

The person's normal reflective detachment from the self and own current mental states collapses. It is impossible to achieve any distance from the current shame and the situation that activated the shame, which overwhelms the self and feels as if it is going to last forever. The capacity for mentalizing, that is, for having nuanced and fairly valid psychological reflections on how their own and others' actions may be associated with and driven by certain needs, impulses, emotions and internal mental states, is temporarily compromised. All attention and mental energy is directed at the feeling of shame and the situation that activated it: the feeling of the self being exposed, naked and revealed as wrong, inadequate, defective, ridiculous and humiliated by others' intense and (negative) evaluating gaze.

The person is absorbed with themselves and how they are perceived by others while simultaneously feeling 'beside themselves' or alienated from themselves. As the German philosopher Günther Anders (1956, p. 82f.) put it, shame can produce an experience of being simultaneously identical and not identical with ourselves, that we are both 'ourselves' ('I am actually the one doing this') and 'someone else' ('I don't recognize myself, I can't acknowledge that I am the one doing this, this is not what I'm like or how I see myself'); that in the shame, we are confronted with aspects of ourselves that we do not fully recognize (the alien inside ourselves) or are reluctant to own up to. As a woman who was tormented by shame after she was caught shoplifting said with horror in her voice, 'But that makes me a thief', something she obviously struggled to reconcile with her self-image.

Bodily

In a physical bodily sense, feelings of shame may be expressed in the form of a frozen facial expression and blushing of the face or neck – places with maximal visibility to others. In other cases, we might go pale or 'white as a sheet', or we might laugh foolishly (loud, awkward giggling) or smile in a way that appears feigned, 'stupid', like a grimace ('putting on a happy face'). Intense facial blushing in particular can in itself heighten the feeling of shame, because it makes the person feel exposed and reveals that they have lost self-control and control of the situation. The person avoids eye contact, lowers their gaze and makes themselves as small as possible. In some cases, the person may close their eyes or have a blank, unfocused stare, in a sense not seeing, as if they could somehow, magically, escape the shameful situation by 'not seeing anything'. This psychological dynamic may also play out in situations where shame makes the person hide their face in their hands; a manifestation we also see in a more symbolic form, for example in the emojis 'facepalm' and 'see no evil' on social media.

The body may go limp, as the person 'collapses', feels paralysed or 'frozen' (cf. the 'freeze' response that is a manifestation of anxiety). Shame may also be expressed as sweating, a lump in the throat, elevated heart rate and heart palpitations (Tiedemann, 2010, p. 23). All of these responses reflect the connection between shame and anxiety, more specifically: fear of exclusion or abandonment. Shame may also make the person chew on their lip (or engage in other monotonous acts in an attempt to distract themselves from the shame). Someone struggling with chronic shame may engage in this behaviour so frequently that their lips go numb. Based on approaches from evolutionary psychology (Gilbert, 2003), this wide range of bodily manifestations of shame may be regarded as non-verbal communication of submission and acknowledgement of the self's low social status, which may prevent the self from being subjected to further humiliation and attacks from others, or at least offer a hope of such escape.

Behaviourally

Shame typically leads to paralysis and an inability to act and the potential collapse of the self's agency, the ability to function as a mature autonomous individual. In this sense, destructive shame, in particular, may be viewed as the antithesis of autonomous selfhood and thus undermine the sense of autonomy, positive self-esteem and ability to function as a competent individual. This may have contributed to the intense scandalization of the feeling of shame in our modern liberal society, which is based on the assumption of the well-defined autonomous individual with a high degree of self-determination, agency and (at times unrealistically) positive self-esteem. Generally, shame leads to a considerable decrease in functional capacity – cognitively, psychologically and in terms of agency. Lietzmann (2007, p. 99) even speaks of shame as 'a spiritual crisis'. Shame can make us feel powerless, trapped and drained of strength (Brown, 2006, p. 45), incapable of acting in a rational and goal-oriented manner and perhaps relying on various forms of avoidance behaviour. In addition, shame hampers or blocks any form of extrovert and potentially self-exposing behaviour with potentially severe consequences for the self's social function.

Shame will often make us go silent, cause the voice to crack, make us stutter or speak in a very low voice or, alternatively, speak unusually loudly and in a forced way in a desperate attempt to escape or divert attention from the wave of shame washing over the self. In some cases, we laugh in an insecure or embarrassed way as a subtle signal that 'I know something's wrong, but I'm not quite sure why, let alone what to do about it'. We feel an urge to hide or wish that the earth would just swallow us up. We may try to hide, conceal or draw our own and others' attention from the self's exposed defect. At the same time, however, we are painfully aware that this is impossible – the damage is done/revealed and irreparable – and our attempts at a cover-up only risk making us appear even more pathetic and shameful.

In some cases, we may successfully use humour, self-deprecation and over-exposure of our own inadequacy and embarrassing defects to draw attention away from or cover up the shame in a way that makes others less likely to focus on the self's shameful defects. People struggling with severe chronic shame sometimes have a great sense of humour and self-irony that lets them become the 'life of the party', giving the false impression that they are having a great time and are not tormented by shame or a fragile self-esteem. Behind the humorous and self-deprecating mask, however, they are tormented by loneliness, profound insecurity and shame, in part because no one sees or is allowed to see who they really are and how they feel behind the cheerful, entertaining and perhaps rather self-effacing facade.

Relationally

Shame is associated with varying degrees of collapse of our intersubjective (emotional and psychological) contact with others. Some scholars speak of the breaking of the interpersonal bridge (Kaufman, 1985). It is debatable whether shame is the cause or effect of this breach in the intersubjective contact and the sense of a lack of reciprocity (and contact) in interpersonal interactions. In any case, someone who is overwhelmed by shame typically gets a strong urge to withdraw from contact with others, avoid any sort of social situation and be alone. Typically, however, this does not make the shame go away, because the imagined other and the thought of the others' disapproving gaze at the self continue to follow and haunt the self – even after they might have broken off contact with real others and are physically 'alone'. Thus, the feeling of shame is not contingent upon a disapproving gaze from any concrete other. Simply imagining that others see, judge and despise the self can be enough to activate strong feelings of shame. As long as we are dominated by shame, emotional and psychological contact with others (and ourselves) is associated with dis-comfort, so we seek to break off or avoid social contact. As mentioned, how-ever, the feeling of shame is always relational, and it does not go away just like that, even if we withdraw from contact with concrete others. It is, so to speak, perpetuated by the self's inner gaze or imagined others' gaze at the self.

In the case of more chronic shame, the urge to avoid contact may eventually become so profound that the person isolates entirely. A patient with borderline personality disorder put it this way: 'Then I'm just on my own. There is no one to look at me. And there is no one who judges me or has any thoughts'. This strategy comes with a severe risk of becoming overwhelmed by loneliness, lack of contact, a feeling of being all alone in the world and a sense of bearing the sole responsibility for this because the self is wrong and unlovable. The feeling of shame may thus be associated with profound loneliness, as the person feels abandoned and completely left to themselves in an attempt to alleviate and cope with the painful feeling of shame. However, at the same time, the person is not actually alone, as they feel constantly observed, judged and condemned by real and/or imagined others. Contact with others is associated with a high degree of ambivalence: the person needs contact with others to avoid being overwhelmed by loneliness. At the same time, the person is incapable of hand-ling contact, because this leads to overwhelming shame.

Paradoxically, the feeling of shame can be activated both in situations where we feel that the self's defects and deficits are laid bare or exposed and in situations where we feel overlooked and invisible, which makes us feel insignificant, worthless or of no importance to anyone. The latter situation may feel like a humiliating lack of recognition of the self as a person and may range from fairly trivial situations of greeting someone who does not greet us back but looks straight through us, as if we did not exist, to a fundamental and deeply humiliating experience of having our feelings, needs and opinions consistently ignored, twisted or invalidated as irrelevant or wrong by important others; a feeling of being of no importance to important others and that, from their perspective, we might as well not exist.

People who struggle with severe chronic feelings of shame often describe that, as children, their parents repeatedly 'forgot' to pick them up from day care (in which case, either a kind preschool teacher took them home, or they were handed over to child protection services), or they were left to their own devices in a bar or were home alone, perhaps with the responsibility for younger siblings, while their parent(s) went drinking or simply 'disappeared', sometimes for days on end. These sorts of experiences naturally led to a painful and existentially unsettling feeling of being unimportant, unlovable and invisible in the eyes of the parents – a feeling that their subjective experiences, emotions and needs were insignificant, illegitimate and irrelevant to the most important persons in their life. Other people with chronic destructive shame struggle with the long-term effects of intense bullying and social marginalization in childhood and youth, which played a major role in creating a basic feeling of being unlikable. This led to further isolation and the avoidance of deep emotional contact with others or, alternatively, made them act out aggressively in an attempt to achieve some form of respect and stop being seen as weak and passive victims of bullying.

Thus, both being seen ('in the wrong way') and *not* being seen by others can be a cause of shame, which further underscores the social aspect of this affect. In a specific situation when we are overwhelmed by shame, we may have a burning desire to become invisible and avoid others' gaze and attention. However, if we actually manage to become 'invisible', unnoticed by others, in the sense that they appear to look straight through us, do not notice us and seem to regard us as irrelevant or inferior beings, this experience is at least as painful, shameful and unbearable. Of course, it is debatable whether 'being invisible' carries quite the same meaning in the two situations. The shame of being exposed as defective in a specific situation where we appeared in an unfortunate light primarily pertains to those exposed elements of the self that are perceived as defective or inferior and which we might wish were invisible or non-existent. This does not necessarily imply *all* the aspects of the self to the same degree, just as it does not mean 'forever', except in people with severe pathological shame. Besides, being seen as who we are and being met by a loving, caring gaze can actually dampen and, over time, heal even severely destructive feelings of shame (see Chapter 7).

Eye contact and gaze

As mentioned earlier, shame is closely associated with an experience of being observed and being the object of others' gaze and negative attention. In that sense, we may regard shame as the affect of the eye and the gaze. Pride can similarly be associated with the eye and the gaze but is accompanied by fundamentally different, perceived positive attention from others. The great significance of the eye and the gaze in human psychology is reflected in idioms such as 'if looks could kill', the significance attributed to 'the evil eye' in human mythology, religious stories and fiction and the idea that the human soul resides in the eye or that the eye offers sublimely privileged access to the human soul. The eye is both a very direct and powerful path to interpersonal contact and an organ of social and emotional regulation. The other's gaze may be soothing or provoking, it may signal support, care and empathic understanding or intimidating dominance and disapproval and give a powerful hint that someone needs to adjust their behaviour and is wrong and defective, thus giving rise to feelings of inferiority and shame over their ways of being and acting. When Oedipus discovers that he has killed his father, married his mother and does not know himself, he gouges out his eyes. This has been interpreted as an attempt to escape the judgmental gaze of others and as a desperate and illusory attempt to escape unbearably shameful thoughts about how he will appear in the eyes of others (Kilborne, 2002, p. 1f.).

With Winnicott (1971, p. 151), among others, we can say that the child sees and discovers themselves in the mother's eyes. The glow, joy and engaging interest in her eyes when she looks at and is in contact with the child plays a crucial role in the development of the child's self-image and establishment of healthy self-esteem and balanced pride in their own self. Or, as Winnicott puts it, 'What does the baby see when he or she looks at the mother's face? I am suggesting that, ordinarily, what the baby sees is himself or herself ... and what she looks like is related to what she sees there' (ibid.), including her own emotional reactions to the child. The mother's gaze mirrors the child but also conveys a reaction to, and thus a form of judgment of, the child. Naturally, these processes may play out equally between infant and father or other significant individuals in the child's life, just as related processes may take place in a therapeutic relationship and have a decisive impact on psychotherapeutic outcomes (see Chapter 7).

Infants see themselves mirrored in important others, ideally experiencing resonance with and recognition of their own emotions and sensations in congruent and marked mirroring (Bateman & Fonagy, 2004, p. 64ff.) of their true selves, a crucial condition for the development of a stable identity (Tiedemann, 2010, p. 55ff.). This may, for example, happen when the infant smiles at their mother, and the mother returns the smile, as they 'meet' in this smile and the positive contact it implies. By contrast, the mother's and others' 'dead' (unresponsive), disapproving and dismissive gaze can contribute to the child's development of a view of their own self as insignificant, wrong, full of defects and deficits, lacking agency (influence on their world) – experiences that are all associated with shame (Mollon, 2002, p. 10).

Speaking of the 'gaze' and its significance for the self, in narrow one-person psychology, we typically focus either on how I affect the other with my gaze or how the other affects me with theirs or, alternatively, how I am affected by my own subjective experience of others' gaze at me. This subjective experience is, to a high degree, perceived as being determined by internal psychological processes inside me as a delimited individual and may contain both paranoid and grandiose elements that are out of step with the way in which others actually perceive me and with reality overall. Here, the gaze is regarded as a monadic phenomenon, unrelated to actual interpersonal contact. On the other hand, focusing on eye contact leads to a much more relational and intersubjective understanding with the awareness that our perception of others' perception of us, and vice versa, is always already relational and relationally constituted. Eye contact is associated with potentially great psychological and emotional closeness and intimacy and is one of the most potent channels of emotional interpersonal communication (Ayers, 2003, p. 3). It is a key channel of communication for emotions and other mental states and involves something other and much more than simply looking at each other, perhaps at each other's face and eyes. Eye contact requires both parties to be emotionally present in the contact that is established with the eyes as the primary channel of communication. The founder of modern affect theory, Silvan Tomkins (1963, p. 180), even argues that there is no greater intimacy than that which can be achieved through eye contact. To some degree, he associates eye contact with sexual contact (ibid., p. 158ff.). When we engage in deep eye contact with a concrete other, we may also suddenly become very self-conscious, as we are thrown back upon ourselves, turn our gaze at ourselves and become overwhelmingly preoccupied with how the other sees and judges the self. Suddenly, we turn away from what we were doing and focus all our attention on how we are and appear to the other (what the other sees) and, not least, what is being communicated in the eye contact with the other in the moment. This is a process that may allow for great depth in the contact with the other but which may also result in confusion, embarrassment and even destructive shame if we find, with eye contact as the central medium, that deeply shameful aspects of the self were revealed and exposed to the other.

Desire for and fear of emotional contact

A woman in her early 40s, who had grown up in a family where she had been subjected to neglect and abuse took away the lesson that she must be self-reliant and generally protect herself by avoiding close psychological and emotional contact with others. Whenever contact with someone else might be about to move beyond the merely superficial state, she immediately becomes very nervous and appears frightened and scared. She avoids any and all eye contact, apart from occasionally signalling briefly with her eyes that she is frightened, that she is yielding and withdrawing or, at least, in no way seeks to challenge the other. She has perfected the ability to appear anonymous and nearly invisible when she is among other people in an attempt to avoid their evaluating (disparaging) gaze and minimize contact with others. The problem is that the more she perfects the strategies she relies on to be invisible and avoid contact, the stronger becomes her sense of loneliness, social isolation and being misunderstood. She then clings to a dream or a secret wish for someone to 'find' her, see her and meet her; someone who can liberate her from her painful feelings of loneliness and her sense of being disconnected from the human community.

Eye contact and contact in general are thus associated with great ambivalence: she simultaneously yearns for and dreads being seen. She wants contact with others but is also constrained and plagued by deep fear of what such contact might lead to and the risk of repeating painful experiences from her past. She fears being intimidated, emotionally overwhelmed and, once more, feeling profoundly wrong, inadequate and unbearably inferior in relation to the other. As a specific manifestation of this ambivalence, during a long initial phase of psychotherapy, she 'plays with' eye contact by slowly and briefly seeking eye contact with the therapist before quickly breaking it off. She gradually increases the duration of eye contact – and thus psychological and emotional contact in the therapeutic space – she can endure. Initially, this contact activates feelings of shame (she feels intimidated, exposed as being wrong), which cause her to withdraw again, but the intensity and duration of these feelings gradually diminish, enabling her to remain in contact a little longer. In a very slow and gradual process, she is able to move out of the bubble of loneliness where she has sought refuge for many years in order to keep unbearable shame and feelings of inferiority at bay.

Thus, eye contact is a double-edged sword and may be associated with profound ambivalence because it can lead to intense emotional experiences of both a positive and a negative nature, including shame and deep (initially wordless) emotional contact. Seeing and being seen by others can be associated with containing and being contained, affirming and being affirmed, understanding and being understood, approving and being approved and may thus be accompanied by great joy, happiness and inner calm (cf. Tiedemann, 2010, p. 63f.). This may be associated with an intense experience of being emotionally and psychologically present and available to each other.

Conversely, seeing and being seen can also be associated with power, a sense of being able to invade, control, harm, destroy and annihilate and of being invaded, controlled, harmed, destroyed and annihilated. In this form, eye contact and seeing and being seen by others is associated with deep insecurity, inner agitation, anxiety and a potentially great destructive force that may violate, subjugate, humiliate and ultimately annihilate the self (Wurmser, 1986, p. 27f.). In this situation, eye contact and being stared at are experienced as a threat to the self's fragile boundaries of intimacy and the demarcation between self and others, as the self may be overwhelmed by fear of fusing with the other, losing themselves (control) and being annihilated (see also Gilligan, 1996, p. 74f.). In this sense, eye contact may be a matter of life and death.

The potentially destructive powers of gaze and interpersonal eye contact is a major factor for people who are tormented by severely destructive and pathological shame. In this case, others' gaze at the self is associated with humiliation, invalidation or ridiculing of the self, and eye contact is often avoided because it involves great insecurity and risk to the self. In extension of this, the self may develop various strategies for avoiding eye contact and others' gaze, which give rise to shame. In addition to minimizing deep contact and, not least, eye contact with others, the person may try to 'turn' the shameful judgmental gaze around, directing it at others by using their own gaze to invade, humiliate and intimidate the other in an attempt to regain control of the contact and restore their injured dignity and honour (Weiß, 2008, p. 874). In this way, the person tries to escape a sense of the self as humiliated, worthless and overwhelmed by shame by denigrating and shaming others. This dynamic may also be understood in relation to projective identification (Ogden, 1979; Jørgensen, 2009, p. 418f.; see Section 4.3) and the evacuation of unbearable or unacceptable aspects of the self and mental states, including shame.

When the other's gaze at the self is not perceived as positive, open, welcoming, approving or simply neutral but instead as negative, judgmental and condemning, eye contact becomes potentially shameful and painful. When the other's gaze is associated with being observed and critically judged as an object that is met with cold indifference, contempt or rejection, this experience may lead to shame, self-contempt and destabilization of self-esteem (cf. Tiedemann, 2010, p. 66). As one young woman who was struggling with severe shame due to sexual abuse put it, 'If I have eye contact with others, I feel that they can see how ruined and filthy I am inside. My cheerful front collapses, and I am exposed'. It is thus quite understandable that people who have these very negative experiences with eye contact and with others' gaze at the self withdraw from or try to avoid eye contact and other forms of close emotional and psychological contact, which they reflexively associate with the risk of actualizing feelings of shame and other threats to the self.

Avoiding eye contact in an attempt to keep feelings of shame at bay may be a sort of 'magical gesture', based on the belief that averting one's own gaze can avert the shame of being seen (Kilborne, 2002, p. 33); as if not seeing means we cannot be looked at or unveiled as being all wrong. This is related to magical beliefs that if we simply close our eyes, we can eliminate the existence of an unbearable reality and its impact on the self – like a young child trying to hide from others by closing their eyes. On the other hand, everyone needs this deeper contact with others to avoid feeling lonely, marginalized and excluded from the human community. Everyone needs the appreciation, validation and approval that can come from seeing and being mirrored in the positive, containing and lovingly approving gaze of important others.

One young woman with borderline personality disorder and a tendency to become flooded with shame at the mere suggestion of deeper emotional contact with others explained that she is well aware that people are expected to look at the person they are talking to. However, she panics and is incapable of handling eye contact; she is overwhelmed by the many confusing emotions this gives rise to and feels intimidated by the other. As a solution, she has developed a strategy of focusing slightly to the side of the other's eyes when she looks at someone. Thus, at no point does she establish real eye contact, with the authentic psychological and emotional contact this involves and which she feels incapable of containing and managing. One of her main challenges is that she is very lonely and, not least, feels completely alone with her difficult experiences and unbearable emotional states, which she is left to try to handle on her own.

Our response to eye contact and others' gaze may, on the one hand, be largely determined by aspects of the specific situation and concrete others' actual gaze at and reactions to the self in the moment. This includes, for example, the specific other's clearly critical, judgmental or generally intimidating gaze and otherwise explicitly communicated disapproval of the self, which makes the self feel humiliated, despised and shameful. On the other hand, our perception, decoding and interpretation of others' gaze may be decisively influenced by our own fearful thoughts and negative self-image, which are easily activated across a wide variety of situations. This may be manifested as overwhelming self-consciousness and a sense of being the centre and object of everyone's critical and judgmental attention; a feeling that others feel contempt for the self, whether or not this is actually the case. Thus, our interpretation of others' gaze at the self may be considerably influenced by projective elements, just as we always, to varying degrees, encounter our own feelings and thoughts in our interpretation of others' gaze at us and in our thoughts about how others see and judge us (cf. Weiß, 2019, p. 21). In this case, we may speak of shamefulness or shame-proneness as a character trait associated with past negative experiences in interactions with important others and with our largely negative self-image and fragile self-esteem.

When we witness someone else being overwhelmed by shame, we may feel the urge to lower our gaze, avoid looking at the person, perhaps even withdrawing from contact with them. On the one hand, this may be regarded as being considerate and as a way of protecting and respecting the other's boundaries of intimacy; a way of affording the person privacy and giving them a chance to compose themselves. On the other hand, however, there might also be less selfless motives at play. As mentioned earlier, shame can often 'infect' someone who is related to or merely witnesses someone being overwhelmed by shame. Because this may in itself be quite unpleasant, we may feel a strong urge to move away from the situation and from the person who is overwhelmed by shame. In this case, we withdraw primarily for our own sake, driven by an urge to protect ourselves and our own boundaries of intimacy, while the other may feel abandoned rather than being afforded privacy out of care and concern.

The interaction between someone who is suddenly overwhelmed by shame and the person who witnesses it may be complicated by several factors. One is that we may differ in our perception of what is shameful, both as a result of cultural differences and inherently different individual experiences with incidents that activate shame. This can make it more difficult for someone witnessing another person's shame to understand how the other's reaction in the moment is driven by shame. Another factor is that the person experiencing shame may sometimes need an empathic and understanding other to see and help them contain and process the shame – rather than having others step back and leave them alone with their shame. This can be particularly significant in the psychotherapeutic space, if the patient needs to be contained and empathically mirrored in a situation that involves shame, where the patient feels extremely naked and vulnerable in the contact with the therapist (see Chapter 7).

3.5 The content focus of shame

Shame can be divided into several categories based on what seems to be the primary cause of the perceived shame, that is, its primary content or focus (cf. Hilgers, 2013, p. 26f.; Hell, 2018, p. 86f.; Scheel, Bender et al., 2013; Scheel et al., 2020). The object of shame – the element that activates the shame – will often be associated with elements of contemporary culture as well as aspects of the individual's personal history, including the specific experiences that caused the person to perceive certain situations and experiences as particularly shameful. In case of severely destructive shame, this can have a deep impact on large parts of the individual person's psychology, as a wide range of experiences and incidents are perceived as shameful and activate strategies to dampen or escape the shame. Furthermore, as mentioned earlier, the source of the shame experience may be predominantly internal or external, as we might be ashamed because we are not living up to our own expectations of ourselves, typically associated with perceived inferiority and powerlessness, or we might feel shame due to our perceptions or fears of how others perceive and judge our ways of being and acting in the world, associated with others' violation, humiliation, disrespect and disapproval of the self (Benecke & Peham, 2007, p. 24).

Precisely because the object of shame is related to aspects of the individual's personal history and (sub)cultural norms and values, there is, in principle, no limit to what might cause an individual to feel shame. We may feel shame over anything from specific characteristics of our own selves to our family or the social (ethnic, religious or national) group we belong to and identify with. That is another reason why it is difficult to measure shame via standardized questionnaires, which will by definition be restricted to a fairly limited spectrum of potentially shame-inducing experiences, aspects of the self and the self's identification with various social groups. However, we can identify the following general forms of shame (see also Brown, 2007):

- Shame related to the person's own body, including a sense of not living up to their own and/or the outside world's ideals about appearance, fitness, clothing, sexuality or personal hygiene. This category of shame relates to a perception of the body, or parts of it, as wrong, defective, inadequate, unattractive or even disgusting and revolting. It may also include shame over physical or mental disabilities, shame because of the person's age and imperfect body, shame because of having an unhealthy, overweight and passive body that is far removed from prevailing ideals of the healthy, fit and well-groomed body of a person with a healthy lifestyle and a high degree of body awareness (Reckwitz, 2017/2020, p. 235).
- Intimacy shame stemming from a sudden and uncontrolled exposure of the person's own or someone else's body; a lighter form of shame bordering on 'ordinary' bashfulness or modesty. This does not include sexually motivated exposure.
- Shame related to the person's own and others' sexuality, including sexual practices, needs, fantasies and preferences. The perception that different aspects of human sexuality are shameful may be rooted in cultural or sub-cultural norms and values related to sexuality, or it may spring from specific experiences and aspects of the individual's family and upbringing, such as homosexuality or a very active and outgoing sexuality being associated with shame. More intense and destructive shame will typically block sexual desire and may be a contributing cause of impotence, frigidity or other sexual dysfunctions (Nathanson, 1997, p. 135). On the other hand, a certain amount of non-destructive shame can arguably heighten sexual arousal and desire associated with revealing oneself to and observing others and with challenging conventional boundaries of shame and intimacy associated with human sexuality, provided this happens in ways that do not involve traumatizing violations of the person's own or others' personal boundaries (Hilgers, 2013, p. 312). Thus, sexual desire may be associated with the temporary suspension or shifting of normal boundaries of shame and intimacy that enables self-exposure and being present in the encounter with the other at a level and with an emotional intensity that would otherwise not be possible.
- Shame activated by severe and perhaps recurring violations of the person's own or others' boundaries of intimacy, including undesired exposure, particularly of the sexual organs, and physical and sexual abuse. Having been subjected to traumatic experiences – and failing to prevent them – can in itself feel shameful. These traumatic events may be perceived as the concrete reason why the self is supposedly defective, and the person may try to hide them from others to avoid being met with contempt, rejection or unwanted pity.

- Generalized shame associated with the self as a whole, with the self's personal characteristics, ways of being and acting in the world and, not least, behaviour in interpersonal interactions; a form of shame that is associated with who the person is and, thus, with the core of their sense of identity. This may include shame over inviting a particular form of contact or relationship with others that is turned down and leads to a feeling of being generally unwanted, invisible and insignificant. More destructive manifestations of generalized shame are related to existential shame (see below).
- Shame because of specific experiences, in which others view the person's thoughts, emotions, needs, sexual preferences, fantasies or thoughts as illegitimate, invalid, wrong or ridiculous.
- Inferiority, cognitive or competence shame related to a sense that the self falls seriously short of the person's own or others' expectations/demands of its performance and abilities as well as experiences of the self failing in its attempts to achieve set goals. When the person identifies with particular skills, and their identity relies to a high degree on having certain characteristics and skills which they are found to lack in a specific situation, the person will often experience competency shame and loss of self-esteem (Tugendhat, 1993, p. 57). This variant of shame may also occur in situations where the self is inferior in competition with others or when the self reveals a lack of cultivation – not knowing what is appropriate behaviour in social contexts – and exposes a general inability to measure up to others. This may also involve experiences of saying or doing something stupid (in the person's own and/or others' eyes) or violating prevailing social norms and conventions; situations in which the self falls seriously short of others'/the outside world's reasonable expectations of age-appropriate behaviour and performance.
- Shame associated with loss of self-control in front of others, for example in situations where the self panics, is seized by anxiety, cries or is overwhelmed by desperate rage (yelling, screaming, being physically violent) in ways that are perceived as highly inappropriate in the situation. This also includes various forms of physical and bodily or mental and emotional loss of control, when expressions of emotions are perceived as being 'too intense' or 'inappropriate' in relation to prevailing cultural norms and ideas.
- Shame associated with being exposed as 'abnormal' in front of others or generally feeling abnormal and different from others in a negative way. This may also include exposure of substance abuse or mental illness; situations, where the person is afraid of being regarded as crazy, insane or on the verge of a breakdown. This form of shame may also occur in situations where the person tells others about a trauma that they are, for various reasons, unable to deal with – and hence the person trivializes or diverts attention from it or shuts down any emotions related to the trauma.
- Shame stemming from perceived social exclusion, as the self is excluded from or not allowed into social communities; situations where the self

appears inferior or wrong in relation to others in a social group that the self identifies with and aspires to be a part of. This form of shame may be associated with a profound feeling of not belonging, a sense of internal and external homelessness.

- Ideality shame driven by discrepancy between ideal self and real self.
- Conscience shame associated with a recurring pattern of behaviour that the self perceives as wrong, failing to live up to their own norms, values and ideals for correct behaviour and feeling guilty over their actions. This form of shame may be difficult to distinguish clearly from destructive guilt.
- Shame activated by others' explicit shaming, scandalization or disparagement (stigmatization) of the self or a social group that the self is a part of and strongly identifies with (see Sadek, 2017). This may be associated with varying degrees of loss of face and perceived violation of the self's honour and dignity and core aspects of the self's identity. It may also include experiences of not being seen and met as a person (as 'oneself') but as a deindividualized representative of a (typically unnuanced, stereotyped) social category attributed certain – typically inferior – characteristics (based on gender, religion, nationality, ethnicity and so forth).
- Status shame activated by a loss of social status or generally low status, poverty or belonging to a socially marginalized group, such as 'homeless people', 'migrants' or 'welfare recipients'. In some cases, extreme wealth may also be associated with shame. This form of shame may also include shame associated with the self's (lowly, stigmatized) social class, language, dialect, habitus (being, body posture, hygiene, social behaviour/manners, humour and what and how to eat), appearance (clothes, make-up, hair-style, tattoos, jewellery) and education (cf. Tisseron, 1992, p. 134ff.).
- Shame because of the self's dependence on and need of others or over ruptures in the self's significant relationships. Shame because of being lonely, lacking a social network or being or feeling unwanted.
- Shame by proxy may be activated, for example, when the person witnesses others being subjected to humiliating treatment or putting themselves in a shameful situation and being overwhelmed by shame. Alternatively, it may occur when the self observes others' shameless self-presentation and/or disrespectful and shameless behaviour. In some cases, this shame may be accompanied by toxic Schadenfreude, a sense of pleasure or satisfaction derived from seeing others humiliated or humiliating themselves (Schultz-Venrath, 2022, p. 90).
- Existential shame related to a more persistent experience of the self being defective, inadequate, irrelevant, worthless and unlovable. Perceiving that the self is ignored and that, as far as others are concerned, the self might just as well not exist. May be associated with recurring experiences of the self being overlooked and feeling treated as an inanimate object; of others having no regard for the self's individuality or even acknowledging the self as a human subject that has its purpose and instead treating the self as an object for satisfying the needs of others. We may also speak of others'

soul blindness in their encounter with the self (Wurmser, 1994, p. 41f.); in its worst form, this soul blindness may result in soul murder and be perceived as an assault on the core of the self's sense of identity (Hirsch, 2022, p. 62f.).

Roughly put, the subjective experience of shame is the same across the categories outlined above. Moreover, the different forms of shame will often occur side by side, to some extent. In practice, it may therefore be difficult to draw clear distinctions between them. The above list of possible categories of shame is far from exhaustive and is intended primarily as an illustration of the many diverse types of experiences, incidents and situations that can give rise to shame. Furthermore, the definition of different subcategories of shame can often be helpful in the diagnostic assessment of and psychotherapeutic work with patients who are struggling with shame.

After this discussion of how feelings of shame are experienced and how we might distinguish between the sense of shame and constructive feelings of shame versus destructive shame, the next chapter will address, among other topics, how we might distinguish between different forms of shame, how people typically respond to or try to defend against painful feelings of shame and what is the fundamental difference between feelings of shame and guilt. Furthermore, the feeling of shame is attributed a central role in human psychology, especially with reference to the philosophers Jean-Paul Sartre and Max Scheler.

4 The basic structure of shame in relation to human sociality

There are many possible perspectives on the nature of shame and its role in human psychology. For example, modern affect theory focuses, to varying degrees, on biologically driven primary/basic and secondary/derivative affects, while at best assigning minor significance to a more dynamic psychological understanding and the relational context of the shame. A similar understanding, based mainly on one-person psychology, can be found in evolutionary psychology (Gilbert, 1998, 2007), which, among other topics, takes an interest in what human beings have in common with 'other animals', especially the higher mammals, and which describes how shame can be seen as an expression of submission and affirmation of existing social hierarchies. Another focus is how shame can dampen the others' aggression towards the self, especially from individuals who are stronger and occupy a higher position in the social hierarchy than the self.

In this view, human beings are seen as driven by a need for attachment and embeddedness in social groups and by persistent competition for social status (position in social hierarchies), in which the feeling of shame is regarded as a significant signal that the self and its identity appear negative in the eyes of others and, not least, that the self may therefore be at risk of social exclusion or attacks from others; that its social status may be jeopardized (Matos et al., 2013, p. 480). Finally, cognitive psychology offers an understanding of how shame relates to recurring thought patterns and the activation of certain – mostly dysfunctional – cognitive schemas in people who tend to experience and react with shame in certain situations (Lammers, 2016). These models for understanding the psychology of shame, some of which are quite narrow in focus and lack complexity, will not be further explored in the present context.

In the following, human shame is understood as a fundamental social, relational and intersubjective affect that is related to how people are constituted or created as subjects in interpersonal interactions and which helps to regulate social interactions and relationships. The feeling of shame cannot be reduced to a self-conscious emotion that simply plays out in the inner life of a single individual (cf. one-person psychology). It is a fundamentally social emotion related to human sociality. The particularly human affect of shame

DOI: 10.4324/9781003521174-4

is inextricably linked with the fundamentally social nature of human beings. This understanding of shame is based, in part, on one of the French philosopher Jean-Paul Sartre's principal works, *Being and Nothingness* (1943/2018), relational psychoanalysis (Mitchell, 1993) and the German philosophers Max Scheler (1957) and, to a lesser degree, Helmuth Plessner (2003, 2019). Each in their way, these writers have addressed issues of direct or indirect relevance for a deeper understanding of the nature of shame and its basis in some of the fundamental elements of human psychology (Lietzmann, 2007; Rutishauser, 1969).

In various ways, these writers describe a unique duality of human nature and existence, which means that we are never quite identical to ourselves, and it is precisely when this duality is 'revealed' or manifested in our ways of being and acting in interpersonal interactions that shame emerges. People are extended between a bodily and a spiritual being; as spiritual beings, we have, on the one hand, a certain degree of freedom to shape our being and existence, freedom to manifest ourselves, but on the other hand, we never have full command over our body (our nature or physical-bodily essence) and thus our whole selves. As a result, we are repeatedly confronted with the fact that we are never just who we thought we were; we are something other and more. Roughly put, a lower animal *is* its body and nature, while a human being *has* a body and a nature which we can, to some extent, distance ourselves from, observe and reflect on, just as we can attempt to regulate how our nature manifests itself (or is barely held in check) in our concrete actions. The feeling of shame also exposes the cracks in modern human beings' self-image as subjects characterized by a very high level of self-insight and self-control; it manifests the limits to the rational subject's self-control and independence of others' perceptions and judgments of the self.

Our bodily and spiritual beings are not identical, and we may be confronted with aspects of 'ourselves' that we did not know or which we have managed to deny, sometimes when we least expect it. When we are confronted with concrete manifestations of the duality of our being or with alien parts of ourselves, we may be overwhelmed by shame: 'I'm not like that', 'I don't want to be like this', 'I don't recognize myself' and so forth. For example, aspects of our desires, sexuality, lack of control of our own bodies, emotions and impulses or selfish needs might suddenly overwhelm us and control our actions and thus give rise to shame. At the same time, shame confronts us with the limits of our (often omnipotently overrated) freedom to manifest ourselves, the limits of our (similarly often omnipotently overrated) self-awareness, self-reflectiveness and ability to command or control every part of ourselves. We encounter something in ourselves that we do not immediately recognize or do not wish to acknowledge; we are confronted with ourselves as an 'it', an object, and with something alien inside us (Anders, 1956, p. 86). Precisely because the feeling of shame brings us into contact with aspects of ourselves that we do not normally have easy access to or which we deny, it can also be a potential source of self-insight – in addition to forcing us to reflect on how we appear in the eyes of others. Thus, in its less overwhelming non-destructive forms, shame can be a 'teacher' inviting us to look into and reflect on ourselves, examine our possible defects and deficits and seek to correct them (cf. Nathanson, 1992, p. 211).

4.1 The psychological elements of the feeling of shame

As mentioned earlier, there is no clear consensus about whether shame should be understood as a more or less innate and biologically determined affect that human beings may experience, at least in a rudimentary form, from an early time during the first year of life (Tomkins, 1963), or whether it is a more complex feeling that only emerges and manifests itself during the first years of life along with the development of more advanced self-awareness and mental representations and the human capacity for more sophisticated inter-subjective exchanges with others (Lewis et al., 1989; Broucek, 1997, p. 48; Czub, 2013). This question will not be discussed here. The main focus in the present context is on the more complex interpersonally determined feeling of shame in young people and adults, a time when normally developed cogni-tive human abilities – including the ability to construct mental representations of self, others and the world in general, the ability to attribute characteristics, intentions and other mental states to self and others and, not least, the ability to imagine how we are perceived by others – are always already involved in the experience of shame, albeit to varying degrees.

As mentioned earlier, the feeling of shame essentially springs from an experience where the self feels observed and wrong or inadequate in the eyes of 'others' or 'the world'. The 'other' may be a specific person or a more generalized or vaguely defined (imaginary) entity. The key issue is that the self has an experience of failing to live up to what others, the world at large and itself expects, along with thoughts about how 'one' ought to be and act. With age, the experience of failing to live up to and violating more complex and partly abstract common social standards, norms, values and ideals through our ways of being and acting comes to play an increasingly central role in the activation of shame. The feeling of shame is also closely related to a sense that the self's social ties and relationships with others are at risk, and that the self is at risk of being marginalized or excluded from the social community (Scheff, 1994, p. 43f.). As fundamentally social beings, we perceive these experiences as an existential threat. The feeling of shame may signal that our social selves are threatened, that the persons we think we are and which we hope or imagine others see us as are at risk of collapse (ibid., p. 51).

Like guilt and pride, among other feelings, shame is a complex self-conscious emotion that requires a certain degree of self-awareness and self-reflectiveness as well as a certain level of mental representations of self and others. Furthermore, these mental representations of self and others need to be fairly distinct from one another (cf. Zahavi, 2013, p. 320). The norms, values and ideals that the self's actual ways of being and acting are compared to are central elements of a normally developed human identity, which are thus also involved in the experience of shame.

With German philosopher Sonja Rinofner-Kreidl (2012, p. 167ff.), among others, we can point to certain elements of human psychology that need to be developed and present for us to experience shame. In addition to the ability to engage in intersubjective relationships with others (Stern, 1985, p. 88ff.) who are fairly distinct from our own selves, we can only experience more complex forms of shame if we have the ability to step away from ourselves and observe ourselves from outside, including observing and judging ourselves from the perspectives of concrete and generalized others. In this mode, we perceive 'others' not simply as objects of our own gratification but as independent subjects, distinct from our own selves and with their own inner lives and perspectives on reality and thus on our selves and our ways of being and acting in the world.

Only beings who are capable of transcending themselves (moving beyond their own immediate needs and egocentric subjective experiences), step away from themselves and observe themselves from outside, from someone else's perspective, are capable of experiencing shame (Rinofner-Kreidl, 2012, p. 169). In order to experience shame, we need to be able to attribute mental states and qualities to ourselves and others. We also need self-awareness – awareness of our own appearance and behaviour – as well as the awareness that others, too, have self-awareness. In addition, we need to be capable of fairly realistic thoughts about – and the ability to imagine and decode – how others see, perceive and judge who we are and how we act in specific situations. Finally, we also need to consider this to be significant to us.

Our normal tendency to care how others perceive us stems both from our fundamental social nature and from the fact that others' perceptions of us are important elements of our ability to judge whether our bonds with important others and our membership of social communities are at risk. The feeling of shame is thus a concrete manifestation of our basic human emotional sensitivity to others' experience and judgment of the self, which in its constructive forms is a crucial element of our capacity for social functioning. The feeling of shame can thus be regarded as a concrete manifestation of internal social control and as a form of moral sensitivity that helps us navigate in the social reality and is a necessary condition for human self-regulation and relational regulation.

In order to judge whether we are living up to ordinary expectations, conventions, norms, values and ideals – and feel shame when we do not – we need to know them and, to some extent, internalize them, just as we need to have some idea about who and what we want to be, in our own and others' eyes. We need a fairly realistic sense of prevailing ideas about what constitutes acceptable and unacceptable, normal and abnormal and even potentially stigmatizing ways of being and acting in various contexts, particularly social ones. Furthermore, we need to be able to compare our actual ways of being and acting with these common and widely acknowledged social standards and conduct a fairly realistic assessment of whether we are living up to them. This includes a fairly realistic assessment of whether our ways of being and acting may have violated normative standards, and if they have, how others feel about this. In the case of severely destructive shame, this sense of ordinary normative standards and the self's ability to live up to them may be distorted.

Our internalization of values and normative standards reflects the fact that we live in social communities that represent and impose certain standards for how people should be and act in order to be accepted members of the community. We have to generally acknowledge these standards, with their associated values and worldviews, as legitimate and, to some degree, make them our own or at least try to comply with them. On the other hand, it could be argued that the feeling of shame can help clarify – and potentially serve as an entry to challenging – prevailing social conventions and notions of what is normal and what is not. When we are overwhelmed by shame in a concrete situation, we realize that we have transgressed against social expectations, norms and conventions that we might have been complete or partially unaware of.

However, the experience of shame is not based solely on purely cognitive and rational processes, and if we wish to understand the feeling of shame from the perspective of humans as moral beings, we have to apply a very broad concept of morality. As mentioned earlier, the feeling of shame ranges from constructive shame, which often has a clear and obvious link to the human capacity for moral behaviour, to clearly destructive and pathological forms, which have a more ambiguous connection to human morality. Destructive shame will often stem from a basic sense of being wrong, inadequate, insignificant and unlovable that has been instilled from an early age and especially in interactions with caregivers and important others. This feeling will influence the self's understanding of specific interpersonal interactions, to varying degrees, and make the self hypersensitive to possible signs that others perceive the self as wrong, inferior or insignificant. In addition, the self may have internalized a critical and judgmental or even sadistically punishing other as the basis of inner object relationships. When this is the case, the self feels constantly observed and judged by a judgmental and shaming imaginary other. This will make the self highly likely to experience and respond with shame in many different situations, and the feeling of shame may develop into a more fundamental dysfunctional character trait.

In more extreme cases, recurring early experiences of shame may cause the self to interpret almost any situation to suggest that (concrete or imagined) others are observing, condemning and despising the self. As a result, the self may react with shame or various defences against shame (withdrawing from contact, attacking others and so forth). This happens even in situations where there are no obvious reasons for the self to feel wrong or inadequate and become shameful. Similarly, the person may have established completely unrealistic expectations of and ideas about what they need to be like in order to be okay (cf. perfectionism as an illusory attempt at avoiding shame), which may further contribute to chronic shame and feelings of inadequacy. Finally, a person who is tormented by severe destructive shame may be fundamentally insecure about who they are and should be in order to be accepted as an equal subject, like everybody else. The only thing that seems certain is that the self is wrong, unattractive and inferior.

Sartre's view: Shame and alienation

In *Being and Nothingness*, Sartre (1943/2018) addresses human self-consciousness, the experience of becoming an object of others' and our own gaze. He views the feeling of shame as perhaps the strongest manifestation of what happens when we find that the self is regarded as an object, and we are compelled, in a sense, to give up our illusion of being the unaffected centre of our own subjective universe (Landweer, 1999, p. 39). Shame confronts us with being a simple object in the eye of the other, being observed and judged. Paradoxically, this conversion of the self to an object of observation and (self-)reflection is what forms the foundation of and condition for human subjectivity. With Sartre, we can understand how an individual is constituted as a subject the very moment they find themselves to be an object of another person's gaze; initially, this typically involves the parents observing and, to varying degrees, evaluating the self and sending signals to the self about how it is seen by others.

This process is the underlying source of human self-consciousness and our ability to step away from ourselves and view ourselves from outside, from the perspectives of both concrete others and the generalized other (cf. Mead, 1934). This ability is fundamental to human self-reflectiveness and the ability to self-regulate in accordance with outside demands and expectations. As formulated by Sartre (1943/2018, p. 308), the other is 'the indispensable intermediary between me and myself'. We are not objective observers of ourselves; we see how others see and judge us, we compare ourselves to others, we see ourselves through the eyes of others, and we use this as a basis of our self-image and self-assessment (Meyer, 2011, p. 36).

Human self-consciousness, our ability to step away from and reflect on ourselves, is thus always already intersubjectively mediated via others' gaze at the self. We need the other's gaze at us in order to attain the detachment from and outside perspective on ourselves that allow us to reflect on and attempt to understand ourselves. The feeling of shame is also grounded and arises in this selfsame interpersonal process. Thus, shame is always already an intersubjective affect that springs from interactions with concrete or imagined others. Shame arises when we are confronted with being objects of others' observation and judgment – a judgment we are helplessly exposed to and have no control of. As French philosopher Emmanuel Levinas (1961/1969, p. 84) puts it, shame 'does not have the structure of consciousness and clarity. … its subject is exterior to me'. Shame is activated when we sense that we are being observed, judged and, for some reason, found to be inferior or defective or when we fail to live up to our own or others' expectations; all of which happens without us having any clear understanding why or the ability to step away from ourselves and reflect on how we might understand the shame that is overwhelming us.

Thus, shame confronts us with the fact that we are distinct from others and that we are the object of their observation and judgment without having any control of this. We are, so to speak, at the mercy of the other's evaluating gaze; an other whose gaze gives them power over us. With Sartre, we can say that 'hell is other people', because we have no control of others' gaze and judgment of us – because we are at the mercy of their perception of us. 'Inherently, shame is *recognition*. I recognize that I *am* as the Other sees me' (Sartre, 1943/2018, p. 308), although this recognition must often be regarded as forced. Also, 'With the Other's look the "situation" escapes me ...: *I am no longer master of the situation*' (ibid., p. 363). Shame is thus associated with a loss of control, as the self is subjected to the other's evaluating gaze. Typically, this also means that the self is emotionally overwhelmed, feels exposed and loses control of their emotional and other immediate reactions, without knowing why. The other sees who I am, and I have no control of how the other sees me or what they see. Fundamentally, thus, shame occurs when the self is reduced to an object of the other's gaze; the self is reified and locked or frozen in the other's gaze (cf. Sartre, 1943/2018, p. 233).

To Sartre, the unbearable quality of shame does not spring primarily from the specific way in which the self appears wrong or inferior in the eyes of the other but rather from the fundamental experience of being unavoidably subjected to the other's gaze and judgment (cf. Holzhey-Kunz, 2007, p. 19), unable to hide behind masks or facades in an attempt to 'show' that the self is not as it is revealed to be and confronted with being in the encounter with the other (cf. Schäfer & Thompson, 2009, p. 14). We often try to control how others see us – as part of our attempts to regulate both our selves and our self-esteem – but the feeling of shame lets us know that this is not possible, or only to a very limited degree.

Shame is, so to speak, woven into the basic fabric of human existence. As we notice the other's gaze at us, we discover how the other, to varying degrees, attributes us a certain being and certain characteristics of which we have no knowledge or control. When we see the other's gaze at our own selves, we become aware that we are being observed and judged as objects. We are 'thrown back' on ourselves and compelled to consider how we appear to the other; how the other judges us. This process will also, to varying degrees, be influenced by how we as individuals project our own perceptions of who and what we are and how we appear, both in the concrete situation and more generally, on a concrete or more generalized and abstract (imaginary) other – perceptions influenced by our own earlier experiences with how we have been seen, judged and evaluated by others.

Thus, the other's gaze at the self cannot be understood completely separated from the observed individual's self-perception and how elements of this self-perception are projected on the other (Neckel, 1991, p. 34). We might also say that the observed self's own internal objects and superego, stemming from earlier experiences and relationships, are projected on and influence its perception of the other's gaze at the self (Gullestad, 2020, p. 435). The feeling of shame confronts us with and forces us to acknowledge that we are an object which the other is observing, evaluating and judging. This also means that, in a sense, we are alienated from ourselves or that we are not fully identical with ourselves. There will always be 'something' about ourselves we have not seen but which the other sees and may subsequently confront us with. With the feeling of shame, we are suddenly and unexpectedly confronted with sides of ourselves we may find alien, undesirable and incompatible with our established self-image, our perception of who we are and who we would like to be. The other, so to speak, knows the 'secret' of who we really are; this exposes our powerlessness and forces us to acknowledge the obvious limits of our self-insight and our insight into our ways of being in our own or others' eyes.

When I am put in these situations, I am also 'ashamed of myself as I appear to the Other', as Sartre (1943/2018, p. 308) put it. And via the other, I 'pass judgment on myself as I might pass judgment on an object' (ibid.). I internalize the other's gaze at and judgment of me and subsequently observe, judge and perhaps condemn myself in reflection of what I saw in the other's gaze. Thus, I lose some of my freedom when I am observed, judged and locked into something others have defined. 'My original fall is the Other's existence' (ibid., p. 360). In the confrontation with the other's observation and judgment of my self, I lose my innocence and my spontaneous being (a state in which I am unaware of myself) and become ashamed of myself in front of others. This experience and reality, as mentioned above, is described as early as in the biblical story of the Fall.

Shame highlights and is thus a concrete manifestation of our social constitution and relational being, our fundamental being-for-others. Thus, shame springs from the acknowledgement that we are the self that the other sees, from unavoidably identifying with and feeling compelled to relate to the object that is being observed and judged by the other. The other's gaze represents a truth about our selves that is beyond our control and which we cannot escape, even if we might try through various forms of self-deception, including the one-sided objectification of the other as a possible (illusory) strategy for evading the other's objectifying gaze and thus immunizing the self against shame (see Section 5.4). This process is not limited to individual concrete interactions with real or present others but may, in principle, overwhelm us anywhere, anytime. 'The Other is present to me everywhere, as that through which I become an object' (Sartre, 1943/2018, pp. 380–381); an imagined (mentally represented) and generalized (not necessarily concrete) other who is always observing and judging the self. This may, potentially, induce shame because the self might be perceived as inferior, defective and inadequate. The possibility or risk of being 'exposed' and experiencing shame is thus present everywhere and may become reality at any moment.

Thus, in several ways, shame is a fundamentally social affect. It is associated with the self's fear of losing honour, dignity, reputation and social status in the eyes of others. It shows the self's fundamental sociality, its being in the field of tension between separateness and connectedness; between the self's ability to command and manifest itself (the freedom of the self) and its deep dependence on and constitution in interpersonal interactions (the embeddedness of the self in relations and communities). Although we may feel shame by proxy on behalf of others, including people close to us with whom we identify, we mainly feel shame over ourselves, who and what we are and how we appear and act. In any case, it is important to note that we feel shame in front of someone, a real or imagined other; thus, shame implies the existence of an other and, not least, our recognition and acknowledgement of the other's existence as a subject who observes and judges our selves as objects, just as we may similarly observe and judge others as objects. Shame is thus both a self-conscious and a social affect: self-conscious because it is closely associated with self-awareness, and social because it relies on our awareness of how we are seen and judged by others.

As an ontological experience, shame is related to anxiety, not just because shame is often accompanied by anxiety and (ontological) insecurity but also because both affects are related to the human condition, extended as we are between two forms of being: subject and object. Neither affect has a specific content. Both anxiety and shame may, in principle, be triggered by an infinitely wide range of concrete incidents and subjective experiences. Anxiety confronts the self with fundamental uncertainty related to the lack of control of its existence, while shame to a higher degree confronts the self with its existence in the eyes of others and in relation to others, which is similarly uncertain and cannot be determined once and for all. If it could, we would be able to comply and deal with it, which is precisely what we cannot do when it comes to shame and which is the cause of this painful affect (Holzhey-Kunz, 2007).

Because (the ability to experience) shame – and, likewise, anxiety – relates to basic aspects of human existence, we can never eliminate or eradicate shame as a recurring affective reaction and subjective experience. This is true, even though it may sometimes appear that modern humans wish and imagine this were possible; for example, some might think that sufficiently liberal socialization and social structures would give individuals maximal freedom of self-expression and self-realization as autonomous individuals and thus eliminate the feeling of shame. On the other hand, we should naturally do everything possible to limit the development of destructive shame, just as psychotherapeutic treatment can diminish destructive shame and its consequences for individual well-being.

Sartre's one-person-psychology: The need for an intersubjective framework

This is not the place for an in-depth discussion of Sartre's existential philosophy. However, it should be noted that Sartre's predominant focus is on individuals and how they are affected by the other's gaze, while he takes little interest in the capacity of intersubjective interactions and the ongoing dialogue and reciprocity in concrete interpersonal relationships – as opposed to an abstract other's influence on the individual's self-image and self-esteem – to continually change everyone involved in interactional processes that cannot be reduced to how one person affects another (see Chapter 7). Sartre also overstates the alienation of the self from itself in the encounter with the other's gaze.

As discussed by the German philosophers G. W. F. Hegel (1807/2019) and Axel Honneth (1992/1996), among others, in contrast to Sartre's perspective, it could be argued that it is precisely in equal and well-functioning interactions with others that we meet and recognize ourselves (Neckel, 1991, p. 30); that we are constituted and recognized as ourselves in well-functioning encounters with others. In this view, the intersubjective meeting is grounded in reciprocal recognition as the positive condition for human existence, development and well-being (see also Lepold, 2021), not as a limitation. Conversely, of course, dysfunctional and destructive relationships can hamper human well-being and development, including giving rise to destructive shame that inhibits human self-expression. However, that is quite different from claiming that every interpersonal encounter is inherently structured in such a way that it unavoidably limits human freedom and self-expression. These two perspectives represent fundamentally different views of human nature and development; however, this point will not be further explored in the present context (see Jørgensen, 2020, p. 127ff.).

Thus, with Sartre we can argue that the other's judging gaze, which also assigns the self to particular categories, for example as female or male, limits the self's identity and scope of self-expression (see also Butler, 1990, 1997). However, it is worth considering whether this intersubjective process does not also contain positive and structuring elements that might be helpful, at least to some people. The other's open, curiously interested and empathically mirroring gaze at the self thus also allows for the self to feel seen, 'recognized', understood and accepted. This can in itself have a positive effect on the self and may also provide an external framework (order, organization) for the self's being and self-perception in a reality that might otherwise seem overwhelmingly complex, at least to some, who therefore seek external points to navigate by and a stable reference for their self-perception and their ways of acting in the world. In this sense, the other's observing and judging gaze is not necessarily a limitation of the freedom, identity and self-expression of the autonomous individual or unavoidably associated with destructive shame. The feeling of shame may be an inescapable element of the basic structure of human existence, but it is not in itself restrictive, let alone destructive (cf.

the existence of more constructive forms of shame), except as the result of deeply negative experiences in interactions with concrete others that give rise to destructive shame.

Thus, shame is a social affect because it arises in the transitional or border-land between self and other, between known, familiar ground and unknown, alien territory, between internal and external reality. With the German psy-choanalyst Günther Seidler (1995, p. 1ff.), we can regard shame as an inter-face affect that arises when the two worlds meet and prove less than fully aligned (ibid., p. 44). In addition, shame may be regarded as an affect that both marks and manifests the boundary between known and unknown, internal and external, and thus also helps to delimit and stabilize human identity (Römer, 2017, p. 317). Precisely because shame also arises in the transitional space between self and other, it cannot be reduced to a purely individual affect. Shame is not just something that occurs within a sharply defined individual; it also contains important intersubjective dimensions. And although shame is a universal affect, inextricably linked to the human con-dition, sociocultural conditions will always influence what activates shame, the intensity of the shame affect and our ability to detoxify and manage shame. Even though shame is an intersubjective affect that is always already associated with human beings' fundamentally social nature, it is, of course, the individual subject who has the concrete experience of shame, possibly with others. The 'locus' of shame is the subject who feels shame, although it could be argued that entire cultures and societies may at times struggle with destructive shame, as was the case for Germany during the interwar years, for example (see Section 6.2). Through psychoanalysis, we may get a little closer to what specifically happens in a subject who is experiencing shame. As mentioned earlier, human beings have a unique ability to step away from and judge themselves from outside, from the perspective of others, as they see themselves through their eyes. The ego contains and is able to alternate between an experiential and an analytic perspective. We can jump back and forth between a mode where we are primarily simply present, experiencing what is happening in the moment, and a mode where we are able, to some extent, to observe and judge ourselves (and the current situation) from out-side, as an object; not necessarily objectively or from a neutral position but with an external gaze that we have developed by internalizing important others' and, to a lesser degree, strangers' gaze and judgment of the self.

As Seidler (1995/2000, p. 23) puts it, the shameful subject undergoes a doubling, becoming a self consisting of two separate but connected func-tional modes, as the subject is, to varying degrees, swallowed up by an overwhelming sense of shame in the moment (cf. the experiencing self) while simultaneously observing themselves from outside as a defective, inferior, humiliated and hence shameful self (cf. the analysing self). The self alternates between being (in) the immediate experience and objectifying themselves, observing and judging themselves from outside. Several writers have also highlighted how the feeling of shame delimits the self and marks and protects the boundary between self and others that is so crucial to human identity and mental health (Hilgers, 2013, p. 311; Scheler, 1957).

Having and experiencing a boundary between self and others that is flexible and permeable without breaking down is an important condition for our ability, as social beings, to function in social communities, where we need to allow ourselves to be affected by and to consider others' perceptions of the self and our concrete acts without engaging in limitless adaptation to others' perceptions, judgments and expectations of the self, which would put an end to the self's existence as a coherent, delimited and autonomous entity.

Scheler's approach: Shame in the encounter of spirit and nature

Max Scheler (1957, p. 67) begins his discussion of the nature of shame by stating that nowhere is humanity's unique position in between the divine or elevated and the animal (or vulgar) as clearly and immediately expressed as in the feeling of shame. According to Scheler, human nature is characterized by a peculiar duality and conflict between, on the one hand, our animal-bodily nature, with all its associated 'lower' (or more immediate, non-spiritual) needs, and, on the other hand, our spiritual existence (in German: 'Geist'). To Scheler, this internal conflict or disharmony between our bodily and our spiritual nature is the foundation that enables the feeling of shame.

With Scheler, we can argue that because human beings have a body with immediate (bodily) impulses and needs, we may end up in situations where we are affected or even overwhelmed by shame. Because our spiritual existence is always already embedded in a body with an associated animal or animal nature and lower, non-spiritual needs, we may experience situations where we experience shame over concrete manifestations of this 'nature', which is a part of the self but is also in conflict or out of step with our spiritual existence. It is solely due to our spiritual existence – the fact that we are and perceive ourselves as persons or subjects who are relatively independent of our bodily beings – that we may experience situations where we might feel shame. This shame may be activated by an essentially infinite variation of concrete experiences and situations (see later) and range from brief constructive shame to chronic destructive shame. However, the human capacity for experiencing shame and the fact that we do so across a wide variety of situations are related to basic structures of human existence, which Scheler can help us describe and understand.

It is easy to argue that Scheler's understanding of shame contains both obsolete and obviously problematic elements, including naively romantic, religious and racist (during his time, widespread antisemitic) ideas about human nature. Furthermore, Scheler's philosophy represents a somewhat narrow one-person psychology (Jørgensen, 2019, p. 123ff.). In his understanding, we primarily feel shame in front of ourselves, which ignores the fundamentally social aspect of shame. Despite these limitations, his philosophically oriented approach to shame contains an original kernel of truth about the possible constructive elements of the feeling of shame and its positive functions in human psychology – as both a reflection and a defence of elevated and valuable aspects of human beings and our existence; a defence against falling into ways of being and acting towards others that is dominated by lower values and immediate impulses and needs (Scheler, 1957, p. 80).

As Scheler (ibid., p. 69) put it: no animal and no god can feel shame. Only humankind, which bridges the gap between the two worlds, are capable of feeling shame. Our being plays out in the borderland between the two spheres of being, and human nature is equally grounded in the spheres of spiritual and bodily being. With inspiration from Sartre's existentialist philosophy, somewhat rhetorically put, we can say that human ways of being play out in eternal tension between an existence as free and spiritual subjects and an essence or nature that is grounded in a physical body with related impulses and needs which we continually need to attempt to regulate and manage. Shame represents an interface and a conflict between the two worlds, or, as Scheler (ibid.) put it, as human beings, we are ashamed of (and in front of) ourselves and in front of God (or the elevated aspects) in ourselves.

It is, naturally, debatable whether Scheler's conceptualization covers all types of shame, but with Scheler, we can say that certain forms of shame (related to the human body, aggression and sexuality in a broad sense) arise when our spiritual existence and our bodily grounded being (nature) meet and clash in mutual conflict. At the same time, according to Scheler, we can view constructive shame as a reflection of our spiritual existence and ability to strive for goals, norms, values and ideals that go beyond ways of being and acting that are driven by our own immediate impulses, affects and needs (our lower, animal nature). Shame protects our own and others' honour, dignity and reputation. It prevents violations of our own and others' modesty, boundaries of intimacy and 'untouchability zone', and it prevents both the self and others from being put in shameful situations as a result of transgressive and shameless behaviour. Constructive shame signals that there are certain things we should avoid doing in order to prevent the self and others from being put in situations that cause overwhelming (destructive) shame. In this sense, the feeling of shame protects our own and others' integrity, boundaries and self-esteem.

A certain level of shame or sense of shame – proneness to shame when we have failed or offended others and an ability to tolerate and manage feelings of shame – is thus a sign of maturity and a high level of psychological functioning. Conversely, shamelessness and the absence of shame in our ways of being and acting in interpersonal interactions is a marker of immaturity, psychological dysfunction and, potentially, even psychopathology, including dissocial and narcissist disorders. Based on Scheler's distinction between elevated and animal human existence, we can also argue that the feeling of shame manifests the body's and (animal) human nature's veto or 'rebellion' against the (alleged) dominance of reason and rationality in human existence; shame sows doubt about the omnipotence of human reason and marks our indisputable bodily existence (Meyer-Drawe, 2009, p. 38). Without resorting to the primitive drive theory of classical psychoanalysis, it is worth noting the power – including the potentially liberating power – of human sexuality; a power that could also be mobilized, for example, in younger women's fight against destructive shame and perceived shaming of their sexuality.

In Scheler's somewhat narrow interpretation, shame is thus a feeling that defends higher spiritual values in human life, and with Scheler, we can speak of constructive shame as contributing to the human capacity for self-regulation; our ability to avoid letting lower needs and impulses control our ways of being and acting and instead aim for higher – or, to use Scheler's terminology, elevated – values. The feeling of shame diminishes the ability of lower impulses and mundane needs to dominate human existence and gives us the freedom to engage with spiritual values (Scheler, 1957, p. 112). It gives us access to the elevated and valuable qualities within ourselves (ibid., p. 115) and is also ethically significant, as it is associated with human conscience and our ability to act in accordance with social norms and obligations (Zahavi, 2013, p. 324). With Scheler, we can argue that constructive shame – related to human modesty and the tendency to become embarrassed when we or others violate normal boundaries for civilized acting or violate the prevailing social conventions of a community – is a reflection of our humanity (cf. Schneider, 1987, p. 194).

4.2 Different forms of shame

Shame as a transient state or a generalized reaction

One category is momentary or highly fleeting states of shame. In contrast to this situational shame, we also need to include a category characterized by shame-proneness, a more general tendency to experience and react with feelings of shame across different types of incidents and situations. This latter category represents a general vulnerability to experiences of shame that is related to more fundamental character or personality traits or more generalized shame. Finally, some writers include a category of shame that is regarded as a more specific reaction to or result of traumatization (Saraiya & Lopez-Castro, 2016), including sexual and other forms of abuse.

In addition, it can be helpful to divide people with increased shame-proneness into two groups, with one group defined as particularly bashful, shy and likely to become embarrassed but in ways that are primarily associated with experiences of constructive or not severely destructive shame. These individuals might also be described as highly sensitive or as persons with an extraordinary sense of shame, which can be both a blessing and a curse. The other group includes people who are affected by more or less chronic destructive shame or who tend to react with intense and destructive feelings of shame across a very wide range of incidents and situations. In this latter group, destructive shame leads to considerably diminished quality of life and psychological functioning. This category of shame, which sometimes manifests itself as a permanent underlying subjective experience of one's own self being inferior and defective or a heightened tendency to react to even minor humiliations and missteps with severely destructive shame, is found mainly among people with more severe mental illness, for example certain eating disorders and disorders of personality organization at a borderline level (Kernberg, 1993). Chronic destructive shame may be masked and outwardly manifested mainly as self-destructive behaviour or aggressive attacks on others as a defence against unbearable shame.

Internal and external shame

The Danish word for shame includes at least two slightly different phenomena (see also Chapter 2), which can be described as internal versus external shame, both of which involve a wide range of subjective experiences. Internal shame (corresponding to the German 'Scham') is primarily about the self's negative perception and judgment of itself; the individual's self-critical gaze, condemnation of and disgust with themselves or even self-hatred. In its more destructive forms, internal shame should be viewed as internalized shame with roots in earlier experiences which involved the self being shamed, subjected to varying degrees of neglect or feeling wrong and inadequate in the eyes of important others. Internalization of perceived shaming and shame in interpersonal interactions thus gradually cause us to shame ourselves. We come to perceive and judge ourselves in the same negative ways that others have viewed and treated the self, in our experience – as a worthless, inadequate and defective person who deserves to be humiliated and excluded. In some situations, internal shame may also serve as a form of defence against or a strategy for managing external shame by, so to speak, pre-empting others' shaming and exclusion of the self by shaming and disparaging ourselves. In this way, we signal that we perceive ourselves as clearly inferior and subject to the others' judgment and control.

External shame refers to a person's general perceptions – and possibly their concrete subjective experience in the moment – of having others observe, disapprove of and disparage the self. In this category, the primary focal point of the shame is real or imagined others' concrete or imagined condemnation and contempt for the self. Compared with internal shame, this external feeling of shame may be associated with a more pronounced fear of the self being exposed or revealed as inferior and consequently rejected or excluded from the community. Analytically, we can discern two subcategories of external shame: (1) external shame associated with specific incidents or recurring patterns in significant relationships, where concrete others actually shame, humiliate and scandalize the self or subject it to degrading and disrespectful treatment (German: 'Schande'), and (2) external shame that springs from the person's subjective perception that others view the self as inferior and defective, but where this subjective experience seems highly influenced by the person's tendency to project their own negative self-perceptions on others. This is primarily found in individuals with low self-esteem and a strong tendency to experience and react with shame in a variety of situations. In some cases, it can be difficult to distinguish the latter subcategory of external shame clearly from internal shame.

Drawing a distinction between internal and external shame may have a certain theoretical relevance, but in practice, it is often of less significance. Perceptions of others' critical and condemning gaze at the self will often contain projective elements and are thus closely related to the person's self-condemnation (projected self-contempt, which is then subjectively perceived as others' contempt for the self and so forth). Furthermore, over time, recurring experiences of others condemning and shaming the self will often be internalized and contribute to the development of a more chronic form of internal shame, including shame-proneness across a wide range of social situations.

Empirical studies suggest that perceived internal and external shame are so closely related (their mutual correlation being very high) that in practice, it is not always possible to draw a meaningful distinction between them (see, e.g., Øktedalen et al., 2014, p. 610). However, a small number of studies have found, for example, that symptoms of anorexia are more closely correlated with a high level of external shame, whilst symptoms of bulimia, on the other hand, seem to have a stronger correlation with internal shame, especially excessive preoccupation with own body weight and appearance (cf. Goss & Allan, 2009, p. 305). Individuals with a lower level of psychological functioning may be particularly prone to having their own and others' critical gaze at the self fuse into one, causing them to imagine or even being convinced that others see and judge the self as critically as they do themselves. Conversely, they may also 'take over' others' (real or imagined) gaze at and judgment of the self in a self-perpetuating destructive process, where it may be difficult in practice to draw a clear distinction between internal and external shame.

On the other hand, it can also be argued that in some cases, whether the subjectively experienced shame is primarily internal or external can affect whether a person develops more severe relational difficulties and what types of mental disorders the person might develop in connection with destructive shame. It makes a difference whether the person mainly shames and condemns themselves or whether they find that others observe, condemn and perhaps abuse and humiliate the self. When the responsibility for the perceived shame is placed outside the self, for better or worse, the person can avenge and defend against the perceived shame by attacking others, which can sometimes (temporarily) diminish the shame. On the other hand, this may give rise to new problems, including additional shame when the person takes revenge on and attacks others in shameful ways. Similarly, it is possible to achieve some defence against external shame by avoiding contact with others, but over time, this strategy may cause the person to become socially isolated and tormented by loneliness.

The subject and object of shame

In relation to the above-mentioned distinction between internal and external shame, we can identify two poles in the experience of shame (Seidler, 1995/ 2000, p. 107): (1) what the person is ashamed over (the subject pole), and (2) the factor in front of which the person is ashamed (the object pole) (see also Wurmser, 1981b, p. 43f.). Roughly put, in internal shame, the self is both subject and object: 'I am ashamed over (and in front of) myself' (or an internalized other). In the case of external shame, the self is still the basis of the subject pole of the shame, while the object pole, the factor in front of which the person is ashamed, is a concrete or imagined other who observes, judges and condemns the self. 'The other' may be a concrete person to whom the individual attributes some form of authority or considers an ideal that the self strives to realize, or it may be a more generalized other or a mental representation of a wide range of interpersonal interactions that has been generalized or combined into a general idea about how others see and judge the self (cf. Stern, 1985).

From the perspective of modern psychoanalysis, which views shame as a basic social affect, we should naturally be cautious about taking these somewhat rigid categories too literally, as no one is ever really ashamed only in front of themselves. Even in situations where we might feel that this is the case, the experience will always stem from having internalized others' gaze at and judgment of the self based on the sum of earlier experiences of others observing and judging the self. The self's own gaze at itself is thus always already relational and the result of important others' earlier perceived gaze at the self. When the self condemns and despises themselves, this is always a result of earlier experiences when important others either overlooked the self and signalled that it is wrong or worthless or expressed their disapproval of, disgust with or contempt for the self in various ways.

When someone is overwhelmed by shame, with a dominant subjective experience that can be captured by the phrase 'I feel ashamed', they are in a largely passive position. This may be because the person is presently the passive victim of shaming by others. In that case, the passive self will be experiencing primarily external shame, as the other acts. On the other hand, someone who feels overwhelmed by shame without being able to relate the feeling to shaming by concrete others may appear to be in the position of a passive victim of a feeling of shame that seems to spring solely from the person themselves: their own negative self-perceptions or persistent rumination over the self's defects and deficits and the person's own self-hatred and self-contempt.

In relation to this distinction, it may again be helpful to include the classical psychoanalytical distinction between the person's (1) perceiving self and

(2) analytical or reflective and evaluating self. If someone is overwhelmed by shame without being able to identify an external other shaming, they are shaming themselves and should therefore, in a sense, be understood as dealing with internal disintegration and conflict, as one (active) part of the self disparages, despises and shames another (passive) part of the self. Earlier, concrete others humiliated and shamed the self, but now, the feeling of shame has become a part of the person themselves, continuing this painful humiliation and shaming of the self, often in the form of explicit self-hatred, self-stigmatization, severe self-neglect and disparagement of the self or core aspects of the self: 'I hate my body', 'the only thing I like about myself is my hair, everything else is shit', 'I'm just so fucking stupid', 'I am a loser' and so forth. However, 'the other' is always, at least indirectly, involved in the feeling of shame. 'The other' is always, at least, somewhere in the wings, influencing what is visibly unfolding on stage, either in the form of one or more concrete others or of an imagined other. Shame can never be reduced entirely to internal processes in a clearly delimited individual. Furthermore, someone who is struggling with severe internal shame may unconsciously seek and contribute to arranging situations and relationships in which they are degraded, humiliated and punished as a form of concretized and externalized realization of the painful internal shame (cf. masochism, see Section 4.3). At an unconscious level, the self's inner drama is staged and concretized in interpersonal interactions.

Generally, shaming is an active act directed at the self, concrete others or, in some cases, entire groups who share a common characteristic or a common social identity that is made the object of shaming and contempt. This may, for example, be people who are unemployed, immigrants, prostitutes or people who are mentally ill. On the surface, active shaming (of others or of parts of one's own self, for example, the body) may be accompanied by a sense of strength, agency and power, as illustrated, for example, in the earlier passage from Dostoyevsky's novel *Notes from Underground* (see Chapter 2). In fact, however, aggressive shaming, whether directed at the self or others, is often a sign of a fragile, vulnerable and shameful self's desperate attempt at escaping an experience of shameful weakness, powerlessness and perceived insignificance (Hell, 2018, p. 70). Ultimately, it is thus far from a sign of strength and instead a shameful manifestation of our own weakness when we shame or humiliate others who are typically in a weaker position than ourselves and violate their boundaries, honour and human dignity without any interpersonal empathy.

Time perspectives

When we experience shame, the feeling may be characterized by different time perspectives. Based on this, Wurmser (1981a, p. 13; 1981b, p. 50f.) defines three categories of shame, all of them to some degree associated with deep-seated fear or perceived risk of being seen as weak, insignificant and inadequate or met with contempt, rejection, ridicule and signals suggesting that the self is invisible and of no importance to anyone:

- A largely *forward-looking shame anxiety*, fear of the self being scandalized. (Anticipatory) fear of being exposed, found out and humiliated as an inadequate human being. This fear of others' contempt may also serve as a warning signal and help the person prevent the self from being dishonoured, brought into disgrace and overwhelmed by shame by avoiding certain (potentially shameful) acts and instead acting in ways that protect the self, mark the self's boundaries of intimacy and avoid situations where the self is unnecessarily exposed in front of others. This may make the person more restrained and respectful in interpersonal interactions. In less adaptive forms, this may make the person overly restrained, inhibited and withdrawn from social contact in an (illusory) attempt to avoid others' judging and shame-inducing gaze. Shame anxiety may also manifest itself as acute and overwhelming panic anxiety due to fear of being affected by shame (Wurmser, 1986, p. 17). Arguably, less severe, non-destructive shame anxiety can be seen as related to our constructive sense of shame: the human capacity to anticipate own and others' reactions and pause before we speak or act in interpersonal interactions.
- *Shame affect proper, in the moment*, when the self feels revealed, humiliated, exposed as weak and defective and feels that they are met with contempt from others, which causes the self to be overwhelmed by painful shame. This is shame about something that has already happened or which is happening in the moment that marks tension or a gap between how we wish to be and how we actually see ourselves or perceive that others see us; between what we or others expect and what is actually happening in the moment. According to Wurmser (1986, p. 17), the shame affect contains a depressive core driven by not wanting to be the person who has been exposed in the self's shameful appearance and a desire to disappear; in more extreme forms, it involves a (typically non-concrete) perceived desire to stop existing, although this feeling is not necessarily associated with suicidal thoughts or intentions.
- *Shame as a character trait*, referring to general shame-proneness. A reaction formation intended to prevent both the shame anxiety and the shame affect proper from emerging by persistently activated psychological defence mechanisms and strategies aimed at covering up the shame. This may, for example, apply to someone who is socially isolated and generally tries to avoid any kind of emotional contact with others, driven by a persistent undercurrent of destructive shame that threatens to increase precipitously and overwhelm the self in close interpersonal contact.

This form of reactive shame may cause the self to hide behind a mask or facade in order to protect their inner life from others' gaze, just as it may limit the self's curious and intimidating gaze at others; a mechanism that protects others from shame. This reaction formation may also involve the develop-ment of certain character traits aimed at preventing the self from being put in situations where it will be exposed as unworthy and scandalous, such as character traits related to restraint, veneration, awe, social judgment and rev-erence. Similarly, the feeling of shame can be masked behind indignation and anger over what the self perceives as primitive, illegitimate or inferior ways of being and acting by identified others. In this case, the self's own shame is hidden from both self and others. However, these different strategies aimed at avoiding or diverting own and others' attention from shame do not make the shame go away. It lives on behind the facade, behind the masks. Based on classical psychoanalysis, we can say that the shame is, to some degree, repressed and pushed into the unconscious (or the non-conscious), from where it will continue to influence the self's experiences and actions in the world, until it is drawn back into the light and acknowledged, and the self perhaps receives help to deal with their shame in a more psychologically mature manner.

Wurmser's concept of shame anxiety can aid our understanding of the distinction that was introduced earlier between constructive and destruc-tive (toxic) shame and the dynamic psychological processes related to the feeling of shame. Shame anxiety can be understood from the perspective of the development of anxiety theory in classical psychoanalysis. Initially, in his early and rather primitive anxiety theory, Freud viewed anxiety as the result of repressed drives, but in his later work, he wrote about so-called signal anxiety. Freud compared signal anxiety to a vaccination, as the ego imagines a situation or incident that threatens it. This is accompanied by a weakened version of the anxiety that will arise should the imagined situation actually occur.

The key function of signal anxiety is thus to enable the ego to act in ways that let it avoid dangerous situations and other related incidents that, were they to become true, would be accompanied by much greater anxiety (Freud, 1926/1949, p. 150ff.). In other words, signal anxiety reflects an anticipated situation or incident that would be stressful to the self, allowing the self to avoid this experience while exposing the self to a weakened version of the anxiety reaction that would overwhelm it if the imagined event were to happen (ibid., p. 158). In addition, signal anxiety may also indicate a current or emer-ging imbalance in the individual's life. In the latter case, the anxiety helps to motivate the self to examine and address these possible life imbalances. As long as the signal anxiety is not so intense and destructive that the self is overwhelmed, it thus provides an opportunity for the self to anticipate and prevent future difficulties, provided the self is open to and curious about what the anxiety might signal. Predominantly constructive shame, which is not so intensive and persistent that it overwhelms and destabilizes the self, holds similar potential provided the person allows themselves to feel it, examine it and reflect on its possible implications rather than immediately pushing it away or activating defensive strategies.

Parallel with Freud's understanding of signal anxiety, which, in a sense, has a functional purpose, we should strive to adopt a nuanced and reflective stance towards the feeling of shame and view constructive shame or shame anxiety as a less overwhelming non-toxic form of shame that might motivate us to avoid situations where we risk being overwhelmed by much more intense and destructive shame. It gives us a chance to modify our behaviour, for example in order to minimize our risk of being abandoned by important others or excluded from social communities. Shame anxiety and constructive shame may thus have psychological functions that are closely related to Freud's thoughts on signal anxiety.

In his later anxiety theory, Freud (ibid.) also distinguishes between objective anxiety – fear of known (conscious) threats – and neurotic or more obviously irrational and dysfunctional anxiety – fear of (unconscious) threats we are not (readily) aware of. In extension of this point, Freud describes situations where it might be difficult to draw a clear distinction between objective and neurotic anxiety, as the two seem to fuse into one. In this case, the object of the anxiety is known and real, but the scope and intensity of the anxiety seems out of step with 'reality'; the discrepancy between the real threat to the self and the intensity of the anxiety thus gives away the neurotic and irrational character of the anxiety. When we seek to distinguish between constructive and adaptive shame versus destructive, toxic and pathological shame that erodes the self, we must similarly focus on the relationship between, on the one hand, the scope and intensity of the shame and, on the other hand, the actual situation and the self's actual being, behaviour and actions that seem to have activated or underlie the feeling of shame. Destructive shame is irrational in both content and intensity and is associated with unrealistically negative and unnuanced ideas about the self as fundamentally bad and wrong. Thus, it represents irrational experiences springing from past experiences, such as not feeling seen and loved by important others, that will typically be out of touch with how concrete others actually see and act towards the self in the present.

4.3 Defences against and reactions to shame

As mentioned earlier, shame is a negative and unpleasant feeling that we generally always wish to dampen or escape. This is particularly true of more destructive shame, which is difficult to contain and often feels like a threat to the self, in some cases even an existential threat. Consequently, we develop psychological and behavioural strategies to defend against, dampen, manage or eliminate feelings of shame or, alternatively, to prevent feelings of shame from arising in the first place. Most of these strategies are largely unconscious and are activated almost reflexively and outside our conscious control. Some of them are also maladaptive and destructive, to both the individual and others, including social communities.

Most of these strategies for dealing with shame can also be regarded as (secondary) manifestations of a feeling of shame. As explained earlier, we normally attempt to cover this feeling up. Someone who is shameful withdraws from contact with others and 'shuts down' psychologically, which may be seen as an attempt to dampen or escape the shame. Often, this means that the shame goes unnoticed, by the self and by others. Thus, it can sometimes be difficult to understand behaviours driven by underlying shame, for example why some individuals and large social groups react to certain, seemingly trivial situations or incidents with a level of anger and aggression that seems disproportionate compared with the activating factor. From a dynamic psychological point of view, anger, rage and aggressive outbursts may be seen as attempts at escaping unbearable shame and restoring fragile self-esteem (see Section 6.2). With Wurmser (1981b), we can also see these defences against and reactions to shame as some of the 'masks of shame', veiled or covered-up expressions of shame. The American psychiatrist Donald L. Nathanson (1994, p. 795ff.) has identified four main categories of individual psychological strategies for managing and defending against shame, organized into the so-called Compass of Shame model, which is briefly outlined in the following.

Withdrawal (hiding from others)

A person who is overwhelmed by shame in a concrete situation or who is generally prone to unbearable shame might withdraw from or try to avoid emotional and psychological contact with others, in part as a way of avoiding their judging gaze. Because eye contact can activate shame, the person seeks to avoid it or quickly breaks it off. The person may go silent or walk away from the situation that activated the shame and seek solitude. As mentioned earlier, eye contact can be a very powerful and potentially emotionally overwhelming form of contact that may be experienced as very intimate, penetrating and revealing, for better or worse, if the person leans into and stays with the emotion. Hiding – attempting to conceal one's true self or vulnerable inner life from others – may be manifested in many other ways than the avoidance of eye contact. For example, the person may appear enigmatic, 'incomprehensible' or 'strange' and thus 'unapproachable'. They may also display a rough, threatening, aggressive and intimidating attitude or facade (without actually attacking others), which may seem frightening and thus push others away. Or they may try to be as anonymous and 'invisible' as possible in the company of others. The person may remain physically present in a potentially shame-inducing situation while maintaining their emotional distance and attempting to keep any contact with others at a formal, superficial level. In more extreme forms, this may include entering a dissociative state, in which the person's own emotional reactions are 'frozen' and the person is mentally and emotionally absent. This is all part of an attempt to escape shame the person has difficulty containing and dealing with; reaction forms that may, over time, give rise to painful experiences of inner emptiness, contactlessness and social isolation, which are particularly common in more severe personality pathology.

These largely defensive, introverted and internalizing strategies for coping with shame may also involve proneness to ruminating on own defects and deficits and on the experience of repeatedly making mistakes and thus deserving condemnation from others. Withdrawing from contact may range from temporary withdrawal with the purpose of protecting interpersonal ties (constructive shame); to withdrawing in order to avoid more painful rejection from concrete others; to, ultimately, more prolonged social isolation or general avoidance of close contact out of fear that it might lead to repeated traumatic violations of the self and its boundaries (destructive shame). In more clearly destructive forms of shame, the person may isolate socially, which may over time contribute to deep loneliness, alienation from others (perhaps behind a facade of self-sufficiency) and the development of mental illness. Anxious avoidant attachment will often be associated with a tendency to avoid and withdraw from contact.

Furthermore, such attempts at escaping destructive shame by withdrawing from contact may be self-maintaining and self-perpetuating. The person flees, hides or isolates in an attempt to prevent, escape or dampen the shame. However, this also robs them of social contact, which might have had a healing effect and which is necessary for dampening and escaping painful and destructive shame in the long term. In healthier, briefer versions and particularly for highly sensitive individuals, withdrawal may be seen as a strategy for protecting the self and its boundaries of intimacy by protecting the self's inner life and integrity from being overburdened. Generally, however, the positive effect of withdrawing from contact with others is limited and typically very fleeting, in part because shame is not just activated by the concrete other's critical judging gaze at the self in the moment – which we can escape at a concrete level by breaking off contact – but also by imagined others, the self's own ideas about how others generally view and disparage the self.

In the psychotherapeutic space, the avoidance of shame may be manifested in a variety of ways, including the patient's silence and persistent focus on seemingly irrelevant topics with a striking absence of emotional engagement, which typically reflects the patient's severe difficulties with verbalizing and revealing shameful parts of the self to others. On the other hand, speaking loudly and profusely or being in constant activity may also be used as defence against dreaded silence, in which the self's being – who the person is behind a facade of verbosity and hectic activity – might become more apparent and 'exposed'. In this latter case, the patient's intense efforts to keep some sort of conversation going serve as a defence against getting into contact with aspects of themselves and with the therapist, which the patient might associate with the shameful exposure of defective or repulsive parts of themselves.

Similarly, recurring absences or other violations of the treatment structure and the psychotherapeutic space – which in a very concrete sense diminish the possibilities of establishing deeper and more continuous emotional and psychological contact between patient and therapist – may be driven by shame and attempts to escape it. These are all elements that in the therapist's countertransference (the therapist's emotional and other forms of subjective experiences and reactions in the interaction with the patient; see Chapter 7) may lead to emptiness, boredom and a lack of emotional engagement with the patient and their difficulties. The therapist needs to be aware of and attempt to decode these manifestations of countertransference by maintaining their psychotherapeutic stance towards the patient and the presented material and contact as well as towards the therapist's own emotional and other reactions in the therapeutic space. In concrete terms, this means that the therapist needs to ask themselves why they feel empty or bored or have trouble engaging in a specific patient: What might this tell the therapist about the patient's difficulties and the typical ways in which these play out in the patient's interpersonal interactions (see Chapter 7)?

Attack self

Another way to attempt to escape shame is by attacking, denigrating and ridiculing oneself. Subjectively, this may feel like having a strict and unforgiving inner judge who despises and humiliates the self. It may be understood as an attempt to pre-empt others' critical gaze at the self and thus (re)gain a degree of agency and control of the situation: 'I attack, disparage, despise, ridicule and humiliate myself so you don't need to'. This kind of broad criticism of, attack on and contempt for one's own self can also be seen as a form of submission. The attacks on one's own self may also be related to internalized anger or aggression directed at the self. In its more pathological forms, this may be manifested as various forms of self-harm, including humiliation and disparagement of one's own self in front of others, explicit self-contempt, disgust with the self and direct or indirect bodily self-harm. The therapist should also consider how these types of self-attacks might be related to the lack of loving and caring feelings for and thoughts about one's own self based on past relationships in which important others, for various reasons, have not met the person with the loving, validating and appreciative attention that is necessary for developing positive self-esteem and loving self-compassion.

As described by Wurmser (1981b, 1993), certain forms of masochism, in which a person to varying degrees seeks humiliation or punishment for acts or situations that they have no real control of, let alone responsibility for, may be understood as an attempt by the shameful self to diminish, escape or achieve some degree of control of a vague and diffuse feeling of shame; the masochist seeks suffering, pain and humiliation in an attempt to earn some form of love and respect (Wurmser, 1997, p. 367). By inviting or provoking others to humiliate, degrade and punish the self, the person may, in a sense, concretize and manifest a more diffuse feeling of shame in very concrete humiliations of the self. The person seeks and stages sexually – or otherwise – humiliating situations that can both produce a sense of having some degree of control of one's own shameful humiliation and provide the self with real and concrete reasons to feel wrong, inadequate and socially isolated. Furthermore, the self may experience a form of – typically perverted – interpersonal contact with their 'tormentors'.

This behaviour may represent a more or less unconscious interpersonal effort to stage or externalize inner dramas and mental states, which also help the socially excluded and isolated shameful self to (re-)establish a form of contact with others and to become (re-)embedded in some form of community. Diffuse overwhelming shame, loss of control and social isolation feel so unbearable that the person prefers others' concrete and tangible humiliations and punishments of the self. At the same time, masochism may also contain elements of the self identifying with their 'attacker' and the person who is humiliating the self (aggressor). With this more or less deliberate external staging of their own inner dramas, the masochist, in a sense, moves from the position of passive victim to a more active position, where the position of the humiliated victim and the suffering are somehow associated with pleasure and power ('I have the power, and I use it to make you humiliate me'). Finally, masochism can sometimes be driven by an urge to seek forms of contact that are characterized by strong emotional intensity as a counterbalance to a sense of emptiness, boredom, inner death, irrelevance and numbness.

From a psychological point of view, one of the problems in this dynamic is that in its more destructive forms, it locks the self into a very self-destructive pattern which is in fact out of the person's control (Wurmser, 2015, p. 1627), and in which the other is not in fact perceived as a subject but is merely used as a (subjectless) object or instrument in staging and re-enacting certain specific interpersonal patterns driven by severe and destructive shame. Thus, there is a reason why Wurmser calls masochism the 'theatre of shame' and views it (and sadomasochism) as a form of contact and sexuality that might bring individuals together who for various reasons struggle to contain and cope with shame (Nathanson, 1992, p. 333).

Over time, however, the inflicted pain and punishment are more likely to increase than to diminish perceived shame, in part because they can lead to a perception of the self as an innocent victim of unfair violations and abuse (cf. Gilligan, 2003, p. 1164). This may bring a certain masochistic pleasure in being the constantly and extraordinarily degraded victim, perhaps combined with an idea of one's own moral purity in comparison with the person or persons involved in degrading and abusing the self. With German psychoanalyst Christa Rohde-Dachser (2020, p. 115f.), we can argue that what the typical masochist in fact primarily seeks is not pain or suffering but to be met by an empathic other who can diminish the person's unbearable shame (as the good self-object alleviating an inner defect or emptiness). However, suffering, pain and humiliation are the masochist's dominant strategy for gaining access to an empathically understanding other: 'When you see the degree of my suffering – my pain and humiliation – you will have to show me the empathy and loving care I yearn for'. In some cases, the masochist may perceive inflicted pain as expressions of loving care, which brings us into the borderland of perversion. In *King Kong Theory*, the French feminist writer

Virginie Despentes (2006, p. 42f.) argues that when some women fantasize about being sexually (and otherwise) dominated (and even raped), this is not based on any biologically determined female receptiveness to masochism. Instead, she argues, it stems from elements of modern culture, which may socialize women into associating sexual pleasure with their own powerlessness and another's (a man's) superiority, especially to avoid being seen as disgraceful whores with an excessive and overly active desire. In relation to this point, it should be noted that human sexual desire can sometimes have the character of an 'inner abroad', a domain where a person's sexual desires are not necessarily in accordance with their self-perception or how they wish to be or be perceived.

Similarly, albeit less radically, in her autobiographical novel *A Girl's Story*, Annie Ernaux (2016/2020, p. 36) describes how a woman submits to a man's desire: 'She has surrendered all will, entirely absorbed by his', and she dares not express her own boundaries and needs: 'She does not ask him to [do what she would like]. It's a shameful thing for a girl to ask. She only does what he wants' (ibid.). 'She expects none [no pleasure] for herself. ... She ... simply waits for him to want her, one night ... Her need to give him mastery of her body makes her a stranger to any sense of dignity' (ibid., pp. 44–45). 'You wait for the Master to grace you with his touch, if only one more time ... with the absolute supremacy you've begged him for with all your being' (ibid., p. 8). The desire to be taken by 'the man' comes to control her entire being in the world: 'The hope of seeing him again has become your reason for living, for putting on your clothes, improving your mind, and passing your exams' (ibid.). At the same time, she finds this experience to be deeply shameful: 'It is the shame of having once been proud of being an object of desire' (ibid., p. 83). Parallel with this, Ernaux's narrator reflects on how the more general gendered dynamic plays out in her first sexual encounter with a man: 'Her submission is not to him but to an indisputable, universal law: that of a savagery in the male' (ibid., p. 47).

We should be cautious to pathologize all forms of masochism and rather view masochism as a dimensional phenomenon ranging from the playful exploration of dominance and submission to extreme submission and an invitation to humiliate the self driven, in part, by severely destructive shame. Although masochism is typically associated with a sexual practice – and, in its more destructive versions, is considered a sexual perversion – the concept can also refer to a broader character structure, including moral masochism (Wurmser, 1997, p. 368). Among others, Danish psychotherapist Maria Marcus (1974, p. 270) similarly argued for a distinction between a broader authoritarian masochism (a general tendency to submit to perceived authorities) and more narrowly defined sexual masochism, in which sexual desire is associated with coercion, pain and varying degrees of personal subjugation and degradation. In a very general sense, perverted and destructive sexual masochism can be defined as related to a dehumanized form of sexuality and/or sexualized dehumanization (ibid.,

p. 376). Thus, the character of the intersubjective contact is a crucial element in distinguishing between normal and destructive/pathological masochism. With their affordance of faceless contact (which may in fact represent an absence of contact) and widespread presence of dehumanized sexuality, social and digital media bring with them a significant risk of an explosive growth in the prevalence of perverted masochism and other perverted forms of sexuality.

In somewhat less problematic versions, a person may manifest attacks on the self and self-staged humiliation or ridicule by signalling submission: signalling that the person does not wish to challenge others' superior position in relation to the self and that they generally consider themselves insignificant and inferior in relation to the other. The person does this in order to avoid feared humiliation and abuse of the vulnerable self or simply to earn the other's acceptance. Similarly, the 'clown' or stand-up comedian who ridicules themselves through self-deprecating jokes and stories about their own embarrassing behaviour may initially avoid feared experiences of shameful humiliation and ridicule from others by, so to speak, making others laugh at them and thus preserve a certain sense of agency and control: 'I make others think I'm awkward and funny/ridiculous at a time and in a way of my own choosing'. In this way, the person breaks down their own boundaries of intimacy in a 'voluntary' overexposure of themselves, their personal space and their own mistakes and defects; a phenomenon that has the potential to go viral on social media. These strategies for coping with shame, which can sometimes be adaptive, rely on a delicate balance and risk tipping over into self-destructiveness, for example if they make the self give up their own dignity, social status and personal integrity in their attempts to dismantle others' critical and potentially shame-inducing focus on the self.

In the Danish writer Cecilie Lind's novel *Pigedyr* [Girl Animal], the first-person narrator, Sara, offers a painfully nuanced description of how she gives herself up and subjugates herself in an attempt to escape shame and be loved, or at least tolerated, by the other, her friend Rosa:

> This is how I make friends with other girls: I appoint the girl to mistress [put her up on a pedestal, elevated high above the self], I am subservient and grovelling, throw myself at her feet. Beg for friendship, her favour. I become a loyal subject, I suffer and rejoice. The more terse her reception of my adoration is, the more reverent I become. ... I am wretched. I am ugly [the dark side of subjugation: shame]. I don't care. I am a suitor. I sacrifice myself. And am rejected. ... Become a doormat. Put up with anything if only I can be included. If only Rosa will suffer my company. Fetch me a glass of water, Sara, says Rosa, with a devilish glint in her eye, and I fetch it, and Rosa says, I'm not thirsty after all, take it back. This is the game of submission that we always play.
>
> (Lind, 2022, p. 35f.)

In the therapeutic space, attempts to escape shame through attacks on the self may be manifested as explicit self-hatred ('I am a fool, a loser'), self-stigmatization ('I am useless, good for nothing, will never amount to anything') and ironic detachment from one's own difficulties and a tendency to trivialize them or talk about them in ways that make them seem amusing or ridiculous. The therapist may be tempted or seduced into laughing at the patient's often amusing stories about situations where her core difficulties played out. It can be tempting to follow the patient's emotionally distanced trivialization of her own difficulties and thus overlook the deep psychological and emotional pain and perhaps loneliness that might hide behind the light-hearted, joking facade. In people with mental illness, self-stigmatization always involves an element of shame, even if the shame might be covered up, hidden behind various masks (self-hatred, self-irony). The patient's self-contempt and self-stigmatization may also involve the therapy process itself, which some patients view as a shameful reflection of their failure to deal with their problems and the fact that they need help. Similarly, the therapy may, at worst, become yet another painful exposure of the defective self and yet another humiliation of the self, which de facto repeats maladaptive patterns in the patient's relationships, without the therapist catching on and effectively intervening to prevent it. Thus, therapists must remain attentive to elements of the therapeutic relationship that might represent a repetition of the harmful interaction patterns that are at the heart of the patient's difficulties.

A patient who, with a certain degree of self-contempt and no sign of self-care, let alone empathic understanding of themselves (self-compassion), describes themselves as worthless, insignificant and inadequate may use this negative self-image to try to cover up and cope with painful underlying shame; shame that may initially remain hidden from the therapist behind one of the many possible masks of shame, the negative self-image. Alternatively, the patient may humiliate themselves and overexpose their own defects and deficits in the therapeutic space in ways that make the therapist find the patient repulsive, activate a strong urge to correct or control the patient or cause the therapist to be overwhelmed by sympathy and pity for the poor, 'pathetic' patient.

In this case too, the therapist's primary task to decode what these reactions to the patient in the therapeutic space (in the countertransference) can reveal about the patient's current mental state, typical strategies for coping with painful mental states and general difficulties, as they play out in interpersonal interactions (see Jørgensen, 2019). This must be approached with a clear awareness that the therapist's countertransference is always already intersubjective and thus reveals insights pertaining not just to the patient but also to the therapist and their tendency to react in certain ways in certain situations. The therapist also needs to bear in mind how self-harming behaviour, suicidal ideation and suicide attempts can be related to deep-seated shame and represent attempts at regulating unbearable shame that the patient may not even be fully aware of and has never communicated explicitly to the therapist, perhaps because the patient lacks a language for speaking about their shame. Naturally, this situation will be exacerbated and further complicated if the therapist also lacks sufficient knowledge of the language and masks of shame or is not in contact with and sufficiently capable of containing their own feelings of shame.

Avoidance (hiding from oneself)

Another approach to shame is through various forms of avoidant behaviour, denial or attempts to reinterpret (distort) a shameful situation into a neutral or even a positive incident. In concrete terms, this might involve, for example, denying events and others' acts and reactions that could lead to humiliation of the self and expose the self's powerlessness, weaknesses and defects, thus activating shame and destabilizing self-esteem. We may also attempt to avoid paying attention to the feeling of shame by diverting our own and others' attention from the shame and anything that might activate it, for example by using humour, apparent competence or distraction (constant and compulsive activity, persistent participation in 'events', workaholism, persistent and intense efforts to achieve self-perfection), as we act in order to avoid sensing and noticing feelings of shame that we do not know how to manage.

Avoidant behaviour may also involve substance abuse, using intoxication as a temporary escape or relief from perceived shame. One of the problems of this strategy is that in itself, it often leads to new shame or exacerbates existing shame because substance abuse is widely perceived as shameful. Promiscuous sexuality, sexualizing contact with others, compulsive shopping, excessive physical training and eating disorders can also serve as strategies for escaping unbearable shame. More generally, impulsive behaviour may be driven by shame and be an attempt to divert one's own and possibly others' attention from underlying shame. A common aspect of these defensive strategies is that they can be regarded as attempts at avoiding or diverting attention from more or less unconscious shame without doing anything to make the shame and its underlying causes go away. Shame does not go away. However, at best, these avoidance strategies can temporarily push the consciously perceived shame into the background. The price is the need to expend a big share of our psychological resources on keeping the feeling of shame in check, at great cost to our self-expression, well-being and development.

Attack other

Finally, we can divert our own and others' attention from our own shameful self by showing contempt for, attacking, humiliating, mocking, disparaging or ridiculing others in an attempt to boost our own self-esteem and escape shame by activating shame and a feeling of inferiority in others, perhaps the people who are seen as the cause of our perceived shame (Elison et al., 2006b, p. 162). This is an attempt to regain some self-respect and social status by humiliating others and making them appear (and perceive themselves as) weak and inferior in relation to the self (Nathanson, 1992, p. 313f.). On this point, Wurmser (1986, p. 34) speaks of anger, rage, contempt for and indignation over others' acting as 'cover affects' that divert attention from painful perceptions of the self as weak, humiliated and vulnerable. A shameful fear of being 'abnormal', weak and inadequate is alleviated by pointing at, shaming and stigmatizing others (migrants, sexual minorities, women and so forth) as defective and inferior in comparison to the self or 'us': a social group with a common social identity (cf. Nussbaum, 2004, p. 219, see Chapter 6). Like the two strategies discussed above – 'withdrawal' and 'attack self' – this may be considered an interpersonal strategy for regulating shame and other affects or for interpersonal self-regulation (see Horney, 1945, p. 42ff.). It may become a core element in the development and maintenance of psychopathology if it is gradually extended to more areas of a person's life and is rigidly implemented across a wide variety of situations.

This strategy is a form of externalized anger and aggression in an attempt to deal with perceived defects and deficits, inadequacy, shameful vulnerability, inability and powerlessness by labelling others – individuals or social groups – as inferior, repulsive, ridiculous or otherwise unworthy and thus scandalized (sub)humans. We try to escape our own shame, wounded pride and perceived powerlessness and helplessness by putting others in a similar situation and activating the same emotional states in them, especially feelings of shame and inferiority. This dynamic is related to projective identification, as we evacuate feelings of shame by projecting shameful elements of our own selves on others and then show contempt for these self elements in concrete others (Ogden, 1979; Broucek, 1991, p. 72). A small number of empirical studies have found that heightened shame-proneness is associated with a heightened tendency to react with anger and maladaptive strategies for dealing with anger, including an increased tendency to blame and take revenge on others who are perceived as having caused the self's (shame and) anger. Conversely, an increased tendency to experience guilt is typically associated with a lower tendency to angry reactions and with more constructive strategies for regulating anger (Tangney, Wagner, Fletcher et al., 1992; Tangney, Wagner & Gramzow, 1992, 1996).

Abuse of others as a form of defence against one's feelings of shame may also be manifested as objectification of others and failure to recognize others as equal persons and subjects. To the extent that the person is able to dismantle others' subjectivity and define them as inferior and insignificant in relation to the self, the consequences of their objectifying gaze at and judgment of the self may be diminished, which will sometimes diminish the feelings of shame stemming from others' gaze at and judgment of the self. The person may construct an ultimately illusory perception that the self's ways of being and acting are more or less independent of (inferior) others' gaze at and perception of the self. Outward aggression as an attempt to escape the self's shameful defects and inadequacies also appears as cynical contempt for shared values and ideals that the self is, for various reasons, unable to live up to and as shameless and aggressive insistence on the self's right to 'be who I am' and pursue their own needs with no concern for others.

In the therapeutic space, intimidation of and attacks on the therapist in defence against the shame associated with a perceived loss of control, exposure of the self's vulnerability and inadequacies and actualized inferiority in the therapeutic space may take many different forms. In addition to the patient's aggressive and explicit attacks on the therapist's person and professionalism, the patient may repeatedly violate the therapist's personal boundaries, for example by shifting attention from themselves to the therapist through direct and personal questions or comments about the therapist, the therapist's personal life, professionalism and subjective experiences in our outside the therapeutic space. The patient may also violate the therapist's boundaries of intimacy in a variety of ways, for example through invasive or intimidating behaviour, a tendency to 'occupy' the therapeutic space in a very concrete way by bringing in and scattering belongings throughout the office when they come in for a therapy session or through other types of behaviour that may be viewed as the patient's attempt to 'take up room' and take control of the therapist and the therapeutic space.

Generally, these behaviours should not be interpreted as deliberate, let alone malicious attacks on the therapist and the therapeutic space, but as therapeutically valuable illustrations of how the patient typically tries to protect themselves and deal with unbearable feelings of shame in interpersonal interactions. The patient may try to protect their fragile personal boundaries against dreaded shameful violations by shifting the joint attention to the other and challenging their boundaries (cf. the idea of offence being the best defence).

The therapist may find themselves repeatedly caught wrongfooted and brought slightly out of balance emotionally at the beginning of each session with a patient, for example if the patient initiates each session with deeply personal comments about the therapist, criticisms of the previous session or questions about the therapist's clothes, professionalism or current mood which the therapist might not have a ready professional response to. This may give the therapist a shameful experience of losing control and failing as a therapist. When this happens, the therapist needs to focus on the patient's actions as a representation of how they defend against the fear of shame in connection with meeting and reconnecting with the therapist, thus maintaining focus on the patient's psychological life and difficulties under the shadow of shame. The patient's behaviour may also be seen as attempts to achieve and mark agency in the therapeutic space, which may also help diminish the patient's sense of inferiority and shame (see Chapter 7).

Envy: A specific attack on others

In some cases, envy can be a relational manifestation of shame over and dis-paragement of the person's own inferior self (Orange, 1995, p. 103), often accompanied by a more indirect and discreet form of outward aggression. The shameful perceived inferiority in relation to a specific other is 'converted' into a perception that the other received unfair advantages and preferential treatment compared to the self. The other's perceived positive attributes, higher social status and advantages may be interpreted as the result of unfair benefits or as devaluation of the self. At the same, the focus is discreetly shifted from the self's inadequacies and inferiority to the other's (possibly discreetly disparaged) positive attributes and unfair advantages (Tiedemann, 2013, p. 98; Gilligan, 1996, p. 69). In this sense, envy can be considered a defence against shame, as the conscious attention is shifted from the person's own inferior self to the specific other who has what the self lacks (Kilborne, 2002, p. 18). This may be accompanied by notions of the person's own moral superiority: 'Perhaps the other has something I don't have and would like to have, but at least, I am morally pure'. This psychological dynamic is often grounded in the painful awareness that the person's own real self is far from living up to the person's own expectations, goals and ideals. The person may try to avoid or deal with this awareness by focusing instead on perceived differences and inequalities between the self and a specific other, as the self's diffuse sense of inferiority is perceived as (or magically redefined to be) a reflection of the other's unjust and illegitimate advantages.

Both shame and envy are self-conscious affects associated with comparisons of self and other or comparisons with an ideal self. These comparisons expose the self as inadequate, defective or flawed unless the person implements strat-egies for escaping this painful recognition (cf. Lansky, 1994, p. 438). Normally, envy is regarded as an unambiguously negative feeling. However, it may also be interpreted as being driven by painful deprivations and shameful deficits and yearnings in a fragile self, which gives reason to reconsider the often mor-alizing reactions to expressions of envy.

Perceived injustice in the wake of toxic envy can lead to destructive bitterness, indignation, grievances and resentment over the advantages others have enjoyed in comparison with the self, which are thus perceived and disregarded as illegitimate. On this basis, the person no longer primarily views their own shameful inferiority and inadequacy in comparison to others. Instead, the focus of attention is on specific others' unfair advantages, which have 'nothing' to do with the self's own defects and deficits but are regarded as the result of an unjust world or specific others' contemptible actions, including unfair preferential treatment, a lack of regard for the self and so forth. In addition, perceptions of one's own inadequacies, defects and painful experiences of being unlovable because of these defects may be transformed into a perception that the other has certain qualities and possessions the person also desires – and, not least, that the existence of these disparities or examples of unfair preferential treatment represents injustice (cf. Wurmser, 1981b, p. 199). To most people, these experiences will be less painful than destructive shame, but they may also colonize large parts of the self and poison its being in the world. General and pervasive feelings of envy are typically toxic and threaten to break down the self from within while also polluting and ruining the self's relationships to others.

Reaction formation: Converting shame to its opposites

To this, we might add a fifth (or sixth) category, which is related to the latter of Nathanson's four categories – Attack Other (to recap, the other three are Withdrawal, Attack Self and Avoidance) – but is still considerably broader and extends far beyond it: various forms of reaction formation which handle shame by converting it into its opposite in the form of shamelessness, grandiose and arrogant actions towards others or the construction of a facade of pretend-pride over the self and the person's own accomplishments. Self-asserting, arrogant and disrespectful behaviour towards others may thus be driven by a need to cover up or escape from a state characterized by identity insecurity, shame and low self-esteem. Extreme arrogance is often the sensitive and vulnerable self's attempt to construct a shield that provides distance to others and superficially signals strength, self-sufficiency and independence of others and their gaze at the self, usually without basis in reality (being highly dependent on others' attention, recognition and approval). Furthermore, shameless and tactless behaviour without consideration for prevailing norms, values and ideals, let alone others' boundaries, is seen as (in effect illusory) rebellion against common boundaries of shame and an attempt to escape the (effectively inescapable) reality of the self being subject to social norms and others' judging gaze.

Alternatively, we can see shameless behaviour as an expression of defects in a person's normal position in the symbolic order of their culture and the development of critical self-reflection, which normally helps to regulate the self's behaviour and enables the self to act largely in accordance with prevailing norms and rules of acceptable social behaviour (Gullestad, 2020). Shameless behaviour may also relate to an inability to decode – or cynical disregard for – others' feelings, boundaries and reactions to the self's behaviour. The public behaviour of the 45th US President, Donald Trump, may be seen as a globally familiar example of this issue. However, we do not have the necessary basis for assessing the psychological or possible political strategic basis of Trump's openly shameless behaviour. Thus, it is not possible to offer a qualified opinion on the extent to which his shameless behaviour is a reaction to deep-seated shame (see, perhaps, Trump, 2020).

The discussion of shamelessness typically includes normative elements in the sense that we often use the term in negative classifications and judgments of a specific person's ways of being and acting, because they violate the normal norms and rules of 'our social community' – although it should be noted that these norms and rules do show variation across (sub)cultures and society and are thus a somewhat relative phenomenon. Besides, it cannot be ruled out that Trump's popularity among some sections of the American population is in part due to his shamelessness in a culture in transformation, where shame is increasingly viewed as a scandalous constraint on individual freedom and self-expression; Trump dares and, so to speak, lives out what some of his voters wish they dared to do themselves.

Precisely because shameless behaviour often violates others' boundaries in a sudden and startling way and thus may feel highly intimidating (and induce shame), it has the potential to bestow power over and control of others (Pines, 1995, p. 349). We are all, to some extent, susceptible to the shameless person's intimidating and transgressive behaviour, which represents pro-found disrespect for normal norms and interpersonal boundaries. However, this power also destroys relationships and thus, in the long term, harms the shameless self. As the Swedish psychoanalyst Else-Britt Kjellqvist (1996, p. 22) put it, the mask of shameless behaviour often hides a wasteland of loneliness, just as the wall of callous or seemingly insensitive and arrogant behaviour towards others can undermine any chance of establishing deeper emotional contact. The narcissistic mask of apparent invulnerability, emotional impas-siveness and cold may be driven by a great need to protect the self against unbearable shame (Wurmser, 1986, p. 20).

In relation to this point, it is worth considering whether the explicit exhib-itionism and boundless self-exposure and sharing of intimate details from the self's private space that some people engage in on social media and in unfil-tered reality shows on TV represent attempts to cope with or escape shame by converting it into its opposite in the form of self-chosen (counterphobic) shamelessness and the construction of a grandiose self that is 'something spe-cial' and stands out from the crowd by virtue of its 'extraordinary' openness, 'honesty', lack of personal boundaries, sexualization and authenticity and, perhaps, 'courage' to engage in this sort of self-exposure. In some cases, this courage is presumably more likely to reflect a lack of psychological bound-aries and a denial of the self's own need for boundaries of intimacy, which may have severe long-term destructive consequences for the person (cf. Marks, 2021, p. 101; Akhtar, 2015, p. 103). Seen from the other side of the screen, there is also reason to consider whether the widespread success of reality TV (talent shows, dating programmes), especially among a younger audience, is partially driven by ambivalent (pleasure/displeasure) shame by proxy and Schadenfreude over seeing others being ridiculed or making fools of themselves on camera (Köhler, 2017, p. 77).

In some cases, what is widely perceived as shameless exhibition or sexualized exposure of one's own body and intimate life on social media may also be an attempt to cope with a shameful perception of one's own insig-nificance, sense of abandonment and invisibility by attracting attention from the many imagined and (perhaps) real viewers on social media (cf. Wurmser, 1981b, p. 260). However, it is easy to lose control of this strategy, as there is no way to control or predict the response – or lack of response – from faceless and often disrespectful others. This strategy may thus be associated with risk for the self in the sense that the received response or lack of response from others can lead to additional shame and further destabilize the person's already fragile self and self-esteem.

When someone constructs a facade that expresses demonstrative and exaggerated self-confidence, overstated belief in their own abilities, own worth and independence of others, this may thus be an attempt to escape painful shame and low and generally fragile self-esteem. In that case, it represents an overcompensating defence against shame, low self-esteem and profound dependence on persistent attention, affirmation and recognition from others (cf. Kohut, 1971, 1985, p. 136f.).

It has been argued that especially men and individuals with narcissistic disorders who live with a feeling that they need to appear strong, invulnerable and self-sufficient in order to protect a fragile self, including their fragile and jeopardized masculinity, may be particularly prone to hiding shame and vulnerability behind an aggressive facade of toxic masculinity and primitive macho attitudes (Tiedemann, 2010, p. 112), including aggressive attacks on homosexuals (Hilgers, 2013, p. 342). These people may also have a great and often unacknowledged need for others' admiration, 'respect' and continual affirmation of the self's grandiosity in order to keep painful feelings of shame and inferiority at bay. They may experience it as a personal violation and unacceptable betrayal if important others show signs of independence and refuse to play the role of uncritical admirers of the self's grandiose facade and self-perception. When that happens, the grandiose self's defence against shame may lead to aggressive attacks on the other, who is threatening the grandiose defence by failing to provide the admiration and affirmation that the self hungers for and feels entitled to.

Perfectionism

Exaggerated and compulsive perfectionism can also serve as a defence against chronic and destructive shame, both as an inner psychological defence against internal shame and as an attempt to attain the positive attention, empathic mirroring, appreciation and love from important others the person has been missing all their life. The person seeks to achieve this through accomplishments and diligent (often exhausting) efforts to live up to (often unrealistic) ideals (Lessen, 2005, p. 22). More or less unconsciously, the person tries to compensate for or escape being viewed as defective, inadequate and wrong by themselves or others by being especially accomplished, virtuous and flawless (Skårderud, 2001c, p. 1615).

Dynamically, these attempts at being or appearing perfect can also be seen as an attempt to compensate for perceived inferiority by trying to live up to own ideals and making one's real self appear as a one-to-one realization of one's ego ideals (Tiedemann, 2010, p. 80). An attempt to realize the grandiose idea of their own ideal and real self being perfectly aligned is a typical defence against unbearable shame for someone who has a narcissistic disorder. This may also involve uncritically adapting and doing everything possible to please and live up to others' expectations and needs, perhaps supplemented with strong denial of own needs and trivializing own difficulties in an attempt not to be any trouble and avoid being seen as demanding. In this way, the person seeks to maximize the chances of being accepted and avoiding rejection or exclusion despite their many (self-perceived) defects and deficits.

A meta-analysis of studies of possible correlations between perfectionism and various psychological symptoms – unfortunately, mostly based on non-clinical populations, which weakens the generalizability of the findings to individuals who have mental illness or struggle with destructive shame – concluded that perfectionism is associated with higher scores on dimensional ratings of anxiety, depression, OCD and eating disorders (Limburg et al., 2017). In relation to this point, it is relevant to ask what might be the dynamic psychological driver behind this correlation. An obvious possibility might be shame, as the self strives for perfectionism in an attempt to cover up or compensate for shameful perceptions of the self being inadequate or defective. There is reason to assume that this form of shame-driven perfectionism could contribute to both the development and the maintenance of psychopathology.

On the other hand, it could also be argued that even exaggerated perfectionism implies a sense of agency, hope and notions of a possible path out of the shame and psychological pain that are the dynamic psychological drivers of perfectionism: 'If only I work hard enough to overcome my defects and deficits and perfect myself and my performance, I will become lovable and gain the love and approval from important others that I yearn for' (cf. Landmark, 2018). The main problem of this strategy is, first, that it is based on an illusory idea that it is possible to escape shame and other painful emotions through concrete accomplishments and acts. Second, the specific ideas about what the self should be like in order to be lovable are often uncritically accepted replicas of ideas about the ideal self circulating in contemporary culture. In addition to not matching the self's actual characteristics and needs (constitutional self), they are also unrealistically high and in fact unattainable for most people. In practice, this means that the individual can put all their efforts into living up to these ideals without ever getting close. A meta-analysis of cohort studies among young people in the United States, Canada and the United Kingdom suggests that the tendency towards perfectionism among young people has been steadily increasing in recent decades (Curran & Hill, 2017). This suggests that perfectionism in response to growing external demands and expectations and shame related to the failure to live up to these expectations may also be related to aspects of contemporary culture.

Destructive shame and other painful affects with deep roots in individual psychology and history cannot be effectively diminished, let alone eliminated, through concrete acts, although someone with a focus on rational and resolute problem-solving might think so. This misperception may, however, become a driver of compulsive behaviour and actual mental illness (OCD, eating disorders). Instead, the person needs to engage with the painful affects and examine their close relationship with the individual's unique history and interpersonal experiences and reaction patterns as well as the perceptions of self and others that they have developed as a result of this history.

One young man struggling with severe destructive shame and very low self-esteem – both rooted in a deep-seated conviction that he is defective, inadequate and unlovable – tries desperately to become 'good enough' in the eyes of others and thus diminish his shame and self-contempt by spending many of his waking hours in the gym to build an ever stronger, more muscular body. He is also extremely preoccupied with his hairstyle and with the use of tattoos, jewellery and clothing to appear rugged and attractive. He explains that it is easier for him to imagine that he will be able to stand up for himself if someone abuses or attacks him when his body appears strong – and that women will be interested in him and find him sexually attractive when he is fit and has optimized his appearance through his choice of clothes and jewellery. Furthermore, he is driven by an idea – or a hope – that if he could only optimize certain parts of his body and his appearance, he would be okay and thus escape his shame, his self-contempt and his conviction that others look down on him and despise him. As the therapist gradually develops a closer relationship with him, it becomes clear how compulsive much of his strategy really is, as well as self-destructive in the sense that his training exceeds what his body can handle. He keeps developing injuries and also takes various illegal substances in order to optimize his muscle mass. In his world, continual measurements of muscle mass and percentage of body fat offer concrete ratings of his worth as a person. Similarly, even minor, casual comments about his training and body from random others at the gym can have a big impact on his self-esteem, which can rapidly soar and become almost euphorically high (albeit only briefly) or collapse, accompanied by suicidal ideation.

In his attempt to escape chronic and unbearable shame, he identifies minor, concrete details of his body and appearance as the 'cause' of his feelings of being defective and inadequate and then focuses all his efforts at improving these tiny aspects of his appearance. Gradually, however, he has to acknowledge that he will never be good enough, and that he will constantly discover new details about himself (his hair, his tattoos, his skin and so forth) that are unsatisfactory (imperfect) and the 'cause' of (new) shame and self-contempt; his percentage of body fat could always be lower, and his muscle mass could always be further enhanced.

He acknowledges that his feelings of shame and self-contempt stem from the fact that for much of his life, he has had to fight to be seen and accepted as being good enough, especially in the eyes of his father, by being physically strong, mastering physical challenges and generally being self-reliant and not being 'in the way' as his parents pursued their own needs. None of this can be resolved through ever harder physical training, which essentially only perpetuates and repeats patterns from the way he fought for his father's approval as a child by appearing strong and tough – unsuccessfully and with shame and low self-esteem as a result. We cannot change our inner psychological reality with the related affects, including painful feelings of shame, through concrete acts or attempts to change the external physical reality, however much we might wish we could. Major changes in our inner psychological reality often require a prolonged psychological process, including working with a qualified psychotherapist.

Normopathy

In a reaction related to compulsive perfectionism, we may also try to diminish or escape our shame and create a lovable self by constructing a facade or a false self characterized by exaggerated 'normality' and adaptation to perceived external expectations of the self. This effort aims for a self-obliterating conformity, where we in fact give up or cover up our individuality. Every effort is made to create a superficial impression and appearance that makes us 'fit in'. This normopathic effort is in fact an attempt to diminish a shameful experience of being wrong or a fear of standing out in a negative way; typically at the cost of our own boundaries and needs (see Bollas, 2018, p. 42ff., 1987, p. 135ff.; Skårderud, 1998, p. 136f.). Such a strong urge to 'just be normal', 'like everyone else' and to 'fit in' is especially common in individuals with severe personality disorders. For them, it can be both a defence against destructive shame and an attempt to escape a painful fear of being irreparably crazy, insane or defective.

Overstated pride

Finally, pride in the self, own accomplishments and characteristics and the self's perceived connection to or identification with valuable external objects (idealized others) and authorities (religious or national communities and so forth) can serve to diminish or divert attention from perceived shame. For example, we may try to escape a shameful feeling of inferiority by defining a particular personal characteristic, such as our nationality or ethnicity, as a particularly valuable attribute and source of pride (cf. Neckel, 1991, p. 14). Both shame and pride are affects associated with judgment of the self and thus central to the regulation of self-esteem. In many ways, the two affects are each other's opposites, which also explains why (overstated) pride may sometimes (superficially) compensate for and serve as a counterbalance to shame.

Shame is typically associated with the exposure of a seemingly great discrepancy between the real and the ideal self and with a tendency to isolate or feel excluded from the community, just as it makes the self feel incompetent, defective and unlovable (Tiedemann, 2010, p. 32). Pride, on the other hand, is associated with a feeling that the self is approaching its own ideal – or that the tension between who we want to be and how we actually think we are is (temporarily) eliminated (cf. Wurmser, 1986, p. 20). It connects the self with others and makes the self feel like a competent, admired and beloved member of the human community. Furthermore, pride is normally accompanied by joy and an urge to show oneself to others, to be seen; unlike shame, which is associated with a strong urge to withdraw, hide and cover up in order to conceal the self's defects and deficits (Nathanson, 1987a, p. 184).

It is important to distinguish between healthy pride – which is balanced and realistically associated with the self's actual accomplishments and valuable qualities – and false, assumed and defensive pride. We feel healthy pride when we succeed at something and receive positive attention from others for our real accomplishments or basic character traits. Assumed, defensive and arrogant pride appears much more grandiose and unrealistic, a fragile and vulnerable self's often pathetic and desperate attempts to prop up an unstable or generally low self-esteem. 'Wounded pride is lied into exaggerated pride and irascible contempt' of everything and everyone (Schmidt, 2006, p. 46). As Karen Horney (1950, p. 95) wrote, false pride can be 'as insubstantial as a card house and, like the latter, collapses at the slightest draft'. In order to defend the fragile self, the person abandons the 'truth of the self' and turns to a self-righteous sense of pride accompanied by a strong urge to avenge or defend against even the most minor perceived humiliations: 'Nothing short of triumph *can* restore the imaginary in which pride is invested. It is this very capacity to restore pride that gives neurotic vindictiveness its incredible tenacity and accounts for its compulsive character' (ibid., p. 104).

The person who is eternally searching for major or minor triumphs in what is perceived as ongoing competition with others can invest everything into striving for personal success, power, money and material possessions, which are seen as concrete expressions (evidence) of the self's value. This persistent quest may thus be driven by a need to avert shame and find something to be proud of and admired for, as a counterbalance to painful underlying doubts about the person's self-worth. This is an overstated, defensive form of pride, characterized by a superficially strong sense of self-satisfaction combined with underlying anxiety and fragility, which typically means that the person can only see themselves, is highly self-centred, has no concern for others and tends to have an instrumental view of relationships, which are solely seen to serve the purpose of affirming and stabilize their own self and thus keep the underlying shame in check (cf. Nussbaum, 2021, p. 25f.). This is an internal and interpersonal dynamic driven by a narcissistic need to feel superior and admired in order to curb feelings of shame and inferiority that strain and ruin relationships with others. Exaggerated and assumed pride may give rise to experiences and behaviour in interpersonal interactions that compel the person to avoid deeper emotional attachment to others out of fear that the attachment might threaten their fragile pride (narcissistic balance); fear that others, so to speak, will discover that the apparent strength and pride are false and built on shaky foundations.

From a passive to an active position

A common feature of most of the outlined strategies for coping with shame is that they make it possible, to some degree, to move from a position as the passive object of others' critical judging gaze to a more active position, in which the person regains some degree of perceived agency, control and empowerment, even though this is often illusory and may have long-term negative or even severely destructive consequences for both the self and the people around the person, for example in the form of social isolation, self-destructive behaviour and attacks on others, with destructive consequences for both the self's relationships and social communities. In addition, the strategies are all mainly action-oriented and characterized by a striking lack of self-reflection and curiosity about the person's own self and the insights perceived feelings of shame might provide about the self and their own being. Thus, the defensive strategies described above may be regarded as manifestations of psychological and emotional avoidance behaviour: rather than face the shame and attempt to understand what it is based on and what insights it might offer about the self and the person's own relationships with others, the person attempts to run away from or shut down feelings of shame.

Generally, the different defences against shame will primarily be activated in connection with more destructive shame and in people who, for various reasons, have a heightened level of shame-proneness and also have difficulty containing and dealing with shame by means of more mature psychological processes. Individuals who are overwhelmed by destructive shame and who perceive this as a threat to the self as well as individuals who find that shame destabilizes their identity and self-esteem and who have not developed sufficient adaptive strategies for processing shame, guilt, remorse and related painful affects (for example using the capacity for mentalizing perceived affects) will be more likely to use the more primitive strategies outlined above in their attempts to diminish or escape their shame.

The above descriptions of reactions to and defences against shame also illustrate how shame can be hidden behind different masks or disguised as other affects, especially anger, *ressentiment* and contempt for others but also guilt, envy, pride and self-hatred. The different defensive strategies are all, to some extent, associated with fear of being shamed, humiliated, ridiculed and met with contempt if the person shows who they really are, with all their defects and deficits. Instead, the person feels compelled to withdraw or hide behind a facade of arrogance, grandiosity, pretend-independence and self-sufficiency, toxic masculinity or aggressive contempt for others. This contempt for weakness and defects in others is typically associated with deep (underlying) contempt for the person's own weakness and inferior parts of their own self and may serve as a shield for the sensitive and vulnerable self, used to create distance and superficially signal strength and self-reliance that has no basis in the self's actual psychological reality. More generally, these strategies may be seen as reflections of an effort to deny the person's own humanity in the sense that all human beings have defects and deficits, and as social beings we have inherent sensitivity to others' critical gaze at the self, which means that from time to time, we may be overwhelmed by shame.

4.4 Shame and guilt: Two inherently different moral affects

Historically, there has been little effort to distinguish between the two central affects of shame and guilt, which weakens the applicability of especially the older theoretical writings and empirical studies (Dost & Yagmurlu, 2008, p. 110). Shame and guilt have both traditionally been considered humans' moral and self-conscious affects, which make us reflect on and evaluate (judge) the morality of our ways of being and acting in the world. Thus, they can help regulate, guide and correct our actions and self-image (Tangney & Dearing, 2002, p. 2ff.). They intervene in our relationship with ourselves and can thus, in a sense, be perceived as potentially intimidating, invasive and damaging (destructive versions) but also as emotions that invite us to take ourselves and our own ways of being and acting more seriously (constructive versions). In addition, both affects may emerge in reaction to violations of social conventions and moral standards for what is desirable and what is ethically and morally unacceptable behaviour. Normally, we regard both guilt and shame as negative affects that we would rather be without. They generally emerge in interpersonal contexts where the person is, to some degree, confronted with an external gaze at themselves in relation to past and present interactions with a real or, perhaps, imagined other. Both can be viewed as affects that, to varying degrees, help individuals act in accordance with prevailing norms, values and ideals and thus support social integration.

In this sense, shame and guilt have several features in common, and in some situations, it can be difficult to distinguish between, especially, the positive effects of constructive shame and non-pathological guilt on people's behaviour and long-term interpersonal functioning and well-being. Similarly, it is not always easy to distinguish between the potentially very negative impact of severely destructive shame and pathological variants of severe guilt on people's psychological well-being and the development of actual psychopathology. In a sense, shame is related to our fundamental being as singular individuals, while guilt springs from our concrete actions (Hirsch, 2022, p. 137). However, since our being often is often reflected in our concrete actions, it can be difficult to draw a clear distinction between the two emotions (ibid., p. 148), and we should instead focus on the phenomenological differences between the two emotions, including their concrete manifestations in our subjective experiences and perceptions of ourselves and our appearance in the eyes of others. Generally, the main challenges in our understanding of shame and guilt and, not least, the borderland between these two central moral affects stem from a very imprecise use of the two constructs and from the widespread use of insufficiently precise instruments for measuring shame and guilt in empirical studies. There are several decisive – and, to varying degrees, empirically founded (Tangney & Dearing, 2002, p. 24; see also in the following subsections) – differences between shame and guilt that we need to know and apply as a basis for the assessment of persons who seem troubled or even overwhelmed by one or, perhaps, both moral affects.

'I am wrong' versus 'I have done something wrong'

Boiled down to their most essential difference, the core of shame is an all-encompassing sense of being wrong – 'I am small, defective, wrong' – while the core of guilt is a sense of having done something wrong – 'I lied to my best friend, I regret that and feel remorse'. This is a basic distinction between the inadequate and the guilty self. When we experience guilt, we implicitly distinguish between the self and its concrete acts – a distinction that seems absent in the feeling of shame, in which the whole self is the object of critical attention and destabilization. The cause of guilt is always the individual's concrete acts, often in a specific situation, which the individual themselves and/or the people around them consider morally reprehensible, undesirable or unacceptable. The individual feels guilt over what they did – or what they did not do but ought to have done – in a given context and then typically determines to act differently and more 'appropriately' if a similar situation were to arise in the future. The feeling of guilt is related to making a mistake, while the feeling of shame relates to a perception of *the entire self* as defective. Guilt relates to something that already happened and which the self is often able to distance themselves from and reflect on, while destructive shame in particular overwhelms the self and its capacity for rational reflection. Although we may, of course, also be overwhelmed by guilt, it is often easier to attain and maintain a reflective distance to feelings of guilt, which do not similarly encompass and overwhelm the entire self, including the capacity to reflect on what we feel and why we feel the way we do in the moment.

Generally, the feeling of guilt is temporary, although it may sometimes develop (exacerbate) over time and become destructive. Its core is always the individual's concrete acts, rather than everything the self stands for, let alone the self in its entirety, and even when we are troubled by guilt, we normally maintain a certain sense of agency. The self is intact as an autonomous and actively acting subject. We feel that we did something wrong but also that we could have acted differently and thus prevented the perceived guilt. Our sense of agency remains intact, and we are also able to achieve some distance to our own flawed behaviour by acknowledging our guilt and taking responsibility for our actions. This also means that through our own actions going forward, we can restore our social reputation and positive self-image. Through our actions, we can diminish and, so to speak, work our way out of guilt.

In addition to deciding to change our future behaviour, we can also show remorse for our actions, apologize and ask for forgiveness from the people who were affected by our unacceptable behaviour. Similarly, we can take steps to atone for or redress our unfortunate actions by trying to repair the damage we inflicted on others. Feelings of guilt can even strengthen the self's sense of empowerment and urge to improve and make amends for the damage done, even though feelings of guilt also typically limit certain types of actions that involve aggressive, potentially abusive and dissocial behaviour towards others. Roughly put, guilt generally dampens aggression, while destructive shame in particular, as mentioned earlier, can sometimes raise the level of aggression, in part because destructive shame is associated with a feeling that the self needs to defend against imminent danger.

Thus, shame generally leads to a very different situation than guilt. In connection with shame, it is the entire being and core of the self – which the individual cannot readily change – that is perceived as inherently wrong, defective, ridiculous and the object of disapproval, mockery and contempt from others. This experience often arises suddenly and unexpectedly. In case of severely destructive shame, we are typically dealing with a more chronic condition. Being overwhelmed by shame feels like a never-ending, all-encompassing negative state, which the person is just as passively and help-lessly subjected to as they are to others' disapproving gaze. Generally, there is nothing the person can do to alleviate shame, except try to hide, disappear, withdraw from contact with others and thus attempt to escape their gaze, dis-approval and contempt.

If we initially disregard the outlined destructive strategies for coping with shame by attacking others, the self is in fact paralysed, passive, powerless and unable to take proactive action when they are overwhelmed by shame. The person's sense of agency is severely compromised, and the person feels help-lessly subjected to this overwhelming affect and external gazes that follow the self wherever the person goes. Someone who is ashamed will typically disparage and despise themselves and ask themselves, how did *I* come to be this way? The entire self and its being are at stake and the object of critical and negative attention. The shameful person's identity, basic self-image and self-esteem are destabilized, preoccupied with the self's defective or inferior character – a state that is associated with the perceived loss of honour, dignity and social status.

Consequences for social function

As mentioned earlier, guilt has been associated with a state of inner tension between the individual's ego and superego or conscience, which typically heightens the self's concerns for what they did to others or in front of others. In extension of this, feelings of guilt will normally increase both the self's empathy with others and the self's fear of being associated with and punished for morally reprehensible acts. Feelings of guilt heighten the self's attention on and sensitivity to the possible consequences of their actions, especially the consequences for others. Someone who is troubled by guilt will thus typ-ically feel the urge to confess, to show remorse and perhaps to accept just punishment for their morally reprehensible acts. The person might punish themselves, which may include an urge to almost overexpose their morally reprehensible acts, sometimes in an attempt to earn others' forgiveness, which may also help the person forgive themselves. More radical and potentially pathological versions of this simultaneously inner and relationally psychological dynamic is seen in people with a masochistic urge to be punished by others as a very concrete and non-mentalizing way of soothing, (temporarily) escaping or controlling strong feelings of guilt (or shame).

Conversely, as mentioned earlier, shame has been associated with an inner state of tension between the real ego and a collection of often rather diffuse ego ideals, which it may be difficult to realize, as well as a state of tension between the self and real or imagined others' critically judging or condemning gaze at the self. While someone who is troubled by guilt will thus typically have the urge to reveal and face the consequences of their actions, shame is primarily accompanied by a characteristic urge to hide, 'disappear' and cover up or divert others' (and their own) attention from the self's defects and deficits.

A person who is overwhelmed by shame will be egocentrically preoccupied with themselves, their relationship with themselves and how they might 'save themselves', while their empathy with and sensitivity to others is diminished, sometimes dramatically so. The narrow focus on what others are thinking about the self, which is a key characteristic of shame, has nothing to do with empathy or with any actual interest in others (cf. the old joke about the shameless narcissist who suddenly becomes aware that they have been talking exclusively about themselves: 'Well, enough about me, what do *you* think of me?'). Besides, shame is usually associated with a fear of rejection, ridicule, contempt and abandonment or exclusion from the human community; a fundamental fear of the loss of love and of being left all alone in the world that is also seen in connection with guilt.

The other as victim or condemning observer – and anger

Both shame and guilt can be said to involve an internalized object, an internalized other, who influences how we perceive concrete others in the moment. In case of guilt, the internalized other is primarily a victim of the self's actions, who in some situations may be angry with the self and make the self worry about the consequences of their actions. Sometimes, it may also involve a strict, authoritarian, punishing other, but the main focus of the other's judging gaze is still the self's concrete actions, not the entire self and its being and existence as a whole. The distinction between destructive guilt and shame can become porous when the source of guilt is, to a high degree, projected on concrete others, who are thus perceived as bad, punishing objects that pursue the self and make it almost impossible for the self to escape. However, this is not the case with normal, non-pathological guilt (see below). In the experience of shame, the internalized other is a witness, a critical observer who judges the entire self, causing the entire self to feel completely laid bare, exposed and subjected to the other's contemptuous gaze (cf. Williams, 2008, p. 219). In the case of guilt, it is primarily the other's integrity that is perceived to be at risk and in need of protection; in the case of shame, it is the self's own integrity.

This difference in the subjective experience of and reactions to feelings of shame and guilt relates, in part, to the fact that we typically perceive the source of guilt to lie within our own selves, while the source of shame – the source of degradation, contempt and blame directed at the shameful self – to a much higher degree is perceived to be outside the self; the person feels disparaged, despised and shamed by concrete others or a more abstract other (perhaps God). As mentioned earlier, destructive shame can give rise to anger and powerless and desperate rage at the other, who is perceived as the source of unbearable shame; this reflects an urge to take revenge on the condemning other in order to restore the self's honour, escape the passive, powerless and inferior position associated with shame – and thus escape the shame.

The Danish writer Rachel Röst gives a very apt description of this dynamic in her novel *Grundvold* [Foundations]. The protagonist, a young woman raised in a family of Jehovah's Witnesses, is having a religious, morally edifying talk with her dad:

> I shrunk in dad's crosshairs. I felt that my sins were projected on my face like a film that revealed everything to dad, even though I was trying to control my facial expression. … I'll do better, I said to dad as I felt my cheeks burn with shame … He held my gaze and looked deep inside me. I wanted to rip off his glasses and crush them against the floor so that he couldn't see me as clearly.
>
> (Röst, 2021, p. 60)

In other cases, the anger is directed at the person's own self in the form of intense self-contempt and self-loathing: 'I am unworthy, I am homeless, a drug addict, I have done things you could never even imagine. I am pure shit, scum', as one of the main characters in the Danish writer Mikael Josephsen's novel *De Andre* [The Others] (2021, p. 135) says of himself. Self-contempt is sometimes acted out as actual self-harm or even suicidal behaviour. This destructive anger directed at the self and/or others is not normally seen in (non-pathological) guilt, although guilt, as mentioned earlier, is often associated with an urge to confess and be punished for concrete actions, which contains an element of (more mature) anger towards the self. However, in this case, it is the specific acts that the self is willing to accept punishment for; it is not the self as a whole that is so defective, reprehensible and loathsome that it – seen from the person's own perspective – deserves to be struck by devastating anger or deserves to be punished simply for existing.

Shame and guilt can weaken or strengthen the perceived social order and integration

Generally, feelings of guilt are thus less painful and easier to cope with than shame, because guilt is normally associated with negative attention on some of the self's concrete actions, not on the self as a whole. Furthermore, it is usually less difficult to deal with guilt and potential punishment because this is based on and in itself affirms a sense of order and meaning in the world. By contrast, severely destructive shame is often associated with a more profound feeling that there is no meaning or any stable order in the world; this sense of anomy or normlessness opens an abyss of perceived lack of meaning and orientation that it can be difficult for the self to cope with, especially because shame is also associated with a sense of being abandoned, excluded and cast out (cf. Lynd, 1958, p. 58).

While the feeling of guilt implicitly affirms the existence of certain moral standards and thus a feeling that there is a social order and a degree of predictability, which is often accompanied by a sense that it is meaningful to seek others' forgiveness and to act in order to improve ourselves and the world, these constructive perspectives are more or less absent in connection with shame, especially in destructive shame. Shame is, first of all, accompanied by a sense of emptiness and disorientation and a feeling that even if there is some sort of social order, it is inscrutable and opaque, unfair, illegitimate and harmful to the self (cf. Lindsay-Hartz, 1984, p. 701); a perception that leaves room for conspiration theories as a desperate attempt to 'see through' the opacity and escaping the shame of feeling powerless. In normal feelings of guilt, the core of the self is still okay in the person's own eyes and in the eyes of others, despite the person's mistakes. The belief in a moral and social order is intact, and the person still implicitly supports this order in their efforts to improve and act more appropriately in the future. These constructive elements are also absent in more persistent shame.

While the feeling of guilt typically increases the integration of the self – internally and in the human community – destructive shame has a powerful disintegrating effect, both on the individual's identity and on the self's embeddedness in social communities (cf. Tisseron, 1992, p. 11). The guilty self still perceives themselves as part of the human community, even if the person is weighed down by others' condemnations of their actions and fears the potential punishment. Severe and destructive shame can overwhelm the person with a much more fundamental fear of being, or already having been, excluded from the human community – a fear of complete abandonment, solitude and resulting psychological annihilation, cf. the fundamentally human need for others and belonging to a social community as a condition for our physical and, not least, psychological survival (cf. Marks, 2021, p. 59).

Constructive and destructive guilt

In order to distinguish precisely between shame and guilt, we also need to distinguish more constructive feelings of guilt from those that are unambiguously negative and destructive, corresponding to the previously discussed distinction between constructive and destructive shame. Constructive feelings of guilt are, to some degree, associated with what we might call 'objective' facts, in the sense that the self has in fact failed to live up to its obligations and reasonable expectations of the person's actions in a given context. The self has committed a mistake, offending or harming others or violating social norms, rules and conventions for acceptable or dignified behaviour in ways that the self could and should have avoided (cf. also guilt in a legal sense). In this situation, the self had both the necessary resources and the knowledge and judgment to have acted differently. It is thus realistic and legitimate to assign guilt to the self for mistakes and negative events that the self could reasonably be held responsible for and could have avoided.

In the case of destructive and potentially pathological feelings of guilt, the situation is very different. Here, in an almost omnipotent and self-tormenting manner, the self assumes responsibility and guilt for events that they had little or no influence on, including the person's own traumatic experiences. The self assumes guilt and responsibility to an unrealistic degree that goes far beyond what the self actually has or could have any influence on and could thus reasonably be assigned responsibility and guilt over. This form of guilt is, to a high degree, detached from the self's actual, concrete acts and may therefore be difficult to distinguish clearly from destructive shame. More extreme manifestations of this are seen, for example, in people who are tormented by painful guilt over the very fact that they exist, as if they were responsible for their own conception.

With the German philosopher Ernst Tugendhat (1993, p. 238), we can understand destructive feelings of guilt more generally as an irrational and internal (self-imposed) sanction that is incomprehensible (without psychodynamic insight), and is not based on clear and readily understandable criteria for judging the self's actions and moral status. We can also speak of destructive feelings of guilt when these feelings are very easily evoked and thus dominate a person's emotional life and reactions to a degree where they severely hamper or disable the person's capacity for constructive actions that diminish perceived guilt, for example by making amends for actual missteps.

Although it is important to distinguish between shame and guilt, this does not rule out the possibility that some people may be prone to both destructive shame and guilt, just as the two destructive affects may, to varying degrees, activate, exacerbate and spill over into each other. For example, recurring experiences of destructive feelings of guilt may over time contribute to the development of more persistent destructive shame. In addition, overwhelming shame may prevent adaptive coping strategies, including psychotherapeutic processing of guilt, because the very act of acknowledging mistakes, especially to others, including a therapist, will be perceived as further humiliation and loss of dignity and thus intensify already unbearable shame (cf. Steiner, 2006, p. 40f.). Furthermore, destructive feelings of guilt can sometimes feel less unbearable than more diffuse (not concrete) destructive shame, just as even very severe and destructive feelings of guilt can serve as a defence against even more unbearable powerlessness and helplessness; this is seen, for example, in victims of physical or sexual abuse, whose conviction that 'it was all my own fault' (which makes the self an active participant) is less unbearable than the acknowledgement of how radically victimized, helpless and powerless (passively victimized) the self was when the abuse occurred (Wurmser, 1997, p. 378).

Empirical studies of shame, guilt and psychopathology

The significance of the distinction between constructive and destructive guilt is borne out, in part, by meta-analyses of possible connections between, on the one hand, guilt and shame and, on the other, depression and anxiety disorders. These meta-analyses found a significantly stronger correlation between shame and depression than between guilt and depression. This difference soon disappears, however, if we look only at especially problematic (destructive) feelings of guilt and ignore the more constructive variants (Kim et al., 2011). Thus, both destructive guilt and shame appear to be involved in the development and/or maintenance of depression.

In largely corresponding findings, a meta-analysis of correlations between shame/guilt and anxiety disorders determined that while shame generally has a stronger correlation with anxiety, more destructive feelings of guilt have the same level of correlation as shame (Candea & Szentagotai-Tatar, 2018). This study also defined two subcategories of destructive feelings of guilt that are just as closely correlated with anxiety as destructive shame: (1) generalized, free-floating feelings of guilt with no connection to a specific context and (2) exaggerated feelings of guilt and responsibility with no connection to the self's actual responsibility, let alone a realistic assessment of the self's actual influence on negative events (ibid.).

Overall, these meta-analyses suggest that if we consider guilt as a single homogenous and uniform affect, we will miss out on valuable information about how guilt, on the one hand, is usually a constructive affect but, on the other hand, can sometimes be so pervasive and overwhelming that it has severely destructive consequences for the self's well-being and capacity for adaptive behaviour. This is a case of destructive guilt accompanied by chronic self-reproach and compulsive rumination on the person's own missteps with no realistic connection to the errors the self may have actually committed in concrete situations and can reasonably be said to bear the responsibility for.

Many empirical studies suggest that a tendency to feel guilt over one's own errors is correlated with subsequent adaptive actions, while it does not seem to increase the risk of psychological difficulties and mental illness, perhaps on the contrary. Thus, there are indications that non-destructive feelings of guilt diminish the risk of developing mental illness (cf. Tangney et al., 1996), although the field is characterized to some degree by an inadequate distinction between constructive and destructive feelings of guilt in existing empirical studies. On the other hand, numerous studies have found that increased shame-proneness is correlated with an increased risk of a wide range of psychological problems (Tangney & Dearing, 2002, p. 119; Tangney, Wagner & Gramzow et al., 1992).

Similarly, we see that shame-proneness in situations where the self missteps seems to be correlated with a heightened tendency to blame others for one's own mistakes (Stuewig et al., 2010), greater anger and, not least, greater likelihood that the person will try to handle their anger in ways that are not constructive, for example through physically or verbally aggressive attacks on others and maladaptive rumination on their own anger (Tangney et al., 1996). Isolated findings also suggest that a high general level of anger and hostility may be an attempt to protect one's own self against painful shame and low self-esteem (Shanahan et al., 2011). Furthermore, a number of studies suggest that shame does not in itself necessarily lead to increased aggression but only correlates with increased risk of aggression towards others when it is combined with a tendency to assign guilt over the perceived shame to others, thus externalizing the responsibility for the shame and blaming others for it (see Section 6.2 on *ressentiment*). When that happens, shame may lead to increased aggression directed at others in the form of verbal or physical attacks on the concrete other or others whom the person blames for the perceived shame (cf. Stuewig et al., 2010). As mentioned earlier, these attacks on others may be viewed as attempts to restore or defend the self's honour, dignity, self-esteem and integrity, which are perceived as threatened or violated when the self is overwhelmed by destructive shame.

A tendency to experience feelings of guilt over one's own missteps is correlated with a higher likelihood of taking responsibility for one's own mistakes rather than blaming others (Stuewig et al., 2010). It is further correlated with a lower level of anger and with more constructive strategies for handling one's own anger. This is not nearly as damaging to interpersonal relationships as the reaction of people who often experience shame and try to deal with their anger by blaming and attacking others (Tangney et al., 1996; Tangney & Dearing, 2002, p. 96ff.). A constructive way to deal with one's own anger might, for example, include non-hostile dialogue with the person or persons who are the object of this anger and more mature attempts to deal with the causes of it (cf. Tangney & Dearing, 2002, p. 102). Most of the empirical studies in this area are based on self-reported measures of how people deal with their anger, which is not unproblematic. Thus, the outlined correlations between shame/guilt and aggression/anger must naturally be interpreted with a certain degree of caution.

A meta-analysis of correlations between the tendency to experience shame or guilt and the risk of self-harm found that shame-proneness is associated with a heightened risk of self-harm and somewhat higher prevalence of self-harm, while a tendency to experience feelings of guilt does not appear to increase the risk of the prevalence of self-harm (Sheehy et al., 2019). A small number of studies have even found that a tendency to experience guilt is associated with a reduced risk of self-harm and lower prevalence of self-harm among young people (VanDerhei et al., 2013). A tendency to experience both shame and guilt seems to be correlated with an elevated risk of suicidal behaviour, but this connection is considerably stronger for shame (Sheehy et al., 2019, p. 8). However, it is possible that the more specific psychological connection is not the same in the two situations, as suicidal behaviour may be driven by an urge to punish the self in connection with severe feelings of guilt, while suicidal behaviour in connection with severe destructive shame is more likely to be related to the self's urge to escape an unbearable emotional state.

A single longitudinal study that followed a group of young people from the age of 10–12 years until the age of 18–21 years found that shame-proneness during childhood is a risk factor for later deviant behaviour in adolescence, problematic drug use, earlier onset of alcohol use and unsafe sex (although this would hardly be classified as actual deviance in a northwestern European context), while a tendency to experience guilt during childhood was found to correlate with a reduced risk of various forms of substance abuse, unsafe sex and criminal behaviour during youth (Stuewig et al., 2015, p. 222f.). Overall, based on the available empirical research, we may cautiously conclude that, compared with destructive shame, feelings of guilt are the morally and socially constructive affect, as long as we ignore destructive and often pathological destructive guilt. Destructive shame typically has negative consequences for human well-being and social functioning, while we should assume that the often overlooked feeling of constructive shame may be at least as important to the human capacity for acting within morally acceptable norms, avoiding violating others and establishing, maintaining and being part of well-functioning social communities as non-destructive guilt.

Destructive shame is of particular relevance for understanding and treating feelings of shame and guilt in individuals with mental illness. This makes it important to be able to distinguish between constructive and destructive shame (see Table 3.1), just as we also need to determine criteria to distinguish between destructive shame and feelings of guilt. Table 4.1 outlines what we might focus on in discerning destructive shame from feelings of guilt in a broader sense.

Table 4.1 Overview of core criteria for distinguishing between destructive shame and (nondestructive) feelings of guilt

	Destructive shame	Guilt
Subjective experience	I am wrong, small, helpless, inadequate, defective – potential collapse of self-esteem.	I have made a mistake that I regret and feel remorse over – normally no lasting negative consequences for self-esteem.
Focus	The self's interior, core and entire identity; global and associated with the self's being in the world – perceived as being 'forever'.	The self's specific actions (and intentions); mainly exterior, limited in relation to the self – typically temporary.
Inner psychological process	Tension/conflict between ego and ego ideals; between the ideal self and the real self, between (internalized) social conventions and the self's actual ways of being/acting. Is more of an affective state than a reflection of objective facts, that is, the notion that the self is actually defective, deeply flawed and so forth.	Tension/conflict between ego and superego/conscience; guilty conscience. Normally has some connection to objective facts, that is, that the self has actually violated others or common norms, values and ideals.
Status of the self	Reduced to 'small', passive, powerless, paralysed (childish) object of internal or external gaze/authority that evaluates, judges and condemns the self.	Autonomous and active (adult) subject acting freely and taking/accepting responsibility for own actions.
Self–other differentiation	May be/become compromised; may destabilize identity.	Is/remains clear.
Status of the other	Superior, bigger and stronger (adult) person who observes, judges – including despises, humiliates, denigrates and rejects or excludes – the self (often in a position of 'child' or lower social status).	Equal subject whom the self has hurt, insulted or harmed; the self needs to seek forgiveness and reconciliation with the other, needs to compensate for or make amends for the harm the self inflicted on the other.
Associated with fear of	Being exposed, ridiculed, met with contempt, excluded, abandoned, alone; loss of love.	Being punished; being associated with morally reprehensible behaviour.

(Continued)

Table 4.1 (Continued)

	Destructive shame	Guilt
Temporal dimension	Often arises suddenly, unexpectedly – although severely destructive shame is more persistent and potentially chronic.	Often arises in connection with concrete acts and may develop over a prolonged period of time (especially in connection with destructive, pathological guilt) but is typically fairly short-lived and goes away when the self has apologized, made amends or accepted the punishment for their actions.
Possible social sanctions	Scandalization, social marginalization, isolation.	Punishment, demands for compensation or restoration for 'victims'.
Judgment/ condemnation of the self from	External, condemning (concrete or imagined) others whom the self is passively defenceless against.	Primarily the person's own inner self, the self's own self-judgment.
Is especially activated when others	Overlook, despise, mock, devalue, ridicule, expel, do not recognize the self as a result of the self's ways of being.	Accuse, blame, are disappointed in the self – as a result of the self's concrete actions or omissions of desirable actions in concrete situation.
Opposites	Healthy pride (pathological: shameless behaviour, grandiosity).	Innocence, morally 'pure' (pathological: unscrupulousness, dissocial behaviour without subsequent remorse).
Frequent accompanying states	Fear of rejection/isolation, self-loathing, anger/rage.	Grief/sadness, guilty conscience.
Primarily limits	Positive self-esteem, agency/ empowerment, ability to function as a mature and autonomous subject.	Certain actions; limits the self's strength/power in relation to others.
Typical consequence	Simultaneously covers up and exposes the self's inadequacies, defects and weaknesses to others. The self submits, hides, tries to adapt to social norms and community expectations.	The self strives to improve.

Table 4.1 (Continued)

	Destructive shame	Guilt
Individual coping	Not immediately possible to escape or reduce – the entire self is defective and would need to change; may lead to anger, hate towards others; perhaps attempted to be 'converted' into guilt, which is easier to deal with. Increased self-acceptance (self-compassion) as a possible way to reduce shame.	Short term: rejecting, denying, 'undoing what was done' (magical thinking). Longer term: accepting guilt/ responsibility, acknowledging own mistakes, apologizing, asking for forgiveness, atoning, making amends, repairing the damage.
Most important 'antidote' from others	Empathy, 'love'.	Forgiveness and reconciliation.
Relational elements	Preoccupied with/ concerned about others' negative assessment of the self; will often 'infect' others.	Worried about what the self has done to others; seeking to make amends.
Connection with empathy	Introvert preoccupation with own self; reduces empathic interest in others – may block insight and mature ways to deal with actual guilt.	Preoccupation with the impact of own actions on others; associated with increased empathy, especially for the person or persons whom the self harmed/insulted – and supports mature ways to deal with guilt.
Focus	Focused on the self and own psychological pain (egocentricity); weakens empathy and interpersonal sensitivity/ function.	Focused on others, how the self's actions impacted others; strengthens empathy with others and interpersonal functioning.
Behavioural manifestations	Urge to hide, cover up, disappear, become invisible, avoid eye contact, perhaps 'annihilate' oneself. Alternatively: aggression directed at others – compromised capacity for actual problem-solving.	Tendency to confess, apologize, show remorse for morally wrong actions, seek forgiveness, perhaps punish oneself – attempts to discover the reasons for one's own wrongful behaviour and correcting it, 'solving the problem'.
Implications for agency	Paralyses agency, instils passivity (except in case of other-directed aggression).	Is ready to act, is often active, in part in order to compensate for harm done by the self (except in case of destructive rumination).

(*Continued*)

Table 4.1 (Continued)

	Destructive shame	Guilt
Correlation with anger and hostility towards others	May increase outward anger and hostility, including a tendency to blame and attack others – in an attempt to 'escape' the shame.	Inhibits anger and hostility directed at others; increases responsibility for own actions and diminishes tendency to blame and insult others.
Relational embeddedness	Communicates social submission, affirms relational hierarchy; attempts to prevent others from attacking the self and make them lower their expectations of the self.	Compatible with equal/ symmetrical relationships; may be accompanied by attempts to make others forgive the self's reprehensible actions.
Function	Protect/restore the self's reputation and status, avoid further loss of love and social exclusion.	Protect/repair damage done to others and in relationships.
Correlation with psychopathology	Increases the risk of mental illness.	Normally not in itself associated with mental illness, apart from destructive guilt.
Correlation with narcissism	Potentially strong; attention is directed towards the self, not towards the other observing the self.	Little or none; attention is primarily directed at the 'victim' of the self's reprehensible actions.

4.5 Challenges in empirical studies of shame

In interpreting and applying the findings outlined above in relation to connections between shame or guilt and various indicators of psychological dysfunction – and findings from studies discussed elsewhere in this book – it is important to bear in mind that many of these empirical studies of shame have rather serious methodological problems; this is particularly true of the older studies. Thus, many of the available studies are based on student populations and self-report questionnaires aiming to measure people's tendency to experience shame and guilt. In many cases, these self-reported measures of shame and guilt are then compared to dimensional ratings of psychological disorders or symptoms of psychological dysfunction.

Thus, anyone interpreting or applying these studies in a clinical context should always consider to what degree findings from studies based on students' self-reporting are applicable to people who are diagnosed with mental illness, who often experience shame and guilt of much greater severity and possibly of a very different nature. It must be characterized as clearly problematic that many writers uncritically and with little or no reflection generalize findings based on students' self-reporting to people with severe psychological disorders (see, e.g., Currie et al., 2017; Tangney, Wagner, Fletcher et al., 1992; VanDerhei et al., 2013; Peters et al., 2014).

Furthermore, the instruments used to measure guilt and shame have varying degrees of problems with the distinction between constructive and destructive shame and also do not typically distinguish between constructive and destructive feelings of guilt. In many cases, there is also reason to consider whether the questionnaires are more likely to document the participants' moral standards and ego ideals than their actual feelings of guilt in concrete situations.

Similarly, it is important to bear in mind that the applied measures of shame often conflate shame with anxiety, depression, more general neuroticism, low self-esteem and general negative self-perception, among other phenomena. Moreover, most of the methods used to rate shame are based on an understanding of shame that typically reflects the theoretical understanding of the person or persons who developed these methods (Øktedalen et al., 2014, p. 602). Most of the existing questionnaires for rating shame thus require that the participants have a fairly clear understanding of what is meant by the concept of shame and how shame differs from guilt, which is highly unlikely to always be the case; this reduces the validity of the participants' responses (however, see Rizvi, 2010).

Quite a few studies of shame are based on rather vague, imprecise and, in some cases, virtually absent definitions of shame. Similarly, many of the empirical studies in practice operate with an overly narrow and partially trivialized concept of shame, which may also cast doubt about the validity of the presented findings and their generalizability to people with actual psychological disorders. While most studies fairly universally associate shame with a wide range of negative consequences related to the self's psychological well-being, psychological functioning and capacity for social functioning, when we interpret these findings, it is important to bear two points in mind. One is that the findings do not necessarily apply to brief and constructive shame, which generally has the potential to make a positive contribution to individual self-regulation and ability to function in social contexts. The other is that people with severe mental disorders may be struggling with forms of shame that are far more pervasive, painful and destructive than what is typically captured by the methods that are commonly used. If we consider shame as a dimensional feeling ranging from light, passing and constructive shame to severe, chronic and highly destructive shame, the vast majority of the existing instruments for rating shame will mainly capture what might be loosely described as a moderate or medium level of shame, while both constructive and severely destructive forms of shame will be largely or completely absent from the studies.

Generally, it is also important to bear in mind that far from everyone is able to access or is fully aware of their own shame. As mentioned earlier, attempts to hide and avoid our shame through various defence mechanisms and avoidant behaviour are a core aspect of the nature of shame. We try to hide and forget our shame and avoid exposing it to others. This is particularly true of profound and severely destructive shame (or primordial shame) associated with fear for the self's existence and the fear of being excluded from social communities. Thus, we need to distinguish between, on the one hand, conscious, explicit and easily accessible forms of shame and, on the other, more unconscious, implicit and passing or fleeting ones (cf. Lewis, 1971); the latter are unlikely to be captured with any real degree of credibility by self-reported questionnaires.

That is not to say that studies based on self-reported measures of shame are useless. Far from it. However, it is important to bear in mind what these studies can tell us and, perhaps especially, what they cannot tell us much about, such as severely destructive forms of shame in connection with severe psychopathological states that most of the study participants typically were not experiencing (cf. studies based on students), and/or which the applied questionnaires are not in fact able to capture or offer even an approximation of, because they were developed with a very different focus and purpose in mind, namely to measure more 'ordinary' and less destructive shame in the everyday lives of people with normal psychological functioning.

Finally, in interpreting studies based on retrospective recollection of shame in specific situations in the past, we must bear in mind that recalling shameful experiences, getting into contact with one's shame and, in various ways, revealing it to others can in itself be shameful. As a result, it is not necessarily a simple task to determine the nature of the shame being captured, for example, when a person who self-harms is asked retrospectively to report the presence of shame while they were self-harming (cf. Brown et al., 2009). The same applies to asking a patient with an eating disorder to report the occurrence of shame in connection with overeating or purging. If the patient reports experiencing shame, did this shame actually occur at the time when they were self-harming or overeating? Or is it rather/also a retrospective shame over being 'the kind of person who self-harms or has an eating disorder' and revealing this to others here and now?

While the previous chapters have examined the phenomenology of the feeling of shame, how people experience and react to various degrees and forms of shame and how shame, especially destructive shame, differs from feelings of guilt, the focus in the next chapter is on the potential connection between destructive shame and a wide range of mental illness. The mental disorders discussed in the next chapter have been selected because they would appear to have a potentially significant relationship with destructive shame, based on clinical experience and considerations and in light of the existing empirical studies. The list includes eating disorders, posttraumatic stress disorder, depression, certain forms of anxiety and severe identity disturbances as well as a number of personality disorders, especially borderline, narcissistic and evasive personality disorders. The sole point of examining the potential connections between these mental disorders and destructive shame is to increase awareness of the dynamic psychological impact of destructive feelings of shame in these (and other) mental disorders. Thus, the point is not to claim that shame is the only or in itself a decisive aetiological factor in the development of the selected mental disorders. All mental disorders are characterized by a highly complex, multifactorial and often individually unique aetiology, which means they cannot be reduced to a single or a few causal factors.

5 Destructive shame and mental illness

Generally, there is reason to assume that destructive shame is involved to some degree in most moderate to severe mental disorders. It may be present as a primary issue that contributes to the development of the disorder and which constitutes a core issue in the disorder, or it may be a secondary consequence of the mental disorder, because the person is shameful about being mentally ill or about certain manifestations of the disorder. Naturally, this does not mean that shame is the only or in itself a decisive issue in all mental disorders. However, it will generally be relevant to consider the impact of feelings of shame in conceptualizing mental illness. For example, the patient may be ashamed over lack of impulse control, difficulties with interpersonal contact or problems living up to common ideas about 'the good life' and certain expected accomplishments in education or the workplace.

A small number of studies have found fairly strong correlations between the subjectively perceived level of shame and certain general measures of psychological difficulties, including number of diagnosed mental disorders (how many symptom disorders and personality disorders the person meets the diagnostic criteria for), general symptom level, level of challenges in interpersonal relationships and level of personality organization (Benecke & Henkel, 2021, p. 23f.). Severe and destructive shame thus appears to be systematically associated with more severe mental illness across a large number of parameters, including disturbed relationships and fragile personality organization. This may be related to how destructive shame compromises our capacity for deeper emotional and psychological contact with others (and, to some degree, with ourselves) and thus our ability to enter into mature, equal and rewarding relationships with others. However, it is important to bear in mind that correlational studies do not shed light on causal links, just as the practical applicability of the existing empirical studies is generally limited by the fact that they do not distinguish sufficiently between constructive and destructive shame.

DOI: 10.4324/9781003521174-5

5.1 Eating disorders

Numerous studies have found a correlation between shame and eating disorders (Nechita et al., 2021), as eating behaviour appears to serve as a strategy for self-regulation and the regulation of negative affects, including shame, just as the disturbed eating behaviour in itself may evoke and intensify feelings of shame. Someone who has an eating disorder may feel shame about never being skinny enough, general shame about their own body – which is perceived as inadequate compared to an internalized or imagined other with an ideal that is unrealistic for most people – and about behaviour related to the eating disorder, such as overeating, purging, compulsive exercising and perhaps 'secret' binge eating followed by self-loathing (cf. Sanftner & Tantillo, 2011, p. 278f.). Eating disorders – especially anorexia – are characterized by an exaggerated preoccupation with physical appearance and weight and with various rituals and idiosyncratic thoughts about calorie intake, exercise and other topics related to the body. In addition, individuals with anorexia are particularly sensitive to external (real and imagined) reactions to the appearance, size and weight of their bodies, which has a great impact on their self-esteem. At the same time, for a person with an eating disorder, self-esteem, including experiences of shame and pride, will be closely related to how well they are able to manage their own body.

Someone who has an eating disorder may try to avoid letting others see their body by covering it up and minimizing social situations where it might be exposed and become the centre of attention. These reactions are all driven by body shame. A number of writers (Duarte et al., 2016) have argued that individuals with an eating disorder are very preoccupied with comparing themselves with others and establishing social hierarchies with a focus on weight and appearance. In these comparisons, they often find that they are assigned low status in the social hierarchy, which is associated with shame, extreme self-criticism and low self-esteem. In light of this, the disturbed eating behaviour may have been developed as a strategy for coping with the perceived shame, in a self-perpetuating vicious cycle. As the Norwegian psychiatrist Finn Skårderud has put it, shame is 'a central affect in eating disorders, and shame is always a relational emotion in the sense of always including the idea of others' contempt and disapproval' (Skårderud et al., 2018, p. 200). In this understanding, the boundary between internal and external shame is porous, or both types of shame are involved (see Section 4.2).

Any deeper understanding of the role of shame in eating disorders must include the always-already precarious position of the human body in modern Western culture, with its focus on individual self-control, autonomy and constant self-optimization. Physical drives (sexual desire, the desire for food and other hedonist stimulants), 'impurities' (body hair, faeces, uncontrolled deviations from narrow constructs of what is normal and optimal) and inevitable decay (including the tendency to become 'overweight' and so forth unless we constantly work to prevent it) remind us of our 'animal', non-spiritual being, limited self-control and mortality. These are all elements of our selves that we may come to despise because they are not easily compatible with prevailing notions of optimal selves in complete control.

A meta-analysis (Nechita et al., 2021) based on a wide range of empirical studies (n=195) with a total population of more than 64,000 subjects found a strong correlation between shame and eating disorders across different sub-categories of eating disorders (anorexia, bulimia and so forth). Higher levels of shame-proneness are associated with more severe reported symptoms of eating disorders (ibid.). Unfortunately, the vast majority of the underlying studies included in this meta-analysis were based on non-clinical populations, and their methodology is generally poor, which weakens the applicability of the analysis. A small number of studies also suggest that the correlation between shame and symptoms of eating disorders may be mediated by the individual's capacity for more mature and adaptive self-regulation (Gupta et al., 2008). Thus, the disturbed eating behaviour may be used as an instrument for downregulating negative affects, especially by people who have failed to develop more mature self-regulation strategies. Thus, we have to assume that not just the individual's shame-proneness but also their ability to contain and regulate feelings of shame through mature and adaptive self-regulation strategies affect whether feelings of shame will activate or intensify an underlying tendency for disturbed eating behaviour. Shame related to the body and eating is especially closely correlated with eating disorders (Nechita et al., 2021).

The connection between shame and disturbed eating behaviour is weakened with age (but never disappears entirely), presumably because many (but far from all) people improve their ability to contain and regulate shame as they get older and perhaps a little less preoccupied with others' perceptions and opinions of them. Also, body ideals tend to become less rigid with age. Generally, there has been less research into the connection between shame and bulimia. People with this disorder typically feel shameful about their disturbed eating behaviour (overeating and so forth) and often try to hide it and keep it a secret. At the same time, the disturbed eating behaviour may serve as a primitive and very concrete strategy for regulating negative affects, including shame.

Based on the existing studies, which focus predominantly on simple statistical correlations between the scope or intensity of feelings of shame and the prevalence of eating disorder symptoms, it is not possible to identify any causal links between shame and eating disorders, that is, whether and to what extent feelings of shame might be the dynamic psychological driver of disturbed eating behaviour or vice versa. That would require longitudinal studies that follow a large group of people from youth into adulthood or close, intensive analyses of internal psychological processes in individuals in connection with incidents of very severely disturbed eating behaviour.

However, a small number of studies suggest that more pronounced shame-proneness, especially in regard to body shame, precedes the development of eating disorders (Nechita et al., 2021, p. 34; Troop & Redshaw, 2012) and that the level of perceived shame increases in the lead-up to incidents of disturbed eating behaviour (overeating, purging and so forth) and diminishes immediately after (Blythin et al., 2020). This may indicate that shame is a contributing cause in the development of eating disorders and is not 'just' developed in parallel to or as a secondary consequence of an eating disorder.

Similarly, more recent network studies of possible dynamic connections between eating disorder symptoms and various affects have found a strong correlation between perceived shame (and guilt about eating) and the severity of eating disorder symptoms (Wong et al., 2020). Thus, shame may not just be a contributing cause of the development of an eating disorder but might also play a central role in maintaining it. Feelings of shame may destabilize the self-esteem of a person who has an eating disorder, causing them to use the disturbed eating behaviour in a continual attempt to regain, stabilize or compensate for their low and unstable self-esteem and to regulate unbearable feelings of shame. In addition, the disturbed eating behaviour (purging, perceived loss of control of food intake and so forth) and being diagnosed with an eating disorder can in itself be shameful and thus contribute further to maintaining and exacerbating the mental illness (cf. Oluyori, 2013, p. 54).

A small number of studies of change processes in patients with an eating disorder in psychotherapeutic treatment found indications that reductions in the patient's perceived level of shame precede and predict subsequent reductions of eating disorder symptoms. This supports the notion that shame ought to be a central focus in the psychotherapeutic treatment of eating disorders (Kelly & Tasca, 2016). Similarly, a reduction in eating disorder symptoms and heightened self-compassion are followed by a reduction in patients' level of shame (ibid.). This suggests that enhanced self-compassion can be an important impact factor in the treatment of eating disorders and also supports a possible dialectic interaction between shame and disturbed eating behaviour. However, more and methodologically stronger studies are needed to shed light on these key questions about causality.

Qualitative studies of eating disorders paint a picture of individuals with anorexia in particular feeling that their own selves are inherently wrong and that their own bodies and sexuality are disgusting and revolting (Skårderud, 2007). They describe a self-image characterized by profound shame, severe self-loathing, self-hatred and basic inadequacy (Rance et al., 2017). From this perspective, in some cases, the person will sometimes seek to compensate for this fundamentally negative self-image and low self-esteem through grandiose ideas about not needing anyone or anything (food) and about being unique due to this extraordinary control of their own food intake (Skårderud, 2001c, p. 1616) and thus of their own body and of the self's (the body's) physical (animal) needs. On this point, a small number of studies have found that identified correlations between destructive self-criticism and the severity of eating disorders are mediated by feelings of shame (Kelly & Carter, 2013). This further points to shame as a central element in the development and maintenance of eating disorders. Severe self-criticism bordering on self-hatred exacerbates the eating disorder through elevated levels of shame.

Possible dynamic connections between shame and disturbed eating behaviour

Based on Scheler's (1957) description of shame as a result of the insurmountable internal gap between our spiritual and physical bodily beings, we may view the difficulties of a person who has an eating disorder as manifestations of an impossible battle against or a crazed attempt at gaining control of their perceived primitive and 'filthy' body with its needs and desires (Pines, 1995). This takes the body–mind duality to the extreme, as the person's own body, with its needs, is split off from the rest of the (psychological mental) self and perceived, to varying degrees, as 'not me' and then ignored, punished and subjected to a strict (self-destructive) regime (see Section 5.5). As a parallel issue, in the person's self-perception and the eyes of others, the worth of the self is largely determined by how successful the person is at controlling and subjugating the body.

Sometimes the person's strict self-control and ability to resist the urge to eat may be a source of pride and improved self-esteem, which temporarily counteracts the painful shame (Goss & Allan, 2009). This can lead to a self-perpetuating dynamic interaction between shame and pride, in which the ability to control bodily impulses and the craving for food and the (temporarily) successful rebellion against others' perceived attempts at controlling the self ('you have to eat', 'this is what you should look like'), creates a positive sense of superiority and improved self-esteem and a self-perception that is less dominated by shame (Goss & Gilbert, 2002, p. 242f.). This is sometimes described as a shame–pride cycle (ibid.).

On the other hand, (new and intensified) shame may arise in the cracks that inevitably occur in this regime of controlling one's eating behaviour and realizing the irrational quality of one's own ideas about food and weight (including the feeling of being 'abnormal' or even 'insane') and in the confrontation with the physical consequences of prolonged disturbed eating behaviour. Furthermore, the act of eating may be perceived as a failure, since it means that the self has relinquished control to others (or the body). When this happens, the person returns to a shamed-self-image of being fat, ugly, confused, inferior and wrong (Goss & Gilbert, 2002, p. 242f.). This may be described as a self-perpetuating shame–shame cycle (ibid.). Similarly, the person's tendency to compare with others and rate their own social status based on their body and eating behaviour may trigger extreme feelings of inferiority, a sense of failing or being inadequate, also in a competitive comparison with other individuals with eating disorders. This means that the person is doomed to feel shame over their own inadequacy, since it will always be possible to find someone who seems to be a little better at controlling their weight, their food intake and the appearance of their body (Rance et al., 2017), if not in the physical, then in the virtual world.

Cultural stigmatization of eating disorders can add further shame to the person's disturbed eating behaviour, just as the emphasis on self-control in modern culture can exacerbate the destructive shame that might overwhelm someone with an eating disorder who experiences even a brief and minor loss of control of their eating behaviour. The inherent paradox of eating disorders is that the disturbed eating behaviour is simultaneously the patient's problem and the perceived solution to the selfsame problem; it is both the cause of unbearable shame and the patient's principal tool for escaping or regulating this feeling. The same is true of eating disorders that involve alternating bouts of overeating and purging (especially bulimia). In these cases, the patient may perceive overeating and subsequent purging as an effective (short-term) tool for regulating confusing or painful emotions (stabilizing the self) and achieving a sense of agency and a unique identity (cf. the fact that the practice of overeating and purging is often kept secret from others and may be perceived as a manifestation of the self's uniqueness). At the same time, however, it is also a source of shameful self-loathing ('I'm not normal'), an urge to hide the disturbed eating behaviour (with the accompanying risk of social isolation) and fear of being found out, which in itself may contribute to destabilizing the self and increasing the need for tools for self-regulation and self-stabilization, typically in the form of additional overeating and purging (Goss & Gilbert, 2002, p. 245).

Overall, the key dynamic role of the feeling of shame in people with eating disorders suggests that empathic exposure and processing of shame should be a central focus in psychotherapeutic treatment of eating disorders, just as shame should be included in the diagnostic assessment and general understanding of eating disorders. This is further underscored by the fact that shame is one of the main barriers for people to seek help and open up to a therapist, including their willingness to talk to a therapist about the core of their perceived difficulties and disturbed eating behaviour; difficulties which they often try to keep 'secret' (Nechita et al., 2021, p. 2). Furthermore, it is important to bear in mind that the disturbed eating behaviour is often embedded in relational dynamics, where, for example, a self who refuses to adapt and submit to directions about particular behaviours from others – including authority figures – may manifest this resistance through stubbornly and rigidly controlled eating behaviour.

The disturbed eating may thus be a manifestation of rebellion and autonomy and generate a sense of pride, victory, superiority and control in relation to others, such as the person's relatives, partner or therapist, who, by contrast, feel powerless and unhappy. This is the case even if the person's behaviour is often completely or partially outside the self's rational and voluntary control and has severely self-destructive consequences (cf. Goss & Allan, 2009). Egosyntonic symptoms are symptoms that the patient does not perceive as problematic. When these are embedded in complex relational dynamics, the patient will, at least, feel ambivalent about their symptoms and will not be unambiguously interested in receiving help to alleviate them. Thus, to have a real chance of helping the patient, we must first understand how the disturbed eating behaviour might be associated with shame and relational challenges in this particular individual. The therapist also needs to understand that disclosing and talking about disturbed eating behaviour may in itself be associated with shame and with a perceived risk of losing access to strategies for coping with unbearable emotions that were, in a sense, necessary and might even be perceived as 'successful' ways of regulating shame and other painful affects. If the therapist considers a quick reduction in the patient's most obvious eating disorder symptoms as an indication of treatment success and, similarly, views an absence of symptom reduction as a sign of their own (shameful) inability to help the patient, while the patient, conversely, sees a reduction of symptoms as sign of a shameful loss of control and as a defeat in a malign power struggle with the therapist, the groundwork has been laid for a destructive relationship between patient and therapist. In this destructive game, both parties may be driven by more or less unconscious shame, which makes it very difficult or impossible for the therapist to help the patient recover from the eating disorder. First of all, the patient needs a therapist who tries to understand and validate the dynamic psychological background of their disturbed eating behaviour, including the close link between the patient's eating behaviour and destructive shame and attempts to escape this shame, in part by taking pride in being able to resist external attempts to control the self and in the demonstrated control of bodily impulses and needs.

5.2 Posttraumatic stress disorder (PTSD)

PTSD has traditionally been perceived as a disorder that is mainly based on anxiety and fear, while the possible role of other affects has been overlooked or understudied. This changed somewhat with the introduction of DSM-5 in 2013, where negative changes in cognition and emotional state, including shame, are included as one among a fairly wide range of criteria for the diagnosis of PTSD (APA, 2013, p. 271f.). Similarly, the ICD-11 diagnosis of complex PTSD (cPTSD) includes diagnostic criteria that are quite closely related to shame and associated with negative self-perception and a perception of the self as failed and worthless (Brewin et al., 2017). Many patients with complex PTSD will have been exposed to numerous traumatic experiences or persistent traumatization over time, resulting in severe limitations in psychosocial functioning (Brewin et al., 2017). In relation to these changes in diagnostic criteria, a number of writers have discussed what they view as growing recognition that PTSD is in fact characterized by a wide range of negative affects, including shame and guilt (Badour et al., 2017; Lee et al., 2001). Some have advocated for the need for a special shame-based variant of PTSD, which should be expected to have avoidant behaviour as one of its prominent characteristics (Saraiya & Lopez-Castro, 2016, p. 14).

A review of the literature on shame in relation to PTSD based on 47 empirical studies concluded that overall, there is clear evidence of a connection between shame and PTSD, although there is considerable variation in the quality and design of the existing studies, the definition of shame and the methods used to measure it (Saraiya & Lopez-Castro, 2016). Both the development and the severity of PTSD symptoms thus appear to correlate with shame. There are also indications that the level of shame is higher in individuals who have experienced (1) sexual trauma, (2) multiple traumatic experiences and (3) partner violence, compared to other types of traumatization. A meta-analysis based on 25 studies similarly found a clear, if moderate, correlation between self-reported shame and self-reported PTSD symptoms (Lopez-Castro et al., 2019). In interpreting both this meta-analysis and the literature review mentioned above, it is important to bear in mind that the underlying empirical studies have significant methodological problems, including imprecise measures of shame, the inclusion of populations with significant differences in make-up, inadequate distinctions between constructive and destructive shame and inadequate differentiation between shame and guilt.

Nevertheless, these studies suggest a significant correlation between shame and PTSD, with the degree of shame correlating with the severity of PTSD symptoms (Cunningham, 2020, p. 145; Bash & Papa, 2014). However, the nature of the underlying causal links is yet to be determined, and we have no basis for determining whether shame is a contributing factor in the development of PTSD, whether it emerges as a secondary consequence of PTSD or whether the two develop in parallel in a dialectic interaction.

A small number of longitudinal studies (Saraiya & Lopez-Castro, 2016, p. 15) suggest that shame may be a contributing factor in the development of PTSD and generally lower psychological functioning in patients with PTSD, just as feelings of shame may contribute to maintaining a PTSD disorder (Cunningham, 2020, p. 145), in part through various forms of avoidance behaviour aimed at escaping unbearable feelings of shame. This avoidance behaviour in itself hampers the processing of traumatic experiences and limits access to help and support from others (ibid., p. 149). On this point, studies have added support to the idea that individuals who generally rely on maladaptive strategies to regulate their emotions and other mental states (such as a tendency for catastrophizing and self-reproach) are more likely to experience and react with shame (Szentagotai-Tatar & Miu, 2016) and that this may be a significant mediating factor in the connection between early trauma and the subsequent development of destructive shame and psychopathology.

Finally, a study of young psychiatric inpatients (aged 12–17 years) found indications that early sexual and emotional abuse influence the subsequent development of depression and suicidal ideation via the development of feelings of shame and guilt (Sekowski et al., 2020). The authors interpret this finding to mean that after experiencing abuse, the young people may have identified with the abuser's humiliation of and aggression towards the self and subsequently direct humiliation and aggression at themselves, partially manifested as destructive shame and guilt. As yet, however, these potential dynamic psychological connections lack sufficient empirical support.

We might imagine related dynamic relations between early abuse and the subsequent development of PTSD, as the development of severe shame and guilt following abuse increases the risk of subsequent development of PTSD. This may in part be mediated by shame-driven self-stigmatization, as the patient blames themselves for the abuse (including the self's failure to prevent the abuse) and perceives themselves and their body as filthy, repulsive and unlovable due to the abuse, which makes them feel damaged or defective. This self-stigmatization may also keep abuse victims from talking about and seeking help to process the experiences, especially if the abuser threatened the victim with repercussions if they told anyone about the abuse as well as fear about how others might see the shameful, 'filthy' and 'damaged' self if they 'find out' about the abuse.

In relation to this point, children who were subjected to neglect during their early years (first six years of life) are subsequently (around the age of seven years) more likely to experience shame and a higher level of depressive symptoms than children who did not suffer neglect (Bennett et al., 2010). Furthermore, the children's depressive symptoms seem to be at least partially driven by shame-proneness. In this case, too, self-stigmatization and the development of negative self-perceptions as a result of important others' expressed contempt for and humiliating treatment of them (including the caregiver's persistent lack of empathy and responsiveness) may be a significant factor in the development of destructive shame. A small number of studies which followed the development of at-risk children and young people over a number of years suggest that the connection between early childhood neglect and adolescent shame-proneness is mediated by the behaviour of key caregivers during adolescence. Dismissive parenting behaviour during adolescence thus appears to increase the connection between early neglect and later susceptibility to shame. It also increases the risk of depressive symptoms (Stuewig & McCloskey, 2005). The consequences of early neglect and the resulting shame thus seem to be related to whether the child or adolescent had access to caregivers who were capable of creating a secure space and helping the child and adolescent contain and process early difficult and stressful experiences and the resulting affective reactions, including shame.

Shame as a long-term consequence of sexual abuse

In what she calls 'the five laws of rape', the Danish novelist Johanne Bille writes that 'the person who is raped by someone has their body contact and body awareness confiscated … as compensation, the person who is raped by someone is awarded self-loathing and body-loathing' (Bille, 2021, p. 97).

> I [the woman who was raped] do not know what to sense, think, feel, and yet, I have never been as self-conscious as I am now. Shame over being me makes me yearn to be someone else. Anyone else would be better.
>
> (ibid., p. 101)

She also asks,

> What is the value of the faithless, raped woman? She is worth nothing, I am worth nothing, and the best way to keep this secret from the Idealist [her new boyfriend] is to pretend the opposite is true. I want to be the most attractive, the one who does the most, the one who is so considerate and attentive to other people's needs that she herself seems to disappear entirely.
>
> (Bille, 2021, p. 106f.)

In addition to the first-person narrator jumping in and out of and, to some extent, hiding in her own text – in itself a good illustration of how the raped subject often feels the need to hide – in this passage, Johanne Bille offers a very precise description of the tendency of victims of sexual abuse to become overly sensitive to others' expectations and needs while forgetting about or ignoring their own. This marks an attempt to gain the recognition and love that she yearns for but is worried she cannot have because she is 'damaged', defective and worthless after being subjected to abuse.

A small number of studies suggest that chronic shame can sometimes be a long-term effect of sexual abuse, which also increases the risk of long-term PTSD symptoms and should generally be considered a serious vulnerability factor for the development of psychopathology (Feiring & Taska, 2005; Feiring et al., 2002). A study of adult interpersonal trauma survivors found that significantly more women (12%) than men (3%) meet the DSM-5 PTSD criterion of shame; a remarkable gender gap that seems to be primarily driven by women who have suffered both sexual and physical abuse (Badour et al., 2017, p. 1628ff.). Many abuse survivors experience shame just after and in relation to the abuse being revealed to others. In most cases, the shame then gradually diminishes, but sometimes it lingers, for a variety of reasons (Feiring & Taska, 2005), including insufficient access to qualified help with processing the abuse and the related shame. Another reason may be the inability of the victims' relatives, friends and important others to handle the revealed abuse in a helpful way; instead, they might ignore, trivialize or otherwise signal their inability to contain the traumatic experiences the victim is trying to share with them (see also DeCou et al., 2017).

Studies have shown that the level of shame just after the occurrence of sexual abuse correlates with the severity of PTSD symptoms six months later, and that shame is closely related to avoidant and maladaptive coping strategies (Alix et al., 2020). These strategies in themselves increase the risk of developing mental illness and long-term pathological consequences of sexual abuse. In extension of this point, research has also found that a high level of shame one year after the abuse took place correlates with significantly elevated risk of a high level of shame six years later and, thus, the development of chronic shame; conversely, a low level of shame feelings one year after the abuse occurred appears to correlate with a good prognosis (Feiring & Taska, 2005; Andrews et al., 2000; see also Herman, 2011, p. 266). Thus, there are many indications to suggest that destructive shame reactions in relation to traumatic experiences are a significant risk factor for the development of psychopathology. Shame may also play a significant role in relation to elevated risk of suicidal ideation and suicide attempts among people with PTSD (Cunningham, 2020, p. 156). More specifically, research has found a correlation between the level of shame and the prevalence of suicidal ideation among women who were subjected to childhood sexual abuse (Kealy et al., 2017). Together, these findings suggest that individuals who have been subjected to sexual abuse or other types of relational trauma should quickly be offered qualified help to process the shame and other painful affects that arise in the wake of traumatization.

In relation to this point, it is important to consider how the individual understands why the abuse took place, included whether the person assigns responsibility and guilt to themselves, to the abuser or, perhaps, to an absent/ neglectful caregiver (who should have prevented the abuse), or whether the abuse is perceived as 'incomprehensible' or 'random'. The risk of developing psychopathology is considerably higher in connection with internal attribution, where the person partially blames themselves for the abuse and for failing to avoid or prevent it ('I should have struggled', 'I just froze and was completely passive'). This connection is mediated by shame in the sense that internal attribution of responsibility for the abuse is related to a higher risk of negative long-term consequences if the person also struggles with persistent destructive shame in relation to the abuse (Feiring et al., 2002; cf. aggression directed at the self rather than at the abuser or, perhaps, at a caregiver who failed to protect and help the self).

Studies further found that shame and self-reproach in connection with women's experience of verbal or physical abuse in the public space influence how likely these experiences are to lead to the development of PTSD symptoms (Carretta & Szymanski, 2020). It is worth noting that identification with feminist values weakens this connection, presumably because women with integrated feminist values are better able to assign responsibility for potentially traumatic sexual abuse to the abuser, rather than to themselves. Presumably, the phenomenon of women (and others) joining forces, for example in the MeToo movement, to break the silence about perceived abuse and other, more severe forms of personal abuse, can in itself help empower them to assign responsibility for the perceived abuse externally, which will help reduce the risk of painful feelings of shame in extension of the experience. It is also relevant to consider how other people's reactions to the victim's story of perceived abuse influence the development of shame, just as prevailing (sub)cultural perceptions of victims of sexual abuse will presumably make a difference (cf. the tendency to 'victim blaming' and so forth). Furthermore, it seems likely that a fragile or poorly developed capacity for mentalizing and self-compassion will generally increase the risk of long-term negative effects of abuse, in part because the victims will be more likely to blame themselves for the traumatic experiences and see themselves as responsible for incidents that they in fact had little influence on.

A small number of studies indicate that psychotherapeutic work with shame and diminished levels of shame are central elements in the efficacy of PTSD treatment (Cunningham, 2020, p. 155). Part of the reason for the significance of shame in maintaining a PTSD disorder and the crucial import-ance of focusing on the patient's shame in PTSD treatment may be that shame generally prevents the patient from seeking help and blocks the processing of traumatic experiences. Both factors may be driven by the patient's urge to hide, avoid emotional contact with others and avoid telling others about their perceived trauma. As long as the patient, for example, experiences shame over perceived abuse, it is extremely difficult to achieve a sense of mas-tery in relation to the experience and their own reactions to it (cf. Herman, 2011, p. 267). Furthermore, shame can hamper the integration of traumatic recollections into the self's identity that is a necessary condition for recovery and may thus diminish the efficacy of the treatment (cf. Saraiya & Lopez-Castro, 2016, p. 2).

Some patients may avoid sharing the most traumatic, humiliating and shameful elements of the perceived abuse with their therapist for fear that the therapist will be emotionally repulsed, disgusted and withdraw from the patient. This could, at worst, make the patient feel that the abuser is the only person in the world who truly 'knows' and understands the patient. If this happens, the patient may, in a sense, become emotionally isolated in a mental space alone with the abuser; an experience that will be extremely painful and harmful for the patient's recovery (cf. Herman, 2011, p. 269). Furthermore, shame can activate maladaptive avoidance and defensive strategies, including social isolation, dissociation, self-destructive behaviour, substance abuse and outward violence, that exacerbate the traumatized person's condition and functioning (Taylor, 2015; Lopez-Castro et al., 2019; Herman, 2011).

In a more general sense, persons who have been subjected to, for example, sexual abuse may develop coping strategies and concrete behaviours that are dynamically shaped by the abuse in the sense that they may either try to avoid all forms of sexuality (avoidance behaviour) or almost compulsively seek (stage) sexual situations that repeat core aspects of their past abuse. In this way, too, unprocessed shame may over time contribute to creating, maintaining and worsening a PTSD disorder. On the other hand, therapists should bear in mind that recalling traumatic incidents in the psychotherapeutic space may (re)activate difficult feelings of shame and recollections of past humiliations of the self (Lee et al., 2001, p. 455f.), which can in itself be quite painful and make the patient withdraw from treatment. Shame and attempts at avoiding overwhelming destructive shame may thus be a decisive factor when some survivors of sexual abuse choose not to tell their therapist about the abuse (McElvaney et al., 2021). This is another reason why qualified work with shame-laden experiences of abuse requires a competent and well-trained psychotherapist, who can help the patient get into contact with traumatic experiences in the therapeutic space at a pace and in ways that do not over-whelm the patient's boundaries of shame.

Based on a qualitative interview study of individuals subjected to sexual abuse (n=19), Pettersen (2013) has proposed a number of subcategories of shame in this patient group. Among other points, the participants described (1) shame related to family members, who knew about the abuse without inter-vening, (2) shame related to their own body, which they perceive as filthy and seek to control by controlling their food intake, and (3) shame in connection with low self-esteem and problems with intimacy. In extension of this, they also describe (4) a variety of sexual difficulties, as they associate sex with extreme displeasure and try to avoid it or get it over with as quickly as possible or perhaps (5) use sex as a way to punish the self. Finally, (6) the participants described finding it shameful to open up to and reveal their vulnerability to a therapist. The researcher does not report whether the participants had under-gone systematic diagnostic assessment, and it is unclear how many of them had PTSD. Thus, we cannot be certain to what extent these subcategories of shame can be generalized to sexually traumatized PTSD patients.

However, there is little doubt that it can feel quite shameful to be the victim of various forms of abuse and other forms of relational traumatization. Being the passive and helpless victim of an abuser, whom the victim perhaps lacked the strength to fight and who may have been a person of trust, can in itself be immensely shameful. This is the case even though the victim's pas-sivity can sometimes be an adaptive response, as it might help prevent an escalation of the abusive situation and thus increase their chances of survival, whether the passivity is a largely conscious and rationally calculated choice or the result of 'freezing' and becoming paralysed during the assault. In add-ition, being seen and treated as an inanimate object for the satisfaction of the abuser's needs, as opposed to being seen and acknowledged as a human subject, can lead to destructive shame during the abuse, immediately after-wards and in the long term, as being a survivor of abuse may be a decisive factor in developing a negative self-image based on shame and difficulties with defending one's own boundaries of intimacy in a balanced way.

Finally, in some cases, it may be helpful to consider psychoanalyst Sándor Ferenczi's (1933/1988) thoughts on what he calls the 'confusion of tongues between adults and the child' in connection with sexual abuse, as the child needs and seeks tenderness and emotional closeness and contact but is met by an adult (abuser) driven by sexual desire. A related 'confusion of tongues' in the sense of a severe discrepancy in the understanding of a relational situation and the absence of emotional and relational attunement can occur in connection with intimate contact between adults, when one party (the victim in a situation that develops into abuse) might seek tenderness, non-sexual physical closeness and emotional contact, while the other (who becomes the abuser) is simply living out more raw sexual passion with no awareness of the other's needs or understanding of their concrete encounter. Both situations must be considered abuse and will often be accompanied by feelings of shame over failing to be seen and met but instead used merely as an object to satisfy the other's needs, which the victim of the abuse might not even understand.

With Wurmser (2015, p. 1628), we can imagine that some abusers suffer from 'soul blindness', in this case, blindness to the abused person's individuality and a lack of acceptance of the abused self's autonomy. Ultimately, the consequences of this soul blindness may lead to soul murder, since a person who is not seen as a human being, a person and a subject entitled to their own feelings, legitimate needs, boundaries and independent volition can suffer fundamental damage and thus be prevented from undergoing normal psychological development. In this sense, sexual abuse is associated with a risk of soul murder, especially if the abuser is one of a small circle of important others in the abused person's life. Finally, being a survivor of sexual abuse may in itself be associated with social stigmatization and contribute to self-stigmatization, which can lead to shame and increase the risk of more chronic feelings of shame.

5.3 Borderline personality disorder

Borderline personality disorder (BPD) is one of the most severe and common personality disorders. Shame is not included in the formal diagnostic criteria of BPD, but several writers (Nathanson, 1994; Crowe, 2004) have argued quite convincingly that destructive shame, including severe problems with containing and regulating feelings of shame, is a core issue in BPD and should be considered one of the most important dynamic drivers behind most of the central elements of the disorder, as they are described in the diagnostic criteria of BPD (APA, 2013, p. 663; see Table 5.1), including severe identity disturbances (see Section 5.6). Conversely, a striking absence of feelings of shame is mainly related to antisocial personality disorder and psychopathy, while extreme shamelessness in interpersonal interactions is primarily associated with certain types of narcissistic personality disorder (see Section 5.4). As mentioned in the introductory chapter, a qualitative interview study of the subjective experience of severe identity disturbances in female patients with BPD paint a picture of shame as a core and very painful feeling in this group (Jørgensen & Bøye, 2022), manifested as a sense of being inherently wrong, condemned by others and excluded from social communities. As one of the study participants put it, 'Hell, I am out of order, like a machine where a bolt is missing, that's me'. Another participant said, 'I feel wrong in relation to everyone I encounter'.

The interviewees describes being constantly 'worried that people don't like me – I feel that they're judging me'. A deep-seated sense of being wrong and different in a negative sense: 'I am inherently wrong, I don't fit in anywhere. No matter who I'm with, I am always the odd one out'. In extension of this, the women describe an urge to withdraw from others and to isolate – 'then I am on my own. There's nobody looking at me. And there's nobody judging me or having an opinion [about me]'. Alternatively, they try to hide behind 'this huge facade of make-up … so that I look as if I'm okay'. Many of them wonder and doubt whether they have a right to live, to exist, or whether it might be better – or perhaps of no consequence – to others if they did not exist: 'I want to feel loved and worthy of being here [in the world], and I don't'. Thus, there seems to be a short path from difficult feelings of shame to suicidal ideation.

There is reason to consider whether the general tendency to overlook shame and treat it as taboo is part of the reason why shame has been largely left out of our traditional delimitation and understanding of BPD. While Kernberg (1993), among others, argued that envy, anger and hate (aggression) form the affective core of BPD, it could be argued that these affects in many cases are in fact secondary manifestations of, reactions to or defences against unbearable feelings of shame stemming from the fundamental feeling of the self being defective, inferior and repulsive that is common among people with BPD. However, in some cases, shame, perceived inferiority and a sense that one's own self is fundamentally defective may be less conscious and, not least, harder to measure through the simple self-reported questionnaires that are typically used in empirical studies. Thus, it is not necessarily straightforward to document the role of shame in BPD using traditional quantitative empirical methods.

Hate of concrete others contains an element of relatedness with these others (Fuchs, 2021, p. 321) and, perhaps, a hope of changing the relationship, unlike destructive shame, which makes the self feel socially excluded, cut off from contact and thrown back on themselves. Since we also know that anger and hate may be reactions to unbearable feelings of shame as well as significant elements of psychological strategies for dealing with unbearable shame, we should consider whether intense anger and hate may be involved in the shame defence of patients with BPD – a defence in which the self's perceived humiliation is converted into an attempt to humiliate, intimidate and shame others. To the extent that the opposite of love is not hate but indifference, hating or being hated by others may seem like a preferable alternative to being abandoned, ignored, left to one's own devices and met with a wall of indifference from others (cf. Fuchs, 2021). There is also reason to assume that shame can both arise and be reinforced as a result of the limitations in the capacity for self-control, affect control and impulse control that are part of the BPD disorder; furthermore, the dysfunctions in subjective experiences (reality testing), memory and other cognitive functions that are common in connection with BPD can also in themselves be shameful (Tiedemann, 2010, p. 465). Occasional and recurring defects in cognitive functioning and the capacity for self-control may make the person appear (or perceive themselves as being) out of control, inadequate, deviant, abnormal or even insane in ways that may feel shameful to the person themselves and in the eyes of others.

Shame in models for understanding BPD

Two of the leading models for understanding and treating BPD, Marsha Linehan's (1993) dialectical behavioural therapy (DBT) and Anthony Bateman's (Bateman & Fonagy, 2016) mentalization-based therapy (MBT), both focus on defects in the regulation of intense and painful affects as the core, or part of the core, of borderline disorder. Linehan (1993) associates the development of BPD with growing up in a family environment characterized by a lack of validation or even explicit invalidation of the self and its subjective experiences and emotional reactions; an environment in which the self's emotions and subjective experiences are disregarded and defined as invalid, wrong or unacceptable, which is shameful in itself. Furthermore, in such an invalidating environment, emotional vulnerability and communication of negative emotions are often met with various types of punishment. This experience can lead to destructive shame over and invalidation of the person's own self and emotions (Linehan, 1993, p. 72).

Growing up, most people with BPD will have experienced invalidation and shaming because of their emotional vulnerability. They will have lacked the opportunity to develop an ability to verbalize and regulate emotional and other mental states and will instead have learned to react with shame to their own uncontrolled and negative emotions (Linehan, 1993, p. 42). Based on Linehan's DBT model, we may thus see shame as a central affect in BPD and as an important mediating factor between early stressful experiences and the subsequent development of BPD and other forms of psychopathology (cf. Buchman-Wildbaum et al., 2021, p. 155), even though Linehan herself does not focus on shame as a primary element of the borderline disorder but focuses more on general difficulties with regulating negative affects, including destructive shame. A few small empirical studies based on Jeffrey Young's schema-focused approach to personality disorders (Young et al., 2003) found that a cognitive schema based on a perception of the self as defective and shameful combined with schemas focused on distrust, inadequate self-control and the abused self, among other aspects, sets BPD apart from other personality disorders (Bach & Farrell, 2018).

In a view related to Linehan's DBT perspective, Bateman and Fonagy view BPD in relation to defects in the capacity for mentalizing (having nuanced and relevant psychological reflections on) emotions and other mental states, including intense negative affects, such as destructive shame. BPD is associated with a fragile and vulnerable self that is easily overwhelmed by transgressive experiences and intense affects which the self has difficulty containing and processing psychologically. This implies, in part, that the self may be flooded and destabilized by shame, which feels much more destructive and life-threatening to the self when the capacity to mentalize the shame and the concrete activating situations is compromised (Bateman & Fonagy, 2004, p. 96f.). Experiences in attachment relationships in which the self was seen and treated as a dehumanized object (prototypically in connection with physical or sexual abuse) in a relationship where the self would normally expect to be seen and appreciated as a person are particularly likely to lead to overwhelming shame and a general tendency to regress to a low level of psychological functioning.

This occurs especially in situations where the self is under pressure and reverts to what Bateman and Fonagy call teleological and psychic equivalence modes: functional modes that make it difficult to step away from, engage in nuanced reflection on and understand painful experiences and affects in the moment, which may therefore easily overwhelm and destabilize the self. One young man with BPD described how, as a young teen, he came home from school one day ecstatic, excitedly telling his mother that he got the after-school job he had long been hoping for. Instead of seeing empathic mirroring, recognition and affirmation in his mother's eyes, his mother was furious and forbade him to take the job, telling him it was unacceptable and counter to the agreement she insisted they had: that he promised to spend more time on his homework. This incident repeated a pattern that the patient had experienced over and over during his upbringing, as his excitement and enthusiasm met with angry rejection (rather than empathic mirroring and emotional resonance), which instantly killed his joy and replaced it with destructive and unbearable shame. Later, he said that this situation marked the first time that he reacted with such intense anger that he subsequently hit his mother in a desperate attempt to escape or alleviate his unbearable feeling of shame.

When a person with BPD is operating in psychic equivalence mode, perceiving their self to be defective and imagining that others feel contempt and loathing towards the self, they are convinced that they are defective and that others find them revolting. This internal reality (including imagined others) and the external reality (including concrete others) fuse into one, and the person is unable to develop any detachment and distance to the subjective experiences that caused the self to be overwhelmed by shame. The patient also struggles to reflect on how these subjective experiences, infused with anxiety-filled perceptions and past experiences, relate to the actual reality here and now, including how shame and unbearable subjective experiences in the moment may be influenced and, to some extent, determined by traumatic past experiences. When something that is playing out in the patient's relationships with others – including therapists – makes the patient feel inadequate, humiliated and shameful, in the psychic equivalence mode, they may feel (and be completely convinced) that these others deliberately intended to make them feel humiliated and shamed. This subjective experience can give rise to intense anger and an urge to attack these others in order to escape the unbearable anxiety and defend against or avenge the perceived shaming.

Shame as an affective driver of diagnostic criteria

Shame can activate and is intimately associated with two of our most anxiety-evoking thoughts, as social beings: the fear of being abandoned, excluded from the social community and left to ourselves and the fear of being inherently wrong, inadequate, abnormal and different from others in a negative way (cf. Lammers et al., 2007). Both these anxiety-evoking thoughts are very prominent elements of the BPD disorder. The patient's fear of being abandoned and the accompanying, often desperate attempts to prevent this from happening can be understood in relation to a persistent struggle to avoid social isolation, unbearable loneliness and exclusion from social communities that is driven by shame, among other affects. We may view this as a struggle to belong, to feel and be recognized as part of a community and to engage in a form of contact and attachment with others that may be simultaneously driven and jeopardized by shame. In order to escape a feeling of abandonment and loneliness that might be both a cause and an effect of shame, patients with BPD may feel an urge to embrace an other's agenda and ignore their own boundaries and needs in a desperate attempt to maintain contact.

Similarly, the characteristic tendency of patients with BPD to alternate between idealizing and devaluing the self and others may be viewed as a defence against shame, as the idealization of others may deflect attention from their own shame. As long as the self feels some form of contact with, access to or control of the idealized other, this can help diminish the sense of shame and inferiority. Idealization of the concrete other driven by – often unconscious, unacknowledged – shame can also result in a high degree of dependence on the other as a way to suppress the underlying shame and stabilize the self. At the opposite extreme, intense devaluation of others may be driven by shame stemming from a feeling that these others have failed, abandoned or been abusive towards the self. Alternatively, these others may be seen as being far superior to, disparaging and humiliating the self. The intense displeasure of seeing themselves in the mirror that is common in individuals with BPD may similarly stem from a mechanism where confrontation with their own reflection leads to self-consciousness, self-devaluation and a shameful experience of the self as defective that is so intense that it threatens to overwhelm the self. Therefore, some patients with BPD deliberately try to avoid 'meeting' their own reflection (see Winter et al., 2015).

Devaluing and attacking others can help deflect attention from the person's own shameful defects and deficits and (re)create a sense of agency and control or power (which is typically severely compromised when the self is overwhelmed by shame). These attacks on others may also be seen as acts of revenge or counterattacks on others who are perceived to be to blame for the self's unbearable shame (because they misunderstand, humiliate, degrade, exploit or do not see the self). Devaluing others may also be interpreted as an attempt to handle the fear of abandonment, as it lets the individual feel (or convince themselves) that being abandoned by this devalued or inferior other does not matter (Nathanson, 1994, p. 799ff.).

Loathing, despising and attacking one's own self and body, including self-harm and suicidal behaviour (see below), may be closely related with a feeling of shame that threatens to overwhelm the self. Concrete physical attacks on the person's own shameful self and body in the form of self-harming behaviour or attempted suicide may appear as the only way to escape the shame or as concrete manifestations of the person's perception of their own self as unacceptably defective, inadequate, repulsive and unworthy. In extension of this, scar tissue and other visible marks of self-harm and attempted suicide can be understood as almost excessively concrete manifestations of the damaged and defective self, which highlight and communicate the self's defects (and psychological pain) to the world.

A lack of internal stability and impulsivity are defining aspects of the BPD disorder and is manifested in actions governed by fleeting and momentary thoughts, affects and impulses. This may take the form of, for example, impulsive sex, spending, reckless driving, disturbed eating behaviour and various forms of self-harm and substance abuse (APA, 2013, p. 663). Seen in relation to shame, the impulsive behaviour of patients with BPD sometimes serves as a form of avoidant behaviour, as attention is deflected from the defective self, and the patient tries to escape unbearable feelings of shame and humiliating experiences in which the self appeared or was exposed as inferior, powerless, defective and thus shameful. In some cases, the impulsive behaviour may also represent attempts at regaining the sense of agency and empowerment that normally breaks down when the self is overwhelmed by shame. In that case, the impulsive behaviour is, so to speak, an attempt to act one's way out of unbearable shame; a strategy that typically only has brief or no effect.

Fleeting and stress-related paranoid thoughts and a tendency to dissociate are often associated with BPD. Paranoid beliefs are based, in part, on a fantasy of others observing, disparaging and threatening the self and are thus, in several ways, related to subjective experiences associated with destructive shame. Chronic shame can in itself be considered a kind of dissociative state that inhibits the capacity for nuanced and rational thinking (Nathanson, 1994, p. 804). In some cases, dissociation can also be viewed as an attempt to regulate or shut down unbearable affects, including feelings of destructive shame that sometimes threaten to overwhelm the self. Dissociation can thus reduce the risk of strong affects flooding the self.

The chronic feeling of inner emptiness and boredom that is another central characteristic of the borderline disorder may be closely associated with shame and identity diffusion. The feeling of inner emptiness is often accompanied by diffuse notions of the self being wrong, defective and abnormal in the eyes of others and 'incapable of figuring out' how the self should be in order to be okay, included and accepted by others. In addition, shame is often silent, blank and empty and difficult to verbalize or concretize, which also relates to characteristics of the inner emptiness in BPD. Finally, in some cases, inner emptiness can arise as a result of a partially intentional attempts to shut down all emotional experiences and reactions in a desperate attempt to escape unbearable emotions, including destructive shame.

Severe identity disturbances (identity diffusion), which are at the heart of the borderline disorder (Jørgensen, 2006, 2010, 2018a), are closely associated with a perception of the self as inadequate and defective and, not least, with persistent shifts between different perceptions of one's own identity. This marks a lack of internal integration of shameful, unacceptable or defective parts of the self, among other elements, which gives reason to consider whether overwhelming shame might sometimes be part of the affective core and the driving force of the lack of integration of elements of the self and its history. As a minimum, identity diffusion and a tendency to experience and react with shame seem to be closely associated with BPD. Both are grounded in an inherent sense of being defective, broken and unlovable and accompanied by a strong urge to construct a facade that may attract positive attention and recognition from others.

One of the tragic aspects of this strategy is that it does not actually help people who have BPD, as the attention and recognition they might achieve by pursuing this strategy is not directed at who they really are. In fact, the recognition is directed at the constructed facade and is therefore false, and the use of this strategy to earn recognition often makes the person even more unsure of who they really are behind the different masks and facades. Furthermore, needing to hide behind or seek contact via a constructed mask, rather than daring to 'be oneself', can in itself feel shameful. This may also be a strong factor when patients with BPD seek contact on social media and dating profiles; an issue that is far from unique to this group.

The characteristic affective instability and occasional tendency to fluctuate between strong and polarized affective states that is seen in patients with BPD may therefore stem partially from shame and shame anxiety occasionally overwhelming the self as a result of varying ego-states and impulsive reactions to events in interpersonal interactions.

Table 5.1 summarizes some possible relationships between destructive shame and the diagnostic criteria of BPD.

Table 5.1 Possible dynamic relationships between diagnostic criteria of borderline personality disorder and shame

BPD, diagnostic criterion	Relationship to shame
Intense efforts to avoid being abandoned or left on one's own	Attempts to reduce or escape shame-related experience of the self as defective, inadequate and at risk of social exclusion and loneliness: 'If I am abandoned, I am nothing, empty'. Contact with 'the other' keeps overwhelming feelings of shame in check. Further complicated when the person humiliates themselves, submits, is extremely subservient, gives up their own boundaries and needs in desperate attempts to avoid being abandoned – which is shameful in itself.
Unstable and intense relationships characterized by constant fluctuations between idealization and devaluation	Related to alternating between shame (devaluation) and pride (idealization). Attempts to cope with the shameful perception of the self as defective by idealizing/taking pride in own self – or idealizing/taking pride in an important other who can affirm, support and stabilize the self and boost the person's fragile self-esteem. Idealization and pride may be attempts at deflecting attention from a shameful self. Inhibits realistic perception/assessment of the self and others. Devaluing, degrading and attacking the other may similarly be attempts at coping with shame by making the other experience shame, which can sometimes alleviate the self's perceived shame.
Identity disturbance and highly unstable self-perception	Associated with inadequate self-integration, including integration of shameful self-aspects, perception of the self as defective/unlovable and shameful traumatic experiences (abuse, severe neglect) in which important others treated the self as a dehumanized object. The person's identity is destabilized and perceived as permanently at risk/jeopardized as a result of perceived humiliations and resulting shame.
Impulsivity	Impulsive and dysregulated behaviour may be an attempt to escape/flee from unbearable shame; avoidant behaviour serves to divert own and others' attention from the defective self and shame.
Suicidal ideation and suicidal behaviour	Self-harm and suicidal behaviour may be both a reaction to and a consequence of the self's perceived shameful defects, inadequacies and disgust with their own self and being.
Emotional instability and a high level of emotional reactivity	May be driven by incidents in which the self is overwhelmed by shame and shame anxiety and reacts emotionally to this shame/shame anxiety which the self lacks the necessary psychological resources to contain and cope with at a more mature level (verbalizing, mentalizing and understanding the perceived shame in dialogue with others).
Sense of emptiness	May be closely associated with intense feelings of shame, including a perception of the self as defective and inherently wrong, and an inability to determine what the self should be like in order to be 'good enough' in others' eyes and to be accepted as an equal member of a social community. In some cases, the inner emptiness may be a defence against overwhelming shame, as the person attempts to shut down all affects/emotions (possibly intensified by harmful use of alcohol/drugs).

Table 5.1 (Continued)

BPD, diagnostic criterion	Relationship to shame
Intense anger and difficulties with anger regulation	Dysregulated anger, attacks on and an urge to take revenge on others who are blamed for the self's feelings of shame, perceived betrayal and the threat of social exclusion and for not sufficiently seeing and recognizing the self. Over time, dysregulated anger (loss of control) can in itself lead to shame. Acting out anger/rage is used as a way to feel alive and affirm the self's right to exist (avoid unbearable feelings of emptiness and shame) and temporarily stabilize the identity. Outward anger may also be a strategy for deflecting attention from one's own shameful self and evoking shame (by proxy) in others (cf. also projective identification) who are the object of the self's anger.
Stress-related dissociation and paranoid beliefs	Paranoid beliefs associated with the shameful perception that others observe and (negatively) judge, despise, condemn or ridicule the self. Dissociation arises as an attempt to escape shame and emotional flooding of the self, alternatively, chronic shame as a dissociative state.

Sources: APA, 2013, p. 663 (borderline personality disorder). Nathanson, 1994, p. 799ff.; Stanghellini & Mancini, 2018 (shame).

Empirical studies of shame in BPD

A meta-analysis based on ten studies of self-reported shame in patients with BPD found a significantly higher level of shame among this group compared with healthy controls. The analysis also found that a higher level of shame in patients with BPD correlates with lower levels of self-esteem and quality of life (Buchman-Wildbaum et al., 2021). Among patients with BPD, shame-proneness is further associated with disturbed relationships and an elevated level of anger and hostility (Buchman-Wildbaum et al., 2021; see also Scott et al., 2017). The level of shame does not appear to diminish with age, unlike most other BPD symptoms. This might indicate that a targeted focus on shame should be a central element of psychotherapeutic treatment of BPD. A single study found a correlation between subjectively perceived shame and the number of diagnostic BPD criteria a patient meets (Benecke & Peham, 2007, p. 29); roughly put, this suggests that the more severe the borderline disorder is, the more likely the person is to struggle with severe feelings of shame.

Unfortunately, the available empirical data about possible relationships between BPD and shame, including the extent to which shame may be particularly pronounced in or characteristic of BPD, is weakened by some of the previously discussed methodological problems. One such issue is that most of the existing studies are based on students and examine possible correlations between dimensional measures of BPD, often fairly weak measures of shame and various measures of accompanying issues, such as hostility and self-harm. In relation to this, it is worth noting that perhaps the most widely used measure of shame, the Test of Self-Conscious Affect (TOSCA; Tangney et al., 2000), seems to have extraordinary difficulty distinguishing between guilt and shame in patients with BPD (Rüsch, Corrigan, Bohus, Jacob et al., 2007). Thus, if we want real insight into the possible relationships between shame and BPD, we need studies that look at destructive shame in a larger group of patients with BPD, rather than more studies that compare more general and, at best, imprecise measures of shame with BPD traits among respondents who do not have any actual personality pathology.

However, a small number of studies based on patient populations have found higher – often considerably higher – self-reported levels of shame among patients with BPD than among patients with depression (Scheel, Schneid et al., 2013, 2014), ADHD (Scheel et al., 2014), social anxiety (ibid.), social phobia (Rüsch, Lieb et al., 2007), narcissistic personality disorder (Ritter et al., 2014), obsessive-compulsive personality disorder (Rizvi et al., 2011) and other non-BPD personality disorders (Unoka & Vizin, 2017; Karan et al., 2014). Furthermore, a single experimental study found signs that shame-proneness in connection with interpersonal challenges is significantly higher among patients with BPD compared with patients with depression or bipolar disorder, and that feelings of shame are significantly more persistent over time among patients with BPD than in the two affective disorders (Mneimne et al., 2018). Overall, these findings support the notion that shame is a particularly pronounced problem among patients with BPD. A small number of studies have examined the role of comorbid PTSD in BPD. For now, however, the possible significance of PTSD for perceived shame in people with BPD must be viewed as unresolved (Rüsch, Corrigan, Bohus, Kühler et al., 2007; Buchman-Wildbaum, 2021).

So far, heightened shame-proneness among patients with BPD has been found to be associated with a heightened risk of self-harming behaviour (Brown et al., 2009), with the degree of identity disturbance (Unoka & Vizin, 2017, p. 327) and with lower levels of both psychosocial and interpersonal functioning (Cameron et al., 2021). This also points to shame-proneness as a key problem area in people with BPD. Thus, an inability to contain and cope with shame may be a core element in the persistence of low levels of psychosocial functioning in patients with BPD long after they no longer met the diagnostic criteria of the disorder (Cameron et al., 2021, p. 15). Conversely, a lower tendency to experience guilt seems to be associated with lower levels of social and interpersonal functioning in patients with BPD (Cameron et al., 2021). In this regard, too, non-destructive guilt thus appears to have a positive influence on the person's social and relational life. Attempts to diminish or eliminate unbearable negative affects are also a frequently reported motive for self-harm, including among patients with BPD.

Conversely, a study of self-harm among patients with BPD found shame to be the only negative affect that often worsens in connection with self-harm;

only 17% of the participating patients with BPD reported finding that their feelings of shame diminished in connection with self-harm, while as many as 53% reported that they worsen with self-harm (Kleindienst et al., 2008). Among the participating patients with BPD, shame was the only negative affect that was found to get worse after episodes of self-harm. This might be because many find self-harm inherently shameful, which may be part of the reason why they try to keep it secret from others. On the other hand, some patients almost seem to overexpose their self-harm and its concrete consequences, in some cases as a very concrete manifestation of their psychological pain and a cry for help, in others as part of almost masochistic self-exposure and disparagement of their own defective and repulsive self.

A single study (Cameron et al., 2020; see also Wiklander et al., 2012) found that shame-proneness among patients with BPD is related to the frequency and severity of suicidal ideation and behaviour independent of the severity of other BPD symptoms. This may suggest that shame is a central factor in suicidal behaviour. It is therefore important for therapists to focus on feelings of shame in the diagnostic assessment and psychotherapeutic treatment of patients with BPD who have strong suicidal ideation and behaviour. Thus, there are strong indications of a complex relationship between shame and self-harm in BPD. Self-harm appears to be a frequently used strategy to diminish or escape shame, although it usually has limited positive effect on the shame of patients with BPD, and its effect may even be negative.

Patients with BPD may view self-harm and suicidal ideation as their only way to deal with extreme and unbearable feelings of shame, with self-harm and suicidal behaviour as possible desperate attempts at self-regulation and affect regulation (cf. Brown et al., 2009; Cameron et al., 2020). In addition, self-harm may in itself lead to shame – because of the person's self-harm and, perhaps, suicide attempts – and thus increase the risk of subsequent self-harm in an attempt to escape or down-regulate the resulting/intensified shame and other negative affects (cf. Spitzen et al., 2020) in a self-perpetuating vicious cycle. Although self-harm may thus sometimes offer temporary relief and help reduce shame and other negative affects, over time, it may also exacerbate these negative affects and thus become a driver of new self-harm (ibid., p. 635).

Studies based on students and other non-clinical populations found that BPD traits, problems with anger and a tendency to externalize symptoms/behaviour are associated with a higher level of shame-proneness, a higher level of shame and a lower level of guilt (Peters & Geiger, 2016; Currie et al., 2017). Furthermore, the traits of both BPD and evasive personality disorder appear to be related to an implicit or non-conscious tendency to avoid shame (Currie et al., 2017). In extension of this point, a small number of studies found that BPD traits (related to the diagnostic criteria of BPD, see above) are not only associated with an increased tendency to experience shame and anger but also with rumination on anger. This rumination means that the anger is not acted out but becomes the driver of persistent (but unconstructive) thoughts centred on anger, aggression and hate, with no prospects of a more mature and adaptive way to deal with this internal anger (Peters et al., 2014; Peters & Geiger, 2016).

There is reason to assume that the occasionally intense and impulsive anger seen in some individuals with BPD may be driven by shame, including serving as an outward defence against unbearable shame. Similarly, the afore-mentioned occurrence of self-harm and suicidal behaviour may sometimes be a manifestation of inward anger in response to or defence against shame (cf. Table 5.1). To the extent that this is true, we should assume that empathic mirroring, emotional resonance, verbalization and gentle work directed at shame in the therapeutic space will over time help reduce the patient's anger and the resulting dysfunctional behaviour – provided the therapist is able to do this in ways that do not result in additional and more persistent shame in the patient (see Chapter 7).

Finally, there is reason to assume that the often difficult relational problems experienced by individuals with BPD – including difficulties with establishing and containing/being in deeper emotional and psychological contact with others – are sometimes related to severe shame and fear of being overwhelmed by shame if they leave themselves open to deeper con-tact with others and thus make themselves even more vulnerable to being abandoned and to perceiving themselves as wrong and inadequate in the eyes of others. Thus, their feelings of insecurity in, varying degrees of with-drawal from or avoidance of close contact and social contexts may be related to a fear of and an attempt to avoid potentially shame-inducing situ-ations. Furthermore, the often painful sense of inner emptiness in BPD may be associated with a blank or empty shame which may be immensely diffi-cult to capture, contain and verbalize (cf. Janin, 2015, p. 1604) – even for experienced psychotherapists.

5.4 Narcissistic and evasive personality disorder

For most personality disorders, there may be reasons to consider the pos-sible significance of feelings of shame on at least three levels: (1) shame as an immediate affect that overwhelms the self and destabilizes the identity and self-esteem of a person who has a personality disorder, in part because the ability to contain, digest and regulate shame is inadequately developed; (2) development of strategies for avoiding or compensating for shame (for example, masochistic submission, intimidating behaviour, avoidant behav-iour), which often lead to maladaptive acting in various contexts and generally reduced levels of functioning (especially social functioning); and (3) develop-ment of secondary feelings of shame as a result of the self's maladaptive ways of acting, recurring experiences of defeat/failure and so forth driven by (other) primary elements of the personality disorder, including impulsivity (reduced capacity for self- and affect regulation), identity disturbance and difficulties with handling interpersonal relationships.

In the following, the focus will be on two personality disorders, in which feelings of shame appear to play a prominent role as the driver of the patient's symptomatology and behaviour: narcissistic personality disorder and evasive personality disorder.

Narcissistic personality disorder

When working with narcissism, it is important to bear in mind that there is no professional consensus about how narcissism should be delimited and defined, just as there is far from always a sufficiently precise distinction between narcissism as (1) a fairly normal character trait and part of normal psychological development, (2) a cultural phenomenon in modernity and (3) a manifestation of severe personality pathology. In the literature, all three categories of narcissism are associated with varying degrees of shamelessness, boundless self-promotion or self-positioning and the pursuit of own individual needs with little concern for others or social communities (see Jørgensen, 2025). In the present context, the focus is solely on the fairly severe narcissistic personality disorder (NPD).

We may distinguish between at least two forms of NPD (Gabbard, 2017, p. 486f.). Thick-skinned, grandiose NPD is characterized by arrogant and aggressively dominant behaviour, obviously grandiose self-aggrandizement and self-absorption and a need for attention and admiration from others, combined with apparent emotional imperviousness to other' negative reactions to the self. From a dynamic psychological perspective, with this variant, we should always bear in mind that shame might be hidden behind a facade of grandiosity and intimidating behaviour. Thus, the shame may be covered by dramatic and self-aggrandizing behaviour, as others are seen and treated with the same contempt, disrespect and lack of empathy that the person frequently perceived experiencing from important others in the past. In thin-skinned or vulnerable NPD, the person's grandiose self-image is less obvious and only becomes apparent in closer contact, while the person often appears vulnerable, socially shy, inhibited, (superficially) self-effacing, depressive and with fragile self-esteem, shame and hypersensitivity to others' negative reactions to the self. In thin-skinned NPD, the feeling of shame and its role are thus slightly more easily accessible, and persons with this variant are quick to feel hurt, humiliated and overwhelmed by shame. In addition, the feeling of shame may be accompanied by more or less pronounced idealization of selected others, which helps to stabilize the vulnerable self. The vulnerable and shameful self may receive a boost to their self-esteem by feeling connected to the idealized other.

In addition, we might argue for the existence of a third category of possibly borderline cases of NPD characterized by a high level of functioning in many regards. This group includes often seemingly socially and professionally successful individuals who are remarkably egocentric and who have a persistent need to tell everyone about their own personal talents and successes.

They may be driven by an underlying NPD that only becomes visible when they encounter resistance and defeat in their social and professional life. In this situation, they can no longer rely on their successes – and the positive attention from others that success often enables – as a means to stabilize their fragile self-esteem and keep their painful shame of negative self-perceptions at bay. Overall, NPD thus has several inherently different manifestations which should not be understood or handled in quite the same way. In individual patients, the concrete manifestations of NPD may, to some extent, alternate between the three outlined variants over time.

Wurmser (1981b) viewed shame as the quintessential narcissistic affect but applied a somewhat broader concept of narcissism, which focused on the human need to be seen and met with admiration and recognition (see Kohut, 1971; Karterud, 1995). When others – especially important others – fail to recognize and fulfil this need, the person may feel humiliated and ashamed, which will be destabilizing to their self-esteem, as the feeling of shame affects the self's core, self-esteem, self-respect and integration (Wurmser, 2015, p. 1616). This is the driver of the development (and subsequent manifestations) of NPD, albeit in more radical and potentially traumatic versions than in people without personality pathology. Thus, NPD cannot be reduced to being self-centred or 'a jerk' but is seen in individuals with a great – often unmet – need to be seen, admired and recognized. Individuals with NPD thus have a great need for others to help them regulate their inherently fragile self-esteem and to affirm, admire and thus stabilize their more or less obviously grandiose self-image (see also the alternative model for diagnosing PD: APA, 2013, p. 767).

Therapists in particular need to bear in mind that what we see in patients with NPD is an inherently vulnerable and insecure self plagued by doubt, despair, inferiority and shame. This applies both in relation to patients with vulnerable NPD, where this is more obvious, and in relation to patients with grandiose and arrogant NPD, where it takes a little more work to discover the vulnerable self, which is often hiding behind the grandiose and not always immediately likeable but rather manipulative, seductive or perhaps somewhat pathetically self-aggrandizing facade. In addition, therapists should remember that grandiose NPD may be closely related to dissocial personality disorder, and that the distinction from psychopathy is not always crystal clear. Thus, in some individuals with grandiose NPD, it may not be possible to see, let alone reach and even briefly get into contact with their vulnerable core, whether for the patient themselves or for the people around them. In some cases, there might not be a vulnerable core. Furthermore, some persons with NPD who experience adversity and events that evoke shame and destabilize their self-esteem may perceive this as a narcissistic insult by selected others, who are then met with rage and a thirst for revenge (Kohut, 1985, p. 148). In this case, perceived threats against the self do not immediately activate shame and withdrawal but rather anger, aggression or even hate directed at the other, who is seen to 'improperly' violate, degrade, disrespect or try to humiliate the self and assaults its dignity.

Some writers have argued that virtually all the diagnostic criteria of NPD (APA, 2013, p. 669) may be seen as an expression or defence of a profound and shameful feeling of inadequacy (Benecke & Peham, 2007, p. 27). Furthermore, a small number of empirical studies have found that NPD traits are closely associated with intense self-reported discomfort related to feelings of shame (Schoenleber & Berenbaum, 2012b). However, it is important to bear in mind that these studies are based on students or undiagnosed patients with NPD, and thus, the presence of NPD-related traits and experiences of shame have been measured by clearly inadequate self-reported instruments. Nevertheless, it is worth noting that findings from these studies lend support to the assumption of a significant link between NPD and shame.

Shame in vulnerable versus grandiose NPD

Another study, based on patients diagnosed with NPD, found a high level of explicit shame ('I am wrong') in patients with NPD compared with a non-clinical control group (Ritter et al., 2014), although the level was lower in the NPD group than among patients with BPD. However, the study also found that the NPD group stood out with a high level of latent or so-called implicit shame – a form of underlying, unverbalized shame associated with the person's own self – as measured in an association test (ibid.). At first glance, these findings seem compatible with the idea that especially patients with grandiose NPD may not be in contact with or capable or willing to report the feeling of shame that is assumed to be an often important driver of NPD (see also Bilevicius et al., 2019). Behind the arrogant and self-sufficient facade, the typical patient with grandiose NPD may thus be shameful, in part over their dependence on and need for others and their admiration and recognition. These needs may, at first glance, seem difficult to reconcile with a self-image characterized by grandiosity and self-sufficiency. Psychologically, NPD is often grounded in chronic shame and problems with self-esteem, which the person may try to deal with through arrogant contempt for others.

A small number of studies have found that traits associated with both vulnerable and grandiose narcissism are related to outward aggression and that general emotional dysregulation, including maladaptive strategies for dealing with shame, mediate the connection between traits from both grandiose and vulnerable narcissism and aggression (Velotti et al., 2020). Difficulties with containing and regulating shame thus appear to be associated with dysregulated aggression in persons with higher levels of both grandiose and vulnerable narcissism. Especially in case of grandiose narcissism, more general emotional dysregulation appears to be an important mediating factor in the connection between narcissism and outward aggression. Other studies suggest that shame plays a greater role in vulnerable narcissism, while the link between shame and grandiose narcissism is more uncertain; it might even be negative in the sense that grandiosity (at least superficially, cf. grandiosity as defence) is associated with less shame (Krizan & Johar, 2015). However, the field is generally marred by a lack of empirical studies, and most of the existing empirical data are based on non-clinical populations (however, see Velotti et al., 2020), which makes it problematic to apply these empirical data on pathological narcissism.

As mentioned earlier, while shame and fragile self-esteem are more obvious and observable in vulnerable NPD, as the patient often withdraws from contact and 'competition' with others in an attempt to shield and protect the fragile self, it is often hidden behind a 'noisy' grandiose facade in grandiose NPD. From a dynamic psychological perspective (see Jørgensen, 2019), in the individual case, the therapist should therefore consider whether the omnipotent self-perceptions of a patient with grandiose NPD serve as defence against unbearable envy and shame. In envy and shame, the self feels small and inferior, which is typically an unbearable position for someone with NPD. Furthermore, the feeling of shame is associated with a perception of the self as the passive object of a superior other's negatively judging and exposing gaze (cf. Weiß, 2008). This situation may be difficult to deal with for anyone, and especially for someone who has a narcissistic disorder. In extension of this point, a study based on a wide selection of individuals in psychiatric outpatient care found a clear relationship between narcissistic vulnerability on the one hand and suicidal ideation and behaviour on the other; a connection that is mediated by the patient's level of shame (Jaksic et al., 2017). Presumably, narcissistic vulnerability in combination with a negative self-image driven by shame will thus also increase the risk of suicidal behaviour, just as suicidal behaviour may contain aspects of self-punishment for failing to live up to one's own grandiose self-perceptions or perfectionist standards (ibid., p. 1677); this may in itself lead to self-hatred and shame because of one's own inadequacy, 'unacceptable' failures and inferiority.

By contrast, the grandiose self perceives itself as grand, mighty and superior; the opposite of the shameful self. Furthermore, the apparent – and it *is* just apparent – absence of shame and the arrogant behaviour of a person with grandiose NPD can be understood as attempts to escape shame by not acknowledging others as equal persons (subjects) who observe and judge the self as an object. Patients with NPD try to defend against a relational constellation that is (potentially) associated with shame and threats to their fragile self-esteem by reducing others to passive objects that the self can control (cf. Seidler, 1995/2000, p. 263).

The arrogant and intimidating behaviour that someone with grandiose NPD displays in interpersonal interactions may thus be viewed as an attempt to put others into a position of passive objects who exist to satisfy the self's need for uncritical attention and admiration and promote the person's fragile pride (the antipole to shame) over their own accomplishments and characteristics. At the same time, the person denies the existence of the others' independently observing and judging gaze at the self as an object or tries to annul it – which is inherently impossible (see Section 4.1). In the case of grandiose NPD, the patient seems to implicitly say to others, 'You are so insignificant and inferior compared with me that it holds no significance to me and is generally entirely irrelevant if you were to see or think differently and meet me with anything but positive, admiring attention'. This also means that it may be dangerous for the person to allow others – including a therapist – to become emotionally important to the self. This implies a risk of the self becoming clearly dependent on the other, which in itself is perceived as shameful and hazardous to the self. It also means that the constructed defence against shame could collapse, and the other's gaze at and 'judgments' of the self could take on significance and authority, which might result in shame and destabilize the self.

A patient with NPD is trapped in a paradox described by Hegel (1807/ 2019) and discussed in Honneth's (1992/1996) theory of recognition (see also Benjamin, 1996, 2019), which is that if we do not see and recognize the other as an independent subject – whose gaze at and judgment of our own self we cannot control, with the inherent risk of experiencing shame and destabiliza- tion of our self-esteem – then we cannot achieve the authentic recognition of our self from the other that we fundamentally need in our existence, as self- reflective social beings with an identity that is always already embedded in relationships of recognition:

> If I don't recognize you as someone capable of observing and judging me as an object from a position as subject independent of me, I fundamentally also cannot feel authentically seen and recognized by you as the person I really am.

Because individuals with NPD – for a number of reasons – are incapable of containing and regulating shame, they struggle to engage in the equal relationships of recognition that are crucial for them to develop and to escape their narcissistic prison. That is why working with shame and the gradual inte- gration of the patient's self – tensioned between the self's poles of grandiosity and worthlessness, idealization and devaluation – is a key focus in psycho- therapeutic treatment of NPD.

Evasive personality disorder

Most of the diagnostic criteria of evasive personality disorder (EPD) can be associated with manifestations of shame or efforts to avoid shame and protect a vulnerable self characterized by insecurity and fragile self-esteem (Benecke & Peham, 2007, p. 26). A tendency to avoid social situations and new activ- ities for fear of criticism, disapproval or rejection and a fundamental per- ception of the self as socially inferior, unattractive and inferior in relation to others forms the core of evasive personality disorder and can be associated with fear of humiliation of the self and of being overwhelmed by shame. In addition, there is a general sense of inferiority that leads to behavioural inhib- ition in social situations as well as a pronounced tendency to feel inhibited and uncomfortable in intimate relationships, as the person fears becoming overwhelmed by shame, feeling inadequate and ridiculed (APA, 2013, p. 672f.). These elements of diagnostic criteria of EPD too may be seen as near exemplary descriptions of how the shameful self may act and appear in interpersonal interactions.

The DSM-5 system's alternative model for diagnosing PD (AMPD) mentions frequent and exaggerated feelings of shame as one of the diagnostic criteria of evasive PD (APA, 2013, p. 765). Thus, it can be argued that a central part of the core and dynamic psychological driver of EPD is shame, intense discomfort in connection with shame, an inability to contain and regulate feelings of shame and strategies for defending the self against shame, especially various forms of avoidance strategies and self-effacing behaviour. The overall effect is an often considerably impaired level of functioning, including social functioning.

The above-mentioned study of relationships between dimensional measures of disturbed personality traits and fairly primitive measures of shame, based on students, found a strong correlation between, on the one hand, intense discomfort in connection with feelings of shame and shame-proneness across a variety of situations and, on the other hand, EPD-related personality traits (Schoenleber & Berenbaum, 2012b). Despite the study's aforementioned methodological problems, the presented findings may be interpreted as suggesting a presumably significant relationship between shame and evasive personality disorder.

A closely related study similarly found that the tendency to experience and avoid shame is closely related to EPD traits (Schoenleber & Berenbaum, 2010, p. 201f.). The study also found that shame-proneness only appears to correlate with the level of EPD traits if shame is also perceived as an intensely uncomfortable affect that the person will go far to avoid. This finding makes sense, as some of the diagnostic criteria of EPD may be seen as manifestations of avoidant behaviour, including efforts to avoid shame. Finally, as mentioned earlier, EPD traits have been found to correlate with measures of latent or implicit shame (Currie et al., 2017), which may indicate that EPD is related to a level of shame that goes somewhat beyond what the affected persons themselves might be aware of and able to report in a questionnaire or in a conversation with a less experienced therapist who is not trained in uncovering and decoding indications of shame as a possible driver of psychological symptoms and dysfunctional behaviour. However, additional research is needed before we can reach more substantially founded conclusions on correlations between latent or unconscious shame and EPD.

Dissocial personality disorder (APA, 2013, p. 659f.) is often (but not always) associated with a striking absence of feelings of shame and guilt and with shameless violations of others' boundaries and personal integrity, which may be related to severe defects in the normal development of an internal moral and ethical compass, conscience (superego) and the ability to form an understanding of other people's inner life (empathy), including the ability to decode how others perceive and react to one's own behaviour (mentalizing capacity). Furthermore, a person with a dissocial personality disorder may have learned early in life that deeper emotional interest in, need for and dependence on others and psychological reflection and openness to being emotionally influenced by others reflect a weakness that is contemptible or dangerous to the self and incompatible with a self-image characterized by strength, independence and agency (cf. Gilligan, 2003). This perception of self and world does not leave room for developing the emotional and interpersonal sensitivity that is part of the foundation of shame in social human beings.

There is also reason to consider whether the tendency to avoid social contact that is a characteristic aspect of schizoid and schizotypal personality disorders (APA, 2013, p. 652ff.) and the social anxiety that is seen especially in schizotypal personality disorder may in some cases be related to shame. Furthermore, the sexualized and seductive behaviour and the pronounced urge to be the constant centre of attention that is typically seen in histrionic personality disorder (APA, 2013, p. 667) may contain elements of counterphobic acting out as a defence against shame. A person with a histrionic personality disorder may, so to speak, actively seek the types of situations they associate with a risk of shame in an attempt to pre-empt and gain control of these situations. Furthermore, the ability to conquer and seduce others sexually may serve as defence against a shameful experience of being defective, inadequate and unlovable; an experience that may be at least temporarily assuaged when the person manages to arouse others' interest in and positive attention towards the self (cf. Nathanson, 1992, p. 357f.).

A similar psychological dynamic may be the driver of the tendency to highly dramatizing and theatrical behaviour in social situations that is also seen in people with a histrionic personality disorder. This behaviour typically prevents deeper emotional and psychological contact with others. As this behaviour might result in shame and more obvious destabilization of the person's fragile self-esteem, the person will try to avoid it with their characteristic intimidating and seemingly inauthentic and superficial behaviour. In dependent personality disorder (APA, 2013, p. 675f.), the self's agency and capacity for independent functioning are inadequately developed, causing the self to appear weak, incompetent, helpless and highly dependent on others' persistent and highly explicit affirmation. This may be perceived as shameful by modern adults.

Finally, in some cases, there may be reason to consider how the extreme perfectionism and urge for order and predictability associated with obsessive-compulsive personality disorder (APA, 2013, p. 678) may be related to and part of an action-oriented defence against shame, including how these individuals' strong urge for control may be a defence against shame and the fear of being put into situations where they are overwhelmed by shame; an urge for control that may have developed in reaction to past traumatic experiences associated with loss of control, for example in connection with physical or sexual abuse or severe neglect (see also Sections 5.1 and 5.2).

5.5 Depression, anxiety, self-harm and substance abuse

As mentioned earlier (Section 4.5), several meta-analyses have found clear correlations between mainly destructive feelings of shame and, respectively, depression (Kim et al., 2011) and various types of anxiety disorders, including social anxiety/social phobia (Candea & Szentagotai-Tatar, 2018), self-harm and, to some extent, suicidal behaviour (Sheehy et al., 2019). Although these relationships are mainly based on correlation studies, which do not shed light on potential causal links, shame does appear to be a significant factor in the development and maintenance of these disorders. Furthermore, research has found some – albeit weaker – associations between perceived shame in the moment and various forms of substance abuse as a strategy for reducing or escaping unbearable feelings of shame (Luoma et al., 2019).

Depression

Meta-analytic findings of a fairly strong correlation between destructive feelings of shame and depression suggest that shame should be attributed significant relevance in our understanding and treatment of certain types of depression, just as it should also be included in our understanding of dynamic psychological processes related to depressive symptoms. Some writers have argued that we should distinguish between different subcategories of depression dominated by destructive feelings of guilt or shame (Nathanson, 1987b), with the former characterized more by internal conflict, painful rumination and feelings of guilt over the self's questionable acts, and the latter associated primarily with a more fundamental and painful perception of the self as damaged, defective, worthless, inferior and deeply inadequate, with no chance of improvement. The latter is also described as narcissistic depression, because it involves depressive symptoms related to severely destabilized self-esteem and, thus, disturbances of the self's narcissistic balances (Hilgers, 2013, p. 107), feelings of inner emptiness and shame, while the latter is sometimes labelled melancholic depression (Zabel, 2019, p. 13f.). However, these narcissistic imbalances should not be confused with the far more severe narcissistic disturbances in NPD (see Section 5.4). Others have distinguished between anaclitic and introjective depression (Blatt, 1974; Blatt & Zuroff, 1992). The former is primarily characterized by painful feelings of being weak, helpless and alone and by a pervasive fear of being abandoned and left to oneself without support, care and love from others (Blatt & Zuroff, 1992, p. 527f.), while introjective depression is associated, in part, with intense self-criticism, unrealistically high demands of oneself and a pervasive feeling of being worthless, inferior and characterized by defects and inadequacies; a state the person may try to escape through perfectionism and (over)performance (ibid.). Both types of depression may be associated with shame, to varying degrees, but it seems particularly apt to imagine that introjective depression may be related or even partly driven by destructive shame.

In addition, it can be argued that persistent worrying about and rumination on specific events and acts may represent an attempt to cope with or defend against negative emotions, including shame, as the person turns their attention to concrete concerns, situations and own mistakes rather than the more painful and diffuse (non-concrete and partially unconscious) feelings of shame. In relation to this point, it is notable that destructive (excessive or inappropriate) feelings of guilt are part of the formal diagnostic criteria of depression (APA, 2013, p. 160f.), while destructive shame is not, although there do seem to be indications that destructive shame may be an equally strong driver of depression as feelings of guilt (see also Section 4.4).

As proposed by Kelly and Lamia (2018, p. 91) destructive shame may block the experience of positive affects, including the self's ability to have corrective emotional experiences capable of balancing and providing a normal counterweight to a negative self-image and negative perceptions of the world. Similarly, severe feelings of shame can inhibit the self's openness to and curiosity about the world. Together, these elements may increase the risk of developing and maintaining depression. Thus, there is reason to view shame both as a possible risk or vulnerability factor in the development of depression and as one among many manifestations of depression, just as unregulated destructive shame may contribute to maintaining depression. Finally, therapists' lack of understanding of the role of shame in patients with depression may help explain why treatment for depression might not have the desired effect (cf. Kelly & Lamia, 2018, p. 89).

It should also be noted that several studies have found a connection between recollections of early traumatic experiences of shame and depressive symptoms during adulthood; this connection is mediated by a heightened level of shame in the present (Matos et al., 2013). Conversely, recollections of early positive experiences, when the self felt they were in safe and caring hands, appear to moderate the effect of early experiences of shame, provided these were not so severe that they would be classified as actually traumatic (Matos et al., 2015). Finally, an overview study based on studies of parents who lost a child suggest that shame (along with self-reproach and feelings of guilt) might be related to more intense and severe grief reactions after a loss (Duncan & Cacciatore, 2015); these reactions may inhibit or block the affected parents' normal and healthy grief processing and thus contribute to the long-term development of depression, among other problems.

Anxiety

'Anxiety' is a term that is often used with insufficient precision. As a result, it is sometimes difficult to distinguish anxiety clearly from Wurmser's concept of anticipatory shame anxiety – anxiety focused on the risk that the self might be put into situations where it is humiliated and overwhelmed by shame (cf. Freud's concept of signal anxiety; see Section 4.2) and thus a form of anxiety that may contain clearly constructive elements in the sense that it can both warn the self that it might be at risk and motivate it to improve and thus appear in a more positive light to others (Kelly & Lamia, 2018, p. 76). Anxiety can have many and inherently different expressions, including fear of being abandoned, overexposed, found out or laid bare in front of others, losing control and death, with some of the manifestations of anxiety being more obviously related to shame than others.

As mentioned earlier, a meta-analysis found a clear correlation between anxiety and shame (Candea & Szentagotai-Tatar, 2018), and it can be argued that shame should have a much more central place in our understanding and treatment of some forms of anxiety. Numerous studies have found a relationship between shame and social anxiety (ibid., p. 80), just as shame may be involved in the development and maintenance of obsessive-compulsive disorder (OCD) (ibid., p. 85). In generalized anxiety, a focus on concrete worries can help divert attention away from shame and other negative emotions, as it allows the feeling of shame to remain 'hidden' or to some degree unacknowledged by the self.

Feelings of shame are not explicitly included in authorized diagnostic criteria of anxiety disorders. However, for example, the diagnostic criteria of social anxiety (social phobia) do include the fear of being put into humiliating and embarrassing situations (APA, 2013, p. 202f.) that may be associated with shame anxiety and feelings of shame. Social phobia is related to evasive personality disorder (see Section 5.4) and is typically manifested as pronounced social inhibition, avoidance of social situations, feelings of inadequacy and heightened sensitivity to perceived criticism, rejection, ridicule and disapproval of the self, which may over time cause the person to isolate and withdraw from large parts of their social life. These elements are all difficult to distinguish clearly from manifestations of shame. In extension of this, several writers have argued that social phobia is more aptly viewed as a shame-based disorder than as an anxiety disorder (Tiedemann, 2010, p. 378).

People with social phobia often conflate the negative and shameful self-perception they developed in early relationships with their own (projective) perceptions of how real others see and (negatively) judge the self (Hilgers, 2013, p. 81). This may lead to self-perpetuating vicious cycles, which it can be difficult for the person to break without acknowledging and examining their own shame. Similarly, social phobia may be related to the self projecting their own high demands, expectations and ideals (ego ideals developed and internalized in earlier relationships) on concrete others or turning them into generalized beliefs about what is demanded or expected of the self by others or the world at large, which are subsequently perceived as others' great and legitimate expectations of the self, which it is shameful not to live up to.

Self-harm and substance abuse

Destructive feelings of shame are related to an increased risk and a somewhat higher prevalence of self-harm across a number of mental disorders.

This refers strictly to non-suicidal self-harm (Sheehy et al., 2019; see also VanDerhei et al., 2013; Schoenleber et al., 2014; Cameron et al., 2020), in which a general tendency to internalizing behaviour (aggression directed at one's own self) may also play a certain role (VanDerhei et al., 2013). Possible connections between shame and suicidal ideation or attempts and actual suicide have been insufficiently studied. However, there are indications of a certain relationship between feelings of shame and a heightened risk of suicidal behaviour (Sheehy et al., 2019). This includes a small number of studies, mentioned above, that found a strong correlation between shame and suicidal behaviour in borderline personality disorder (Cameron et al., 2020; Brown et al., 2009). A small number of studies also found, among other connections, a relationship between suicidal ideation and shame-proneness in women who have been subjected to childhood sexual abuse and are now receiving treatment for depression (You et al., 2012).

As this issue has similarly only been addressed in small-scale correlation studies with methodological weaknesses, it remains unclear whether or to what extent self-harm and suicide attempts should be viewed primarily as – perhaps impulsive, unpremeditated – attempts to escape or regulate unbearable feelings of shame (and other painful mental states), or whether feelings of shame (also) arise as a result of self-harm and/or suicide attempts. The person may concretize and attempt to deal with shame by attacking their own body, as diffuse shame about being wrong, defective and inadequate is concretized, localized and thus made manageable and associated with the person's own body (or specific parts of it) that the person perceives as defective, ugly, gross and repulsive. In extension of this, the person may try to reduce feelings of shame by harming or altering their body, in extreme cases by changing their gender or undergoing cosmetic surgery based on more or less conscious beliefs that the self will receive the positive attention, recognition and love from others that the person yearns for ('everything will be fine'), if only their body is brought closer to an imagined ideal.

From a dynamic psychological perspective, self-harm and suicidal behaviour may be seen as attempts to regulate shame, which may in itself give rise to or intensify an existing feeling of shame in a self-perpetuating vicious cycle. We can also speak of shame-based syndromes, as attempts to reduce or escape shame instead end up exaggerating it. Similar dynamics may be seen, for example, in people who, in addition to obvious self-harm (see Curtis, 2016), try to escape shame over past sexual abuse and regulate general overwhelming negative affects through pronounced ('shameless') sexualization of relationships, acting out or exposing their sexuality or seeking various types of sexual contact containing aspects of repetition of past abuse.

It is important to bear in mind how the exposure of both extreme forms of self-harm and deeply shameless behaviour on social media, including in special online forums for self-harmers, may be associated with a particular (perverted but, in a sense, comprehensible) form of pride and social status. As such, it offers a kind of counterbalance to unbearable shame through pride and the achievement of social status. In these forums, the members compete for attention, significance, social status and recognition based on who can be most shameless, most unbounded in their self-exposure or violation of others or, alternatively, carry out the most extreme form of self-harm or series of self-harming acts or come up with the most sophisticated and extreme self-harm ritual.

Self-harm and suicidal behaviour may also be seen as related to aggression stemming from unbearable shame being directed at the self rather than at others, as the person seeks to regulate shame through a largely internalizing (inward) defensive strategy rather than through more externalizing and outward behaviour. Pronounced self-hatred, self-contempt and attacks on the person's own self may thus represent desperate attempts at protecting relationships with others, as fear of rejection, abandonment or exclusion and perceived inferiority fuse into one (Tiedemann, 2010, p. 103). Finally, more diffuse and impulsive self-destructiveness may be driven by attempts at escaping unbearable shame for lack of better options.

Austrian writer Stefan Zweig (1939/2016) described these psychological processes in his masterpiece *Impatience of the Heart*. At a ball, the novel's protagonist, the young Lieutenant Hofmiller, invites a young woman to dance. He does so without knowing that she has a severe disability and is incapable of dancing. When he becomes aware of her disability, he is shocked, and the situation is so painful and shameful to him that he feels compelled to flee. Overwhelmed by shame over his behaviour, the following day, he sends a large bouquet of roses to the woman whom he put in this painful situation. Driven by shame and pity for the young woman, after a series of incidents which he perceives as shameful, he is eventually engaged to her but is unable to acknowledge their engagement to his fellow soldiers. When the woman accidentally discovers that he denies her, she commits suicide. Once again, Hofmiller is overwhelmed by shame and flees from his feelings of shame and 'from himself', this time by going to war. Fleeing from shame and himself, he acts impulsively and destructively rather than acknowledging and confronting his shame and his own shameful acts (Greiner, 2014, p. 302f.). Similarly, the shame of the situation causes the young woman to take her own life, as she discovers that the young lieutenant to whom she declared her love never saw her as an equal but as a cripple whom he cannot possibly love. The unbearable shame thus drove the young woman to her death.

There is reason to assume that various forms of substance abuse may also serve as strategies for escaping shame and other unbearable negative affects. Thus, the use of alcohol or drugs may serve, in part, to regulate shame and negative self-perceptions. However, the development of substance abuse may over time lead to secondary shame because of the self's addiction and the loss of control in situations where the self is heavily influenced by alcohol or drugs. The person may then attempt to reduce their shame through additional abuse in a self-perpetuating vicious cycle similar to what we see in other forms of self-harm. A meta-analysis of this topic did not find systematic relationships between shame and the development of substance addiction (Luoma et al., 2019), although a small number of studies do suggest that such a connection exists (Cook, 1988; Dearing et al., 2005). However, the area is characterized by significant methodological problems, including few and small studies with great variation across studies and the use of weak measures of shame that do not distinguish between constructive and destructive shame. Nevertheless, substance abuse treatment should always include shame as a possible central driver of the individual client's abuse and consideration of whether the substance abuse might serve as a strategy for avoiding or escaping shame (Nathanson, 1997, p. 136).

5.6 Identity disturbances

Shame, especially destructive shame, may be perceived as a threat to a person's identity. Shame and identity are both related to our fundamental self-perception, self-beliefs and how real and imagined others see and judge who and what we are as persons. Our identity is also shaped by how we would like to be and how we are actually perceived by others, and it may be destabilized if we are overwhelmed by destructive shame. Furthermore, shame and identity are core elements of human sociality, constitution and existence in interpersonal relationships and social groups. However, the relationship between shame and identity is highly complex.

We may experience light, passing and constructive shame, which does not overwhelm the self but merely confronts it with the fact that it appears inadequate, slightly incompetent or laughable in a concrete situation in ways that are, nevertheless, perceived as manageable. In some cases, this may lead to a slight, temporary identity crisis without leading to a severe identity disturbance (Jørgensen, 2020). Instead, the feeling of shame will serve primarily as further motivation for self-improvement and efforts to realize our own ideals and be a sociable and likeable person who acts in accordance with prevailing expectations, norms and values, including, not least, our own (internalized) norms and values. The self is confronted with the possibility that it might not be or be perceived the way we would prefer and, thus, with the need for change. Constructive shame, which defends the self's boundaries of intimacy as well as our own and others' personal integrity also helps to protect and stabilize our identity. Conversely, destructive shame may destabilize and erode our identity, especially if it develops into more chronic destructive shame.

Constructive shame as a foundation of a well-developed identity

A healthy and well-developed identity is associated, in part, with stable and pervasive positive self-esteem with stable, integrated self-beliefs and stable, well-integrated goals, norms, values and ideals as a foundation for our sense of meaning and order in the world and in our own life overall. The main elements of a well-developed identity also form the basis of our unique human ability to step away from ourselves and observe and judge ourselves from an external perspective. A well-developed identity's inherent notions of 'normality' and of prevailing norms, values and ideals thus form the standard and the stable internal criteria that a self-reflecting person compares their own ways of being and acting to in order to determine whether the self is okay and acting more or less in accordance with prevailing (sub)cultural demands, or whether they need to correct their ways of being and acting, for example in order to prevent social marginalization and shame.

The human capacity for self-reflection is key to our persistent search for answers to the basic questions of identity: Who am I, and who do I want to be (Jørgensen, 2020)? This self-reflection is also the foundation of the unique human capacity for experiencing shame when we sense that we are failing to live up to our and (real or imagined) others' expectations, norms, values and ideals. In this sense, human identity and feelings of shame can be said to be intimately connected. Both are grounded in the unique human capacity for self-reflection and ability to compare our real self with internal or external beliefs about the ideal self and with concrete or generalized others' (real or imagined) expectations of the self.

The internalized goals, norms, values and ideals of a mature identity serve as an internal frame of reference for navigating in the world and form and indispensable condition for the mature human being's agency – our ability to be competent and goal-oriented actors striving to realize our long-term goals without acting in ways that violate prevailing norms and might risk social marginalization or exclusion. Severe identity disturbances are typically associated with significant inadequacies in the ability to internalize stable norms, values and ideals in accordance with the social community and prevailing trends in contemporary culture. Thus, individuals with severe identity diffusion have a greater risk of appearing and acting in ways that others find abnormal, inappropriate, offensive or even morally reprehensible. Inadequate internalization of normal beliefs about expected and desired behaviour (cf. inadequacies in the development and integration of the superego, mature values and ideals) thus means that individuals with identity diffusion are at greater risk of being shamed, ostracized and socially excluded; they are also at much greater risk of perceiving themselves as wrong, inferior and defective in their own and others' eyes, which may lead to destructive shame.

One of the unique characteristics of human identity is that it is always, in principle, undetermined and is never settled once and for all. As pointed out by existentialist philosophers, in particular, human identity and being is never completely determined by our biology or bodily processes; it is historical and variable and never reaches an ultimate settled form. As human beings, we will always, to varying degrees, continually need to ask ourselves who and what we are, just as we are compelled to 'create ourselves', building our own identity and struggling to earn others' approval of it. This is a project that might fail and be met with disrespect, indifference or a lack of resonance and recognition (non-approval) from others. When that happens, it will often give rise to shameful experiences of being wrong, defective, abnormal or different in a negative way (Lietzmann, 2007). This may lead to painful and shameful experiences of not feeling at home, both in concrete situations and in the world in general, experiences of homelessness and of a lack of embedded-ness in human communities.

Shame as a threat to our identity

The feeling of shame throws a stark, negative light on who and what we are, in both our own and others' eyes. It can make us feel completely alone, laid bare and exposed to (concrete or imagined) others' condemning and humili-ating gaze – a gaze that may also, to a high degree, be associated with the notion of a merciless inner judge, distorted ego ideals and our own deeply negative self-perceptions and self-expectations that are clearly out of step with reality. In this light, we may perceive our own ego ideals as an internal other or an alien force in relation to our own ego, which in the case of a severe identity disturbance may be associated with inadequate internal iden-tity integration. This state may give rise to an internal split between parts of the self that might identify with certain higher norms and ideals and other parts of the self that are more likely to be governed by the person's own immediate spontaneous impulses and needs.

When we are struck with shame, the core of our self and identity and, not least, our flawed ability to live up to our own and others' expectations is exposed and laid bare and becomes the focus of our own (and, in many cases, also others') attention in a way that is unpleasant and may be associated with painful perceptions of our identity as inferior, inadequate, defective, repulsive and/or contemptible. Our sense of who and what we are and our sense of being fundamentally okay is destabilized. This experi-ence may be accompanied by internal disorganization, as we suddenly begin to question central aspects of our being and identity. Our identity becomes unmoored and may be overwhelmed by anxiety, confusion and disorientation. This situation may lead to sudden drops in our level of psy-chological functioning, including a loss of agency, capacity for self-control and impulse control and capacity for containing and regulating affects and other mental states. The rug is pulled out from under our sense of security and ontological certainty (Neckel, 2009, p. 106), revealing what may sub-jectively appear as an unbridgeable gulf between, on the one hand, how the self wishes to be and be perceived by others and, on the other hand, how the self actually is and appears to and is perceived by (real or imagined) others. This gulf between, on the one hand, the self's desired identity and being and, on the other hand, its actual identity and being is 'revealed' in and by the other's gaze at the self.

Severe identity disturbances and destructive shame may play out, for example, in relation to human sexuality, as the person's sexual desires and needs may feel wrong, repulsive or humiliating. The person's gender identity, sexual orientation and boundaries of intimacy may be perceived as being out of step with what is held up as normal and right in mainstream contemporary culture. When this is the case, the person will typically perceive their fantasies and their perceptions of themselves as a gendered and sexual being as shameful. Conversely, the absence of sexual desire and sexual fantasies may also be perceived as wrong, abnormal and shameful, even when the lack of sexual desire and the apparent absence of sexual fantasies might stem from earlier (in themselves shameful) traumatic experiences that led to sex being associated with intense displeasure, abuse and humiliation of the self. Finally, the person may associate sex with being exploited and used as a voiceless object for the satisfaction of others' needs or with the cynical use of others as objects for satisfying one's own needs, as sex and emotional contact, for a number of reasons, are kept strictly separate. All these limited ways of living out one's sexuality and attempting to have one's need for contact and physical intimacy met are associated with shame, precisely because they are limited and involve splitting off parts of one's own and others' selves. It may thus in itself be shameful if the person, for various reasons, is unable to be fully psychologically and emotionally present during sex.

In situations where we are overwhelmed by destructive shame, the presented self – the self-image we seek to present to others – might crack. It is revealed as a pitiful facade or 'a lie' that is out of step with reality. Our self-esteem may collapse. We may find that the self's honour, dignity, social status and bonds with others, which are so crucial for delimiting and stabilizing our identity, are under threat. Being overwhelmed by destructive shame blocks our access to validating mirroring, appreciation and recognition from others, which are central to the development, integration and stability of our identity. The psychological and emotional contact that is our bridge to others may develop deep cracks and threaten to collapse entirely. This may leave us overwhelmed by a feeling of profound social isolation and loneliness and a sense of being all alone in the world (Ayers, 2003, p. 13). This may also be related to the way in which someone struggling with severe destructive shame might try to reduce unbearable shame by becoming 'invisible': hiding and trying to avoid others' gaze at the self in order to avert shame (cf. the close connection between shame and the other's gaze). One of the drawbacks of this defensive strategy is that it cuts the self off from vital contact with others. The self becomes socially isolated and tormented by loneliness, and the access to mirroring and recognition from others, which is crucial to identity development and stability, is severely weakened or disrupted entirely. 'Without some continual input from an intersubjective matrix, human identity dissolves' (Stern, 2004, p. 107). Thus, destructive shame may overwhelm the self in ways and to a degree that potentially destabilize the structural elements of identity in self-perpetuating vicious cycles, as identity destabilization leads to additional shame.

Confrontation with 'alien' parts of the self

As mentioned earlier, overwhelming shame may be related to the self being confronted with parts that it has tried to repress, deny, fight or 'keep down'. Generally, this can be partially explained by the way in which human existence is tensioned between spiritual and bodily ways of being, which means that shame may confront us with 'the other and alien' (the unconscious, taboo and so forth) part of ourselves (see Chapter 4). When we are overwhelmed by shame, especially destructive shame, we are confronted with unintegrated and possibly denied or repressed aspects of ourselves and our identity that we, so to speak, have no access to or control of, which may in itself be frightening and shameful (Lietzmann, 2007, p. 48). This may also involve being confronted with shameful acts from our past that make us feel alienated from ourselves, suddenly insecure, confused and disoriented. We may be compelled to ask ourselves, 'Is this what I'm like? Is this the real me, or is it not me?'

These experiences are related to the fundamental structure of human existence, as we feel at once identical and not identical with ourselves; we feel that we are at once ourselves and 'someone else' due to 'the alien' part that suddenly seems to take over or is revealed in situations where we are overwhelmed by shame. The unity of the self is disturbed, different parts of the self and our identity turn out to be in opposition to each other, and we lose control of parts of ourselves and our being in the world. The 'alien' element within, which we do not have full access to or control of and have difficulty acknowledging and integrating with the rest of our identity, may, for example, include strong impulses, aspects of our sexuality, parts of our history and affects, fantasies or thoughts that we normally repress. With the French psychoanalyst Jacques Lacan (1966/1985), we may say that in shame, we are confronted with what is real, that which we cannot readily control or even verbalize (cf. the symbolic), the unknown that we cannot have precise ideas about (cf. the imaginary) and hence may struggle to understand – and which, for these reasons alone, seems scandalous to modern human beings, who require and expect themselves to have full insight into and control of all aspects of their being and existence, body and mind (Wilden, 1968; Copjec, 2022).

It might be experiences related to the person's own body or a strong dependence on others that suddenly breaks through, 'takes over' and overpowers the self and causes shame. These are the types of experiences we try to capture when we say, 'I wasn't myself', or 'I didn't even recognize myself'. The 'alien' part of our own self that suddenly pokes its head out and causes overwhelming destructive shame may also be grounded in past traumatic experiences that could not be integrated into the self's internal structures and narrative about itself and are associated with severe feelings of shame. These experiences will typically be accompanied by a fundamental perception of the self as worthless (or bestial, scandalous, bad) and unlovable that are kept out of our conscious awareness by means of various forms of dissociation, denial or attempts at repressing the experiences and the related unbearable affects. However, suddenly this is no longer possible, and the experiences and their related affects break into our conscious awareness, accompanied by shame. In a sense, the feeling of shame may thus confront us with ruptures in our identity and unintegrated parts of our identity that we are not normally able to verbalize but which come to the surface when we are overwhelmed by shame (Rinofner-Kreidl, 2009, p. 160). When this happens, the feeling of shame may provide a valuable opening for psychotherapeutic treatment of these split-off parts of the self and identity – but only if the therapist is able to handle this psychotherapeutic task with the necessary sense of pace, timing and attunement with the individual patient's momentary states and needs (see Chapter 7).

Development of more chronic destructive shame and recurring experiences of the self suddenly and unexpectedly being overwhelmed by unbearable and potentially traumatizing destructive shame may be a contributing cause of the severe identity disturbances that are seen, especially, in individuals with moderate or severe personality disorders. Generally, we should expect the identity of individuals with a high general level of destructive shame – alternatively, a pronounced tendency to react with destructive shame in connection with stress or mistakes – to be unstable, fragile and vulnerable to major destabilization in connection with the activation of destructive shame (Czub, 2013, p. 250f.). This may include situations where the self remembers or otherwise comes into contact with past traumatic experiences and is overwhelmed by unbearable affects related to these experiences, including destructive shame. This is obviously relevant to psychotherapeutic work with traumatized patients. Unfortunately, we do not have sufficient empirical research into the relationships between shame and identity disturbances. As mentioned earlier, one study based on individuals with a borderline personality disorder (BPD) found a strong correlation between the level of shame and identity disturbance and also found that of the nine diagnostic criteria of BPD, identity diffusion had, by far, the strongest correlation with shame (Unoka & Vizin, 2017). This finding supports the idea that identity diffusion and shame are central elements of the borderline disorder – so central, in fact, that they should presumably be core focus areas in psychotherapeutic work with BPD.

Overall, there are strong indications suggesting that destructive shame is a key affect and driver of a wide range of, especially, moderate and severe mental disorders and that focusing on and processing shame should be a central focus of psychotherapeutic treatment of these disorders. Shame thus appears to be both a contributing cause and a significant maintaining factor of a wide range of mental disorders that must be addressed for any treatment to have long-term effect. We should also expect that in many cases, it will be necessary to focus on improving the patient's capacity for acknowledging, containing and dealing with destructive feelings of shame. Otherwise, these feelings may continue, even after the conclusion of treatment, to overwhelm the patient and give rise to potentially self-destructive and interpersonally problematic (impulsive and so forth) behaviour, including social withdrawal, which may over time undermine the patient's possibility of living a well-functioning life with fruitful interpersonal relationships.

People who experience or react with overwhelming and destructive shame either chronically or in the face of minor psychological or stress-related challenges, including conflicts that arise in interpersonal relationships, will struggle to handle close psychological and emotional contact with others. As a result, they will often feel lonely, socially isolated and wrong, even if they might superficially appear to have – and give the impression of having – a fairly well-functioning social life with 'lots of friends'. Furthermore, most mental disorders will, to some extent, make it harder for the self to live up to others' expectations and prevailing ideas about the optimal or good-enough human being, which may in itself cause secondary shame over struggling psychologically and needing help, a situation that is not necessarily compatible with the notion of optimal functioning in our meritocratic performance society (see Section 6.1). In the treatment of any mental disorder, it will often be helpful to address this particular source of shame. However, due to the nature of shame, we are often unaware of it or, if we are aware of it, will often do anything to shut the feeling down and hide it from others. In order to address it, the therapist therefore needs to continually pay attention to when the patient (or the therapist) is struck by destructive shame in the therapeutic space.

After examining how destructive shame may be an important factor in a wide range of mental disorders, we will now turn our focus to how shame might be associated with destructive processes in modern Western culture. Among other issues, we will examine how the internal logic of individualistic and meritocratic societies can intensify feelings of shame among some groups of the population, in part due to stigmatization and lack of recognition of socioeconomically disadvantaged groups. Furthermore, the chapter will argue that societies with a high level of unacknowledged and escalating shame may develop escalating internal polarization and, at worst, become involved in acts of war driven by an urge to avenge or redress perceived shameful humiliation. In the next chapter, we also examine how social dynamics driven by shame, among other affects, are converted into and sought to be managed through *ressentiment* and anger directed at selected individuals or social groups who are perceived as being to blame for other groups' vulnerability and vulnerable social position.

6 Shame and contemporary culture

For those of you who have been directing racist abuse at some of the players I say: 'Shame on you!' And I hope you will crawl back under the rock from which you emerged.

> (British Prime Minister Boris Johnson about racist attacks
> on players from the England football team after their defeat in the
> final of the UEFA European Football Championship; 12 July 2021)

We still see groups of all ages in far too close proximity. There are even some who still hold parties and celebrate special birthdays. That is not a decent way to behave. It is thoughtless. And, first and foremost, inconsiderate.

> (Danish Queen Margrethe II in national appeal to the
> Danes to follow the authorities' directions during
> the first wave of the coronavirus; 17 March 2020)

As illustrated by the quotations above, shaming is still a widely used as means of regulating human behaviour. This includes modern Western societies, where some argue that shaming should be abolished as a method for controlling human behaviour and, more broadly, that we should generally seek to eliminate the affect of shame by all means possible, because it can be so painful and limiting for human self-expression and well-being. In fact, however, shame is an emotion that plays a key role at many levels of modern Western culture, whether we like it or not. We need a better understanding of how the feeling of shame – often very discreetly and outside the conscious awareness of the persons involved – is manifested and impacts our ways of being and acting in the world. In the debate about whether it is reasonable to use certain forms of shaming and inducing (constructive) feelings of shame as one of many possible tools for regulating human behaviour and maintaining a social order, we should understand shame as a dimensional emotion, ranging from constructive to severely destructive shame. The latter not only has the potential to destroy the life of individuals but can also be a crucial driver

DOI: 10.4324/9781003521174-6

of escalating and destructive processes in social groups, human communities and between nations.

In some (sub)cultures, shame is associated with profound injury to the self's honour and dignity. Here, people may attempt to deal with a shameful loss of honour and restore their own and their family's (own social group's) honour, social esteem and dignity by punishing, ostracizing or even killing individuals who, in the eyes of the family or the specific (sub)culture, brought shame on their family, clan or social group. This occurs, for example, in so-called honour killings, which typically primarily involve the slaying of young women who are believed to have brought shame on their family through some form of socially unacceptable behaviour. In such a case, a single family member's shameful behaviour is perceived as being so shameful, not just to the individual themselves but to the entire family, that the person must be excluded or, at worst, killed to restore the family's honour (Gilbert, 1998, p. 22). A man who does not do everything in his power to stand up for and defend the family's honour may be viewed as weak and similar expelled (Marks, 2021, p. 161). This is a form of (sub)culturally accepted and sanctioned attacks on others as a strategy for dealing with shameful defamation that is completely unacceptable in a modern society founded on the rule of law and in individualistic cultures. The occurrence of honour killings illustrates how significant honour and shame can be in human psychology and cultures and, not least, the tremendously powerful nature of shame, which may even amount to a matter of human life or death.

Similarly, individuals who feel that they are being treated with disrespect and viewed as insignificant and with inferior social status may try to cope with the overwhelming shame such an experience can cause through physical violence towards others. Outward violence may also be seen as an attempt to attract the desired attention, sense of importance and a form of (perverted) respect and recognition by violating or intimidating others (Gilligan, 2003, p. 1157). Others try to deal with the shame associated with a loss of face, perceived humiliation, insults to the self's honour and low social status through an aggressive demeanour and behaviour or through psychological violence towards others. In this case, the person attempts to handle their own shameful powerlessness by gaining power over others through various forms of intimidation and transgressive behaviour (cf. Marks & Mönnich-Marks, 2008, p. 1021f.). The other person's frightened gaze and fear in the encounter with the self is then perceived as expressing a (perverted) form of respect for the self that undoes the loss of face (honour). This dynamic may also be understood in relation to projective identification, as parts of the self (for example, perceived shame and powerlessness) are projected on a concrete other, who is then treated in ways that activate the evacuated emotions and experiences in the other (cf. Ogden, 1979).

6.1 The dark side of individualistic and meritocratic competition societies

Modern Western societies are often described as individualistic, meritocratic, performance or competition societies. They are built on a notion of the clearly delimited, strong and independent individual who, for better or worse, is responsible for their own fate, life and accomplishments. This applies both in good times, when the person has reason to be proud of their achievements, and in less successful times, when the person loses out in the ongoing competition with others and has to face the burdens of defeat, including, at worst, the shame of having lost and thus being a potentially inferior person with low social status.

Modern individualistic societies are typically characterized by great material wealth, internal dynamics and change – characteristics that are often understood in light of extensive internal competition and a focus on individual accomplishments. The internal logic of these societies is presumed to maximize individual performances and contributions to society's material prosperity and continued development. The German sociologist Andreas Reckwitz (2017/2020) has described modern individualistic societies as societies of singularities, where everyone is expected to be and strive to be unique, singular individuals. Uniqueness is generally perceived as a value in itself, while anything that is average, conformist or ordinary is considered uninteresting or even worthless. Furthermore, there is an expectation – which most members of society internalize – that everyone continually strives for self-optimization and is ready to undergo evaluation across a wide range of different contexts. Typically, this evaluation is undertaken by faceless clients or users who, at no cost to themselves (and sometimes shamelessly), can vent their dissatisfaction and frustration at individuals who do not necessarily have much to do with the customers' pent-up frustration. Often, these evaluations are not restricted to concrete performances but also include the individual's personal qualities (whether they are sufficiently accommodating, service-minded, creative problem-solvers and so forth). This increases the risk that the person being evaluated will perceive the results as humiliating and shameful. In these anonymous and impersonal evaluations, many of the factors that normally minimize the risk of unnecessary violations of people's boundaries and dignity are partially or entirely suspended. This includes the individual's empathy and eye for the fact that the target of their humiliating, shaming and disparaging digital evaluation, or the evacuation of their unfiltered opinion about the other person's actions, is a concrete human being. This is seen in more extreme forms in connection with 'shitstorms' on social media, which can result in profound feelings of shame in the targeted individuals.

Winners and losers of the meritocracy

In modern performance and competition societies, individuals gain social recognition through accomplishments and competitive success. A meritocracy is based on the idea that everyone's social status, economic and material wealth and social recognition are determined by their concrete merits and accomplishments (Sandel, 2020). It is further assumed that individuals are driven by mutual competition in a never-ending struggle for social status and material wealth. Society is fundamentally viewed as a marketplace, and all interpersonal exchanges are understood through the lens of marketplace mechanisms and the concept of fair competition, where everyone is viewed as equal and thus logically get what they deserve. The central focus is not on universal equality but on everyone having equal opportunities to succeed. Anyone who really wants it can achieve attractive positions in society, and those who are in the upper echelons of society have basically earned their place at the top. They are the winners in what is perceived as a fair competition, which also legitimizes why some people have a higher status and much better living conditions than others.

In a natural extension of this view, individuals can convince themselves that they have earned their attractive position and their economic and material wealth and thus deserve it, which legitimizes their much more advantageous situation. On the other hand, this may also be seen as a particularly egocentric form of blindness to their own reliance on help from others and well-functioning public institutions in attaining their elevated social status and material wealth. This blindness to how we are always already embedded in social relationships and communities also contains a risk of arrogant disrespect for and lack of empathy with others who were less fortunate and successful in life (cf. Sandel, 2020, p. 95f.). When this translates into more explicit disrespect, humiliation and contempt for disadvantaged groups in society from people in society's elite, the result may be escalating conflicts and destructive internal polarization of society driven by shame and anger in response to shame (see Section 6.2). There are numerous cases of political leaders who aggressively distance themselves from their opponents through more or less unveiled contempt for their allegedly low cultural level and primitive or uncivilized actions. Examples include Danish Prime Minister Poul Nyrup Rasmussen, who directly addressed the members of the (right-wing) Danish People's Party in the Hall of Parliament, saying, 'You will never be fit for polite society', and American presidential candidate Hillary Clinton, who called some of the later President Trump's supporters 'a basket of deplorables'. Statements like these do not contribute to society's internal integration but instead to unnecessary humiliation, shame, anger and destructive internal polarization (see also Jones, 2011). Since meritocratic performance societies view winners as individuals who earned well-deserved victories in fair and even competition, conversely, this also means that the losers in this performance-driven competition for attractive positions in society more or less deserved to lose: they have only themselves to blame and thus, more or less, bear responsibility for their inferior social status and possible economic and spiritual (cultural) poverty. To the extent that this specific view of society's functional logic becomes dominant and is internalized by all citizens, socially marginalized or excluded citizens will come to see themselves as responsible for their marginal position in the organized meritocratic community, based on participation through individual accomplishments. Their status is seen as reflecting their own defects and deficits in a community where there is no demand for what they have to offer, no one has any interest in their thoughts or opinions, and no one shows any real interest in their experiences or feelings in the slow lane of society. This lowly social position may be accompanied by intense shame (Lesmeister, 2009).

Late modern performance and competition societies are closely related to the two social affects of shame and pride. Both emotions are driven by people's continual evaluation and comparison of themselves and each other based on dimensions of what is valuable and may give cause for pride or, conversely, is perceived as worthless and useless and may therefore be a source of shame (Wurmser, 1981b, p. 32). The winners of the mutual competition have reason to be proud. The losers have reason to be shameful about their humiliating defeat (Nathanson, 1987a, p. 188), especially if they lack the psychological resources and the resilience and psychological maturity to be able to handle defeat without risking collapse of their self-esteem and shameful feelings of inferiority. Poverty, unemployment, poor education and lack of cultivation tend to be regarded as the results of individual character flaws or, at least, as indications that the affected individuals did not try hard enough in the struggle for the attractive positions in society. Since responsibility is primarily assigned to individuals, they may come to feel inferior and inadequate. They may also become increasingly concerned and afraid of failing, coming up short in the competition and thus ending up shameful losers in the competition for good marks, education, jobs and partners (Sandel, 2020, p. 180f.).

As pointed out by, among others, the American philosopher Michael Sandel (2020, p. 24), one of the key problems of the meritocratic narrative is that it is far from universally true that everyone in modern society has equal opportunities and chances of doing well in the competition for wealth and attractive positions. Furthermore, this narrative has a built-in tendency to inspire arrogance and self-sufficiency among the winners and humiliation, shame ('I am inadequate, inferior'), anger and *ressentiment* ('this is unfair and unjust') among the losers in the mutual competition (ibid., p. 25). And even though all modern welfare states feature some degree of wealth redistribution between the wealthiest and the poorest citizens, the problems that arise as a result of the meritocratic view of society's winners and losers are far from solved simply by compensating the most disadvantaged citizens economically in the form of various social services and provisions, especially if society is permeated by implicit or more explicit perceptions that the failure (or unwillingness) to be self-reliant and to be (or to make oneself) independent of outside assistance is the sign of shameful weakness or a repugnant parasitic lifestyle (Nussbaum, 2004, p. 193). Generally, equality and justice in a society cannot be reduced to a matter of the distribution of economic and material wealth. It must also include access to social recognition and, thus, opportunities for self-expression and real freedom to realize a valuable life.

Generally, modern Western societies are arguably organized in a way that systematically produces both winners and losers in an eternal competition for economic and cultural resources and for attention, social status and recognition. The winners can be proud of their accomplishments, attained wealth and social status, while the losers have only themselves to blame (and typically do so) for not trying hard enough or for underperforming. What is of note in the present context is how being a loser in society's competition for social status, coveted positions and economic wealth – without appearing to have any particular personal characteristics or any individual merits (accomplishments) that are valued by society – may give rise to acknowledged or unacknowledged shame.

This functional logic may result in a society where everyone continually strives to improve and optimize themselves in order to avoid the shame associated with falling behind and in the hope of earning a fleeting moment of pride by doing well in the competition and achieving impressive merits. In order to avoid shame by failing and losing, everyone must do everything they can to become 'a success', a 'winner', and to hide the weaknesses, faults and defects we all have, simply because we are human (DeYoung, 2022, p. 121). It is a logic that not only systematically generates losers and individuals who feel that they have failed and are inadequate when they compare themselves to prevailing demands and expectations but also causes widespread exhaustion, low well-being and increased risk of psychological difficulties in a large share of the population (see Sundhedsstyrelsen, 2022). To some extent, we have all internalized the meritocratic competition society's belief that the worth of human beings, and thus our worth as human beings, is measured on certain accomplishments and the ability to do well in competition with others. As we internalize this assumption, we will come to feel inferior, inadequate and wrong, at the risk of being overwhelmed by shame when we fail to live up to these beliefs and (often obviously unrealistic) expectations of never-ending accomplishments and victims in competition with others.

6.2 From 'I have done something wrong' to 'I am wrong and inadequate'

Until not terribly long ago, modern societies were based on fairly strict norms, rules, clear expectations and requirements which individuals internalized in the form of often demanding ego ideals and an authoritarian superego or strict conscience. Thus, individuals made society's requirements and demands their own. Roughly put, the way the psychology of modern human beings worked, when someone failed to live up to the fairly clear standards of morally and socially acceptable behaviour, they would develop a guilty conscience and might be overwhelmed by feelings of guilt. Most people had strict internal and external authorities (including God) that set clear boundaries for their self-expression and self-realization. In fact, most of the population had little personal freedom to pursue their own needs and self-realization. Many struggled with a guilty conscience and feelings of guilt (or, we might say, internal conflicts) because they felt they had done something wrong. Today, that is no longer nearly as common.

In late modern Western societies, for better or worse, what is expected of individuals is far more diffuse. Many people have a high degree of freedom to pursue their own vision of a good and happy life. At the same time, there is a widespread expectation that people then actually do achieve self-realization, happiness, family life, a wide circle of friends and a large social network – now that they have the freedom to pursue these goals and are no longer limited by strict norms and rules, let along authoritarian (internal and external) father figures. The late modern self is a performative self, continually exposing and positioning itself to a real or imagined audience, with social media as a particularly popular and powerful stage (Reckwitz, 2017/2020, p. 3). Lacan-inspired psychoanalysts (Soiland, 2022, p. 10ff.) say that modern societies have developed from an oedipal to a post-oedipal organization; they have changed from being organized around a strict work ethic, prohibitions and guilt to a much greater emphasis on the expectation that everyone should enjoy themselves (consume), be happy, pursue self-realization and optimize their self-expression. However, in this post-oedipal society we may be overwhelmed by shameful feelings of inadequacy when this project fails, for whatever reason. Our superego is no longer organized to impose maximal self-discipline but rather aims to maximize perceived pleasure and self-expression, which we may be seduced into perceiving as the expression of maximal freedom. The drawback of this seemingly paradisical condition is that these cultural changes not only reflect newfound freedom and unlimited possibilities of self-expression but also new, strict requirements for us to be happy, enjoy ourselves and attain self-realization in certain specific ways. As a result, people in late modernity live under the tyranny of practically unattainable visions of happiness, enduring pleasure and limitless self-expression. These visions are out of step with reality, which always contains numerous (internal and external) limitations. However, we tend to deny these limitations, which may lead to shameful experiences of inadequacy when we discover their concrete impact on our lives (cf. Soiland, 2022, p. 38). In extension of this point, we may lose and overburden ourselves in persistent (illusory) attempts to cover up or repair the self's perceived defects and inadequacies by performing, consuming (enjoying, seeking concrete objects to fill the self's perceived deficits) and attract others' attention and recognition. Some writers have also described the late modern individual as an entrepreneurial self that aims to keep their options open, remain flexible, focus on their own successes and continually invest in themselves with a view to future payoffs in the form of attention and affirmation (King, 2016, p. 82). This is a self that persistently tries to appear in the best possible light and to attract and keep others' attention and interest.

The drawback of this seemingly high degree of latitude to realize and be ourselves without restrictive demands to be or act in certain ways is that it can be associated with feelings of shame and inferiority and a painful sense of inadequacy if we fail to live up to (our own and others') expectations of self-realization, success, family and children, happiness, lots of close friends and a wide social network. The main human challenge in late modernity is not the torment of internal conflicts or certain dysfunctional thoughts, as described in classical psychoanalysis and parts of cognitive psychology. Rather, it is a sense of basic inadequacy and of being wrong as well as related efforts to be or appear in certain ways in order to be seen and recognized as good enough (Mitchell, 1993, p. 22ff.). This is also a recipe for overburdening the self, developing a false self and self-alienation.

When we fail to live up to our own expectations and those of others (our environment, contemporary culture), we take this to mean that we did not try hard enough and that we could have done better. Feeling unhappy, a little depressed, burnt out, lonely and insecure about our own future is shameful. So is failing to complete an education or get the job we were dreaming of – or not really having any dreams, perhaps because we have seen our dreams shattered too many times, so that we no longer dare to dream because we are afraid of yet another disappointment. It can also be shameful not to be unique, exciting and interesting enough to succeed in the competition for attention and dedicated followers on social media.

Thus, the psychological pain of a typical late modern individual is not primarily about feelings of guilt over violating specific bans or requirements. To a much higher degree, it comes from failing to live up to our own (and others') expectations, goals and standards, which are mostly quite diffuse (and constantly changing). Modern human beings are ashamed of failing and feeling inadequate, inferior and defective. We should always be extremely cautious about positing very close causal links between trends in contemporary culture and the development of specific mental disorders. However, it is worth at least considering whether these developments in modern society might diminish people's psychological resilience to mental disorders when shame plays a certain role in the aetiology of the disorder and its underlying dynamic psychological processes.

One of the key characteristics of our highly individualized modern society is that problems that would be considered common social issues when seen through a less individualistic lens are largely viewed as individual problems that it is up to individuals to solve. The modern assumption that anyone can do anything they put their mind to or that anyone can achieve their dreams if only they try hard enough seems delusional. Nevertheless, the individual is assigned most of the blame when they fail in their efforts to achieve unrealistic goals and ideals. Individuals are systematically made responsible for their own fate and success in life, even though far from everyone has the requisite psychological and other resources to manage their own life (Neckel, 1991, p. 170).

In line with this individualization of common problems in society, which is internalized to the point where it is considered an almost self-evident view of societal and cultural problems, individuals tend to see themselves as failures and losers in the general competition for positive attention, social status and recognition when they do not (as is the case for the vast majority of us) make it to the top tier of society, with high social status and privileged access to positive attention and recognition from others but instead end up much further down the social ladder. This may feel shameful and difficult to share with others, not just because of our almost instinctive urge to hide feelings of shame but also because it is regarded as a strictly individual problem that it is up to the individual to solve. It is a problem that tends to be seen as indication of a possible character flaw and individual weakness and thus grounded in individual characteristics (Jones, 2011, p. 10ff.). As a result, failure is considered shameful and taboo in a culture where the strong and self-reliant individual is held up as the common ideal.

Without necessarily doing so intentionally, meritocratic societies may also tend to assign shame over failing and feelings of inadequacy to the lower social classes, which are then, at best, ignored or marginalized but may also be met with contempt because they failed in the competition. They are subjected to dehumanizing treatment, met with suspicion and required to take part in humiliating meetings, training courses and assessment procedures (cf. Nussbaum, 2004). At the same time, they represent our common fear of inadequacy and failure in the mutual competition that forms such a terrifying undercurrent of the meritocratic performance society (Hoggett, 2017, p. 376). For someone who is already under pressure, it can be a heavy burden to thus become a vessel of anxiety, shame and feelings of inadequacy that the meritocratic society at large is trying to eschew. This dynamic only works in societies built on the common repression of our inherent human vulnerability and our awareness that any one of us might fall victim to the societal logic by which people who are underperforming tend to be seen as worthless or even as a scandalous burden to the community.

The outlined changes in the fundamental elements of the psychological challenges faced by human beings in late modernity are, arguably, reflected in related changes in the modern psychoanalytic understanding of and approach to the treatment of mental illness. Roughly put, over time, the focus has shifted from so-called conflict pathology, rooted in Freud's (1923/1961) structural personality model, towards growing attention on what psychoanalysis often calls deficit pathology, with roots in Kohut's self psychology, among other schools of thought (see Killingmo, 1989). Conceptually, deficit pathology refers to fundamental deficits (often including various forms of traumatization) in early relationships and resulting deficits in the development of individual personality organization. By contrast, the concept of conflict pathology refers to internal and, to a high degree, unconscious conflicts in individuals who otherwise have a well-defined and functioning ego, with the basic personality structures fully developed and in place. Central drivers of conflict pathology are anxiety and guilt, in part because the ego has done something wrong and fears being punished (by the superego or forces outside the self), while shame and an inherent sense of being wrong, defective and inadequate are the dominant aspects of the deficit pathology.

To some extent, this development in modern psychoanalysis can also be seen to reflect a historical movement from the more classical psychoanalytic understanding of the so-called tragic human being engaged in a constant inner struggle between, on the one hand, primitive human nature and imma- ture needs (the pleasure principle) and, on the other hand, the potential for developing reason, rationality and autonomy (the reality principle) to what has been called a more romantic understanding, which views human beings as inherently good and social beings who may become damaged and broken down in the encounter with an uncaring external world, including others who lack empathy and violate the individual's boundaries (Strenger, 1989; Jørgensen, 2008, p. 347ff.). Finally, this historical development may also be seen as a shift from a predominantly one-person psychology approach, which bases its understanding of the psychological development of mental disorders primarily on inner psychological processes in clearly delineated individuals, to an approach based more on a two-or-more-person psychology (or intersub- jective) understanding. In this latter approach, human psychology and mental disorders are informed much more by a view of humans as inherently social beings who are constituted and developed in interpersonal relationships and who are always already embedded in a particular culture (Jørgensen, 2019, p. 123ff.).

Table 6.1 provides a rough outline of the central elements of and differences between the two psychoanalytic models for understanding and treating psy- chological illness with a primary focus on either conflict or deficit pathology. The main focus of the table is on elements that are relevant in relation to the historical changes and related differences in the understanding of shame and shame-related mental disorders (for elaboration, see, e.g., Killingmo, 1989). In clinical practice, this is not a matter of exclusively choosing one or the other model but of remembering that elements from both approaches to the understanding and treatment of mental disorders can be relevant in the encounter with the individual patient (see Chapter 7). However, it will often be necessary to place a greater emphasis on the deficit approach in the treatment of patients who are struggling with destructive shame living in a late modern Western culture. As pointed out by Kohut (1971, p. 181), among others, people with destructive shame are rarely characterized by extraordin- arily high ego ideals, compared with others, which argues against the use of the conflict approach as a basis for treating this patient group.

At this point, we do not have the necessary empirical basis for judging whether – and if so, to what extent – the historical shift from a focus on conflict pathology to a stronger emphasis on deficit pathology reflects real changes in the prevalence of different types of mental disorders. Thus, we do not know whether the occurrence of deficit pathologies (also referred to as

Table 6.1 Central elements of the understanding of mental illness with a focus on conflict pathology versus deficit pathology

	Conflict approach	*Deficit approach*
Central affects	Guilt and anxiety.	Shame – feelings of inferiority and inadequacy.
Concept of shame	Springs from a discrepancy between the real ego and the ideal ego; an inability to live up to/realize one's own (in part internalized) ideals.	Always activated by and embedded in intersubjective relationships; activated by real or imagined others' negatively judging gaze at the self and a lack of loving and empathic mirroring of the self – at times, the self may even take the blame for others' failure or neglect, in which case shame is 'converted' into feelings of guilt as a defence.
Psychotherapeutic approach to shame	Shame is not seen as a central affect; general focus on putting the patient in touch with their affects through clarification, confrontation and interpretations.	Shame is seen as a central affect. It is important to help the patient verbalize feelings of shame – but also to dose and structure the actualization of and contact with shame in the psychotherapeutic space to avoid having the fragile self overwhelmed by destructive shame.
Central aetiological factor related to drawing boundaries	The self is limited by rigid outer boundaries and a strict/punishing superego; inhibits self-expression.	The self is confused because there are too few boundaries, or because the boundaries are too vague, and due to deficits in important others' responsiveness and empathic mirroring of the self; has difficulty managing their individual freedom, is plagued by feelings of emptiness, disorientation, lack of meaning.
Central therapeutic strategy	Confronting the patient with and interpreting the self's defects, deficits and negative affects (with the risk that the shameful self may feel overexposed, 'found out', under attack, threatened and shamed).	Helping the patient contain and accept their own perceived defects and deficits – and view painful affects (including shame) as a natural consequence of past events and being human. Emphasis on affirmative and validating interventions.

Table 6.1 (Continued)

	Conflict approach	Deficit approach
Treatment focus	The patient's inner conflicts and history.	What plays out in the therapeutic relationship/ contact between patient and therapist in the psychotherapeutic space.
View of the patient	The patient is mainly regarded as a clearly delimited and empowered individual who might be challenged and limited by inner (emergent) conflicts.	The patient is mainly regarded as a more passive victim of abuse, caregiver deficits and a 'bad' external world; the patient's difficulties are always viewed as being embedded in (dysfunctional) relationships.
The patient's idealization of the therapist	Viewed as the manifestation of a primitive defence, unrealistic and distorted image of the therapist.	Viewed as a possible manifestation of the patient's hope of change and an attempt to satisfy basic emotional needs and find a counterweight to painful shame and feelings of inferiority.
Pride, grandiose self-perception	Viewed as the manifestation of a primitive defence, unrealistic and distorted self-image.	Viewed as a possible manifestation of the patient's hope of change and an attempt to create a counterweight to painful shame and feelings of inferiority.
The therapist's engagement with the patient	Emphasis on the therapist's emotional neutrality and position as an objective observer of the patient (with the risk that a patient struggling with shame may feel lonely, abandoned and left to themselves in the therapeutic space).	Emphasis on the therapist's authentic presence in the contact and engagement with the patient; accommodates the patient's need for attachment, empathic response and emotional/ psychological contact.
Central treatment goals	Strengthening the ego's ability to manage inner conflicts (between drives/ needs, superego, external demands); bringing impulses and primitive needs (urges) under the control of reason (the ego).	Strengthening the self's ability to relate and to be in emotional and psychological contact with self and others.

(Continued)

Table 6.1 (Continued)

	Conflict approach	Deficit approach
Central therapeutic impact factor	The patient's achievement of insight strengthens the ego.	The patient's corrective emotional experiences in the interaction with the therapist, which compensates for deficits in early relationships and strengthens internal structure and integration; non-repetition of maladaptive interpersonal patterns, the therapist's empathic-loving mirroring of the self.

Sources: see, among others, Killingmo, 1989; Strenger, 1989; Lesmeister, 2021; Jørgensen, 2008, p. 350f.; Jørgensen, 2019, p. 123f.

early, pre-oedipal and structural disturbances) has actually been on the rise in modern meritocratic competition societies, or whether this change should be seen primarily as a result of the ongoing development of psychoanalytic theory; alternatively, it might also be related to changes with regard to who is offered psychotherapeutic treatment or to culturally conditioned changes in our basic understanding of human nature (Lesmeister, 2021, p. 14ff.).

The key point in the present context is that in today's society, destructive feelings of shame seem to be assigned relatively greater significance in the understanding of (especially more severe) mental disorders, compared to earlier. It is tempting to view this in relation to trends in late modern Western culture, where only perfect seems good enough. In such a culture, we are all at risk of feeling inadequate, wrong and shameful in an exhausting (cf. Ehrenberg, 2004) and inherently doomed effort to realize unreachable self-aspirations (Lesmeister, 2021, p. 40f.) in the slipstream of constant comparisons and competition with others, including on social media.

6.3 Recognition, disregard and shame

Human subjectivity, self and identity are constituted in relationships characterized by mutual recognition (Honneth, 1992/1996; Benjamin, 1996, 2018). We all need important others to acknowledge us as subjects, as persons with our own volition and intentions as well as meaningful and significant inner lives. This need for social recognition goes beyond the social esteem and respect for the person as an autonomous individual who should always be seen and treated as an end in themselves and must never be instrumentalized or reduced to a means in relation to others' goals or needs. In addition to this fundamental respect for individual autonomy, social recognition also involves an element of positive evaluation of the individual's person and characteristics that is crucially important for the person's psychological development, basic trust, self-esteem and well-being. Roughly put, this significant distinction and expansion can be traced back to the two German philosophers Immanuel Kant (1783/1992, 1785/2018) and G. W. F. Hegel (1807/2019). While Kant focused primarily on the necessary respect for the individual's autonomy, Hegel laid the foundation of recognition theory's focus on the inherently human need for others' positive gaze at the self (Schmetkamp, 2012). When someone is overwhelmed by shame, we might say that this positive gaze is jeopardized, has collapsed or may even have been replaced by a negative and disparaging gaze.

This striving for recognition can be a double-edged sword that confronts us with a difficult choice. In order to earn recognition for who we are, rather than a constructed facade or assumed mask, we need to be ourselves and authentically present in our contact with the other. We need to dare to reveal and be ourselves and be open to the other, just as we need to see and recognize the other as an independent subject, which also means that we have no control of the other's reactions to our own selves. This is a condition for establishing an intersubjective meeting with the potential for psychological and emotional contact and actual mutual recognition.

However, when we open up as ourselves in contact with other, rather than hiding behind facades, masks and social roles, we also leave ourselves open to the other's possible negative reactions. If we hide behind a constructed facade in our meeting with the other, it feels less painful to be overlooked, disregarded, ridiculed or met with indifference by others. If this happens, it is not our actual or true self as a whole that is disregarded and humiliated, it is merely a facade or the parts of the self we have chosen to show. The key problem of such a strategy for self-protection is that when we do gain recognition, it is of limited value to us, since it does not apply to our actual self but only to the mask or facade we were hiding behind. We are recognized for our ability to play a certain social role, not for who we are.

Similar problems may occur when someone is tempted to lie or embellish the truth in order to create an unrealistically positive self-image in an attempt to attract interest or appear significant as a way to earn someone else's recognition (Kilborne, 2002, p. 61f.). The lie creates distance to others. It leads to internal disintegration and means that any recognition cannot actually be used to support or bolster the person's actual self and identity but instead is more likely to lead to shame over feeling the need to lie or embellish. Due to its relational consequences, the lie increases the self's loneliness, social isolation and difficulties with being authentic with others.

If the person instead engages in contact with the other with all or much of their self, without hiding behind a mask or a facade, they may be hit much harder if the other fails to see, let alone recognize and appreciate the self but instead disregards, humiliates or disparages the self. This sort of experience can be associated with considerable psychological pain and shame. The most extreme form of this is when a person declares their love for someone who responds with mockery, ridicule or humiliation: 'How could you possibly think that I'm interested in you and find you worth loving?'

A somewhat related situation may occur when a young child runs over to mum to show her a pretty pebble, and the mother responds with complete indifference, continuing to chat on her mobile phone without paying any attention to the child. This may give the child the impression that mum not only has no interest in the pebble but in fact does not care about the child. The child's enthusiasm and joy will then typically collapse and may be replaced by shame, stifling the child's joy, enthusiasm, curiosity and ability to play. Conversely, to gain access to the rich emotional and human experiences of being in psychological and emotional contact with others and feel seen, understood and recognized in this contact, we need to engage without hiding behind a mask. Unfortunately, this will often be a major challenge for people struggling with destructive shame. As several writers have pointed out, what might appear to be positive recognition of someone's being and behaviour may sometimes be a manifestation of de facto disregard or a display of force aimed at making the other be and act in certain specific ways (Lepold, 2021, p. 20ff.). This relational dynamic may, for example, play out when we find that others explicitly recognize some of our characteristics, acts, emotions or other mental states which are not, or only partially, in accordance with the way we actually are or feel in the moment. Typically, this will at least make us feel misunderstood and perhaps even unappreciated, disregarded or subjected to intimidating manipulation.

For example, a father may express his pleasure in seeing that his daughter is strong enough to deal with her psychological difficulties, when the daughter in fact feels tremendously vulnerable and alone and really needs her father's help. For various reasons, however, the father is unable to see, contain and deal with this. Instead, he tries to define his daughter as – and make her be – someone she is not. In this situation, it may be tempting for the daughter, who yearns for her father's approval and love, to adapt to his expectations and try to be someone she is not, in an attempt to earn some form of recognition and love. In some cases, this form of disregard disguised as recognition may implicitly convey that the other would like the person to be in a certain way and that they will only recognize them if they comply or, at least, appear and act as desired. In practice, this shows disregard for the other as a subject, and for their actual self and identity – even if it might superficially appear as positive recognition.

These types of psychological and relational dynamics not only play out in dyadic relationships but also at a societal level, where people may be emotionally affected and feel shame, both as individuals and as members of particular social groups. This can happen, for example, if political leaders, representatives of public institutions and other prominent individuals act in ways that implicitly or explicitly express disrespect, disregard and contempt for an individual or for a social group the person is a member of or identifies with. When this happens, the group's lifestyle, honour, dignity and (sub) cultural norms, values and ideals may become the object of disrespect, contempt and various forms of humiliation or degradation, which may lead to shame and destabilized self-esteem in members of the affected social group. This happens, for example, when prominent politicians refer to migrants as 'welfare seekers' or claim that people who are unemployed are too lazy to want to take on an ordinary job, disregarding the fact that many who are unemployed would like to find a job but, for various reasons, are unable to handle a job on normal terms given the often high requirements in terms of working capacity, efficiency and qualifications.

The German social philosopher Axel Honneth (1992/1996) describes three levels of social recognition and their respective significance for human self and identity (see Table 6.2). The first level is focused on recognition of the self's emotions, needs and boundaries of intimacy and recognition of what makes the individual feel unique and special. This level of recognition primarily plays out in dyadic relationships with important others. During the

Table 6.2 Dimensions of social recognition

	In close dyadic relationships	Through embeddedness in social groups	Through embeddedness in a modern society governed by the rule of law
Focus of recognition	Emotions, needs, the self, identity; seen, mirrored and validated.	Personal qualities, skills and contributions to the community; seen and attributed positive value.	Seen and awarded legal rights as an equal, rational, autonomous and accountable subject.
Mode of recognition	Emotional and cognitive.	Cognitive and, to some extent, emotional.	Cognitive.
Crucial significance for	Self-esteem.	Confidence, social appreciation.	Self-respect.
Manifestations of disregard, disrespect	Violations of the self's boundaries of intimacy and personal integrity.	Social exclusion, exclusion from or dismissal of significance for the community; disparagement of the self's central characteristics, skills and contributions to the community.	Formal exclusion, suspension of ordinary legal rights and autonomy; suspension of the right to welfare state services on equal terms with others (negative discrimination).

Source: Honneth, 1992/1996, p. 130ff.

early years, this includes parents and other key caregivers; later, it includes the person's partner and close friends. Level two has a primary focus on recognition and positive appreciation of the self's characteristics, skills and constructive contributions to social communities. Finally, level three concerns the degree to which the self is seen and treated as an accountable legal subject on equal terms with everybody else in a modern society based on the rule of law.

While recognition in close dyadic relationships is crucial for individuals' self-esteem, recognition of the self's characteristics and skills is primarily significant for the person's confidence, while the legal recognition of the self as an accountable, responsible and rational autonomous subject influences the individual's self-respect. Lack of recognition, disregard and actual violations of the self on either of these three levels may lead to subjective perceptions of the self as inferior, abnormal and worthless in the eyes of others. These experiences all have the potential to be associated with and cause painful shame. In extension of this point, it is worth considering whether the human need for recognition, social status and a good reputation in significant social groups is stronger than our striving for economic and material wealth (Mishra, 2017, p. 192). Thus, this need may also partially be understood as a need to avoid the potential shame related to lack of recognition and low social status. If this is true, it has significant implications for the ideal organization of a well-functioning society and what should be the focus of social policy initiatives. Decent societies seek to combat socioeconomic conditions that give their citizens reason to feel disregarded and violated (such as profound social disparities, discrimination and marginalization of certain population groups). They meet all citizens with the same degree of respect and recognition, simply because they are human and members of our community (Margalit, 1996, p. 42). This involves, in part, that public institutions can never contribute to violating, marginalizing, humiliating or demonizing individuals or groups of people, including people who are highly dependent on society's help and support (ibid., p. 90). For example, a decent society will never make sweeping generalizations defining all welfare recipients as lazy or labelling migrants from war zones and dictatorships as 'welfare seekers' or subject people who receive assistance from the welfare state to humiliating control and 'activation' measures that undermine their autonomy and self-respect and make them feel ashamed for being seen and treated as inferior individuals. Generally, Honneth's three forms of recognition and manifestations of disrespect with their related significance for different parts of the individual's psychology are summarized in Table 6.2.

6.4 Inequality

Formally and legally, all citizens in modern society are equal and attributed equal human worth. However, in some regards, reality looks a little different. With Mishra (2017, p. 336), we can argue that '*Ressentiment* was inherent in the structure of societies where formal equality between individuals coexists with massive differences in power, education, status and property ownership'. These are all potential drivers of perceived injustice, envy and shame. The chances of attaining social recognition are not necessarily equally, let alone equitably, distributed in modern societies. As for the possibility of attaining more emotionally grounded recognition in close dyadic relationships, people with a wide range of well-functioning relationships, a stable social network and good contact with their family are clearly in a better position than people who, for various reasons, are socially marginalized, have a weak network and generally have fragile relationships with others.

Loneliness, social anxiety, shame and limited access to recognition in close relationships can be a toxic cocktail for people with psychological difficulties and lead to self-perpetuating vicious cycles as shame because of loneliness, psychological difficulties and own perceived inabilities generally exacerbates an existing tendency to withdraw from contact with others. These individuals begin to withdraw from contact in an attempt to protect the self from further shame, which may in fact end up intensifying the already painful destructive shame, loneliness and problems associated with lack of contact with others that would allow the self to feel seen and recognized. Self-perpetuating shame-related processes such as these can be seen in people with personality disorders, among others (see Chapter 5).

Similarly, there may be considerable levels of inequality in the distribution of opportunities for social recognition of personal qualities, skills and contributions to communities. Generally, for example, people with higher levels of education and key positions in society or local communities and members of the cultural, media-related or economic elite will have much better opportunities for finding that they are seen and recognized as significant members of one or (typically) more communities, in which their personal qualities and skills are recognized, compared with people who have limited education, are at the margins of the labour market or live in disadvantaged or marginalized geographic areas. The culturally and educationally lower classes may also be implicitly or explicitly shamed as being uncultivated, uneducated, coarse, vulgar, primitive, retrospective and provincial (Reckwitz, 2017/2020, p. 200). Social processes of this nature are de facto expressions of disparagement of these people's qualities and, at worst, of their existence as equal human beings.

As pointed out by Honneth (1992/1996, p. 162ff.), when people with shared experiences in terms of perceived disrespect, disparagement and shaming – Honneth also speaks of social shame – meet and join forces, this may contain the potential for collective liberation and a common struggle to combat degradation, abuse and disparagement of certain social groups and people with particular social identities. This may contain the potential for a social movement for recognition, as heightened vulnerability to shame is replaced by opportunities to feel pride over being part of a social group with a specific social identity (see also Jørgensen, 2020). This may also change society in a more democratic direction, with everyone being entitled to the same levels of freedom, respect and recognition, simply because they are human. One example of this is Muslim women banding together to fight religious and patriarchal norms that limit women's freedom and sexuality (Al-Mersal, 2022), or when women from large sections of modern societies get together to fight sexual and other forms of abuse and unacceptable use of power directed at women (cf. MeToo and so forth).

Many writers have argued that economic and cultural globalization has benefited the more privileged sections of modern society far more, while large groups of people at lower levels of society may feel left behind, abandoned, forgotten and marginalized in a tenuous situation without power and with a social status that is, at best, precarious (Sandel, 2020, p. 17). This situation is further exacerbated when the access to normal sources of pride and self-esteem, such as education, career, job and raising a family, is blocked. Cosmopolitan identities characterized by a multicultural outlook and a high degree of openness and flexibility are often held up as progressive and valuable, while, for example, national and other identities with roots in smaller and more local communities are implicitly or explicitly devalued as being obsolete and backwards (Goodhart, 2017). The latter must be considered a reflection of disrespect and lack of recognition of the individuals in question and their identity, which may contribute to their feeling of being humiliated and shamed. Alternatively, it may lead to aggressive reactions (Sandel, 2020, p. 20), including becoming a strong emotional driver of an oppositional contempt for a distant elite who are perceived as being out of touch with 'the people' and with real life (see Meier-Carlsen, 2000).

Roughly put, societal disparities are associated with an increased risk of disparities in the access to social recognition, which in turn is associated with a heightened vulnerability to perceived shame over not being seen and appreciated as a person and as a central and valuable member of a community. To the extent that access to humiliating others and the risk of being humiliated is unevenly distributed in society, the risk of experiencing and being overwhelmed by shame is also unevenly distributed. This includes, especially, shame related to lack of social recognition of one's skills and contributions to the community. Thus, some people live under social conditions associated with a considerably heightened risk of destructive shame (Neckel, 1991, p. 36). In meritocratic societies, individual accomplishments are the main entry to being recognized as a valuable member of the community, just as the value of the self is often closely associated with certain types of accomplishments and value in different markets. This may present special challenges for people who may not have the educational qualifications or personality qualities to succeed in the late modern labour market and other platforms of individual competition (Neckel, 2009, p. 115).

6.5 Social media as an accelerator of shame

The advent of new digital technologies and social media sparked an explosive development in human possibilities for social contact and exposure of the individual's thoughts, emotions and everyday life, including exposing the individual's private space and intimate life to a potentially very large and unknown audience. The number of potential contacts is growing at an explosive rate, and the character of these contacts may also change significantly, since, unlike real-life contacts or contacts in the physical realm, these are not confined by time and space. Many people feel quite ambivalent about this development. On the one hand, it seems to offer a huge expansion of our social life, including our opportunities for attention and recognition. On the other hand, it is associated with, at least, an equally huge increase in the risk of new forms of humiliation and violations of our integrity and boundaries of shame by faceless, anonymous others.

Although social media are sometimes presented as a means of solving some people's social and relational problems, it is probably more accurate to say that the range of challenges in connection with interpersonal contact in real life has largely followed us into the digital world, where the scale of challenges may in fact be multiplied many times over, simply due to the potentially much greater number of contacts. Besides, the potentially faceless and anonymous contact on social media can undermine psychological mechanisms that would normally inhibit the tendency to humiliate and abuse others in interpersonal contacts in the concrete-physical realm (Frevert, 2017/2020, p. 138; Löchel, 2019, p. 37). People with low self-esteem and weak real-life networks may be especially vulnerable to new shameful humiliation on social media (Frevert, 2017/2020).

Social media can be regarded as a new marketplace, where people compete for attention and singularity, in part by presenting the most interesting profile and the most interesting or spectacular stories about themselves (Reckwitz, 2017/2020, p. 179f.). In order to attract and maintain others' attention – important currency on social media – and receive some form of recognition through this, people have to continue performing. They need to persistently update their profile and personal stories in order to keep appearing exciting and interesting.

In this context, some may be tempted to shift and gradually dismantle the boundaries of their own private and intimate space. On the one hand, this may be interpreted as a new level of honesty and authenticity. On the other hand, it may also stem from a poor sense of their own boundaries and a poor ability to protect themselves and their private space. Personal weaknesses and elements from the person's 'imperfect life' may increase the viewer's sense of uniqueness and authenticity, which is typically perceived as positive and is an effective way to attract attention. However, the balance is extremely delicate. If the person does not manage to incorporate the revealed weaknesses into a story about a self with a fairly good grasp of themselves and their life and if they are not also, generally, an interesting and attractive person, sharing very personal aspects of life may be perceived as desperate and trashy (Reckwitz, 2017/2020, p. 182). Even though the development of social media is normally seen to open new spaces with the freedom to be and express what we want, they also arguably impose a heavy pressure for conformity with related risks of shaming in case someone violates the typically tacit rules for what is valuable, normal and socially acceptable (Küchenhoff, 2018, p. 333).

Decades before the advent of social media, the American sociologist Richard Sennett (1974, p. 427) described the obsession with intimacy as a characteristic of an uncivilized society. He based this view, in part, on a concept of civilized society as a society where public and private life are separate, and private life is protected from anonymous others' intimidating gaze; a society where people are not always expected to be personally and authentically present in the public space, and individuals can hide more private and intimate parts of themselves and their (inner) lives behind social roles and by wearing different masks in public.

Sennett associated late modern societies with what he called a 'tyranny of intimacy', as the boundary between public and private life is continually challenged and dissolving, and it becomes increasingly difficult or challenging to protect the self's inner, private life from others' judging and potentially shame-inducing gaze (Greiner, 2014, p. 47f.). In many ways, Sennett anticipated some of the difficulties in distinguishing between public and private – with new tyrannies of intimacy, authenticity and visibility (Han, 2012, p. 24) – that have increased at an explosive rate with the emergence of social media, including the growing risk of shameful exposure of private and intimate parts of the self that is related to life on social media. This development is in conflict with the human need for a space where we can be ourselves, free from others' judging gaze (Han, 2012, p. 8), and where we do not share and expose everything, with the related risk of shame that this involves.

When navigating on social media, we can decide and control what parts of ourselves and our lives we want to share, and we are free to hide any parts of ourselves, our lives and our history that we perceive as shameful. On the other hand, we have little or no control of how others perceive, judge and react to what we do choose to share. This is particularly true of more open forums, where we do not necessarily know or have any reason to trust most of the people who have access to what we share. In addition, self-disclosure and self-exposure on social media can become quite comprehensive, since, in the moment, we often perceive this as something we choose for ourselves and which is therefore associated with a sense of freedom and agency (Han, 2012, p. 80). Thus, we are simultaneously victims and perpetrators. This is also true when our self-disclosure is driven as much by a (not necessarily consciously acknowledged) need for attention and recognition from others in order to stabilize our fragile self-esteem. In a sense, we may feel that disgracing ourselves is preferable to being invisible and insignificant (Köhler, 2017, p. 77).

Overall, this creates a situation that may potentially involve extensive loss of control and an invasion of people's private space, where others can mock, disparage and ridicule what we share about ourselves, and we have no way to control this feedback (Hofstadler, 2019). On the one hand, there can be something disarming about exposing intimate details and revealing our own inadequacies. On the other hand, this may represent naive exhibitionist self-exposure and seemingly voluntary violations of our own boundaries of intimacy, which becomes obvious when these intimate details are subsequently used by others as a weapon to humiliate and ridicule the self (Köhler, 2017, p. 90), which obviously involves a risk of experiencing feelings of shame over how others see and disparage the self.

It can feel shameful if the content we share on social media appears to be of so little interest to others that no one reacts to it, and we are simply met with silence and indifference. That may activate or exacerbate a perception of the self as insignificant, invisible and uninteresting to others: 'I have nothing to offer, I am uninteresting, I might as well not exist'. Similarly, it may be associated with shame if we repeatedly find that others systematically misconstrue and misinterpret the self-image we try to present on social media; that others try to impose their perception of us and their truth about who we are. This intensifies the general challenges and feelings of shame that may be associated with being attributed a particular identity, with related ideas about who we are that do not reflect or match how we see or perceived ourselves.

On digital media, the number of friends, contacts and positive reactions can be seen as very concrete measures of the self's worth as a human being. This means, in part, that a very low number of contacts and reactions can be perceived as an indication of the self's insignificance and worthlessness, which is associated with shame. On the other hand, a person may also have many social contacts and followers on social media without really feeling that they are being seen and met as who they are. This will be particularly true if the person presents a highly edited and embellished version of themselves that does not really reflect who they are. In an attempt to spark interest, attract attention and be considered an interesting person that others want to connect with, the person may then present with a mask or a facade that covers up or hides large parts of their self, which means these parts are not seen and met, let alone recognized.

For someone with deep and close relationships outside social media, this is unlikely to present a problem. However, it can be a double-edged sword for someone whose life on social media plays a dominating role and, to some extent, serves as a replacement of real-life relationships which the person, for various reasons, finds challenging and may therefore tend to avoid. The previously discussed problems with experiencing social recognition of the self may also play out on social media. If the person only presents carefully curated and edited parts of themselves online, any positive attention or recognition is not in fact directed at the real self. If, on the other hand, someone is ruthlessly honest and fairly uninhibited in their self-presentation, disclosing very intimate details about their life, self and private space, it may be emotionally overwhelming and associated with massive destructive shame if the reactions they encounter on social media are largely characterized by indifference, mockery, disparagement or ridicule.

Social media also offer ample opportunity for comparing our own, rarely perfect reality with others' seemingly perfect lives, which cause feelings of inferiority and shame in people with an insecure sense of self and fragile self-esteem (Löchel, 2021, p. 96). Furthermore, social media enable new forms of shame by proxy when we – voluntarily or involuntarily – witness other people's shameless behaviour and uninhibited self-exposure with no real sense of how their behaviour is perceived and judged by others. In addition, people with very different boundaries of intimacy and shame may 'meet' on social media, where something that some people find fairly normal behaviour may be perceived as offensive, shameful and a violation of their personal boundaries.

Naturally, this is not a challenge that was created by social media, but it can be hugely increased for people who spend a great deal of time online, where it is fairly easy to get into contact with people from other (sub)cultures. Furthermore, there is a heightened risk of more radical forms of shame by proxy online, for example when unedited recordings of ISIS fighters decapitating captives or material from war zones circulate on digital media and people may be – in some cases inadvertently – confronted with extremely humiliating and degrading treatment of human beings. This can be emotionally overwhelming, unbearable and lead to shame on behalf of both the victim and the perpetrator. Furthermore, the perpetrators of these types of acts are almost always male, which, in a sense, can be seen as shameful to all men.

Social media are also used, for example, by people taking revenge on ex-partners by uploading intimate or otherwise humiliating pictures or recordings. This can be extremely shameful to the victims. Similarly, phenomena such as cyber-bullying and 'happy slapping' performed in front of faceless audiences on social media expose people to humiliating and degrading treatment. Happy slapping is a phenomenon where others, typically a group of people, put someone in a situation characterized by extreme powerlessness and subject them to deeply humiliating treatment in the form of rape, physical violence and even homicide, while the act is recorded and uploaded on digital media. Here, the material will often find a large audience, who treat it as entertainment and make it the object of ridicule, which may lead to extreme shame in the victims (Frevert, 2017/2020, p. 138). Furthermore, social media make it possible to subject people to public shaming on an unprecedented scale and intensity, for example in the form of various forms of shitstorms.

Social media may accelerate and intensify tendencies towards objectifying and dehumanizing people. This is the case, for example, when women – sometimes in more closed forums, sometimes in open ones – are reduced to their bodies as one-dimensional objects of men's sexualizing gaze and desire. To be reduced to an object of others' gaze is in itself shameful (cf. Chapter 4 on Sartre's views), but this experience takes on a new and far more severe dimension when a woman with an inner psychological life and her own subjectivity (a person who is entitled to respect, solely by virtue of being human) is reduced to a dehumanized tool for satisfying others' needs and, moreover, is exposed to what is, in principle, an infinitely large, faceless audience (Nussbaum, 2011, p. 69f.).

Finally, the concrete manifestations of 'cancel culture' often play out on social media, where individuals are cancelled, ostracized and expelled, often with reference to their presumed low and reprehensible moral character. This may be associated with shame for the targeted individuals. As mentioned earlier, it is in itself shameful to be socially expelled. This shame is exacerbated if the individual is de facto cancelled as a person (is no longer recognized as an equal subject) because their ways of being and acting are allegedly so morally reprehensible and scandalous that no one wants anything to do with them or is interested in hearing what they might have to say in their defence.

6.6 Stigmatization and self-stigmatization

Historically, the term 'stigmatization' has referred to physical branding and the social categorization of individuals or groups in ways that are negative and which may undermine or damage their social identities (Goffman, 1963, p. 9ff.). The term has been explored especially by Canadian sociologist Erving Goffman (1963, 2004). Typically, stigmatization targets people who for various reasons are labelled as 'abnormal', inferior or dangerous or associated with socially unacceptable behaviour. The underlying term, 'stigma', is a mark or specific characteristic that for some reason is associated with social condemnation, disgrace, infamy and shame in a given culture (Lewis, 1998, p. 131).

Assigning a stigma to someone is perceived as discrediting and associated with some degree of social marginalization or exclusion. This can in itself be shameful and cause the affected individuals to perceive themselves as abnormal, inferior and defective. Whether the stigmatization is based on more personal physical and bodily characteristics (for example, a physical disability or mental illness) or the target's race, religion or nationality (collective identity), it will often hamper the targeted individual's access to social recognition and make the person feel abnormal, which is associated with shame. Furthermore, stigmatization often involves varying degrees of soul blindness and dehumanization, as the subjects of the stigmatization (the person or persons doing the stigmatizing) do not see or recognize the objects of the stigmatization (the person or persons who are stigmatized) as equal subjects but instead view them as inferior and, at worst, subhuman or nonhuman. To be subjected to this can in itself undermine a person's identity and is associated with shame.

Although stigmatization is typically directed at a person's specific characteristics, it applies to the self as a whole, marginalizing it as inferior and defective, in a similar effect to the feeling of shame. The specific consequences of stigmatization for the individual depend, in part, on the degree to which the stigmatized self is assigned responsibility for their stigma, for example whether someone who was subjected to sexual assault finds that others believe that they were to blame for what happened (cf. Lewis, 1998, p. 134).

Stigmatization gets under the skin of the targeted persons and influences their self-perception (Tyler, 2020, p. 7f.). In some cases, people can be brought to internalize the perceived stigmatization to such a degree that they subsequently stigmatize themselves. In self-stigmatization, the person has introjected and identified with an external aggressor and with the contempt and humiliation they experienced in previous relationships in a way that now makes the person despise and humiliate themselves to at least the same degree. In many cases, this self-stigmatization closely resembles the contempt they previously received from others, in terms of the characteristics of the self that are despised. The person hates themselves, overexposes their perceived faults and deficits and may actively seek situations where they are likely to be humiliated, degraded and subjected to various forms of abuse.

This may involve elements of counterphobic self-stigmatization, as someone almost shamelessly exposes their own shame and actively seeks dreaded situations. Dynamically, this may be seen as a manifestation of a masochistic or sadomasochistic external enactment of an internal drama and repetitions of interaction patterns from the person's past, as others are invited, provoked or seduced into degrading, humiliating or attacking the self. All of this unfolds in an attempt to achieve some form of control of perceived shame and stigmatization. In addition, the person may attempt to manage perceived stigmatization through apparent indifference, bordering on demonstrative and grandiose rebellion, towards how someone is expected to act in interpersonal interactions and in the public space. To varying degrees, this strategy may be associated with the choice of a negative identity, as the person tries to attract attention and establish a personal identity (delimitation from others) by incarnating what the environment generally signals as being undesirable and socially unacceptable (Schafer, 1997, p. 96).

The struggle for destigmatization may involve attempts to redefine the stigma assigned to a person or a group as a positive expression of a unique identity and efforts to improve the community's perceptions and view of the person or group ('impression management') (Goffman, 1963, p. 73f.). This may also help reduce the perceived shame of the stigmatization. The more the stigmatized person or group is defined as being radically different from 'normal people' (in a process of 'othering'), the less empathy and understanding they will typically encounter from others, and the greater the risk that the person or group be subjected to more comprehensive social exclusion by being placed outside the human community, which will be associated with a shameful loss of social status and attachment. This may affect, among others, certain categories of inmates in correctional facilities, people with severe mental illness and people with severe physical or mental disability.

As several writers (Tyler, 2020) have pointed out, stigmatization can also be an instrument of social control, which may be used, for example, to secure the social status and position of powerful individuals and groups. It may also be involved in shaming and marginalizing minority groups and people who, in various ways, deviate from or challenge what is perceived as normal and socially acceptable in a given (sub)culture. Arguably, stigmatization is always associated with the use of power and cannot be fully understood detached from it, just as it cannot be reduced to an exclusively psychological process. In this sense, Goffman's (1963) classical concept of stigmatization is too narrow and lacks the necessary awareness of the connection between stigmatization and power in relationships and social groups. Public shaming and stigmatization of a selected other demonstrate and affirm the power of the person who is doing the shaming, just as being the object of shaming and stigmatization demonstrates and exacerbates the person's powerlessness (Frevert, 2020/2023, p. 9).

6.7 Shame as a driver of escalating conflicts and cultural polarization

As mentioned earlier, several empirical studies have lent support to the notion of a close relationship between destructive shame and aggression at an individual level (see Section 4.5). In addition, analyses of communication between couples have demonstrated how unacknowledged and destructive shame as a consequence of perceived abuse can contribute to escalating conflicts and violence in close personal relationships (Retzinger, 1991). To some degree, this relationship between shame, aggression and violence also pertains to processes at the level of society. A systematic review of school shootings in the United States from the 1990s on found that this extremely violent category of crime is predominantly carried out by young single white males who kill more or less random people in order to take revenge on what they perceive as an unjust world but also, in many cases, to avenge perceived humiliation and ridicule of the self; thus, the violent act is potentially grounded in and driven by destructive shame (Kimmel, 2013, p. 73ff.).

Others have pointed to severe interpersonal and narcissistic disorders in young men who have a long history of feeling rejected by others, fearing humiliation in interpersonal contacts and developing into outsiders (meaning that unacknowledged shame may be a key driver), as risk factors of school shootings and other types of extreme acts of violence (Hilgers, 2013, p. 92f.). Finally, it could be argued that these types of mass killings, where someone with a narcissistic injury goes on a frenzied killing spree, should sometimes be understood as a form of revenge on individuals (teachers, other pupils, figures of authority) whom the perpetrator perceives as being to blame for their perceived shame and humiliation (Manne, 2014, p. 74). The perpetrator seeks to escape the resulting unbearable shame and humiliation through extreme and uncontrolled aggression. In any case, unbearable destructive shame is one of the affects driving these mass killings.

Similarly, the so-called incel movement ('incel' being short for involuntary celibacy) can partially be understood from the perspective of shame. Incel males, who feel like losers in an imagined struggle for access to attractive women, attack (often completely random) women whom they perceive as being to blame for their perceived defeat and humiliation (Kaiser, 2020). Their attacks – which, in extreme cases, include violent assault or even homicide – on random women may, to some extent, be driven by unbearable feelings of shame and inferiority stemming from feeling like losers who are rejected and excluded by women. At the same time, they are attracted to these women, and given their particular masculine worldview, they feel entitled to have access to them, simply by virtue of their self-perceived status as (mostly White) men. They try to deal with the feelings of shame and inferiority stemming from their de facto low social status through aggressive statements and attacks against the women who, in their view, are to blame for their embarrassing and shameful situation (Nussbaum, 2021, p. 35). Some aspects of their behaviour may also be seen as manifestations of shame-based self-hatred as a result of perceived humiliation and personal defeats, which is converted into hatred of women whom they are unable, for a number of reasons, to attract or have contact with.

Based on decades of experience with inmates in correctional facilities serving sentences for severe acts of violence, the American forensic psychiatrist James Gilligan (1996, 2003, 2016) has argued that violence is always triggered by – often fairly trivial – incidents where the self felt humiliated, ridiculed, disrespected and threatened by overwhelming shame. From this perspective, the violence may be seen as an attempt to undo loss of face and to evade or defend against shame (Gilligan, 1996, p. 110f.). Although Gilligan views shame as the primary cause and driver of violent attacks on others, shame is not in itself sufficient to trigger severely violent behaviour. In addition, shame has to be 'secret', unacknowledged and denied or hidden behind a facade of arrogance and toxic masculinity, just as shame typically primarily results in physical violence among individuals who have failed to develop the psychological and emotional resources that normally inhibit violent behaviour and enable a person to contain and deal with shame, threats to their own (generally low) self-esteem, exposed vulnerability and other painful mental states in more mature ways (Gilligan, 1996, p. 111f.). The stronger and more potentially overwhelming the shame is, and the poorer the person's capacity for psychologically containing and coping with painful shame, the stronger is the urge to hide the shame behind an aggressive facade or physical intimidation of others (cf. Gilligan, 2011, p. 99).

A number of researchers, including especially the American sociologist Thomas Scheff (1994, 2007), have described how unacknowledged destructive shame in individuals and in large population groups can drive escalating polarization and social conflicts in individual societies and in international conflicts, including acts of war. Similar psychological dynamics may underlie populist leaders' effective political mobilization of receptive individuals and population groups. Shame and anxiety that people are, for varying reasons, unable to face up to and acknowledge, whether to themselves or to others, are part of the emotional motivation that demagogues typically rely on to mobilize and brutalize parts of the population in political conflicts. These affect-driven strategies for political mobilization will typically be most effective among population groups struggling with unacknowledged shame, a tendency to experience or react with destructive shame in the face of perceived humiliation and, not least, a tendency to deal with unbearable shame through anger directed at selected individuals or social groups who are perceived as being the cause of the self's or the group's perceived humiliation and shame. In this situation, attacks on others help diminish and, not least, deflect attention from shame. The German social psychologist Leo Löwenthal (1949/2021) described the key role of the instrumentalization of perceived inferiority in Fascist propaganda and its capacity for politically mobilizing certain population groups – especially people in precarious situations who were struggling with feelings of inferiority, which is closely related to shame.

This may, for example, include people who are unemployed and feel humiliated and ashamed over not having a job, being unable to provide for themselves and relying on social welfare and who are outraged to see – as it appears through their subjective lens – migrants coming into the country and taking their jobs. Occasionally, they may escape their own unbearable feelings of shame humiliation by directing their anger at migrants and at the political leaders who failed to prevent this perceived invasion of hordes of foreigners coming in or 'the great replacement' (of White people by migrants with a different ethnicity).

Similar dynamics are seen, for example, among groups of mainly young men who share the view that their country and national culture and identity are under threat from Muslim immigration and who direct their anger at Muslims and symbols of Muslim culture, which they attack, disparage and seek to humiliate. All of these behaviours may, to varying degrees, be driven by anxiety and insecurity about the future and by more or less unacknowledged feelings of shame over occupying a precarious position in society and feeling vulnerable and powerless. These experiences are very difficult for them to reconcile with their more traditional perception of masculinity, which is centred on being strong and self-reliant and, in return, earning the respect of their community.

Public shaming and inducing shame in others can also be an important weapon in conflicts of interest and a core element of political strategies. Making others feel ashamed about their being and behaviour can make it possible to gain power over and control of them (Jacquet, 2015). For example, inducing 'meat shame' and 'flight shame' could be part of environmental climate campaigns, just as shaming people (especially women) for their sexuality and desire is common in gender-based cultural conflicts and efforts to preserve the power and position of certain religious institutions (and men in general). Similar shame-driven dynamics can be seen when public actors try to make selected others feel ashamed in order to make them change their ways or fall in line by stating that they feel violated by others' actions (Pfaller, 2022, p. 49). This involves gaining power by deliberately or unconsciously embracing victimhood, which will typically induce shame in others who are identified as transgressors. A similar dynamic is seen in masochism, as the masochist can sometimes be said to gain a form of power through their suffering and their position as victim and the subject of violation (cf. Wurmser, 1997, p. 380). Environmental researchers have also presented concrete proposals for the use of public shaming (or threats of it) to change social norms and human behaviour (Jacquet, 2015, p. 113ff.). Regardless of how noble and morally righteous the cause may be, the ethical defensibility of political campaigns that deliberately seek to induce and exploit people's vulnerability to feelings of shame is definitely debatable.

Ressentiment

The German philosopher Friedrich Nietzsche's use of the term *ressentiment* is often included in the understanding of the psychological dynamics underlying the human urge to deal with perceived suffering and shame by attacking others. Nietzsche writes about *ressentiment* and anger in relation to perceived pain and suffering:

> For every sufferer instinctively seeks a cause for his suffering; more exactly, an agent; still more specifically, a guilty agent who is susceptible to suffering – in short, some living thing upon which he can, on some pretext or other, vent his affects, actually or in effigy: for the venting of his affects represents the greatest attempt on the part of the suffering to win relief, anaesthesia – the narcotic he cannot help desiring to deaden pain of any kind.
> (Nietzsche, 1887/1969, p. 127)

Thus, according to Nietzsche, we should see *ressentiment* and the urge to attack and take revenge on the person who is perceived as being responsible for our pain as an attempt to dull our pain through intense affects.

Rather than consciously acknowledging and dealing with their pain, humiliation and shame in more mature psychological ways, a person may thus direct their attention and anger at others, seeking to use an even stronger affect in order to avoid being hurt and to divert awareness from their unbearable pain. For this purpose, according to Nietzsche (1887/1969, p. 128), they need a wild affect and an excuse for their affect: 'I suffer, someone must be to blame for it'. Nietzsche (ibid.) argues that this logic, this 'self-poisoning of the mind' (Scheler, 1912/1994, p. 45), is stronger the more unaware the sufferer is of the source of their suffering.

A strong person is less likely to be gripped by *ressentiment* and allow it to poison their soul and better at continually taking action to dampen the pain and painful affects that might otherwise gradually build up and lead to an increasingly toxic urge to take revenge on the person that they identify as being responsible for their suffering (Elgat, 2017, p. 42). Thus, a strong person is less likely to become bitter and flooded by resentment towards others when they experience adversity, setbacks or psychological pain. On this point, it is important to bear in mind that *ressentiment* and hate – unlike anger but like destructive shame – can be toxic and all-consuming affects that colonize the entire self and are directed at the other (cf. the object of hate) as a whole, not just their concrete acts. Also, the person who is feeling *ressentiment* does not necessarily have the reflective distance to their hate that is necessary for bringing it under control and preventing it from escalating and being manifested in attacks on others (Fuchs, 2021).

In a broader cultural and societal context, Nietzsche viewed *ressentiment* as an expression of what he called the driver of 'slave morality' – a moral driven by a shameful and hateful urge for revenge. He understood *ressentiment* in the context of the rebellion of the weak and oppressed and their revenge on a selected elite whom they perceive as evil, whilst they view themselves as 'good' people, with justice (and God) on their side (Elgat, 2017, p. 2f.). Nietzsche's philosophy has many problematic aspects, including his association of *ressentiment* with the birth of Christianity as the rebellion of the slaves and their revenge on their perceived oppressive rulers (Ansell-Pearson, 2012, p. 27). One of the key pillars of Nietzsche's philosophy is the will to power, the overman's struggle against the prevailing (Christian) morality, which is also a struggle against normal human conscience (the superego), guilt and shame (Wurmser, 1999). One of the goals of his philosophy was to transform many of the prevailing values of his time (grounded in Christianity) in order to set humanity free. This was also a struggle against what he perceived as weakness, shame and feelings of guilt over the failure to live up to prevailing obligations and requirements (ibid.). According to Nietzsche, human liberation involves no longer feeling shame over our own self. Nietzsche advocated a morality built on strength, self-control, willpower and eschewing all forms of weakness and exposure; a morality that may, in many regards, be regarded as a struggle against shame (Wurmser, 1999, p. 122f.).

Although these and other elements of Nietzsche's philosophy are clearly problematic and debatable, the core of his study of human *ressentiment* is both original and helpful for understanding how shame can be converted into and manifested as aggression, anger or even hate directed at others, including how shame turned into anger and rage can be a driver of populist movements in modern society. Even though he associated *ressentiment* with weak individuals who are unable to contain and deal with their pain in a more mature and dignified manner, he also described it as a natural human reaction (Elgat, 2017, p. 25ff.); a human urge to search for and identify others (something or someone outside the self) to be held responsible for our pain and discomfort. We look for someone we can blame, accuse and attack, and this is presented as being completely legitimate (Elgat, 2017, p. 32f.), as if we are fully entitled to place responsibility for our suffering outside ourselves. This dynamic can also be understood in light of the psychological defence mechanism of identifying with an aggressor, which involves trying to deal with perceived abuse and humiliation (external aggression directed at the self) and the related shame by attacking and humiliating others the way we were humiliated and attacked ourselves (see Section 4.3 and Améry, 1977, p. 114ff.).

Impulsively acting out the urge for revenge will generally lead to barbarism if it becomes the common practice in a society. On the other hand, it is problematic to deny the human urge to avenge perceived offences or to treat this urge as taboo. Instead, we should examine the underlying psychological processes behind it (Bernhardt, 2021; see also Akhtar, 2014), including shame as a driver. There is also reason to consider how this urge for revenge may be manifested in more civilized forms through the punishment of crimes in a modern society governed by the rule of law (see also Nussbaum, 2004) and how it may be dampened through reconciliation between individuals or social groups who have been trapped in self-perpetuating vicious cycles of mutual abuse and shaming. Similarly, it is worth considering what is behind the widespread fascination with stories about violent avengers who restore justice or the social order, as exemplified by Clint Eastwood's *Dirty Harry* films and some of Quentin Tarantino's extremely (aestheticized) violent films, including *Kill Bill* and *Inglourious Basterds*.

According to Nietzsche, *ressentiment* may also lead to more or less sophisticated attempts to reassess prevailing values and notions of reality in ways that are maximally advantageous for our own selves or our social group, for example by (1) elevating the significance of certain values and standards of social status that we do better on or (2) elevating the idea that everyone is equal in the eyes of God or in relation to another elevated power, body or authority (the people, the nation, the particularly authentic) to the highest standard, bringing previously privileged persons or groups down to the level of our own selves or social group. We may (3) embrace an idea of future reward and punishment (cf. the idea of the Last Judgment and so forth) for our own and others' being and actions, which makes us, at least, equal to others, even if others seem to be attributed greater worth and hold higher social status right now (in earthly life and so forth), or (4) we may make others comply with our values and make them feel guilty for previously overlooking, abusing or humiliating us (Elgat, 2017, p. 38f.).

By using these strategies, individuals can try to redefine their previously perceived weakness, low social status and suffering as signs that they are specially chosen or belong to a particularly important group (by virtue of their nationality, religion, ethnicity and so forth). These strategies all aim to dismantle and transform prevailing social hierarchies and criteria of high worth and social status and instead establish a status hierarchy based on, for example, national, ethnic or religious identity, perhaps supplemented with gender identity and sexual orientation, for example being 'a real man' in the sense of being heterosexual and masculine in certain specific ways (cf. Neckel, 1991, p. 168).

The wronged, narcissistically injured person can thus escape their experience of powerlessness and shame and of themselves as inferior and defective by blaming and attacking others (Stuewig et al., 2010, p. 92f.). In this sense, the person's vulnerability and insecurity are transformed into and manifested as anger directed at others. Sadness, anxiety and worries for their own selves become drivers of anger directed at a concrete other or a social group (Kimmel, 2013, p. 32). Instead of withdrawing or fleeing (passive), the person adopts a combat mode, attacking or seeking revenge (active). Taking revenge on the person or persons perceived as being to blame for one's suffering can help to restore self-respect and stabilize one's humiliated ego and compromised self-esteem. Finally, not least, it can reduce or divert attention from one's own shame.

This narcissistic rage may also be associated with grandiose beliefs about the rightful position of one's own self in the world and true (imagined) qualities, as the person tries to escape and defend against feelings of shame and inferiority through an explosive and self-perpetuating mix of rage and hate directed at others and grandiose thoughts about their own self and legitimate right to avenge perceived insults to the self (see Kohut, 1985, p. 141f.; Karterud, 1995, p. 90f.). According to Kohut (1985, p. 149), the most intense shame and most toxic narcissistic rage (urge for revenge) in relation to perceived insults to the self may arise in narcissistically vulnerable individuals with an extraordinary need for complete control of their immediate surroundings and persistent access to unconditional affirmation from others to stabilize their fragile self-esteem and prevent their self from fragmenting or dissolving.

The processes outline above play out in individuals, in dyadic relationships or in larger social groups, where they might be involved in turning shame into a powerful affective driver of political mobilization and escalating societal polarization, as one social group evacuates their own sense of powerlessness and inferiority and the related shame by identifying another group as morally reprehensible, primitive or inferior. When this also involves more explicit devaluation of or attacks on others, the targeted person or social group may suffer what they might be somewhat justified to perceive as unfair abuse and humiliation. Over time, this may lead to similar shame and anger in the target person or group, at which point all the involved parties may be caught up in what Scheff (1994, p. 49) calls 'feeling traps': self-perpetuating loops of escalating mutual alienation (empathy gap) and, at worst, mutual demonization and dehumanization as well as aggression, anger and hate grounded in and driven by unacknowledged and unbearable shame. To break these self-perpetuating feeling traps, the involved parties need to acknowledge their existence and understand how they are themselves driven by primitive emotions that are out of control. Furthermore, everyone will have to work on some form of reconciliation and mutual forgiveness that can serve as an anti-dote to the destructive shame and dampen the inclination to act out the urge to avenge perceived insults (cf. Wurmser, 2008, p. 962ff.).

When social groups form and organize around escalating *ressentiment* and anger directed at others, this process typically involves four key elements: (1) a common experience of fundamental injustice – the group, and thus its individual members, feels subjected to unfair and humiliating treatment; (2) a strong need to see justice restored, perhaps also an urge to be the force that achieves this; (3) a related urge for retribution and revenge for the perceived injustice and in reaction to experiences of humiliation and powerlessness; and (4) the construction of enemy images of identified external adversary or adversaries or abuser(s) (the person or group that is perceived as being guilty of perceived violations against the group and against justice) that, to varying degrees, are based on rigid black-and-white categories and thus contribute to internal and external polarization of reality. Furthermore, social groups' anger, hate and violence directed at others can be associated with and to some degree driven by the shared misperception that this will let them escape unbearable feelings of shame for feeling humiliated, inferior, vulnerable and weak.

At an emotional level, *ressentiment*-driven indignation and attacks on others may offer the added benefit or function of (temporarily and apparently) creating a sense of own agency, empowerment, power and control – in contrast to the passive withdrawal, submission and social isolation that often accompany overwhelming shame. Thus, feelings of weakness and powerlessness are then (at least superficially and temporarily) replaced by a sense of superiority and elevated status in relation to the person or group that is the object of anger, contempt and intimidation. In more extreme cases, shameful impotence is replaced by grandiose omnipotence, which is acted out as hateful attacks on others (Fuchs, 2021, p. 339). Shame is trumped or covered by its opposite: pride. At the same time, the person feels that the anger and attacks on the other are fully justified. They feel that their anger and aggressive actions against others are legitimate because 'the others', in the person's own subjective experience, are acting in ways that are morally dubious or, more specifically, are responsible for the person's own perceived suffering and pain.

Finally, it can be argued that anger directed at others, in contrast to passive resignation, represents a hope of change (Kimmel, 2013, p. 34), notwithstanding the objectionable and problematic aspect of handling one's own pain by blaming and attacking others for no reason besides the need to unload perceived pain and the responsibility for this pain. On the other hand, these attacks on others are rarely driven by anything remotely resembling rational objectives, let alone grounded in a realistic and sophisticated understanding of the object of the attack but in fact by the attacker's own vulnerability and need to deal with perceived humiliation and unacknowledged destructive shame. Hence, the most likely outcome of such a strategy is regressive and destructive behaviour, to the detriment of all involved parties, including the attacker.

Shame-driven polarization of the population: The case of the United States of America

Based on interviews with people from mainly Republican areas in the southern United States, sociologist Arlie Hochschild (2016) attempted to understand the background of the growing polarization of American society, where some population groups increasingly view each other with mutual contempt and a lack of understanding and willingness to even try to see the world from 'the other' side. Hochschild (2016) describes an 'empathy wall' running through American society that hampers mutual understanding and presents a major obstacle for reaching any sort of agreement about common solutions to common social problems. Based on her interview material, Hochschild summarizes what she calls the 'deep story' behind this social polarization. This story is not primarily about conscious and rational concerns in different social groups but about emotions, hurt emotions in particular, and what might be interpreted as manifestations of shame, including various strategies for escaping or coping with shame. It is a story that does not necessarily paint an objectively correct or adequate picture of the actual workings of American society but which feels right to the sections of the population where it is prevalent. In this case, it is the deep story among the lower social classes, especially Whites, in the American South.

Hochschild (2016, p. 136) describes how her interviewees' perception of the world is shaped by a narrative of persistent social progress, where individuals work hard and ultimately receive their just reward. Everyone is expected to show moral character, people take pride in providing for themselves and are proud of their Christian morality and heterosexual marriages. These are all elements that they view as a source of social status. By contrast, it is viewed as humiliating to be in a position of needing handouts or assistance from the state. It is shameful to need help from others, and it is associated with pride not to (ibid., p. 157). Still, some of the interviewees do accept federal aid and seem torn by an inner struggle between, on the one hand, their own precarious position, vulnerability and very real need for help and, on the other hand, the shamefulness of needing help (cf. ibid., p. 11). The deep story that Hochschild derives from her interview material includes the notion that as long as a person shows sufficient patience, they too will be able to realize a piece of the American dream. However, this story is developing deep cracks. Aided by the state – and political leaders – some people (primarily from minority groups) are being moved to the head of the queue, bypassing people who are, so to speak, waiting their turn to achieve the good life. Hochschild's interviewees view this as unfair, illegitimate and unjust and see it as a breach of society's unwritten rules.

According to the deep story, it is mostly women, Blacks and migrants who are given preferential treatment and allowed to skip ahead of others, mainly White males. That sparks indignation and a feeling that they are being betrayed by their political leaders; that the politicians are 'on the others' side'. 'Foreigners' are allowed to jump the queue, and many, especially White men, find that their social status, with its accompanying dignity and pride, is under pressure (Hochschild, 2016, p. 221f.). The values they associate with pride are no longer respected and do not provide the same social status, for example the values of being heterosexual, White and male (ibid., p. 144). They feel culturally marginalized and disrespected by the American establishment, which they think views them as backwards, sexist and homophobic because they value religion, heterosexual marriage and traditional perceptions of masculinity (ibid., p. 157). These experiences contribute to a sense that they are not receiving the recognition they feel they are owed; a sense of humiliation and that their social status is at risk, which are typical causes of shame. Thus, they constantly have to fight to be seen and respected.

Arguably, what Hochschild has uncovered is that her interviewees feel overlooked and disrespected and are struggling with unacknowledged feelings of shame, which they react to with anger towards the state as well as by selected others, including political leaders and various minority groups who are seen as having received preferential treatment (cf. Hochschild, 2016, p. 115). In natural extension of these observations, Hochschild's interviewees express their disgust with political leaders who help minority groups 'cut in line'. They hate the people who need federal and local government assistance, and they deny their own possible need for help and support from the welfare state (ibid., p. 151).

From a dynamic psychological perspective, these people seem to associate the need for help with shameful weakness and dependence. They deny the notion that they too might need help, and they are indignant and hateful towards others who need and accept help. They hate and detest the leaders who – as they see it – take something away from them and unfairly give it to others. These experiences can contribute to destructive divisions and polarization of the American population, especially if these underlying psychological processes, which seem closely tied to an undercurrent of shame and shame anxiety, remain unacknowledged and are thus allowed to shape how people perceive, meet and act in interpersonal interactions in concrete situations in everyday life and public exchanges. Thus, Hochschild's study can be viewed as an exemplary illustration of the basic psychological structure behind escalating polarization and division in a population driven, in part, by destructive shame. Hochschild (2016, p. 226f.) views her study as a contribution to an understanding of the sociopsychological reasons why large groups gather around charismatic leaders who promise to restore the social order and expel the people who are threatening it and the self's social status, and who are adept at instrumentalizing a common feeling of being subjected to unjust treatment, with the related experiences of humiliation and shame.

Donald Trump: Shame as political mobilization

Shortly after Hochschild had completed her study, Donald Trump was elected President of the United States, in part based on vague promises of restoring the country's national pride and thus the people's pride in being Americans ('Make America Great Again'). With his aggressive rhetoric, Trump incarnates the avenger who seeks to restore justice and a social order where the White man in particular regains his 'rightful' social status. Trump uses a highly polarizing rhetoric that pits different groups against each other – college graduates versus people with limited education, urban versus rural, the elite versus the people. He also activates and communicates understanding and recognition of the experience of large voter groups who have felt overlooked, forgotten and humiliated by America's economic and liberal elite. He verbalizes a deep-seated feeling of being unfairly treated and pushed aside in favour of other social groups, whom some groups perceive as less important members of society than themselves, which is both shameful and upsetting (cf. anger). Finally, not least, with his personal performance in the public arena, he embodies a feeling of anger that may spring from and be driven by many people's shame over feeling degraded, insignificant and as strangers in their own land (Hochschild, 2016).

Perhaps the most important affect involved in Trump's appeal to certain sections of the American population is anger (*ressentiment*); anger that is being channelled down (at migrants and people who take advantage of the system) and out (at foreigners, China, the liberal elite and so forth). In this way, he helps to justify the intense feelings of anger and indignation over the current perceived state of affairs, permitting and legitimizing it (cf. Hochschild, 2003, p. 181). As Pankaj Mishra (2017, p. 346) put it, the 'appeal of demagogues lies in their ability to take a generalized discontent, the mood of drift, resentment, disillusionment and economic shakiness, and transform it into a plan for doing something'. All these elements have the potential to bring large groups of people together around issues that offer a counterweight to the insecurity and lurking feelings of shame about their own precarious position in the people who join and identify with the demagogue and the social movement around them; feelings that Trump embodies with his appearance in public and on social media.

Trump has been described as the 'shamer in chief' (Haslett, 2016), instrumentalizing shame among Americans through his political mobilization, as he not only induces and intensifies the feelings of shame in his supporters with messages that 'we' and America have been short-changed (by China, NATO, trade partners and so forth) but also offers to help selected groups escape these painful feelings of shame. He does this, in part, by promising to 'make America great again', thus banking in advance on newfound pride over being American, especially a White American – and deflecting attention from the same people's potential sense of insecurity, uncertain economic situation and attachment to the labour market, which are associated with shame – and by shaming selected others ('nasty women', people from 'shithole countries' and so forth).

Roughly put, Trump helps his followers escape painful awareness of the shame they feel because of their own precarious situation by aggressively shaming selected others. He also contributes to the already escalating polarization in the American people by consistently dividing people into 'good people' (who are often idealized) and 'bad people', who are humiliated, ridiculed and shamed. Shame is translated into or trumped by rage over alleged or real humiliation and injustice (Watkins, 2018, p. 26f.). At the same time, the anger is not directed at the real causes of their precarious situation (profound economic inequality and so forth) but instead targets migrants, cultural liberals or non-White Americans.

As Max Scheler (1912/1994, p. 33) noted more than a century ago, democratic societies that have formal equality but are in fact characterized by widespread inequality in education, economic and material wealth and power are especially vulnerable to the development of explosive *ressentiment* in population groups, as the gap between these group's self-image and expectations of being taken seriously and their actual societal marginalization is particularly pronounced. Their marginalized position may give rise to shame, which can be exploited by populist leaders like Trump. With his aggressive anti-establishment and elite-bashing rhetoric and his articulation of the loss of security and social status of the traditional working class, Trump appeals especially to White men from Americas' lower social classes. He appeals to their shame about perceived humiliation, their socially precarious position and their worries about the future, which thus become a highly powerful factor in Trump's political mobilization – a mobilization that is driven much more by emotions than by substantial political messages or an actual political programme.

Trump's strong appeal in significant sections of the American population cannot be fully explained with reference to a few simple factors. However, his ability to speak indirectly to some Americans' shame about America's shrinking role in the world, both economically and as a result of some not particularly successful wars (Vietnam, Iraq, Afghanistan), as well as individual Americans' shame about their own insecurity, perceived failures and sense of being forgotten or disrespected presumably played a significant role in the emotional mobilization of large voter groups. Similarly, his ability to incarnate a near perfect mixture of shamelessness, narcissistic grandiosity and entitlement combined with anger (aggressive rhetoric) and apparent promises based on his own almost megalomanic ideas of restoring both national and individual pride has served as an emotional driver of his ability to mobilize large groups of voters. He has emerged as the leader of the forgotten and humiliated people (Hoggett, 2017, p. 375). Parts of the American population feel that he understands them, their losses and their precarious situation. In addition, through shared self-aggrandizing narcissism, including megalomanic ideas of restoring a social order where his supporters will regain the social status and worth they feel they deserve, he promises to compensate for or cover up their denied vulnerability and shame and give them renewed self-esteem and pride over being good Christians and law-abiding Americans (DeYoung, 2022, p. 120).

The situation in Denmark

Several writers have expressed concern about the potential for similar internal polarization and division in Danish society based on 'deep tension between cities and "the Danish periphery"' (Olsen et al., 2021, p. 29). In addition, there is a growing gulf between, on the one hand, sections of the population who are preoccupied with Danish national identity, economic redistribution, strengthening the welfare state, more traditional (religious and authoritarian) values and resistance to or concerns about immigration and, on the other hand, a population group that is much more focused on liberalization, tax relief, identity politics and turning Denmark into a multicultural society that welcomes migrants (ibid., p. 171). This concern is articulated, in part, with reference to growing income and psychosocial security inequality in Denmark, 'ghettoization' at the bottom of society, and a political and economic elite who are gradually losing faith in the welfare state and instead support increasing deregulation and economic liberalization, with the possible consequence that the internal cohesion of Danish society will be compromised, and the general population's distrust of society's elite will increase (ibid., p. 51, see also Meier-Carlsen, 2000).

These types of analyses and attempts to predict the future of Danish society invite many critical questions. Danish society is in a very different situation from American society. That said, it is certainly possible to point to early warning signs suggesting that, in the long term, existing divisions may grow to the point where certain population groups will have virtually no daily contact with each other, as they live in isolated socioeconomic enclaves (Olsen et al., 2021, p. 110) and may over time lose any sense and understanding of each other's life. This will provide a substrate for mutual alienation and internal polarization in the population in line with Hochschild's description of an empathy wall with the related risk of escalating fragmentation of society. The interesting point in this context is that it is possible to add significant depth and nuance to such an analysis by including possible underlying psychological processes, including shame, as possible drivers in the development of deeper division in Danish society.

By contrast, polarization and social conflicts in a society driven by shame and anger can be de-escalated if leaders notice, articulate and acknowledge the shame and the related anger and, not least, trade these significant affects to their possible roots in certain subjective experiences, including perceived insecurity and injustice and experiences of feeling overlooked or let down. Furthermore, it is essential to meet and treat all population groups with the same degree of respect and dignity, regardless of their social status, formal success or accomplishments. Leaders who either ignore or explicitly condemn dynamics in the population that are driven by shame and anger risk creating a situation where people do not feel seen and heard but instead condemned, alienated and excluded. This risks exacerbating these dynamics and can also put these leaders out of power. They may lose power to populist leaders who are able to articulate and instrumentalize the shame and anger that are driving social processes. The wise and only viable path to prevent these processes from escalating and getting out of control is for political leaders to explicitly see and acknowledge these strong emotions – without allowing them to control their actions by manifesting the shame and the related anger and hate in the form of concrete abuse of selected others (Scheff, 1994, p. 120f.). If society has a strong undercurrent of shame and anger, it is important to try to understand the underlying causes. Not least, responsible leaders should attempt to address the concrete conditions in society that cause such an undercurrent.

It is too simplistic and out of step with reality to assume that everyone who joins a populist movement is driven by *ressentiment*, shame and anger and either implicitly or explicitly excluding or writing them off as inferior or primitive (Müller, 2016, p. 20). We also should not disregard the ability of some populist leaders to articulate the feelings of disrespect, humiliation, disapproval and shame among certain social groups in a way that gives them a voice and helps them feel that they finally have political representation.

Unfortunately, this often takes a form that is arguably perverted and destructive, since some populist leaders, through their actions, mainly contribute to heightening social conflicts and social polarization rather than actually seeking to address the underlying social problems driving the strong affects in the population and society, which they simply channel and exploit for political mobilization. Populist movements can be driven by an explosive cocktail of perceived humiliation, degradation, injustice, destabilized self-esteem, anger and shame, which populist leaders at best capture, articulate, dampen and channel into constructive problem-solving. Others, however, will intensify the more destructive affective elements of these processes and use them as fuel for destructive attacks on vaguely defined categories of stated enemies, such as 'the elite', the 'deep state', migrants or political leaders who have not done enough to protect the interests of certain population groups (Sandel, 2020, p. 26).

Hitler and the appeal of Nazism

The German social scientist Stephen Marks (2021, p. 9) has described his own effort to uncover the reasons behind the appeal of National Socialism in Germany from the 1930s on. His conclusion is that feelings of shame played a key role. Germany's shameful defeat in the First World War and perhaps, not least, the subsequent shameful insult to and humiliation of the German people and the German nation in the Treaty of Versailles, which placed the blame for war entirely on Germany, helped lay the groundwork for a demagogue such as Hitler to go on to gain widespread support from large sections of the German people. Germany was forced to give up large parts of its territory and its overseas colonies, and the country was demilitarized and thus rendered defenceless. The treaty also required Germany to pay huge reparations to the other countries involved in the First World War. Many Germans found these humiliating conditions to be deeply unjust, which contributed to widespread self-contempt and shame. This in turn made many people receptive to a demagogue promising to restore the nation's pride and self-esteem.

Hitler thus instrumentalized the shame that was presumably widespread throughout large sections of the German population after the humiliating and degrading treatment of the German nation. This shame was so overwhelming and destructive that the German people – for a number of reasons – were unable to acknowledge and process it. With Hitler as their leader – their *Führer* – the German people instead sought to escape their destructive shame by directing anger and hate at selected internal and external enemies. Hitler also (like Trump) promised to rebuild the German empire and restore German greatness and pride. This new greatness would then compensate for or erase the widespread feelings of shame in the population. Nazi fantasies of greatness, including German world domination and the uniquely elevated status of the Arian race, combined with degrading treatment and shaming of inferior peoples and races, can be seen as manifestations of grandiosity, magical thinking and attempts to instil pride in Germany and German identity in order to provide a psychological defence against an underlying and painful sense of inferiority and destructive shame among the German people (Marks & Mönnich-Marks, 2008, p. 1030).

Hitler offered a so-called people's community ('Volksgemeinschaft') centred on being German. This bestowed a certain social status on people solely for being German (in contrast to non-Germans, enemies of the German people), which also offered to help dampen the shame of perceived humiliation. He also promised to restore social order in Germany, which to many people made him a clear contrast to what they perceived as the chaos and moral decay of the Weimar Republic (Scheff & Retzinger, 1991, p. 142f.). Despite Hitler's modest stature and fairly limited talent as a public speaker (in terms of content, most of his speeches are chaotic and incoherent), the National Socialist propaganda managed to present him as a representative of masculine power that could restore Germany's honour and make the nation great again by establishing the Third Reich, the third empire, thus redefining Germany identity as a source of pride, not shame (Marks & Mönnich-Marks, 2008, p. 1028). Similarly, Nazism's well-known contempt for weakness represents how people sought to deal with their own shameful weakness and vulnerability through stated contempt for weakness in selected others and a (cult-like) fascination with the strength of the masculine Arian body (Theweleit, 2019; Ofstad, 1971).

Hitler's emotional appeal to the German people, which was crucial for his impact, was based on his (at times apparently completely uncontrolled) anger and hate. With his often grandiose and aggressive speeches, Hitler incarnated the widespread anger and hatred that existed among large sections of the German population, partially driven by shame. This shame stemmed not just from the perceived humiliation in the wake of the First World War but also from the many concrete consequences of the escalating economic crisis in Germany, as millions of Germans during the years leading up to Hitler and the Nazis' takeover in 1933 were driven into mass unemployment and poverty, with the related feelings of humiliation, insecurity and uncertainty about their own future.

However, Hitler not only incarnated the widespread anger in German society after the First World War. He also exploited it in his political mobilization of the population and systematically directed it at selected population groups, especially Jews but also others who were identified as being responsible for the humiliation and defeat of the German people, including Communists (Bolsheviks) and capitalists. Thus, in several ways, he incarnated both the shame and a way to escape it through anger and hate directed at selected others, who were held responsible for the sufferings of the German people. He told the German people that they were not to blame for their perceived humiliation and shame. Instead, someone else was to blame (Scheff & Retzinger, 1991, p. 159), which in itself offers a form of release that may seem seductive (cf. also Nietzsche's concept of *ressentiment*).

It should be noted that Hitler never spoke about shame among the German people but instead of shamelessness among the German elite, for whom he felt profound contempt. Shame remained tacit and underground. *Mein Kampf* [My Struggle] (Hitler, 1925/1939) contains numerous references to shame but always veiled, as he spoke instead of inferiority or lack of self-esteem and consistently pointed to new greatness and pride as the path to overcoming inferiority and shame (Scheff, 1994, p. 114). By contrast, he was much more direct and explicit when he articulated, incarnated and intensified the anger that arises as a result of and in defence against shame. He also sanctioned and legitimized the hatred of Jews, in particular, and of the victorious Allied nations in the First World War, which subsequently became the driving force of the genocide of the Jews and the start of the Second World War. He did this with reference to the injustice, humiliation and suffering (narcissistic injuries) of the German people after the First World War – for which the Jews and the Allied nations were held responsible.

After expressing his indignation of how, in his description, 'the misfortunes of the Fatherland were even joyfully welcomed in the most shameful manner' by the German elite (Hitler, 1925/1939, part I, chapter X) in connection with the defeat in the First World War – stating that 'the downfall of the Second Empire and the German people has been so profound that they all seem to have been struck dumbfounded and rendered incapable of feeling' (ibid.) – Hitler wrote, for example, that the 'defeat was more than deserved by us', and that the military defeat was a 'well-merited punishment' (ibid.). He then described how he felt the German people ought to have reacted after the First World War: 'with clenched teeth', as 'fury ... filled their hearts against [the] enemy' – and how 'the capitulation would have been signed under the sway of calm reason, while the heart would have beaten in the hope of the coming *revanche*' (ibid.).

Here, as in numerous other places in *My Struggle*, Hitler – seemingly without reflection and completely governed by impulses – fluctuated between (possibly unacknowledged) shame about perceived humiliation (narcissistic insults), furious outbursts (narcissistic rage) against diffuse groups of selected others (the German establishment and elite, internal and external enemies) and an urge for revenge, restoration and new pride. He did this with recurring references to the German empire that had come into being 'with an aureole of historical splendour such as few of the older States could lay claim to' (ibid.). In a sense, large parts of *My Struggle* can be read as an exemplary illustration of how perceived defeat and humiliation and an inability to acknowledge and deal with the potential related shame can inspire some people to hateful attacks on others who are identified as being to blame for the perceived humiliation and to engage in visions of their own omnipotence, greatness and legitimate right to revenge (cf. also Nietzsche's concept of *ressentiment*).

In a more recent context, we may consider whether Russia's attack on Ukraine might be driven by destructive feelings of shame in Russian society and, especially, among the country's political leaders. In connection with Russia's full-scale invasion of Ukraine on 24 February 2022, President Vladimir Putin gave a speech (see en.kremlin.ru) to the Russian people (and the international public) that contains several indications of shame as a possible motivation. In the speech, Putin declared that Western leaders, especially the United States, have no respect for Russia – that they talk down to Russia from an elevated and infallible position and have violated alleged agreements about not expanding NATO to the Russian border. In the same breath as Putin spoke about feeling humiliated, disparaged, cheated and double-crossed, which is shameful, he launched attacks on Ukraine and repeatedly threatened the use of nuclear weapons. All of this was part of what he presented as a necessary and legitimate defence of 'Mother Russia', which, according to Putin, is threatened with extinction by external enemy powers. Thus, Russia's attack on Ukraine could be seen as an attempt to ward off unbearable shame over feeling unrecognized and degraded by others – who should recognize Russia as an equal partner or counterpart – through aggressive outbursts and physical attacks against others who, in various ways, are associated with perceived humiliation and threats to Russia's way of life, identity and existence. In this context, it may also, for example, be significant that former American President Obama stated that Russia is no longer a global superpower but only a regional power. Parts of the political and military leadership of Russia will presumably have perceived this as a grievous narcissistic insult and out of step with their own self-image and their image of Mother Russia – an experience that may in itself cause painful shame and anger, rage and a thirst for revenge. In extension of this point, the terror bombings of Ukrainian towns, cities and non-military targets seems driven by a primitive rage and hatred that might be understood with reference to perceived narcissistic insults and shame, among other issues, including attempts to correct perceived injustices and traumas (cf. the collapse of the Soviet Union) and restore the nation's fragile self-esteem. This self-esteem would have been further injured and destabilized by Russia's abysmal failure to realize its own apparent notions of its own massive military superiority and ability to destroy Ukraine as an independent nation in a matter of weeks or months.

6.8 Individual and societal psychology

Naturally, the actions and fate of an entire nation cannot be reduced to the actions of even the most powerful leader, let alone this leader's individual psychology and potential psychological disturbances, including their difficulties dealing with shame and perceived humiliation and wounded pride (see also Steinberg, 1991, about shame as a motivation behind Kennedy's and Khrushchev's actions during the Cuban Missile Crisis in 1962, when the world might have been on the cusp of nuclear war). However, it may be relevant to consider how prominent elements of the individual leader's psychology matches, acts out, resonates with and perhaps intensify prevailing psychological processes and affects among considerable parts of the population, which enables the leader to gain popular support (Scheff & Retzinger, 1991, p. 162f.).

Several researchers have pointed out how Hitler's ability to muster such widespread support might have stemmed from his ability (or unconscious urge) to externalize his own psychological difficulties and turn them into a resource in the political mobilization of the German people who were subject to some of the same psychological processes (Scheff & Retzinger, 1991, p. 142f.). A point that is often highlighted is Hitler's upbringing in a family dominated by a violent father and a mother who, intimidated by the father, was unable to protect little Adolf against the father's abuse (Scheff, 1994, p. 109f.). During his upbringing, Hitler was repeatedly subjected to humiliating treatment from a seemingly very authoritarian father, which may have contributed to his personal isolation and intense anger, according to contemporary observations. He could fly into a rage when he did not have his way and was allegedly worried about appearing ridiculous, weak, vulnerable or incompetent (ibid., p. 111f.). These features suggest an underlying feeling of shame and fragile self-esteem. Besides, we know that perceived insults and injustice early in life can lead not just to rage, bitterness and a diffuse urge for revenge later in life but also to a rigid and self-righteous attitude that in itself feeds and cements the urge for revenge and may become extraordinarily problematic if it is allowed to guide the actions of a powerful leader (cf. Weiß, 2017, p. 46; Wirth, 2002).

Although this is, naturally, far from an exhaustive explanation and needs to be supplemented with many other factors to provide a full or even somewhat adequate understanding, it can generally be argued that destructive shame was an important element in the fierce emotional factors driving Hitler's political mobilization, takeover and subsequent acts of war. His destructive shame and resulting anger developed into uncontrolled hate and subsequently found its relief in and was acted out as indescribable acts against the Jewish people and the initiation of the Second World War with attacks on Germany's neighbour countries. At an individual level, there is reason to consider whether soldiers who have been subjected to humiliating and degrading treatment during their upbringing or their time in the army will be more likely to dehumanize their selected enemies, ignore the rules of war and commit war crimes, driven by shame and a vague urge to avenge their own perceived humiliation by humiliating others.

After Germany's defeat in the Second World War, when the full extent of Germany's killings of Jews (as well as Russians and other Slavic peoples) became known, one might have feared a repetition of the global society's earlier failed strategy of extensive humiliating and shaming of the German people. In the long term, such a strategy could have become the foundation of another escalating cycle of destructive shame, anger and hatred directed at selected internal and external enemies. Fortunately, the global community chose a very different approach to post-war Germany this time, which aimed to help at least large parts of Germany – East Germany (the GDR) is a different story, and the reunited Germany still struggles with the impact of this – rebuild after the war (the Marshall Plan and other initiatives). Furthermore, (West) Germany was also gradually accepted as an equal member of the global community. This approach probably helped transform Germany into one of the world's most democratic and well-functioning countries, which for years has acted in ways that are far from war-like but even border on the excessively pacifist. Germany has also been among the most welcoming countries to refugees from war zones.

Furthermore, for many years, the German people and society have exposed and processed their widespread collective shame over the horrors of the Nazi regime, including the genocide of the Jewish people. What made Germany's guilt after the Second World War into something more than guilt and led to profound feelings of shame permeating the entire German society is the monstrosity of the actions of the Nazi regime. This made it impossible to find easy ways of atonement; something to restore a form of balance and enable forgiveness (Köhler, 2017, p. 57). Even if individual Germans do not feel individual or personal shame over the actions of the Nazi regime, they may still feel shame over what happened and was done in Germany's and, thus, their name as a people (Frevert, 2020/2023, p. 309). Among other acts, the German

Chancellor Willy Brandt's moving genuflection in front of a memorial in the former Jewish ghetto in Warsaw in 1970 is an iconic expression of the German determination to break the silence around and acknowledge their shame over the killing of Jews during the war (Köhler, 2017, p. 57) and to seek reconciliation with the many peoples and nations that were victims of Nazi Germany's acts of war and other forms of traumatic abuse (see also Walser, 1998).

To keep abusers from reoffending, we need to meet them with offers of help, care and love in order to make it a little easier for them to contain and process the shame they feel for their actions – not with renewed humiliation, exclusion and harsh punishment. All things being equal, that would primarily serve to intensify and give rise to new and more profound shame, with the risk that the abuser, in the long term, might once again be overwhelmed by anger and hate as defence against unbearable destructive shame.

After examining what characterizes the feeling of shame, especially destructive shame, and how it might be associated with individual mental disorders, trends in modern Western culture and societal dysfunction, the book's second to last chapter will address how therapists might detect, address and heal destructive shame in the psychotherapeutic space. The focus here is on individual psychotherapeutic treatment. Naturally, it will also be relevant to address shame in group, family and couple's therapy.

7   Psychotherapeutic work with destructive shame

The intention of this chapter is not to present a specific treatment model or therapeutic method, let alone specific techniques, for treating shame-related mental disorders. As discussed elsewhere (Jørgensen, 2019), with a few exceptions, there is nothing to suggest that any specific therapeutic technique or method is significantly more efficacious in the treatment of specific disorders (diagnoses) or psychological issues than any other, as long as we stick to commonly accepted treatment approaches. Thus, there is no indication that specific mental disorders are best treated with specific standardized methods. Instead, it appears that the main factor for the treatment outcome, especially in more severe mental disorders, including chronic destructive shame, is the personal qualities of the fully trained and well-educated therapist.

I am convinced that the therapist's ability to establish, deal with and maintain emotional and psychological contact that remains continually attuned to the individual patient's current state and needs is a crucial factor in the treatment of patients who, for various reasons, struggle with severe and destructive shame. The therapist's ability to establish and attune their way of acting in contact with the patient is especially crucial in relation to this group of patients, as the destructive shame affects the patient's capacity for being in contact with others, including therapists. The destructive shame is actualized, plays out and becomes evident in the therapeutic contact here and now in the therapeutic space. That may hamper the therapeutic process but also offers unique opportunities for the patient and therapist together to observe and work with the many faces and psychological dynamics of destructive shame, as they play out here and now, in the therapeutic contact.

As suggested earlier, naturally, this does not imply that the therapist should not be educated and trained in the use of one or more approved therapeutic approaches. They should. However, having completed continuing therapeutic training, being experienced and having received a certain amount of supervision are not in themselves sufficient, just as it is not decisive which of the widely approved treatment models the therapist is trained to practise. Thus, fundamental psychotherapeutic skills, including the ability to establish

DOI: 10.4324/9781003521174-7

a secure therapeutic space, to establish and maintain a basic psychotherapeutic stance (see Jørgensen, 2019) and to empathize with the individual patient's subjective experiences and inner world at any given time are crucial for the course and outcome of any psychotherapeutic treatment. These skills are only to a limited extent acquired through formalized education or training in specific therapeutic techniques; instead, they are psychotherapeutic skills that are developed by working in a psychotherapeutic environment, practising psychotherapy under competent supervision and gaining experience with many different types of patients and psychological difficulties. However, to some extent, they also represent more personal qualities which some people develop during the course of their life, and which everyone does not necessarily have the conditions for developing to the same degree or level.

7.1 Established treatment models

Therapy with patients who have light or moderate shame, including secondary shame resulting from a mental disorder where shame is not, inherently, the main issue, may, in principle, be based on any of a wide variety of commonly approved psychotherapeutic treatment models. In relation to this point, it can be argued that some approaches, including modern psychoanalytic psychotherapy (Maroda, 2012; Yeomans et al., 2015; Caligor et al., 2018; Mitchell, 1993), mentalization-based therapy (Jurist, 2019; Bateman & Fonagy, 2016) and compassion-focused therapy (Gilbert, 2009, 2011; Schlander, 2020) are well suited for the treatment of patients who are struggling with shame. However, compassion-focused therapy, which builds on cognitive behavioural therapy and, to some extent, evolutionary psychology, is probably mainly suited for patients without severe and more pervasive psychopathology, such as more severe personality disorders.

On the other hand, compassion-focused therapy was developed to offer targeted help to patients when shame appears to be their dominant problem and is not grounded in deeper personality disorders or severe traumatization (see also Brown et al., 2011). Thus, brief compassion-focused treatment or the involvement of compassion-focused elements may in some cases be appropriate for treating shame issues in individuals who are not showing signs that their perceived shame is associated with more comprehensive relational difficulties (attachment disorders), personality disorders or other severe mental disorders, including severe eating and substance abuse disorders. This approach may also be helpful for patients struggling with shame who, in addition to destructive shame, have developed a tendency for exaggerated perfectionism in an attempt to escape the perceived shame.

In any case, it is important to bear in mind that shame is always embedded in an inner psychological and relational context. This means that there are no quick fixes for feelings of shame based solely on the application of a specific technique or treatment model. Painful feelings of shame cannot be quickly 'removed' through a few technical interventions by a therapist or a pep-talk to convince someone who is struggling with severe feelings of shame that they have no reason to feel this way ('you're a good, likeable and helpful human being with lots of positive qualities').

Shame has to be healed in a healing relationship, as the other (the therapist) listens, pays attention and contains the patient's shame rather than dismissing or trivializing it as 'wrong', 'unrealistic' or 'unreal' (since this is not what it feels like for the patient; to them, the shame is only far too real). This is an effort that takes time and which places high demands on the therapist. The therapist's personal qualities and what plays out in the contact and interaction between the patient and the therapist will always have a key impact on the patient's treatment outcome. This also applies to the patient's benefit from compassion-focused therapy, a seemingly very specific technical approach to shame. If the focus is too narrowly on the effect of specific elements of the compassion-focused treatment, the empirical basis of the effect of these elements must be considered as tenuous. At this point, there are only fairly few and rather weak studies of more specific effects of compassion-focused therapy (Basran et al., 2022; Kirby et al., 2017).

Compassion-focused therapy aims to develop greater compassion with and care for self and others in the patient, including developing the patient's ability to give and receive care to and from real and imagined others (Matos & Steindl, 2020). Part of the focus of mentalization-based therapy is to improve the patient's ability to identify, reflect on and construct meaning in (mentalize) and communicate affects and other mental states, including feelings of shame. Finally, it can be argued that modern psychoanalytic psychotherapy has a particular focus on central elements of the contact between patient and therapist here and now in the therapeutic space with a view to breaking recurring pathological patterns in the patient's relationships and developing the patient's capacity for establishing and being in contact with others (Jørgensen, 2018b), which enables the patient to engage in interpersonal relationships in ways that are capable of detoxifying and ultimately healing destructive shame.

Varying degrees of shame, including severe and destructive shame, cannot be considered to form a delimited and specific mental disorder like, for example, depression or personality disorders. Destructive and socially debilitating shame is an issue that occurs in many different mental disorders, about which we would only occasionally say that the destructive shame forms the core of the patient's psychological difficulties. On the other hand, comprehensive and severely destructive shame may be or ultimately become a central affective driver of severe relational and attachment disorders as well as different forms of behavioural and substance abuse disorders (eating disorders, self-harm and so forth). Furthermore, destructive shame may be involved in certain sexual disturbances. Severe destructive shame will always have a dynamic psychological connection with other issues and should, to varying degrees, be considered as embedded in or a secondary consequence of, for example, attachment or personality disorders, alternatively a long-term effect of different forms of traumatization (see Chapter 5).

At this point, there are a several well-developed and, to varying degrees, validated concepts for the treatment of these more specific disorders, and there is no reason to develop a particular model or method for treating destructive shame. On the other hand, it is important for psychotherapists to be aware of the potentially central role of destructive feelings of shame in their patients' difficulties and to be qualified and able to decode and competently address them when they become evident or, perhaps, invade and threaten to destroy the contact in the therapeutic space. This is true whether the therapist is practising cognitive behavioural therapy to treat depression or mentalization-based treatment of personality disorders and so forth.

7.2 Assessing the patient's shame

When shame may seem to constitute a key issue for a patient in psychotherapy, the therapist should consider the following questions as part of the initial assessment:

- Is it initially possible to establish a deeper emotional and psychological contact with the patient? Is the patient able to talk about and engage in emotional contact with emotionally significant incidents in their life and to talk about their difficulties without becoming emotionally overwhelmed and chaotic and withdrawing from contact? If so, the patient is unlikely to be struggling with severely destructive and debilitating shame. However, if the contact with the patient remains formal and factual despite several discreet attempts to establish a deeper contact, if the patient appears emotionally unaffected (dissociated?), or if the patient, instead, becomes chaotic and perhaps characterized by (inward or outward) anger (expressing hate of or contempt for self or others?) when talking about their difficulties, it cannot be ruled out that the patient's difficulties are associated with destructive shame.
- How comprehensive and intensive is the patient's shame? Does it encompass large/all parts of the patient's life, or does it seem limited to certain relationships and social contexts? Does it present as severely destructive, profound and more or less chronic shame or, rather, more temporary and/ or less destructive shame, which might be related to the patient's temperament (introversion, shyness), fragile social competences, poor intelligence or other psychosocial challenges?
- What do the patient's feelings of shame appear to be about? What is the content focus of the patient's shame? Is it possible to draw a connection between the patient's shame and specific incidents or relationships in the patient's history?
- How does the patient deal with their feelings of shame? What strategies are dominant in the patient's attempts to regulate and defend against feelings

of shame? Does the patient attack self or others, do they withdraw from contact, do they dissociate in an attempt to deal with or escape shame (cf. Section 4.3)?

- Does the patient appear to have grandiose self-beliefs – and might these, perhaps, be associated with accompanying signs of fragile self-esteem? If so, this might indicate that patient is hiding destructive shame behind a mask of grandiosity.
- Setting the patient's shame-related difficulties aside, does the patient appear fairly well-functioning, or are there indications of more comprehensive psychological difficulties that might suggest one or more psychiatric diagnoses? Does the patient meet the diagnostic criteria of a personality or eating disorder? Are there signs of severe self-harm or some form of substance abuse that might serve as a strategy for dampening or escaping destructive shame? All the diagnostic categories mentioned here are often associated with destructive shame (see Chapter 5).

A variety of terms may be used to capture the impact of individual dynamic psychological differences on the individual patient's capacity for containing and regulating affects, including shame – for example, degree of ego strength (Loevinger, 1976), level of personality organization (Arbeitskreis OPD, 2014) and mentalizing capacity (Bateman & Fonagy, 2016). In case of lower levels of personality organization (structural personality disorders), affects are often more primitive or archaic. This includes feelings of shame typically being more destructive and out of step with the actual, current situation rather than largely constructive and less intense. In this case, the patient is more easily overwhelmed and quicker to react with impulsive acts or attempts to shut down, perhaps because they tend to under- or over-regulate affects and other mental states and to perceive negative (shameful) beliefs about self and others as 'the truth'. The patient is more likely to function in a psychological equivalence mode (Bateman & Fonagy, 2016) and finds it harder to maintain a certain reflective distance from and ability to think nuanced thoughts about their own affects and reactions in general (cf. Benecke & Henkel, 2021, p. 22). In this situation, the therapist needs to lower the pace, structure how and how quickly the patient comes into contact with and has their shame articulated (preventing the patient from being flooded by destructive shame and needing to shut down or withdraw from contact) and place a special emphasis – even more than when working with better structure patients – on creating a therapeutic space where the patient can disclose shameful parts of their self while feeling contained and unconditionally recognized, rather than feeling abandoned by a 'neutral' therapist who keeps strictly to rational analysis (Tiedemann, 2010, p. 177; Killingmo, 1989, p. 66).

The following sections describe selected focus points, issues and treatment strategies that might be significant in psychotherapeutic work with patients struggling with destructive shame, who may otherwise have a variety of psychiatric diagnoses. One of the general challenges of working with more chronic and severely destructive shame is that since these feelings of shame are largely hidden or non-verbalized, the therapist needs to be able to sense and decode when the patient's ways of being and acting in the therapeutic space are influenced or perhaps controlled by underlying destructive shame. Another challenge is that shame is generally actualized and intensified in interpersonal contact, including in the patient's contact with the therapist, and this is precisely the contact in which the therapist has the opportunity to register, contain, process and thus dampen the patient's destructive shame. In psychotherapeutic work with destructive shame, the goal is not to erase the patient's shame (which is neither possible nor desirable) but to detoxify its destructive character, make it less comprehensive and less intense and transform it into more constructive forms, where it can support the patient's capacity for social functioning instead of undermining it.

As suggested earlier, the unique possibilities for emotional and psychological contact between patient and therapist that exist due to the particular organization of the psychotherapeutic space and the therapeutic relationship are thus associated with a significantly elevated risk of activating the patient's destructive feelings of shame. Occasionally, the patient will find that their painful shame is briefly exacerbated by the therapeutic process. Destructive shame is closely related to feeling observed and assessed and being in contact with others – elements that are inextricably part of psychotherapy and thus risk factors for activating shame in the therapeutic space. At the same time, however, the psychotherapeutic process offers unique opportunities for the therapist to gain insight into how the patient's psychological life is affected by shame and, in extension of this, to help the patient get better at containing and managing the perceived shame. The fact that the therapist is involved both in evoking the destructive shame in the patient and in helping the patient manage it may seem slightly paradoxical (Bromberg, 2006, p. 90) and places high demands on the therapist's ability continually to strike the right balance between the patient's different concerns and needs. The therapist should avoid acting in ways that contribute to shutting down the patient's shame, which would cause the patient to continue to feel alone with the unbearable shame. On the other hand, the therapist should also avoid exposing and intensifying the patient's shame to a degree that causes the patient to be overwhelmed by destructive shame and needing to activate various types of defences against it.

7.3 Emotional and psychological contact

For psychotherapeutic work to contribute meaningfully to the patient's development and recovery process, both patient and therapist need to be prepared and, to some extent, able to be open to intersubjective emotional and psychological contact in the therapeutic space. As part of this, the patient has to gradually give the therapist access to their inner life and some of their most painful experiences and difficulties, which the patient may so far have kept secret and attempted to deal with alone. This in itself contains a significant risk of inducing shame in the patient – and, to some extent, in the therapist, who may both be 'infected' by the patient's activated shame and feel shameful for having moved a little too close to the vulnerable patient or having moved a little too fast and thus contributed to the patient's experience of suddenly being overwhelmed by icy feelings of shame. Therapeutic work with patients who are struggling with destructive shame thus requires the therapist to be able to structure, dose and help control the pace of the patient's self-disclosure in order to prevent activation of massive destructive shame, which may over-whelm the patient to a degree that approaches a traumatizing experience.

When we interact with others, we will often 'rediscover' our own feelings and beliefs about ourselves as we interpret others' gaze and reactions to us; feelings and beliefs that are grounded in our past relationships and experiences with how important others have seen and reacted to us. In more concrete terms, this means, for example, that a shameful patient who is struggling with recurring feelings of destructive shame will transfer their own negative experiences from past relationships, where they felt wrong and shameful, to their interaction with the therapist. The patient will then be likely to interpret the therapist's gaze in a way that matches how they were previ-ously viewed by important others and how they normally see themselves: as a defective, inferior, insignificant object that others condemn and meet with humiliation and ridicule. The patient will generally perceive the therapist's gaze at and perception of the self as variations on what they are used to seeing in interactions with others and, thus, as an affirmation of what they more or less consciously fear and expect (cf. Tiedemann, 2010, p. 68).

A patient who is used to and afraid of being met with condemnation and rejection will generally perceive the therapist's gaze at and reactions to the self as indications that the therapist rejects and condemns the self, as others have. This is especially true if the patient has disclosed a sliver of their true identity, with all their perceived disastrous faults and deficits. In this way, the patient transfers their negative experiences with emotional contact to the therapist. This may contribute to the patient's feelings of insecurity and make them asso-ciate the therapist's gaze with feeling intimidated, condemned, humiliated, pushed into submission and being overwhelmed by shame. In this light, it is not surprising if the patient initially tries to avoid deep emotional contact with the therapist, avoids eye contact and is reluctant to answer the therapist's deeper questions – or if the patient, instead, becomes aggressive, attacks or tries to control the therapist in response to even minor attempts at establishing deeper contact and any indication that the interaction might activate feelings of shame.

In extension of this point, it is a key task for the therapist to disconfirm the patient's negative expectations of what is going to happen in the therapeutic space and in attempts at emotional contact with the therapist; expectations that repeatedly activate and intensify the patient's shame and other difficul-ties. In this way, the therapist can help the patient gain new, corrective emo-tional experiences in the therapeutic interaction, which is vital to a shameful patient's recovery process. When the therapist acknowledges their own misunderstandings, deficits and faults in interactions with the patient in an open and balanced way (without overdoing it such that the therapist appears incompetent, seems to be angling for the patient's forgiveness and so forth), this not only helps to build trust and promotes the patient's willingness to be open to emotional contact. By providing a contrast to the patient's earlier negative relational experiences, it can also help the patient see how past and current relationships differ and help break a pattern that has been keeping the patient locked into the expectation that all interactions will necessarily be re-enactments of maladaptive past relationships (Ferenczi, 1933/1988, p. 200). This in itself has the potential to enable a new, correctional emotional experience that can help dampen and heal the shame.

It is almost impossible to avoid evoking feelings of shame in the therapeutic process, especially when working with patients who are struggling with destructive shame, regardless of the therapist's attempts to minimize the risk. When it happens, the patient's perceived shame should be the focus of joint attention and the therapeutic process. The therapist should not necessarily do this right away by immediately verbalizing the patient's shame as shame. Perhaps it can be done a little later in the same session or in a subsequent session, when it no longer feels as shameful and emotionally overwhelming for the patient to confront their shame and the fact that the therapist witnessed the patient being overwhelmed by shame. If the therapist is too quick and too explicit, and thus too confrontational, in verbalizing the patient's shame as shame, with the related massive perceived inferiority and humiliation of the patient's self, this can contribute to increased distance between patient and therapist (as the patient withdraws to protect their fragile self). Alternatively, it may make the therapeutic conversation lapse into a joint intellectualization of the patient's (and the therapist's) shame without any real emotional grounding as a common defence against feelings of shame that are too painful to connect with, perhaps for both the patient and the therapist.

As a minimum, however, the therapist should always explicitly communicate to the patient that they notice it when something is difficult for the patient here and now, including when the patient is overwhelmed by shame (or other painful affects) in the therapeutic space. Next, it should depend on a concrete assessment of the patient's current state and needs and of the concrete situation whether the therapist – in close dialogue with the patient – should delve into the patient's feelings and experience. This may include examining, with the patient, what the current shame (or perceived sense of inferiority, inadequacy, own defects) might be about: what the patient feels shame about (for example, 'I am stupid') and what might have triggered it in the moment ('I didn't know how to respond to your question') – such as a topic that came up in the conversation ('something happened at the parent–teacher meeting last week'), something the patient just came into contact with ('my ex-partner humiliated me') or something the therapist said (for example by drawing a connection between what happened at the parent–teacher meeting and 'what always happens when I am in a social setting'), did (for example, noticing that something was getting difficult for the patient) or did not do (not explicitly noticing and empathically mirroring that it was difficult for the patient to talk about a particular topic or experience).

In relation to this point, the therapist needs to remember that it can be shameful for the patient to be seen as they really are and as they feel right now (to feel accurately empathically mirrored) behind, perhaps, many different facades, and avoidance and defensive strategies – with their shame and all their shameful sides – as the person's perceived defective self is exposed and revealed, whether to a therapist or someone else. In fact, however, it may be at least as shameful not to be seen for who we are (the real self, which is not seen and thus has no chance for recognition) and instead being seen as someone else – either as the delusional fronts and facades we put up and hide behind or as the person others want us to be. Similarly, most patients with destructive shame will have an intense experience of duality or ambivalence: on the one hand, they will have a burning desire for contact with others to help them escape deep and painful loneliness, and on the other hand, they are afraid that this contact will once again cause them to be overwhelmed by catastrophic shame. Alternatively, they may also fear becoming too emotionally dependent on the therapist, who appears to be able to see, contain and understand them, or they might be unsure whether they will ultimately end up paying a high price for the desired contact or fear that the disclosed sides of the self will be used against them (cf. their often pronounced lack of basic trust in others as a result of earlier perceived betrayals and boundary transgressions).

In some cases, it may be helpful to work with the patient to develop a common language for how the patient can contain different parts of the self or inner voices and somewhat contrasting emotions. This is relevant in relation to the patient's desire for and fear of contact – as part of the patient reacts very strongly to shame and withdraws from contact, while another part yearns for and values contact – but also in relation to the fact that part of the patient, for example, hates themselves or other parts of themselves, while other parts might be less hateful but have a little more empathic understanding for themselves. Articulating the fact that the patient contains both a very strict and unforgiving inner judge that is closely associated with the patient's destructive shame and a less strict, kinder and more forgiving inner observer or voice, which might be oppressed and has difficulty being heard, may help create an inner space for dialogue: a transitional space in between the internal and the external reality that is crucial for our ability to detach from our rigid beliefs about self and others (Winnicott, 1971). Some patients will have grown up in a family and a social context where they never had the chance to develop a kind, forgiving and caring inner voice. In that case, it is important for the therapist to help the patient develop such an inner voice, mainly by always seeing and meeting the patient with a loving, kind and caring gaze in the therapeutic interactions.

When the patient's inner conflicts are articulated and become the focus of the psychotherapeutic process, in part by making these conflicts and their concrete consequences clear to the patient, this may weaken the patient's identification with more destructive sides of their own self (cf. the notion of the internal saboteur and identification with the aggressor). In more concrete terms, for example, this may be an inner conflict in the patient between, on the one hand, a merciless inner judge or saboteur and parts of the patient's self that are characterized by massive destructive shame, self-contempt and an urge to humiliate and destroy themselves and, on the other hand, parts of the patient's self that are capable of containing incipient compassion with and understanding of the self's not necessarily self-inflicted difficulties and which have sought help and are trying to hold on to a hope for the future. To the extent that the process succeeds in weakening the patient's identification with more destructive parts of the self and the related destructive shame by developing greater awareness of this inner conflict and its roots in earlier relationships and by having corrective emotional experiences in the therapeutic relationship, this may improve the patient's opportunities for expressing more constructive emotions and parts of themselves, for example the ability to experience joy and love and the ability to be playful, open and curious in encounters with the world and other people.

Articulating different sides of the patient can enable a gradual integration (and thus moderation) of these parts of the self. Not least, this can help the patient attain a certain reflective distance from the most destructive parts of themselves and from the inner voices that are most closely associated with the patient's destructive shame. This represents an inner reconciliation of polarized parts of the self that is closely associated with the inner integration of the patient's personality. In some cases, it can be helpful to identify the patient's unforgiving inner judge and destructive shame as a common external enemy who makes the patient hate and despise themselves, while the therapist attempts to form an alliance with the more fragile and vulnerable but also often healthier and more forgiving parts (cf. DeYoung, 2022, p. 234). Finally, the therapist and patient can work together to explore 'who' in the patient's history it might be 'that is talking' (in many cases, it is a parent) when the patient places unrealistic demands on themselves and hates, despises and humiliates themselves for being inadequate, defective and 'a loser', thus inducing and maintaining destructive shame (Tiedemann, 2010, p. 240).

7.4 The patient protects themselves against overwhelming shame

Acknowledging the presence of psychological difficulties which are so profound that the person cannot deal with them on their own but needs help can in itself be associated with shame. This shame may be further heightened when the person sits in front of a concrete therapist and needs to talk about their problems. In this situation, the person reveals their weakness, vulnerability and difficulties to another person. The patient may feel that this other person not only sees, judges and evaluates them but also condemns them, their exposed weaknesses and their inability to solve their problems without outside help (cf. the widespread notion of the ideal human being: a self-reliant, autonomous individual; see Chapter 6). Many people who are struggling with shame despise themselves for not simply being able to pull themselves together and deal with their own problems rather than 'whining', 'exposing themselves' and losing themselves in 'miserable self-pity'. Precisely because it generally takes a considerable effort and commitment (or a temporary truce in an inner struggle) for a patient struggling with shame to seek help, it may be helpful if the therapist from the outset clearly recognizes and validates the patient's desire and decision to seek help.

Furthermore, it is important to note that for most people, it can be overwhelming and involve various degrees of shame to be the object of a therapist's undivided, constant and interested ('nosy') attention and, perhaps, intense personal presence for a full hour or however long a session lasts. In addition, the conversation in the therapeutic space may bring the patient into contact with emotions, memories and parts of themselves that they may have kept shut down for a very long time and that certainly have not been shared with many others (if anyone), which can in itself be emotionally overwhelming and associated with shame. This challenge may be further heightened for people who feel shameful about getting emotional, especially in front of others. This applies especially to people who, for various reasons, struggle with destructive shame and a general tendency to react with shame in a wide range of situations when they find that their inferior and defective self is exposed, revealed and made the object of what they perceive as the therapist's judging (condemning) and humiliating gaze. This experience will generally be driven by the patient's projection of their own merciless inner judge and their own self-contempt on the therapist and now, so to speak, 'meeting' these parts of themselves in their subjective perception of the therapist's gaze.

If the therapist does not manage to register and help the patient regulate the shame that will almost inevitably be activated in the therapeutic space, it can become a serious obstacle in the treatment. Especially with patients who are struggling with high levels of destructive shame, it can be virtually impossible to do psychotherapeutic work if the therapist is unable to help the patient regulate their shame and bring it down to a manageable level where it does not persistently overwhelm the patient, which would make it impossible for the patient to be emotionally and mentally present in the therapeutic space and remain in contact with the therapist. Over time, the state of being overwhelmed can become so unbearable for the patient that it may feel necessary to withdraw from any emotional contact with the therapist and with themselves (to dissociate) or even break off the treatment.

As discussed earlier, feelings of shame are usually masked, and the patient is not necessarily consciously aware of – and thus able to articulate – their shame. This makes it likely that some therapists will overlook feelings of shame in their patients and underestimate the dynamic role of feelings of shame as a driver of their difficulties and of the psychotherapeutic process. Several empirical studies (Hill et al., 1993; Macdonald & Morley, 2001; Hook & Andrews, 2005; McElvaney et al., 2021) have shown how shame can inhibit the patient's openness towards the therapist. Among other consequences, this means that a patient with destructive shame will, to varying degrees, avoid telling their therapist about symptoms and emotionally significant experiences because they find this disclosure shameful. In a study of depression treatment, 54% of the patients (n=85) reported keeping central symptoms and stressful experiences, including physical and sexual abuse, hidden from their therapist. Of the patients who chose not to disclose certain experiences, 69–75% referred to shame as the cause (Hook & Andrews, 2005). Similarly, another study (Macdonald & Morley, 2001) examined to what extent patients (n=34) in psychodynamic treatment tell their therapist about significant emotions in between treatment sessions. In this study, the patients reported that they avoid sharing as many as 68% of these significant emotions in between sessions with their therapist. In more than 90% of the cases, shame was stated as a contributing reason.

Naturally, a treatment session rarely leaves time for the patient to discuss all their significant experiences since the previous session, just as it is far from given that it is necessary or meaningful to work through all the patient's significant experiences. Instead, the key is rather how they are addressed. Nevertheless, these findings underscore how important it is for the therapist to be able to register and address the individual patient's shame in a qualified manner in the therapeutic space. A small number of studies (Black et al., 2013) further found a relationship between, on the one hand, patients' tendency to withdraw from contact and shut down their own emotional reactions in defence against shame and, on the other hand, problems in the therapeutic alliance, which further underscores the importance of the therapist's ability to register and deal with the patient's shame. It is also important to bear in mind that patients may feel an extraordinary degree of shame when talking about strong (positive and negative) emotions and experiences in relation to the therapist. As a result, the patient may not disclose subjective experiences and emotions that might be highly significant for both the therapeutic alliance and the therapeutic process.

Precisely because painful feelings of shame and fear of being overwhelmed by shame will often keep us from opening up to others, what is sometimes referred to as the patient's 'resistance to treatment' or 'lack of motivation for treatment' may in fact reflect a fragile and vulnerable patient's attempt to protect themselves against situations where their self and difficulties are 'revealed', displayed and exposed and the patient therefore – perhaps not entirely without reason – fears being overwhelmed by feelings of powerlessness, inferiority and shame. In some cases, this may also be related to the therapist's inability to register and deal with these difficult situations in the therapeutic space in a sufficiently qualified manner (Lewis, 1987b, p. 24).

Some therapists may even find it 'easier' and less demanding if the patient keeps any strong positive or negative feelings towards the therapist to themselves. In order to avoid coming into contact with, sensing and acknowledging painful past experiences and their related painful feelings, including destructive shame, the patient may avoid engaging emotionally in the therapeutic process and contact. In a more concrete sense, this may, for example, cause the patient generally to appear tight-lipped and evasive and to offer mainly evasive, brief or superficial responses to the therapist's interventions. Alternatively, the patient may be very active and talkative in an attempt to control the therapeutic space and prevent the therapeutic conversation from moving into topics that might activate the patient's shame.

The patient might maintain some distance from the therapist and the therapeutic process in an attempt to avoid feeling exposed and laid bare in the eyes of the therapist – not out of ill will or in a deliberate effort to obstruct or sabotage the treatment and the therapist's interventions but in an attempt to protect a vulnerable self. In fact, this may have destructive consequences for the patient, as it may negatively affect the treatment outcome. Even if the patient is, to some extent, aware of this, they may not dare to scale down these self-protective strategies. Typically, the patient will have developed these strategies over the course of many years and found that they help prevent dreaded violations of boundaries or psychological breakdowns. The patient may also have found that allowing deeper contact can have profound consequences if the contact goes wrong, in the sense that past traumatic experiences or extreme letdowns in contacts with others are repeated in the contact with the therapist. In relation to this point, however, it is important to bear in mind that this does not mean that the treatment of patients with even very severe destructive shame will necessarily be without effect. Far from it. However, it does mean that the therapist must approach the situation a little differently: during some stages (especially the initial stage when the alliance is being established), the main focus of the treatment should be on addressing the patient's difficulties with establishing and remaining in contact – both with the therapist and with shameful parts of the self and their own history. The treatment should also be expected to take considerably longer, the more severely past relational traumas and destructive shame have damaged the patient's capacity for contact.

7.5 The language of shame

As mentioned earlier, shame is associated with a strong urge to hide behind various masks. Patients who are tormented by destructive shame will have learned to survive through emotional isolation, avoidance of deep contact with others and hiding behind a – sometimes rather convincing – facade. Hence, it might be difficult for the untrained eye to register the patient's shame and its immediate psychological consequences for the patient. If the therapist focuses solely on what the patient explicitly describes as their core problem, there is a considerable risk of overlooking any feelings of shame and their consequences for the patient.

Typically, the patient will not explicitly mention their shame or its extent but may offer more diffuse descriptions of feeling inadequate, inferior, invisible, wrong or awkward in social situations. These experiences may be manifestations of destructive shame, but therapists who are unfamiliar with the psychology of shame may be likely to classify them 'simply' as low self-esteem, shyness or introversion. A therapist who works with patients whose destructive shame is likely to be a significant part of the dynamic behind diagnosed psychological difficulties should be familiar with the 'language' of shame (which is not a verbal language, as the patient's feelings of shame have typically not been verbally articulated), including its many diverse manifestations and its tendency to hide behind various masks and constructed facades (Morrison, 1989, p. 196).

The language and many possible masks of shame, which may be manifested both in the patient's stories and in the intersubjective contact in the therapeutic space, include the following manifestations, among others:

- Feeling wrong, ridiculous, inadequate, inferior, invisible, insignificant, worthless, in the way, 'like a loser' – extremely low self-esteem;
- Feeling fake, inauthentic, like a fraud, like an imposter – because the person feels compelled to hide behind a facade, a happy and positive mask that signals a level of self-esteem and self-reliance that is out of step with their inner reality;
- Expressions of anger, rage, hate, contempt and disgust directed at the self or selected others;
- An urge to avenge perceived abuse or injustices (cf. the relationship between perceived narcissistic injury, shame and an urge to avenge perceived violations or abuse in an attempt to escape shame);
- Passivity, silence;
- Avoiding eye contact or, alternatively, maintaining an invasive stare on the other;
- An urge to avoid or withdraw from (emotional and psychological) contact and from social situations – including a general inability to establish deeper psychological and emotional contact with others (including the therapist);
- Submission, masochism (traits and behaviours);
- Grandiose and omnipotent ideas about the self and its significance.

Destructive shame is typically associated mainly with silence, wordlessness and a stronger tendency to withdraw from contact, just as most attempts at examining and talking about the destructive shame – corresponding to what is normally viewed as the core of psychotherapeutic treatment – will activate and intensify the destructive shame and thus hamper or even block the therapeutic process. Conversely, some (often more narcissistic and

acting-out) patients may try to escape destructive shame through externalization, anger and rage directed at others, including the therapist and their faults,
deficits and incompetence in the eyes of the patient. The destructive shame
is anti-dialogical and accompanied by a tendency to shut down close emotional contact with others instead of the effort to open up and seek contact,
which is an important element in a normal psychotherapeutic treatment process (Skårderud, 2001c, p. 1613). As mentioned earlier, this does not mean
that psychotherapeutic treatment of people struggling with destructive shame
is impossible, it merely requires a slightly different approach.

7.6 Dealing with shame in the therapeutic space

Therapists need to be able to maintain awareness of how the patient's
apparent aversion to the treatment process and tendency to obstruct it are in
fact manifestations of a very vulnerable patient's fear of harm to their own fragile self – which makes it necessary for them to protect the patient against too
much and overly intense contact with the therapist and with strong emotions
and other mental states. In more concrete terms, this means that the therapist
needs to lower the pace, proceed with patience and give the patient more
time to develop the trust that is a condition for the patient to dare to come out
of hiding and engage in emotional contact. This also means that the therapist
has to be prepared that effective psychotherapeutic work with patients who
are struggling with severe destructive shame may take quite a long time and
may not readily lend itself to an organizational framework where the duration of treatment is predetermined, dictated by economic constraints or a
rigid idea that all patients with a given diagnosis should be offered the same
standardized treatment.

The therapist must continually adapt their interventions and invitations for
contact to match the patient's current state and what the patient is able to
handle without being overwhelmed by shame, cognitive chaos and emotional
dysregulation. The therapist should continually offer empathic mirroring and
validate both the patient's need to protect their self against harm – and the
concrete strategies they implement to do so – and what appears to be the
concrete background for the patient's self being so vulnerable and fearful
of what might happen if they allow closer emotional contact with others.
The patient's trust in the therapist and their ability to be open to contact do
not emerge in an instant but develop over time as the accumulated effect of
numerous moments or relational exchanges in which the patient felt seen,
heard and met by an empathically responsive therapist (DeYoung, 2022,
p. 81). Conversely, even brief incidents in the therapeutic space in which the
patient feels overlooked, misunderstood or humiliated by the therapist – and
finds that the therapist affirms their own shameful negative self-perceptions –
risk leading to severe ruptures in the patient's trust in the therapist and shutting
down intersubjective contact for an extended period, especially if the therapist fails to register, articulate and address it in a dialogue with the patient.

Often, severely destructive shame and the related fear of establishing emotional contact with others – contact that is crucially important for the patient's ability to escape painful emotional loneliness – stems from early attachment traumas or later stressful experiences in contacts with others, which might have subjected the patient to severe neglect, violations of their boundaries of intimacy (sexual or physical abuse) or severe and extensive bullying in school. This relationship between harmful experiences in early relationships and the patient's current need to protect themselves against the risk of renewed harm in the relationship with the therapist here and now may need to be articulated to the patient repeatedly, with minor variations depending on the concrete manifestations of this dynamic psychological relationship across different situations.

The relational experiences of a patient who is struggling with shame will often involve an extreme imbalance. This means that it takes a fairly high number of positive and trust-building experiences in a new relationship (including a therapeutic relationship) for the patient to build sufficient trust and confidence in the relationship to dare begin to allow deeper emotional contact. Conversely, it takes just a single or a few negative experiences in a relationship to confirm the patient's deep-seated interpersonal distrust and notions that emotional contact is risky to the self before the patient shuts down any initiation of contact and de facto writes off the relationship. This is especially true if situations that confirm the patient's distrust in others are not addressed. In more concrete terms, if the patient has numerous experiences from past relationships of others perceiving their subjective needs and feelings as irrelevant, insignificant or even wrong and inappropriate (ignoring and invalidating the patient's inner life and experiences), the therapist may need to communicate in a very clear and authentic manner that the patient's inner life is significant (that the therapist wants to hear and see it) and that the patient's subjective experiences, boundaries and needs are important, valid and legitimate.

During times when the patient's (and the therapist's) ways of being and acting are dominated by destructive shame, the therapeutic space may be characterized by oppressive silence, inertia and an apparent lack of emotional dynamic. The therapist may find that repeated invitations to contact and efforts to establish some form of dialogue seem to be rejected or ignored by the patient, who hides behind an impenetrable armour of indifference, self-sufficiency, emotional disengagement or such intense sensitivity that the therapist's invitations to contact inevitably overwhelm the patient. When this is the case, the therapist may find it difficult to keep in mind that the patient's shame and its concrete consequences in the form of a lack of emotional involvement and generally evasive behaviour send a message that something is important to the patient but also that this content is vulnerable, fragile and too intimate or overwhelming for the patient to come into contact with and share with the therapist. Furthermore, what happens in the therapeutic space holds valuable information about how the patient normally deals with and attempts to defend against destructive shame and initiations of contact that make the patient feel insecure and concerned.

Similar psychological dynamics may play out in situations where the therapeutic space is permeated by the patient's aggression, hate and, perhaps, grandiose self-perceptions. This may be manifestations of the patient's attempts to escape unbearable destructive shame, as invitations to contact may be met by more aggressive attacks on or contempt for the therapist and the therapist's invitations to contact. By continually engaging in psychological reflections on – or mentalizing – what is happening inside the patient and what the patient is doing to avoid becoming vulnerable and overwhelmed by shame, the therapist creates meaning in the therapeutic space. When the therapist subsequently responds verbally and non-verbally to the patient based on a reasonably adequate and dynamic psychological understanding of the patient's inner life, this will in itself help the therapist to convey this understanding of the patient to the patient, fairly independently of how conscious the therapist is of this understanding or how explicitly it is articulated.

If destructive shame occurs more abruptly and suddenly comes to dominate the patient's contact, this may be a signal that the patient is becoming overwhelmed by what is happening in the therapeutic space (Bromberg, 2011, p. 23). It may also signal the presence of problems in the therapeutic relationship, either because the contact has become too close, challenging the patient's boundaries of intimacy (and, perhaps, the therapist's ability to maintain their analytical distance and psychotherapeutic stance in the contact with the patient), or because it has become too distant, and the patient feels abandoned by the therapist (who is too silent, passive, misattuned to the patient and so forth) and left alone to deal with difficult experiences and affects (Retzinger, 1998, p. 208). In either case, the sudden invasion of shame in the therapeutic space may be seen as an attempt to protect both the patient's boundaries of intimacy and the therapeutic relationship.

When the patient is suddenly overwhelmed by shame, it may thus signal that the therapeutic relationship is jeopardized. The therapist should address this, perhaps by adopting a different strategy and thus accommodate the patient's possible need for changes in the intensity of contact with the therapist and with emotionally intense experiences. In more concrete terms, this may mean that the therapist needs to adjust the pace in the therapeutic process and modify the balance between, on the one hand, more empathically validating and supportive interventions and, on the other hand, the more explorative and confrontational interventions. The latter is often associated with a greater risk that the patient will perceive the interventions in ways that cause the patient to feel wrong. In any case, the therapist may need to offer empathic mirroring and perhaps articulate the patient's sense of inferiority and shame in the present moment.

7.7 An intersubjective affect – also in the psychotherapeutic space

Although patients who are struggling with severe and destructive shame are especially sensitive to shame-inducing situations and extraordinarily likely to experience destructive shame, we should not lose sight of the fact that shame is an intersubjective affect that is activated in interactions between self and others. One implication of this is that when the patient is overwhelmed by destructive shame in the therapeutic space, the therapist and the organization of the therapeutic space have, at least, acted as contributing factors. When the patient withdraws from contact with the therapist, this may thus happen in response to the therapist's stance, ways of being, style, behaviour and concrete interventions, which in various ways contributed to the patient feeling overlooked, inferior, 'found out', overexposed, judged or condemned (diagnosed, placed in reifying categories) rather than feeling met and understood as themselves, which can in itself be shameful and makes it understandable that the patient has to protect themselves by withdrawing from contact with the therapist (cf. Tiedemann, 2010, p. 123).

Similarly, if the therapist implicitly or explicitly signals to the patient that their ways of being and acting are immature, regressive, primitive, abnormal or otherwise wrong, amoral and a sign that the patient is an inferior or defective person, this may also give rise to shame and the urge to protect the self from harm. Even though this was never the therapist's deliberate intention, the therapist must continually monitor any tendency to engage in normative judgments of the patient's ways of being and acting. There are rarely any benefits to allowing such a tendency to have any significant influence on the psychotherapeutic process.

A young man who periodically struggles to get out of bed in the morning and have a functioning everyday life does significantly better at other times. On good days, he spends a great deal of time at the fitness centre, where he works to optimize his body. He is well aware that his fitness training represents an attempt to escape low self-esteem and painful shame about feeling wrong, inferior and as a failure, a perception that is grounded in his relationship with his father. Since his early childhood, he has tried, unsuccessfully, to gain his father's recognition of his accomplishments and to make his father proud of him. He believes that if he cannot complete an education like his peers, he can instead build a stronger and more attractive body. This may be seen as his attempt to prop up his fragile self-esteem and, perhaps, cover up his shameful feelings of inferiority. For some time, he has been using various drugs to help him build muscle mass faster. Part of him is aware that this is both wrong and harmful to his health. Shortly after the conclusion of a session, the patient tells his therapist, with a certain sense of pride, that the previous day, he beat his own personal leg press record.

Without properly considering his reply, the therapist comments that he is a little impressed to see how much the patient has improved his physical performance in recent weeks before adding, in a playful tone, that maybe the patient cut a few corners by using the drugs in question. The patient laughs a little but also defends his achievement, somewhat timidly. Later that same evening, the patient sends a very angry text message to the therapist, writing that he finds the therapist arrogant, insensitive and incompetent by failing to acknowledge in their earlier exchange how hard these intense workouts are for him and how hard he works at improving his body. He adds that he has does not want to return for sessions any time soon and that he is not sure whether he will be able to continue his treatment with the therapist.

The therapist writes a brief text message to the patient, in general terms expressing his regret that the patient perceived his playful remark that way – but that he also understands how that could happen, even though he had no intention of disparaging the patient's accomplishments. This validates the patient's experience, which is especially important in relation to patients who have had multiple experiences of their feelings and subjective experiences being invalidated (mocked, disparaged, defined as invalid or wrong) by important others, which is in itself shameful and may lead to self-hatred, self-stigmatization and distrust in their own experiences (cf. Linehan, 1993). The therapist encourages the patient to come in for the scheduled session the following week, at which time they can discuss how the patient perceived the incident and why it made him so angry with the therapist. The therapist also comments that the issue is important, in fact much too important to discuss via text messages. Initially, the patient does not reply and thus appears to have cut off contact with the therapist. However, after a few weeks, the patient agrees to come in for a talk, so the two of them can determine whether they can continue their work together, or whether the patient wants to terminate the treatment. In this session, the patient is initially completely silent but appears both latently aggressive and frightened. The patient's body is shaking, which the therapist notices. He also explicitly expresses that he is pleased that the patient came in, even though it might have been difficult for him. The patient does not reply but seems to calm down slightly.

Next, the therapist briefly recapitulates what has happened since the previous session. He also describes his own experience and reactions and the conscious intentions behind his comments and actions at central times during this process. The therapist acknowledges that it was inappropriate for him to tease the patient about possibly cutting corners by taking performance-enhancing drugs, especially since he had done it in a way that caused the patient to perceive it as a dismissal of his accomplishment. The therapist explicitly tells the patient that his attempt at joking and teasing the patient was inappropriate and insensitive. At this point, the patient replies and again begins to criticize the therapist but with the stated desire of trying to continue the therapy. During the session – as the emotional contact and alliance between therapist and patient gradually begin to be restored – it becomes clear that the patient has been furious with the therapist for what he perceived as disrespect and ridicule of his efforts to do the best he can. To the patient, this felt like a painful repetition of a recurring pattern throughout his much of his life, especially in his relationship with his father. In this pattern, he never felt good enough but typically felt completely unseen by the father, who was always more interested in himself and his own projects. These experiences are associated with severely destructive shame, which was activated and overwhelmed the patient when the therapist playfully attempted some good-natured teasing but clearly failed in this attempt.

The therapist explicitly validates the patient's subjective experience of the concrete incident and clearly accepts his responsibility for his share of the resulting conflict (what did I, as a therapist, say, do or fail to do that contributed to the patient becoming overwhelmed by shame and reacting with sudden anger, withdrawal from contact and so forth?). In addition, the therapist also needs to reflect on how his own reactions in this incident may be related to his own psychological processes. In this reflection, the therapist has to acknowledge, among other points, that part of him is worried – and, to some extent, appalled – that the patient is taking performance-enhancing substances, and that this feeling probably influenced his clearly suboptimal reaction when the patient proudly told him of his recent accomplishment at the gym.

Furthermore, the therapist feels a certain degree of shame that the patient perceives him as incompetent, especially because the patient is not entirely wrong that his response to the patient's story of his latest accomplishment was not particularly competent. Initially, the therapist attempts to rationalize or make excuses to himself for his response by focusing on the fact that it took place after the conclusion of the session. The therapist has to admit that this attempt at evading rudimentary feelings of shame is not tenable. He also has to consider whether his own feelings of shame may have influenced his actions in the contact with the patient. He needs to heighten his awareness of his own tendency in certain situations to respond in ways that are driven by his own normative beliefs and on his tendency to break off his psychothera-peutic stance in his contact with the patient as soon as the session is over but before the patient has left the therapist's office. This is not a helpful strategy or behaviour. Everything that plays out between patient and therapist is thera-peutic material and should be treated as such, although, on the other hand, this should not lead to the therapist becoming rigid and inauthentic in their contact with the patient. This balancing act, which is not always straightfor-ward, will not be addressed further in the present context.

7.8 Impact factors in the treatment of shame

Roughly put, destructive shame originates in dysfunctional interactions with important others (typically parents, but to some extent also same-age peers during childhood and other important others later in life), is maintained and manifested in stressful interactions with (real and, in part, imagined) others and needs to be treated in and via the interaction with the therapist; an inter-action that is not similarly dysfunctional or a source of the same destructive shame as the patient's past relationships. Shame is an intersubjective feeling or state grounded in dysfunctional relationships and disturbed interpersonal contacts that are most effectively dismantled and cured through new, positive experiences in contacts with important others, including a therapist (cf. DeYoung, 2022, p. 20f.). The possibilities of this happening in psychotherapeutic treatment will be improved as the therapist and the therapy become significant to the patient (when the patient dares to allow this to happen), and as the patient's destructive shame is actualized in the contact with the therapist, where it can be moderated (regulated), detoxified and healed.

As mentioned earlier, our nature as social beings is constituted in intersubjective relationships, which means, in part, that relationships that take on special significance for us can shape and transform who we are (Lyons-Ruth et al., 2018). This typically includes long-term dyadic relationships where the involved parties take on a special quality and significance to each other as unique individuals (in some cases, a social group may take on a somewhat similar role, but this will not be discussed further in the present context). These relationships are characterized by mutual emotional and psychological closeness and involvement, which can help create what the Boston Change Study Group (Lyons-Ruth et al., 2018, p. 541; see also Section 7.9) calls a 'highly charged relation', a relationship that is shaped by the parties' strong and special mutual engagement in each other as human beings. The therapist's contribution to establishing such a highly charged and significant relationship or contact with the patient in the therapeutic space contains at least three main elements (ibid., p. 549f.):

1 A core positive emotional involvement in the patient that, among other functions, can help create a special openness and tolerance to any difficulties that may arise in the psychotherapeutic process and support the patient's ability to perceive themselves as someone who is unique and significant to the therapist.

2 A persistent focus of attention on the patient's needs and what is going on inside the patient, the patient's current emotional state, inner psychological life and history; this will, in part, improve the likelihood that the patient gradually develops basic (and epistemic, cf. Fonagy & Allison, 2014) trust in the therapist and a sense that the therapist 'is on the patient's side'.

3 An engagement in the patient, the relationship with the patient and their common effort to heal the patient that is based on a special sense of continuity, persistence and stability; among other functions, this can help enhance the patient's perception of the therapist and their mutual relationship as a stable and reliable element in the patient's life. Psychotherapeutic change and, perhaps not least, alleviation and healing of destructive shame unfolds through such an emotionally charged and significant relationship. In this relationship, the therapist may gradually become a highly charged other in the patient's subjective perception, and the therapist may similarly come to see the patient as a unique and significant person. However, the

therapeutic relationship will always remain asymmetrical, in the sense that the patient seeks help from the therapist, who is responsible for the therapeutic relationship remaining strictly professional in nature.

Naturally, there may be many different reasons why the individual patient has developed an extraordinary tendency to become overwhelmed by destructive shame. However, a common factor is that the patient has drawn the lesson from relational experiences that contact with others is associated with various forms of shame, including experiences of being humiliated, ridiculed, bullied and subjected to various forms of abuse, betrayals or neglect of their own needs. This happens in various ways – and with considerable individual variation. In relation to this point, it is important to bear in mind that, as paradoxical as it may seem, it can be less painful and unsettling to perceive oneself as wrong, defective and guilty of perceived betrayals than having to acknowledge the profound deficits and failures of vulnerable parents. Thus, the psychological dynamic of the development of destructive shame often involves the patient disparaging themselves while ignoring the faults of parents and others (Nathanson, 1992, p. 340). In a sense, the patient feels that they are to blame for not feeling seen by their parents, having to fend for themselves from a young age, being neglected and being bullied and marginalized in school.

In the typical emotional process of these stressful experiences, the patient will gradually develop a general sense of being inferior, insignificant and unlovable. This dynamic is actualized and risks overwhelming the patient if they again engage in emotional and psychological contact with others, including with the therapist. Generally, the patient thus needs to break this relational pattern to prevent – or limit – its repetition in the contact with the therapist. Instead, the patient should have the opportunity to make new, corrective emotional experiences in interactions with the therapist as an important other. In these experiences, emotional contact does not always lead to overwhelming destructive shame, or not to the same degree, which may help the patient revise their implicit relational knowledge about what goes on in interpersonal interactions and emotional contact with others. At the same time, therapists should be aware that, to some degree, they will inevitably be involved in repeating stressful relational patterns from the patient's life in the therapeutic relationship. The key is for the therapist to remain continually aware of it when it happens and then to take responsibility for their own share and examine, with the patient, what it was that played out in the therapeutic space and how it can be understood.

As the relational psychotherapist Patricia DeYoung (2022, p. 227) pointed out, the therapist's stated point of departure in an engagement with a patient who is struggling with shame should always be that 'Something *happened* to you. We have yet to explore exactly what happened and how you have worked around it, but the net effect of what happened is that you live with constant shame. This curse is real and relentless, but you are not defective. The shame you feel came from relationships in your social-emotional world that have been deeply wrong for you, and whenever something goes wrong again, that shame is right there to whisper that it's your failure, that it's something wrong with you. But it's not. Something happened'. The patient's conviction that they are wrong should gradually and to varying degrees (depending on the individual patient and the anticipated timeframe of the treatment) be shifted towards a joint focus on how the patient was treated and what happened to them in relationships with others, as it is these experiences that underlie the patient's feeling of being defective (cf. Sørensen, 2013, p. 173).

It is always debatable to what extent it is necessary to go back in time to examine the patient's early relationships and whether it might, in many cases, be both sufficient and more appropriate to work mainly with what is happening in the here-and-now contact between patient and therapist. This intersubjective view of the aetiology of feelings of destructive shame assumes that destructive shame is not the initial core of the patient's difficulties. Rather, it is a reaction to severe deficits and dysfunctions in the patient's relationships with important others, which may subsequently have developed into an independent and self-perpetuating problem, in the sense that shame hampers or, in some situations, blocks the patient's ability to establish the contact with others that is a condition for recovery. This applies not just to destructive feelings of shame but to mental disorders in general.

In the therapeutic space, the patient should ideally have the experience that seeing and being seen by someone else, being in psychological and emotional contact with the therapist, is associated with feeling contained, recognized and understood as who they are – that the patient's own boundaries are seen and respected, that they have a right to having and expressing their own wishes and needs. These experiences will often represent a significant counter-image or antidote to what the patient has previously experienced and become accustomed to (Tiedemann, 2010, p. 64). When patients who are struggling with destructive shame have learned to associate contact with threats to the self and their own boundaries of intimacy, they need a form of contact in which their boundaries are respected, and the other is genuinely interested in their inner life and needs. This will provide a fundamental experience of being respected and recognized by the other (the therapist) as an equal (subject), who has inherent worth and is lovable.

A person with a psychology that is strongly affected by destructive shame may have a great need for fairly explicit recognition and validation of their being, acting and entire person (cf. deep-seated conviction of being inherently defective and wrong), including explicit recognition of what the person shares and does in the therapeutic space. This also means that the person may easily feel condemned, rejected and affirmed in their conviction (or fear) of being wrong and inadequate if the therapist tries to be very 'neutral', offer objective analysis and avoid satisfying what the therapist might perceive as 'primitive' or 'regressive' needs in the patient. In my experience, explicit recognition and validation of the patient's subjective perceptions, understandable attempts at self-protection and contributions to the therapeutic process often play an important role in establishing, preserving and expanding the psychological and emotional contact with the patient, which is perhaps the most important single impact factor in healing the patient's destructive shame.

In one of the first conversations in a lengthy treatment process, the therapist notices that the patient repeatedly stops in the middle of sharing something significant (and often emotionally painful), abruptly cutting himself off, saying, 'No, I'm not sure'. After this has happened several times over the course of several sessions, the therapist comments that he has noticed this possible pattern and asks the patient if this is something he, too, has noticed and recognizes.

The patient clearly expresses that this is a pattern he is aware of, and that it happens frequently when he is speaking with someone he does not know and is not sure he can trust. The therapist says that he can easily understand that the patient needs to protect himself, particularly in light of his history (which has given him no reason to trust that others will treat his openness about his own subjective experiences in a respectful manner), and that it is wise to develop a sense of whether the other person can be trusted before possibly opening up to them and sharing more vulnerable aspects of one's life. The therapist also says that this urge for self-protection can of course also become too strong, causing us to keep others at a considerable distance and never letting anyone in, which can make us feel very lonely.

In response, the patient says that, on the one hand, he does want to answer the therapist's questions and open up to the therapist but that, on the other hand, he is worried that if he does, he will feel completely empty afterwards and feel that he has said too much, revealed how wrong he is and have trouble facing the therapist (again underscoring the central role of the gaze and of eye contact).

In very simple terms, the therapist responds by stating that it can be difficult to discover that one is not sure whether to trust one's own feeling (in this case, the patient's feeling that he can trust the therapist) and to be caught up in such an internal conflict. The therapist also suggests that, perhaps, the patient's bad experiences with feeling empty and wrong after sharing something personal and significant might stem from his perceptions of others' reactions (ignoring, being indifferent) on previous occasions when he has done this. In summary, the therapist can be said to validate and recognize the patient's subjective experience in the therapeutic space while also, in various ways, acknowledging the patient's experiences and reactions to these experiences as both meaningful and understandable. At the conclusion of the session, the patient says, 'Can I just say something? I have not been feeling that you were judging me, and I really appreciate it'.

On the other hand, recognition and validation cannot stand alone in the therapeutic process but have to be accompanied by strategies that contribute more directly to improving the patient's self-perception, perception of others and understanding of interpersonal interactions (capacity for thinking in psychological terms, mentalizing). Thus, the therapist always needs to consider what makes for the best possible balance between the concern for the patient's need for help to regulate destructive shame in the moment (keeping it at a level where the patient is not overwhelmed by shame and needs to withdraw from contact or from the treatment overall) versus concern for the fact that the patient cannot achieve recovery through a conflict-free and emotionally satisfying (pleasant) contact with the therapist as the infinitely good object. The process has to alternate, to some degree, between healing destructive shame through the relational contact and working with and strengthening the patient's capacity for reflection.

When the therapist listens with attention, calm, patience and attentive curiosity to what the patient says and shows – in addition to the content of the patient's verbal communication – this can help create a space, an atmosphere and a contact in the therapeutic space where the patient feels that there is room for them to be themselves and feels seen without being overwhelmed by shame. This in itself helps to correct the patient's fixed ideas about the sorts of negative experiences and unbearable shame that follow from contact with others. Furthermore, this might be the patient's first-ever experience with an important other taking an authentic interest in and offering empathic mirroring of their inner life without judging them. This will play a crucial role in gradually enabling the patient to trust that the therapist will contain and respond with empathic validation if they reveal highly vulnerable and shameful parts of themselves. This process may enable the patient to have the courage to share and express previously frozen, split-off or dissociated parts of themselves, their needs and their history in the therapeutic space (Sassenfeld, 2015, p. 155).

In the treatment of patients who are struggling with severe chronic destructive shame, everything that takes place on the periphery of and outside the explicit, verbal communication will have a major impact on the therapeutic process. Sometimes, it matters more than the concrete content of the verbal communication. Most people perceive shame as an 'unacceptable' affect, bordering on the taboo, and so painful that they try to keep it hidden from others – including their therapist. Hence, we should not expect the patient to speak explicitly about their shame. However, the patient will show their shame in the therapeutic space and communicate it through non-verbal communication (DeYoung, 2022, p. 147f.). In natural extension of this point, the focal point of working with destructive shame is the non-verbal communication. This has to do with establishing and maintaining emotional and psychological contact with the patient, movements in the contact and what plays out in the therapeutic relationship in general. In this process, it is crucial to try to prevent patterns from the patient's past relationships – often characterized by distorted contact, lack of contact or contact that was determined entirely on the others' terms and which violated the patient's boundaries of intimacy – from being repeated in the contact with the therapist. When they are repeated (as they will inevitably be), it is important for the therapist to register and seek to deal with it in a way that makes it possible to restore the emotional contact to a form that is helpful to the patient.

The difference between a good-enough and a less good therapist is not whether the therapist makes mistakes and inadvertently engages in repetitions of stressful patterns from the patient's past relationships. We all do. The difference lies in how the therapist handles these missteps – how well the therapist manages to register and acknowledge these missteps as missteps or suboptimal therapeutic actions, both to themselves and to the patient, and, not least, how well they address and deal with them. This has to happen in ways that make a constructive contribution to the patient's psychological understanding of human psychology and interpersonal interactions. The therapist should also model exemplary ways of containing and dealing with one's own mistakes and deficits in a balanced manner. This means not denying or trying to cover up one's mistakes or blaming them on others while also not lapsing into extreme self-reproach, excessive apologies, self-hatred or destructive self-shaming (Tiedemann, 2010, p. 339).

Thus, much of the therapist's work to contain, respond to and help regulate the patient's shame in the therapeutic space may take place outside our full conscious awareness and outside the explicit content of the verbal communication: through eye contact, facial expressions and the ongoing mutual emotional response and attunement to the other's current emotional state and other mental states as well as physical signals and the subtext of the verbal communication (tone of voice, intensity, pace and so forth). In this sense, it is less important exactly what the therapist says to the patient when destructive shame or other painful emotions are present in the therapeutic space. It is also important to note that this cannot be standardized. The key point is how the therapist is and remains in contact with the patient; the therapist's being and signalled stance towards the patient and the patient's shame in the moment.

On the other hand, this naturally does not mean that the content of the verbal communication and the verbal articulation of the patient's shame is insignificant. Far from it. As outlined below, verbal communication is an important tool in establishing and continually regulating the contact between patient and therapist, which, as mentioned earlier, is the focal point of the therapeutic process of dampening and detoxifying the patient's shame. The verbal communication focuses the joint attention on what is significant to the patient and in the intersubjective interactions here and now. Furthermore, articulating the patient's shame and helping the patient – at a pace that is appropriate for the patient – to examine and share their shameful experiences of feeling wrong, unwanted and inferior, together with the therapist, can help the patient associate the destructive shame with and, in a sense, convert it to sadness and grief over what the patient has been missing, lost and been subjected to. This sadness over feeling lonely, unseen and all alone with unbearable experiences is an underlying basis of the patient's experiences of being defective and wrong (cf. Skårderud, 2001c, p. 1617). Destructive shame may thus be accompanied by profound and painful deprivation of the need and yearning for loving, caring contact and attention from important others that it may be almost unbearable to come into contact with and acknowledge.

7.9 The therapist's stance and actions in the encounter with the patient

Patients who struggle with destructive shame and whose early relational experiences made them draw the lesson that their boundaries, emotions and needs are insignificant – that they themselves are in fact insignificant, in the way, difficult, demanding, bad, destructive and toxic to others and wrong in every way – will typically have internalized these self-perceptions to the extent that they take for granted that others view them in the same way. They may also have become 'experts' in (or hypersensitive to) spotting recurring affirmations of these perceptions in interpersonal interactions. Therapists need to meet these patients in a way that maximizes the chance of avoiding yet another experience that affirms this negative self-image and instead offers 'the opposite' experience as a form of antidote to experiences in past toxic relationships.

Throughout his childhood, one young man was repeatedly told by his parents how difficult and impossible he was. Over and over again, he was punished for what the parents appeared to perceive as his bad character and rebellious behaviour but which by all indications in fact reflected that he had no idea how to be or what to do to be 'a good son' that his parents could love or at least accept. During the initial long phase of his therapy, he (or a large part of him) is convinced that he is so (alternately) difficult, boring and rebellious in the eyes of the therapist that he almost terminates the treatment. Over and over, he tells the therapist (albeit not until after the therapist explicitly asks about it) that after each session, he ruminates on and blames himself for the way he was in therapy (being a bad, boring, difficult patient who mostly attends therapy to satisfy the therapist). Over and over, the patient asks in different ways whether the therapist finds him difficult, annoying, provoking or otherwise 'wrong' in the therapeutic space.

The therapist tries to mirror how painful it must be for the patient to have these experiences and to be so convinced that no one can contain him, let alone love him, but must surely perceive him as wrong in every way. The therapist also invites him to engage in a joint exploration of what concrete signs the patient sees to indicate the therapist in fact views him as difficult and wishes to break off the treatment. Similarly, he is invited to engage in a joint look at how the patient might recognize these experiences from the therapeutic space in other parts of his life and history, including whether the patient's conviction of being so defective, toxic and wrong that he is unwanted and unlovable might be related to experiences he has had throughout much of his past life. Gradually, this lets the patient develop a sense that the therapist might not perceive him as difficult, provoking, toxic or unlovable (on the contrary, the therapist finds him easy to like) and helps him trust and believe that there might be people who like him and whose perception of him is very different from his past experiences, which have led to profound feelings of shame. As pointed out by DeYoung (2022, p. 18), in the encounter with the individual patient, the therapist must always consider certain basic questions, including, 'How can I be with you in this relationship so that you can be with yourself in ways that give you more security and well-being?' There are no standard answers to this question, which is fundamental and crucial to the therapeutic process. The answer depends on the individual patient's needs, specific challenges and ways of functioning psychologically and in relationships. What is important is that therapists ask themselves this question in the encounter with each individual patient and try to answer it, partially together with the patient.

Ideally, the therapist should show the patient that their subjective experiences, inner life and emotions, including feelings of shame, are relevant, significant and possible to contain. This happens both through verbal interventions, which articulate central aspects of the patient's subjective experiences, mental states and inner psychological life and through the therapist's way of relating to, accommodating and attuning their ways of being and acting to where the patient is in the moment. To the extent this is successful, the patient will gradually be able to embrace the therapist's more positive and approving approach to their self. Among other points, this means that negative self-perceptions and the related feelings of shame are detoxified and no longer feel so unbearable that they have to be kept hidden, shut down or deflected (Morrison, 2011, p. 33). The therapist needs to communicate to the patient – verbally and non-verbally – that they know or are able to sense, through empathy, how painful it can be to be overwhelmed by destructive shame. The therapist also needs to stay with the patient and prevent their contact from being broken off when waves of shame wash over the patient.

It is not helpful for the therapist to offer the patient concrete 'strategies' or 'techniques' for escaping or regulating their shame through specific behaviours, as these methods rarely have any significant effect outside the moment and do not fundamentally detoxify the patient's toxic shame and self-image. Instead, the therapist should offer to stay with and help the patient contain and regulate shame and other painful affects in their interaction in the therapeutic relationship (DeYoung, 2022, p. 233). The therapist should make themselves available and offer to follow the patient into the dark recesses of their soul and recollections where the destructive shame resides. Shame will not let go of the patient until it is brought into the light, where it loses its toxic power.

Generally, this approach to working with the patient's shame requires the therapist to use a range of empathically validating and mirroring interventions, which primarily involve communicating to the patient that the therapist sees and perceives the patient's shame and other mental states as meaningful and comprehensible and appreciates how painful they must be. Roughly put, the therapist's communicated acceptance of and compassion with all parts of the patient will over time help the patient develop greater self-acceptance and self-compassion, including of their own perceived faults and deficits. With Rogers (1957), we can say that the therapist has to meet patients who are struggling with shame with unconditional positive attention and acceptance (recognition) (Jørgensen, 2018b, p. 72ff.) and strive to avoid interventions that the patient might perceive as an expression of criticism, humiliation or lack of recognition of the patient's self as an equal subject and which may thus indirectly affirm and exacerbate the patient's negative and shameful self-image (Nathanson, 1992, p. 319). When the patient is affected by shame in the therapeutic space or discloses shameful material, the therapist should actively validate (Linehan, 1993, p. 349) and meet the patient with what Ayers (2003, p. 215) called perhaps the most important impact factor in therapeutic work with destructive shame: a loving and caring gaze ('eyes of love'), which was presumably lacking and missed from important others throughout large parts of the patient's past life.

Focusing on non-verbal communication and boundaries

Especially when working with individuals who have personality disorders, therapists need to bear in mind that to a high degree, the patient not only notices and reacts to the content of what the therapist says but also how it is said, how the therapist meets and relates to them, and how the therapist's statements affect the patient, including by activating destructive shame (Tiedemann, 2010, p. 279). For example, one such patient becomes very angry with her therapist when she finds that his interventions define and categorize her instead of inquiring about her experience in various situations. When the therapist expresses his sense of how she is feeling and what she is experiencing right now – impressions that are far from always perfectly aligned with the patient's own experience (which she sometimes has difficulty articulating) – she feels misunderstood, overlooked and disrespected, which has significant elements of repetitions of stressful experiences from earlier relationships. These experiences of being overlooked and of others trying to define who she is, what she is experiencing and how she is feeling activates destructive shame in the patient. In an attempt to escape this shame, she attacks the person (in this case the therapist) whose attempts at defining her experiences activated the unbearable shame.

Even though the therapist's interventions are intended to help the patient articulate her subjective experiences, this is not how she perceives them – which is what matters. The patient finds that the therapist takes over, defines and thus violates – and in fact has no interest in – her experiences, which contains elements of repetition of painful experiences from the patient's past. Until the therapist realizes this and changes his strategy, the therapeutic process is not going to make a positive contribution to the development of the patient's capacity for containing and regulating their shame. Through his way of interacting with the patient, the therapist is – unknowingly – contributing to activating and intensifying the patient's destructive shame.

Working with the patient's shame in the therapeutic space requires tact – a sensitive awareness of others' boundaries of intimacy and judgment that continually enables the therapist to strike the right balance in noticing, reacting to and directing the joint attention to the patient's shame. This includes, not least, the subjective experiences of inferiority and inadequacy, which are often the more concrete expressions of the patient's shame in the therapeutic conversation, without adding unnecessarily to them and having the patient feel exposed, laid bare or humiliated and shutting down emotionally (Tangney & Dearing, 2011, p. 383). This also involves continually regulating the balance between closeness and distance in the emotional and psychological contact to prevent overstepping (violating) the patient's boundaries of intimacy and emotional exposure (which are typically fragile and related to a high permanent proneness to shame and anxiety) and to try to keep the patient's destructive shame (and anxiety) in the therapeutic space at a level that is tolerable to the patient and does not cause the patient to be flooded by destructive shame and to disorganize.

If the therapist withdraws from the emotional contact with the patient, avoids eye contact and avoids intervening in ways that direct attention to the patient's shame, the patient may perceive this as a form of rejection and as affirmation that the self is defective, shameful and impossible for others to contain and understand. The patient may feel that he has been 'abandoned' by the therapist in an emotionally vulnerable and charged situation. This may occur, for example, when a patient for the first time shows the therapist the many scars on his arms and legs after many years of severe self-harm. Another example could be a patient who in working through experiences of physical and sexual abuse begins to reveal that part of him felt a sense of arousal in connection with the abuse or felt a certain 'unique' connection with the abuser – which is shameful to the patient.

In these situations, the therapist – or someone else who is close to the patient – may feel a strong urge to withdraw, avoid looking at the patient's scars or shift the focus away from the patient's perceived arousal because it may be associated with a diffuse sense of discomfort and, not least, shame to follow the patient into these dark recesses of their inner world and life. There are no easy answers as to what is the best response in such a situation – no standardized manual – as it always depends on several aspects of the concrete situation and patient. However, the therapist must avoid acting or intervening in ways that make the patient feel abandoned, alone and socially isolated with their shame and psychological pain.

Whether it is helpful to direct joint attention at the patient's shame depends on a concrete assessment of whether this would further intensify the patient's shame and whether this might overwhelm the patient emotionally, or whether the patient would instead perceive this as helpful in containing and dealing with the painful shame that is currently threatening to overwhelm the self and compel the patient to implement their common avoidance strategies. In this situation, it is also important to bear in mind that it will, at best, be ineffective for the therapist to meet the patient's feelings of inferiority and shame with assurances that the patient has no reason to have these negative emotions and self-perceptions (Landmark, 2018). Statements of this nature, which will often (also) be driven by the therapist's own need to comfort the vulnerable patient and thus shut down intense psychological pain which it can be difficult to contain and witness, carry a high risk that the patient will instead perceive the therapist's response as yet another instance of rejection (invalidation) and affirmation that their experiences and feelings are wrong and unbearable, notwithstanding the therapist's good intentions. It can sometimes be helpful to challenge parts of the patient's very negative self-perceptions by inquiring about more specific details of these perceptions, potential exceptions, concrete situations and experiences that would suggest that the patient also contains other, more valuable and capable elements. However, asking questions is quite different from defining the patient by telling them how they should – in the therapist's opinion – perceive themselves. In many cases, the patient would experience this as another invalidation of their own experiences rather than as helpful support.

Exposing and focusing on the patient's shame needs to be carefully dosed to ensure that the patient is protected from being overwhelmed by shame, preserves their dignity and continues to feel that they have some degree of control of what is happening in the therapeutic space. This sense of control is essential for the patient to develop the sense of security and trust in the therapist and the therapeutic setting that is necessary for the patient to undertake therapeutic work and to open up and engage in emotional contact with the therapist. Typically, this will also involve validating and showing empathic understanding of the unpleasant feelings the patient experiences when they engage in contact with and expose shameful experiences and aspects of themselves. Similarly, the patient's urge to change the focus and the topic of the conversation or to withdraw from the emotional contact with the therapist should also be normalized. The patient's urge to avoid focusing on their shame and feelings of inferiority is quite understandable. However, it is also an important element of the therapeutic process to notice, verbalize and reflect on how we might understand this urge to flee. As the patient becomes more consciously aware of their urge to flee and better at having psychological reflections on when and why they are overwhelmed by it, it will become less pronounced, and the patient will be more prepared to examine their destructive feelings of shame and what they might be about.

It may be shameful for the patient not to feel seen and heard as the person they are or feel that they are. Thus, a patient who feels that the therapist does not notice their painful shame may feel misunderstood and invalidated and feel that the therapist is focusing in the wrong place. They may get the impression that the therapist does not see or does not care about what is important to the patient, which may in itself be associated with shame and intensify their feelings of destructive shame. In concrete terms, this may mean, for example, that if the patient finds that the therapist appears more focused on identifying and examining signs that the patient has a particular diagnosis or on following a particular standardized treatment approach, rather than listening to and seeing what the patient is experiencing, sharing, showing and trying to communicate to the therapist, this experience may inadvertently represent yet another situation in which the patient finds that others do not perceive their subjective experiences and needs as important. This may be associated with shame and may affirm the patient's existing negative self-perception (Wurmser, 2019, p. 36).

Therapeutic flexibility

There may be some concern about whether therapists who are subject to strict requirements to standardize and rationalize their treatment work might develop a form of 'soul blindness' (see also Section 6.6) to the specific patient's individuality, unique challenges and particular needs. This can have severe negative consequences for their psychotherapeutic work. This soul blindness may apply, for example, to what is hidden behind masks intended to hide the patient's shame, and it takes both time and a well-developed sense of nuances in interpersonal contact to prevent it from playing a role in the therapeutic space (Wurmser, 2019, p. 28). This is not readily compatible with the standardization of treatment offers and the idea that all patients with a given diagnosis require the same treatment ('one size fits all'). In working with patients who are affected by destructive shame, the key point is not the use of specific standardized interventions or adherence to a particular treatment model that may have been identified as being especially well suited or having evidence-based efficacy for the given patient's diagnosis. They key point is for the therapist to be and act in ways that make the patient feel seen, heard, understood, recognized and validated as an equal human being.

Any intervention is a relational event, and everything that the therapist says and does in the therapeutic space is part of the ongoing and complex interaction between patient and therapist. Any intervention and act (including any attempts to remain 'neutral' and avoid responding to what the patient says and does) conveys much more than the concrete explicit content of the therapist's verbal communication, including signals indicating how the therapist perceives, judges and relates to the patient as a subject and a person (cf. Aron, 2021, p. 126). These signals may significantly influence the patient's level of destructive shame here and now. That is another reason why the therapist should continually consider how their ways of being and acting in the therapeutic space are perceived by the individual patient and influence the emotional and psychological contact with the patient and the relational interaction with the patient in general.

When working with patients affected by destructive shame, therapists need to be authentically present and emotionally accessible to the patient in the therapeutic space (Orange, 1995, p. 125ff.). This is inherently different from primarily being a technician implementing a standardized method. A therapist who is strictly a technician – from a narrow perspective, perhaps even a highly skilled technician – without being emotionally present in the contact with the patient will have little or no ability to engage fully in the intersubjective meeting in the therapeutic space that is necessary for changing the patient's intersubjective or implicit relational knowledge and, thus, the patient's tendency to become overwhelmed by shame in contact with others (cf. Bruschweiler-Stern et al., 2010, p. 21). Instead, there is a risk that the patient will once more feel like a soulless object, treated as such by an emotionally absent other (a technical authority). This is likely to exacerbate the patient's shame.

Similarly, a fairly silent and allegedly neutral therapist who aims to minimize their emotional presence and visibility as a subject in the therapeutic space will rarely be helpful to patients who are affected by severe destructive shame. This therapeutic style is more likely to increase the risk of the patient being overwhelmed by escalating destructive shame and feeling abandoned and alone with their shame in the therapeutic space. This detachment may make the patient even more alienated from the therapist and cause them to withdraw further from contact with the distant therapist and, perhaps, from contact with themselves (dissociation) (Nathanson, 1987a, p. 204; Bromberg, 2006, p. 91).

Based on the psychoanalytic-interactional treatment model (Heigl-Evers & Nitzschke, 1994; Streeck & Leichsenring, 2015), we can say that patients who are struggling with shame need a therapist who is authentically present in the psychotherapeutic space and who 'responds to' the patient's ways of being and acting as a real person. This has also been called 'Prinzip Antwort' (the treatment principle of 'answering' the patient), which has as a central treatment goal to change the patient's implicit relational knowledge (how is a person supposed to be in interpersonal interactions, and what happens in interpersonal interactions?) in order to enhance the patient's ability to be in emotional and psychological contact with others and have a social life without being unnecessarily inhibited or blocked by destructive shame. The therapist should contribute to making the interpersonal interaction in the psychotherapeutic space transparent and comprehensible to the patient, including by being very visible as a person (without veering into the private sphere) and clearly communicating selected parts of their own subjective experiences and action tendencies (cf. objective countertransference) in the interaction with the patient. This will improve the patient's ability to understand how others actually perceive and react to them and how interpersonal interactions work. This can help dismantle severely negative beliefs about how others see and judge the patient and thus weaken and heal destructive shame (Streeck & Leichsenring, 2015, p. 121f.).

In a concrete sense, this may sometimes require the therapist to articulate parts of their countertransference (self-disclosure; telling the patient how the therapist perceives what the patient says and does and what is playing out in their relationship right now, including how it affects the therapist). In other cases, the therapist should primarily try to contain what plays out in the countertransference. Finally, in some cases, elements of the countertransference can be used as a point of departure for understanding, articulating and offering interpretations of what is happening in the patient, the therapist and the therapeutic space here and now. Which of these strategies the therapist should choose depends on the concrete situation and patient and thus relies on the therapist's judgment.

Patients who go silent, lack words, perhaps dissociate and drop out of contact with the therapist ('freezing' or fleeing) because they are overwhelmed by destructive shame or shame anxiety will not be able to find their own way out of this psychologically painful and often escalating state and have an urgent need for help to deal with this from an active, emotionally present and empathically mirroring therapist (Bromberg, 2006, p. 80f.). On the other hand, it is also important for patients to feel that there is room for them to be themselves in the therapeutic space and not to feel pressured into being in certain ways or playing a specific role. Therapists should not take up so much room or dominate the therapeutic space so much that there is no room for the patient. Similarly, therapists should not be so active in their questions and interventions that their approach feels invasive and intimidating to the patient. As with so many other aspects of therapeutic work, the key is to strike the right balance in a way that is attuned to the individual patient's current needs, state and level of psychological functioning.

In some cases, this may require the therapist to move at a significantly slower pace in an effort to establish psychological and emotional contact with patients and to be much more prepared to wait for the patient to be ready (and helping them become ready) to engage in contact with emotionally intense elements of their story together with another person (the therapist). It is also important to see the patient's withdrawal from contact and efforts to 'hide' as a wordless cry for help, as the patient needs contact but does not know how to establish and handle it. This challenge is related to what happens when someone (a child, a young person or an adult) withdraws from contact with others, isolates and becomes the longing observer of others' social life. The person needs contact but is incapable of conveying and dealing with this need and thus requires help to escape the bubble of loneliness that they have gradually shut themselves into. In this situation, too, the therapist's judgment, ability to sense the patient's boundaries of shame and (emotional and relational) needs and ability to match their actions in a subsequent interaction with the patient will be crucial for the course of the treatment. Typically, this will also, to some degree, involve the need for the therapist to help the patient articulate what is happening inside them and to them, as therapist and patient together approach the patient's boundaries of intimacy and shame – and to invite the patient into a dialogue about this at a pace that matches the patient's capacity and needs in the moment.

Moments of meeting and emotional contact

With the Danish psychologist Lars Sørensen (2013, p. 140), we can perceive shame as a feeling that tells us of 'an unmet, deep-seated wish for closeness and authenticity' in the meeting and contact with others. To the extent that it is possible for someone who is affected by shame to meet and realize this wish in the therapeutic space through authentic, attuned and credible emotional and psychological contact, 'there is a good possibility that the shame will fade away like morning dew without the need to be articulated' (ibid.). It is always debatable whether it is meaningful to separate the verbal contact and communication taking place in the therapeutic space from whatever else is happening in and between patient and therapist, in part because the content of the verbal communication, all things being equal, has a considerable impact on what plays out in the non-verbal communication and wordless contact, just as the different levels of communication will always interact. However, there is no doubt that elements of the deeper emotional and psychological contact between patient and therapist can in themselves help dampen the patient's destructive shame, even if the contact and shame in themselves are not necessarily articulated very explicitly (cf. corrective emotional experiences in the therapeutic relationship as an independent impact factor).

Boston Change Study Group is a small group of researchers, originally including the prominent developmental psychologist Daniel Stern (1985), who got together to explore the impact factors of psychotherapy (Bruschweiler-Stern et al., 2010). The group described what they called 'now moments' and 'moments of meeting' in the intersubjective contact between patient and therapist. These concepts, originally developed based on empirical studies of the interaction between parents and infants, represent an important contribution to our understanding of the specific aspects of the therapeutic contact that may help heal destructive shame.

Now moments are brief, affectively charged and significant moments that arise suddenly in the therapeutic space and which are associated with heightened emotional intensity and an elevated level of anxiety, while the character of the therapeutic relationship is, in a sense, brought into play or destabilized (Stern, 2004, p. 245). These moments may arise, for example, if events in the therapeutic space touch and challenge the patient's (and/or the therapist's) boundaries of intimacy, evoke shame and, to some degree, threaten the contact (perhaps even the relationship) between patient and therapist. Now moments involve a considerable pressure for both patient and therapist to be personally present in the moment and in the intersubjective contact, which also means that the therapist has a (sometimes clear, sometimes more diffuse) sense that a routine technical intervention will not be sufficient to deal with what is happening in the now moment.

A now moment may also be perceived as an exceptional situation or a 'moment of truth' (Bruschweiler-Stern et al., 2010, p. 42) in the therapeutic space, as patient and therapist, to varying degrees, are at risk of dropping out of or deviating from their accustomed roles and being differently and perhaps more intensely emotionally present in the moment. This leads to a special emotional intensity and (potentially) a highly authentic presence in the intersubjective contact. This may in itself increase the risk of shame, but it might also enable a deeper emotional and psychological contact and resonance. Thus, now moments may also be viewed as moments of crisis in the therapeutic relationship (cf. the threat of ruptures in the therapeutic alliance) that can be resolved through a so-called moment of meeting (cf. healing ruptures in the alliance), in which case they will help transform both the intersubjective contact between patient and therapist and the patient's sense of self. Furthermore, any moment of meeting will change the patient's implicit relational knowledge about what to do, think and feel in relationships and how to be in contact with others (Bruschweiler-Stern et al., 2010, p. 31f.; see also Safran & Muran, 2000). The potential for handling the now moment and the significant transition from a now moment to a moment of meeting hinges on the patient's (and the therapist's) subjective experiences and mental states in the moment. The key to success is the therapist's authentic interest in and appreciation of the patient's subjective experiences and inner life in the moment, including the therapist's authentic interest in what is playing out in the intersubjective contact here and now. This is much more important than purely cognitive meaning and the therapist's complex interpretations of the patient and the patient's transferences and so forth (Stern, 2004, p. 226).

Moments of meeting in the therapeutic relationship are moments of authentic contact, in which the therapist does not simply react with a standardized technical intervention, let alone evades the emotional intensity and contact with the patient that is evoked by the now moment. Instead, the therapist is present and reacts as a fellow human subject who is emotionally affected by and puts something of themselves into the contact with the patient here and now. The therapist is open, allows themselves to be intoxicated by the here-and-now interaction and makes themselves available as a sounding board for the patient's inner life and mental states, including the patient's shame (cf. Rosa, 2022, p. 67). In these moments, the patient may have a sense of being significant and being seen, treated and met as a human being (a unique individual), not 'just' as a patient with a specific diagnosis and various psychological problems who is receiving standardized treatment. In this way, the moment of meeting can serve as a counter-image and provide a corrective emotional experience for patients struggling with destructive shame, who for much of their lives have felt that they were treated as soulless objects. As such, it represents a counter-image to the patient's experiences of being overlooked or seen in ways that do not match their self-perception. In the moment of meeting, the therapist becomes visible as a person and shows what they are experiencing, thinking and feeling. Both the patient and the therapist have the experience of being engaged in a meeting and of seeing a common truth, which is often wordless (Rohde-Dachser, 2021, p. 190f.).

In one of the first sessions of a long treatment, the patient tells the therapist that she finds it extremely difficult to establish trust in others and that she is easily emotionally flooded in contact with others, overwhelmed by shame about feeling inadequate and wrong. Furthermore, she often finds that emotional contact oversteps her boundaries and makes her so emotionally overwhelmed and confused (affected by cognitive chaos) that she has to withdraw from contact with the therapist. Because of this, she needs for the therapist to 'look out for her'. This includes that the therapist has to avoid moving too quickly and pressuring the patient to talk about topics and experiences that she struggles to contain emotionally. In a slightly later session, the patient very gradually cracks open the door to some severely traumatic experiences from her past. The therapist immediately seizes the opportunity and initially tries to maintain their common focus and attention on this topic in the conversation, in part by asking for more specific details of these traumatic events in the patient's history. The patient very explicitly and in a tone of indignation lets the therapist know that the process is now moving much too quickly – 'I only just stepped through the door!' This appears to express a very important subjective experience for the patient, which also implicitly communicates that she does not find that the therapist is 'looking out for her'. The therapist immediately realizes that the patient has a point and becomes a little embarrassed (shameful) over not paying sufficient attention to the risk of overstepping the patient's fragile boundaries of intimacy. Moreover, the therapist is aware, at an almost intuitive level, that this situation – which can be considered a now moment – cannot be handled with a couple of standard interventions.

The therapist replies that the patient is right; the therapist did move forward too fast, especially in light of the patient's earlier statement. She also acknowledges that she understands it if the patient found that in this situation, the therapist was not looking out for her sufficiently well, which she regrets. Finally, the therapist says that she views the patient's very clear communication about this issue as a sign of how the patient tries to protect herself by clearly marking her boundary – and that in this sort of situation, it is important for her, as the therapist, to respect the patient's boundaries, whether they are communicated explicitly verbally or non-verbally. (This holds a potential for corrective emotional experiences, as the patient is clearly used to having her boundaries disregarded.) Immediately after this exchange in the conversation, a new and more intense emotional contact between patient and therapist arises (including eye contact, which so far has been a fairly rare occurrence in the therapeutic space), and the patient explicitly states that she appreciates the therapist's reaction. She also says that she feels wrong (shameful) for, in a sense, criticizing the therapist for moving too fast and being a little insensitive in their contact and that she is fully aware how hard it is for her to develop trust in the therapist (and in anyone else), even though part of her really wants to. Thus, there are several indications in the situation to suggest that the now moment was successfully transformed into a moment of meeting.

Over the course of the following sessions, this relational theme continues to play out, with minor variations, giving rise to new now moments that turn into moments of meeting, as their joint attention gradually also turns to how these episodes in the therapeutic space contain elements of repetition from the patient's former relationships. They also talk about how sensitive the patient is to even minor indications that her boundaries might be about to be violated or that a situation may arise in which she might be overwhelmed by unbearable shame, even if this fear may be unfounded. Their conversation also addresses how this sensitivity may contain a duality, in the sense that, on the one hand, it is important for her ability to look out for herself while, on the other hand, it may cause her to reject opportunities for deeper contact with others (including close contact with the therapist) and with parts of herself, her own emotions and her history, which she needs (and yearns for) in order to move forward and be able to live instead of merely surviving. In other words, she may shut down forms of contact with herself and others that part of her longs for because she is afraid of where it might lead, even though this fear may sometimes be unfounded.

If the patient and therapist together manage to handle now moments in which boundaries of intimacy and destructive shame are brought into play in a way that does not shatter their mutual trust, emotional contact and mutual understanding but instead deepens and enhances it, as the now moment is replaced by or transformed into a moment of meeting, this can help detoxify and dampen the patient's shame. The accumulated effect of numerous now moments that patient and therapist together manage to turn into moments of meeting can make a major contribution to the treatment outcome. Often, moments of meeting in the therapeutic relationship can also be a way to repair ruptures in the therapeutic alliance (Safran & Muran, 2000).

Conversely, now moments that are not seized and turned into moments of meeting but instead are missed may have a negative impact on the subsequent therapeutic process and the treatment outcome. This may happen, for example, if a now moment is missed or deliberately ignored by the therapist (perhaps in order to avoid the potential shame that may occur if the therapist gets emotionally involved in the now moment) or if the therapist simply offers a standardized intervention without becoming emotionally involved in the potential emotional contact with the patient (hiding behind the method). Similarly, if the therapist reacts to the now moment with spontaneity and authenticity but in a way that is clearly unhelpful and which affirms the patient's shameful beliefs about themselves and negative perceptions of how emotional contact can be a threat to the self, all things being equal, this will intensify the patient's toxic shame and may thus have anti-therapeutic consequences (Jørgensen, 2019, p. 216f.).

Thus, now moments in the therapeutic space should be considered as potential 'high risk–high gain' episodes. They may have both major positive and negative consequences for the patient and for the treatment, depending on how they are handled by the therapist (together with the patient). Furthermore, the potential therapeutic effects of moments of meeting suggest that the detoxification of toxic shame is based on the patient's lived experiences in the therapeutic space, as the therapist's verbal communication, explanations and stories cannot in themselves lead to decisive change. The therapist's interventions should be embedded in and compatible with the patient's subjectively perceived experiences in the here-and-now contact with the therapist.

The therapist not only needs to tell the patient that they understand them and communicate this understanding through the content of verbal interventions; the patient should also feel seen and understood in the non-verbal intersubjective contact with the therapist here and now. This requires an intersubjective contact between two equal and authentically present subjects, unlike a (non-)contact in which a psycho-technician intervenes with a view to correcting diagnosed malfunctions in a de facto objectified patient (Tangney & Dearing, 2011, p. 393) – to offer a deliberately simplistic summary of the nature of the challenge. This contact mainly plays out in the real relationship between patient and therapist, where transference and countertransference play a relatively minor role (Bruschweiler-Stern et al., 2010, p. 22). In this regard, too, the therapist's personal qualities and ability to engage in balanced emotional contact with the patient are thus key to the treatment. Psychotherapy is essentially a relationship and a unique space for psychological and emotional contact, not a technique that can be manualized.

Good-enough handling of moments of meeting with patients affected by toxic shame relies on the therapist's sense of professional and ethical boundaries, timing, affect tolerance (capacity for containing destructive shame), tact and sensitivity to the patient's boundaries of intimacy and shame and the ability to be emotionally present without violating the other's boundaries (Tiedemann, 2010, p. 307). Therapists need to be able to strike the right balance between, on the one hand, being authentically present and investing themselves (without being unduly inhibited by shame anxiety) while, on the other hand, avoiding stepping out of their professional role as therapist (acting out countertransference) to a degree and in ways that cause their capacity for maintaining a basic psychotherapeutic stance to collapse and turn the therapeutic relationship into a private, intimate relationship with fatal consequences for the psychotherapeutic space (cf. Section 4.2 on shame in connection with ruptures in social role relationships; Rutishauser, 1969, p. 109; Jørgensen, 2018b).

The therapist's countertransference

As mentioned earlier, shame tends to be 'infectious', for several reasons. This is also true in the therapeutic space, where the therapist should expect that they might be strongly influenced by the patient's destructive shame and therefore need to be prepared to deal with this possibility. One reason shame is infectious is that witnessing someone else's shame can be shameful in itself;

an effect that may be further heightened if the witness feels powerless and unable to help someone who is affected by shame. Furthermore, the strategies that people use in their attempt to escape destructive shame can evoke shame in others. Openly shameless behaviour can be intimidating, violate others' boundaries of intimacy and thus cause shame in others. Similarly, aggressive attacks on, explicit contempt for, devaluation of and attempts to humiliate others in order to deal with destructive shame may lead to severe violations of others' boundaries of shame and thus cause shame. Finally, being in a social field characterized by victim–abuser dynamics, as abuse victims try to escape their shame for being victims by violating others, thus leading to alternating positions of victim and abuser, may spark destructive shame, both for being a victim and for having abused others.

All these issues are also at play in the therapeutic space, where the patient's destructive shame and attempts to escape or regulate their shame may induce shame in the therapist's countertransference. In this context, the therapist may also feel shame for their own reactions to the shameful patient and their own apparent inability to understand and help the patient. Naturally, shame in the countertransference is far from isolated to therapy with patients affected by destructive shame. However, all things being equal, it should be expected to occur considerably more often and with somewhat greater intensity in work with these patients, as intense and destructive shame is, so to speak, constantly at play in their psychological dynamic and intersubjective relationships (or, instead, near absence of relationships) with others.

Roughly put, we can distinguish between four levels in the therapeutic relationship: the patient's transference, the therapist's countertransference, the therapeutic alliance and the real relationship (Gelso & Hayes, 1998). In practice, these levels in the therapeutic relationship overlap and continually interact. Thus, the four levels should not be perceived as sharply defined elements of the therapeutic relationship but instead as concepts or analytic categories that can help us understand the many complex processes in the interaction between patient and therapist in clinical practice. As mentioned earlier, the transference concept refers to the interpersonal phenomenon of the patient's (usually largely unconscious) tendency to transfer perceptions and reaction patterns from earlier interactions with important others to the interaction with the therapist here and now (Freud, 1912/1958; Bettinghofer, 2000; Jørgensen, 2009, p. 423f.). For example, a patient who is used to being humiliated and intimidated in interactions with others will expect (and fear) the same to occur in the interaction with the therapist, as a natural and taken-for-granted pattern. This phenomenon can complicate the therapeutic process but also holds a positive potential, as it gives the therapist an opportunity to observe and address the patient's typical perceptions as well as the patient's typical actions and reactions in interactions with others, including what activates the patient's destructive shame and how the patient tries to deal with it when it arises. What is happening in the contact with the patient here and now in the therapeutic space, provides the therapist with an in-depth look at how the patient's destructive shame is activated and how the patient reacts to it in the form of various (internal and interpersonal) defence mechanisms.

Briefly put, the therapeutic alliance refers to a sort of carrier wave in the therapeutic relationship; it consists of a basic (not necessarily fully articulated) agreement between patient and therapist about the goal and method of the therapy and an emotional bond between patient and therapist. This emotional bond may involve both positive and negative emotions and different degrees of trust or distrust (Muran & Barber, 2010; Horvath & Greenberg, 1994). The therapist's countertransference roughly consists of all the sensations, subjective experiences, thoughts and emotional reactions that emerge in the therapist during the therapist's interactions with the patient in the therapeutic space (Gelso & Hayes, 2007; Jørgensen, 2009, p. 416f.).

To enhance our capacity for having more nuanced and dynamic psychological reflections on the therapist's countertransference, it can be helpful to break it down into an objective and a subjective category. In this categorization, the therapist's objective countertransference refers to perceptions and reactions in the therapist during the interaction with the patient that are likely to show – and contain valuable information about – the sorts of perceptions and reactions the patient's ways of being and acting often give rise to in others. The therapist's objective countertransference (Winnicott, 1949; Jørgensen, 2009, p. 365f.) can thus help paint a picture of the sorts of behaviour the patient is used to encountering (and unconsciously contributes to activating) in their interactions with others. For example, if the therapist feels cut off from contact and shut out from the patient's inner world in interactions with the patient, this may illustrate what often happens in the patient's interpersonal interactions and how others feel when they are with the patient.

By contrast, the therapist's subjective countertransference refers to parts of the therapist's perceptions and reactions in the interaction with the patient that, all things being equal, are primarily about the therapist themselves and thus, in a sense, can be understood as a form of transference on the part of the therapist. In this case, the therapist transfers elements from their own past and present relationships outside the therapeutic space – and their own more personal feelings and needs – to the interaction with the patient. For example, the therapist may find it difficult to deal with a lack of emotional contact with the patient and with feeling shut out and alone in the therapeutic space, which may come to govern how the therapist understands and acts in relation to the patient (for example, by 'assessing' that the patient has a great need for emotional contact).

In more concrete terms, this may mean, for example, that the therapist puts an extraordinary effort into establishing contact with the patient in ways that have more to do with the therapist's own need for contact (or difficulties with handling being cut off from contact) than what the patient needs in order to establish contact with the therapist that may, over time, help detoxify the patient's shame. Similarly, a therapist who struggles to contain and deal with feelings of shame that arise continually in the contact with patients may try to avoid or flee from these feelings by changing the focus of the conversation or withdraw from emotional contact with the patient, perhaps under the guise of an (in this case erroneous) 'assessment' that this is in the best interest of the patient. Naturally, the therapist may be correct in the assumption that it might be better for the patient to avoid coming into contact with feelings of shame, because it may overwhelm and dysregulate the patient and lead to excessive emotional intensity in the therapeutic space. However, it is always important to consider whether this concern might have at least as much to do with the therapist's own difficulty in dealing with this. In contrast to objective countertransference, the therapist's subjective countertransference is thus not a similarly credible tool for understanding the patient and what commonly plays out in the patient's interactions with others. In practice, it will rarely be possible to distinguish completely unambiguously and objectively between these two dimensions of the therapist's countertransference. However, this is not a problem, as long as the therapist remains fully aware that this distinction is mainly intended as a basis for the necessary and continuous reflection on how their experiences and reactions in the interaction with the patient may be associated with dynamic psychological processes in both therapist and patient and with processes unfolding in the particular intersubjective meeting with the patient in the therapeutic space.

The real relationship

The term 'real relationship' (Jørgensen, 2018b, p. 334ff.; Gelso, 2018, p. 5f.; Greenson, 1967, p. 216f.) refers to aspects of the contact and interaction between patient and therapist that are not, or only to a very limited degree, determined by transference and countertransference. It describes an authentic meeting between two equal adult subjects here and now that is not shaped or influenced by their respective histories to any major degree, including tendencies to perceive others in any particular way (based on experiences from past relationships) and to react with particular emotions or forms of behaviour, driven by dynamic psychological processes rooted in past relationships and experiences. The therapist's ways of being and acting in the real relationship reflect their subjectivity and emotional responsiveness as a person, which plays a key role for the healing of destructive shame (cf. Aron, 2021, p. 147). As described earlier, establishing contact in the real relationship between patient and therapist and what plays out in the real relationship are significant factors in the process of detoxifying destructive shame. Corrective emotional experiences, which do not affirm the patient's shameful self-beliefs and beliefs about how others perceive the self or which balance them with new and much more positive experiences unfold mainly in the real relationship.

A person who is struggling with destructive shame will need the therapist's help to contain, regulate and detoxify their shame in the therapeutic space, especially to be able to bring it down to a level where it no longer blocks their ability to establish deeper emotional contact with the therapist. Naturally, this is only possible if the therapist is able to contain and manage these destructive feelings of shame. Thus, the therapist has to be familiar with their own feelings of shame and fairly adept at dealing with them in order to prevent them from flooding the therapeutic space and guiding the therapist's actions in situations where the patient's destructive shame is actualized (cf. subjective countertransference). To do this, the therapist needs to have developed the psychological maturity, emotional capacity and capacity for reflection (mentalizing) that are necessary for containing the many different possible expressions of the patient's destructive shame in the therapeutic space and in the therapist's countertransference and, not least, is able to deal with them in ways that facilitate the psychotherapeutic process.

The therapist must be able to maintain the ability to decode how diverse manifestations of the patient's shame (including the therapist's own emotional and other reactions to these manifestations) reflect the patient's psychological difficulties and convey valuable information about them (cf. objective countertransference). Not least, the therapist has to maintain a basic psychotherapeutic stance in relation to what plays out in the therapeutic space without allowing it to be compromised by any evoked shame or other powerful mental states in the countertransference (cf. subjective countertransference). If the therapist struggles to contain and deal with feelings of shame, this presents a permanent risk of overlooking or ignoring significant manifestations of destructive shame in the patient. It also makes the therapist more vulnerable to becoming involved in an unconscious or unstated agreement with the patient to avoid focusing on – or noticing – and addressing feelings of shame. One possible reason for this joint avoidance behaviour is that the therapist finds it almost as unpleasant or even painful to come into contact with and examine feelings of destructive shame as the patient does and is in fact more or less incapable of doing this as a result of unprocessed negative experiences with shame in their relational history.

While it should be fairly obvious that patients who are struggling with shame will find it deeply painful to come into contact with feelings of shame and will resort to various defensive avoidance strategies, psychotherapists who work with these patients should not be expected to find it nearly as personally challenging to come into contact with, contain and deal with feelings of shame. Thus, it will be very unfortunate and potentially destructive to the therapeutic process if a patient affected by severely destructive shame has to work with a therapist who has similar problems dealing with shame (cf. subjective countertransference). In addition to the issues outlined above, the therapist's problems with containing and dealing with destructive shame may be manifested, for example, in an urge to trivialize the patient's shame or encourage the patient to 'think more positively' (see Szentagotai-Tatar & Miu, 2016) and attempts to disregard the patient's shame by insisting that their shameful sense of inferiority is baseless, perhaps accompanied by a general lack of understanding of the presumed roots of the patient's shame in deficits and dysfunctions in early relationships.

The therapist's own shame

When a relationally oriented psychotherapist strives to be authentically present in the therapeutic space and to invite emotional and psychological contact with their patient, this will in itself put them at a higher risk of experiencing shame compared with therapists who place less emphasis on the therapist's personal presence and focus more on the use of certain technical interventions. Basically, there are no limits to what might cause the therapist to feel shame in a concrete situation. It depends on the therapist's personal psychology and history and on what plays out in the intersubjective interaction between patient and therapist. However, certain relational events and dynamics in the therapeutic relationship may be particularly likely to overstep the therapist's boundaries of intimacy or shame and lead to varying degrees of shame in the countertransference (highly dependent on the individual therapist's personal boundaries of shame). Initially, it will necessarily not be clear whether the countertransference is mainly objective or subjective, but it might be helpful to reflect on this question, perhaps in a dialogue with a supervisor, especially if the shame is prolonged and appears to have a negative influence on the therapeutic work with a concrete patient or several patients. For example, the following experiences may spark shame in the therapist (see Hilgers, 2013, p. 209f.):

- Unanticipated events in the therapeutic space when the therapist, to some degree, falls out of their role as therapist and is 'forced' to be more personally present and invest some part of themselves that goes beyond classical therapeutic interventions (cf. now moments and moments of meeting).
- Personal/intimate questions from the patient; in this situation, the therapist needs to be aware that if they explicitly refuse to answer a patient's questions without offering a reasonable explanation, this may make the patient feel wrong, disparaged and disrespected, which can cause the patient to feel shame.
- Personal comments from the patient about the therapist's person, look or behaviour that go beyond ordinary small talk and polite remarks.
- If a patient attacks, disparages or tries to humiliate the therapist verbally; if a patient explicitly questions the therapist's professional competence, says that the therapist is inexperienced, too old/young or insensitive, lacks empathy and so forth (physical attacks are not included here, since, all things being equal, that would lead to termination of treatment).
- If a patient 'takes over' the therapist's office and the therapeutic space, perhaps causing the therapist to feel a loss of control. An example might be a patient who brings in various items (clothes, food, drinks, electronic devices and so forth) and scatters them around the office at the beginning of the session; a patient who checks the therapist's journal or notes or otherwise has an intimidating behaviour in relation to the therapist's

personal items; or a patient who consistently talks loudly and at length and talks over (ignoring) the therapist's interventions.

- If a patient looks up or contacts the therapist outside the therapeutic space and in conflict with the agreed-upon treatment framework.
- Eroticization of the therapeutic relationship; if a patient displays exhibitionistic or sexualizing behaviour in the interaction with the therapist; in this situation, it is important for the therapist to understand how this might be a manifestation of the patient's hope for change and an attempt to establish a form of contact with the therapist and, perhaps, the patient's difficulties with distinguishing between emotional and sexual contact. The therapist should avoid reacting to this eroticization of the therapeutic relationship in ways that increase the patient's shameful experience of being wrong and unwanted. On the other hand, the therapist should also avoid playing along or acting in ways that might further contribute to eroticizing the relationship with the patient. This can be a difficult balance to strike.
- Massive idealization of the therapist, which may activate intense self-consciousness and stimulate an internal conflict between grandiose and more critical self-beliefs in the therapist and may cause the therapist to develop a more encompassing experience of being seen as in a way that does not match the therapist's self-image (cf. perceived disparagement of the self).
- Experiencing negative affects and reactions in relation to the patient that clash with the therapist's own professional ideals and ideas about what characterizes a competent therapist, for example, feeling disgust because of the patient's poor personal hygiene, an urge to distance themselves from the patient's detailed descriptions of self-harm, past abuse, sexual or aggressive desires/fantasies, or irritation with a patient who repeatedly attempts to avoid contact with their destructive shame by attacking and intimidating the therapist.
- A recurring pattern of patients terminating the treatment early, failing to benefit from the treatment or even deteriorating during treatment.
- Generally struggling to understand and/or contain a patient (what the patient says and does in the therapeutic space) and feeling powerless and unsure how best to deal with and intervene in relation to this patient – perhaps feeling inadequate; feeling like a 'bad therapist'.
- Forgetting important information about the patient, key events in the patient's life or other important elements of the patient and therapist's earlier conversations and work.
- Having difficulty, for various reasons (perhaps including more personal ones), adopting and maintaining a position as an observing, assessing and evaluating subject in relation to the patient – which can be part of the therapist's task in connection with diagnostic assessment, formal assessments of the patient and so forth.
- If a patient spots reactions, recurring patterns or other aspects of the therapist in the therapeutic space that the therapist has not noticed or been

willing to acknowledge; this can make the therapist feel 'found out' by the patient and make them want to refute the truth of the patient's observations. A therapist who flatly rejects the patient's observations without self-reflection has 'lost' on at least three counts: (1) The patient will (rightly) feel that that the therapist is not able to be personally present in an equal intersubjective contact; (2) It demonstrates the therapist's problems with handling shame, which can be unsettling for a patient struggling with the same issue; (3) It may contribute to the patient's shameful perception that both the patient and their impressions are wrong. The patient's subjective experience is invalidated, which can lead to shame. Conversely, in some – but not all – cases, it may contribute to the establishment of a moment of meeting and change the atmosphere in the therapeutic space if the therapist agrees and acknowledges the patient's observations (cf. Tiedemann, 2010, p. 356).

- Feeling compelled, for economic or organizational reasons, to offer the patient a treatment that the therapist knows is inadequate but has to some extent taken responsibility for, even though the patient could receive much better help if the resources were available. Having to compromise on their own professional competence and identity due to circumstances completely or partially outside their control.
- Presenting one's therapeutic work in a supervision process, where it is observed and evaluated by an older, more experienced colleague. Shame anxiety in relation to the critical gaze of the supervisor (and perhaps other colleagues in the case of group supervision) can be a driver of an urge in the therapist to embellish the presentation of their work, at the cost of their benefit from the supervision (Küchenhoff, 2018, p. 338).

These are experiences that could be said to be part of the psychotherapeutic task that a therapist has to be able to contain and handle, regardless of how intensely difficulty it can sometimes be. Therapists might temporarily be brought off balance emotionally by feelings of shame, but it is an important part of psychotherapeutic work to generally maintain a psychotherapeutic stance and the ability to engage in psychotherapeutic reflection on what is playing out in the therapeutic relationship here and now as well as in the therapist's own subjective experiences and emotional (and bodily, action-oriented and so forth) reactions here and now (Jørgensen, 2019). This is a condition for avoiding acting out one's reactions in ways that might harm the patient or the therapeutic relationship (cf. acting out subjective counter-transference) and instead using these incidents as therapeutic material and as a source of information about the patient's difficulties. However, it is also important for therapists to be aware of and prepared for the possibility that these experiences not only may but undoubtedly will occur and, not least, to be prepared to acknowledge and accept them when they happen. This is part of the foundation for maintaining the necessary reflective distance to these incidents and one's own reactions to them.

Thus, as much as possible, therapists should allow themselves to have these subjective experiences and reactions in the interaction with the patient and avoid being overwhelmed by intense self-criticism or shame over not always living up to their own high ideals for what characterizes the competent psychotherapist and perhaps feeling the urge to overstep their own boundaries (offering the patient additional help, moving beyond the agreed-upon framework of the therapy and so forth) in an attempt to compensate or atone for their own perceived faults. Naturally, this is predicated on the therapist's ability to avoid acting out these reactions in ways that impose a burden on the patient and significantly hamper the therapeutic process. It also involves being aware how challenging it can be to maintain the psychotherapeutic stance and empathic, understanding approach to the patient in situations where the therapist comes under fierce attack from the patient or otherwise feels that their boundaries are being challenged. In these situations, it is important to try to bear in mind why the patient is acting as they are while also understanding one's own experiences and reactions in relation to this behaviour – without denying one's own contributions to the intersubjective interaction with the patient. It is possible for the therapist to acknowledge that, perhaps, their actions were not optimal in a specific situation while still maintaining an empathic, understanding view of their own actions and preserving the ability to engage in psychotherapeutic reflections on how best to handle any problems that have arisen in the contact with the patient. Good-enough therapists will inevitably make mistakes (perfect therapists who never make mistakes do not exist). This is not in itself a huge problem, as long as the mistakes are not grave and, not least, as long as the therapist subsequently acknowledges and competently deals with the impact.

As mentioned earlier, idealization by the patient can also cause shame and tension in the countertransference, because it places the therapist's person centre stage in a way that may feel uncomfortable, for a number of reasons. This may somewhat hamper the establishment of deep, authentic contact in the real relationship because the patient essentially does not see or relate to the therapist's real person but instead primarily sees and relates to their own imagined transference perceptions of the therapist (DeYoung, 2022, p. 76). Furthermore, the patient may feel intimidated by their own idealized perceptions of a therapist who, in the eyes of the patient, sees and understands everything, which can be a simultaneously pleasant and scary thought for the patient. The patient may also be overwhelmed and feel inferior and shameful in contact with a therapist who is perceived as so much greater, more valuable and better than the patient.

On the other hand, the therapist needs to be able to accept the patient's idealization when the patient needs the therapist to function as a strong and idealized self-object that the patient can lean on and who can compensate for the patient's own perceived faults and deficits. By accepting the role of idealized other, the therapist may thus provide a relational defence against the patient's destructive shame (Morrison & Stolorow, 1997, p. 74). The patient's idealization of the therapist is thus not necessarily a sign of pathology or of an immature level of functioning; it may be a reflection of the patient's hope of receiving help and support from the therapist to escape their shame and other psychological difficulties. Thus, the therapist not only needs to resist the temptation to act out their immediate reaction tendency (to reject or perhaps bask in the patient's idealization) but should meet the idealization with a psychotherapeutic stance and maintain their curiosity. What is happening right now? What is playing out in the patient, myself and our relationship right now, as I feel that I am being idealized? Might the patient's idealization be an attempt to escape or regulate shame? Might the patient experience a form of calm and security by feeling connected to me as the idealized other; a sense of security that might help lay a productive foundation for our therapeutic work? Or does the patient's idealization of me instead present an obstacle to the establishment of authentic and fruitful contact in the therapeutic space?

8 Conclusion

As discussed in the previous chapters, shame is a deeply significant, potentially powerful and highly complex emotion that ranges from a constructive human sense of shame to shame that may be activated in various ways and may limit people's opportunities for self-expression and which is used (exploited) as an instrument of social control to, ultimately, chronic and severely destructive shame which is often a core factor in the development of a wide range of psychological disorders. In extension of this perspective, destructive shame may become part of the emotional driver of self-perpetuating vicious cycles that contribute to the development, maintenance and deterioration of mental illness. Furthermore, psychotherapeutic treatment of individuals struggling with severely destructive shame requires certain special skills of the therapist. Finally, destructive feelings of shame and, not least, our attempts to escape them contain huge emotional power that may lead to severely self-destructive behaviour as well as destructive attacks on and abuse of others who are, consciously or unconsciously, perceived as being to blame for what the person perceives as unbearable shame and unfair treatment of the self. Similarly, huge emotional powers may be brought into play when we feel that our individual or collective identity and way of life are under threat and have an often diffuse sense of the need to defend our identity and take on selected external adversaries with all the seriousness of a life-and-death struggle (Jørgensen, 2020, p. 145ff.).

Activation of the uniquely human sense of shame can help protect our own and others' integrity and boundaries of intimacy. Constructive feelings of shame play an important role in our capacity for self-regulation and our ability to function in social communities. They also help us (sometimes in unconscious ways) to register delicate nuances of various forms of more discreet (non-verbal) interpersonal communication that are important for our ability to handle close psychological and emotional contact. For better or worse, social groups, including entire (sub)cultures and societies, can use shame as a tool for creating a sense of internal cohesion and social order but also to enforce a degree of social adaptation and conformity that appears illegitimate seen from outside and, potentially, as a violation of the autonomy

DOI: 10.4324/9781003521174-8

and rights of individuals. The line between the two forms may be subtle and may become the object of heated discussion and a driver of social conflicts; furthermore, it will also always be influenced by cultural history and subject to change over time.

Shame is an intersubjective and social feeling that is inextricably related to human nature and the fundamental sociality of human beings. Thus, we cannot eradicate or eliminate feelings of shame, even if some might want to because they view shame as an unreasonable limitation of individual freedom or because shame is in fact often a painful feeling. In order to achieve a deeper, more nuanced understanding of shame we need to view shame as a dimensional feeling. This also means that we cannot simply claim that shame needs to be preserved and defended because it serves constructive functions in human life. Conversely, we also cannot claim that shame is an exclusively destructive feeling that we should fight in all its manifestations and at any cost. Regardless of its form, shame will be perceived as a painful feeling that we would rather do without and try to escape, hide or otherwise shut down. As the German philosopher Svenja Flaßpöhler (2021, p. 25) argued, it would be hopeless to demand or expect that modern human beings should simply tolerate any psychological pain, including painful feelings or shame. On the other hand, it also is not sustainable if we end up in a situation where modern human beings expect to be protected from any form of psychological pain and even see this as the task of society at large and feel violated and appalled when society does not embrace or achieve this task. It is neither realistic nor reasonable to make society responsible for eradicating all painful feelings, simply because sensitive human beings presumably have difficulty with tolerating and dealing with them, including painful feelings of shame.

Instead, we need to enhance our ability to distinguish between, on the one hand, the constructive sense of shame and feelings of shame that are an unavoidable part of being human and, on the other hand, destructive feelings of shame. Destructive feelings of shame can be illegitimately exploited by authorities and powerful social institutions to control and limit people's life and are also a key element of the destructive dynamic psychological processes we see unfold in a wide range of mental disorders. We also need to enhance people's ability to recognize, contain, articulate and deal with feelings of shame. This involves socializing children and young people to deal with feelings of shame in themselves and others as well as finding ways to work together to fight the forms of shame that lead to illegitimate limitations of people's lives, psychological development and human well-being. The ability to acknowledge and talk to others about our own and others' shame is an important element in developing psychological maturity, resilience (in contrast to vulnerability to feelings of shame and others' use of shaming to control and restrict the self) and strength of character. Psychotherapeutic work aimed at dampening and healing destructive shame also involves a focus on developing the patient's capacity for recognizing, containing, articulating and handling destructive feelings of shame when they arise and threaten to over-whelm the self.

Based in part on interview studies of shame among women (Brown, 2006, p. 47f.), the American professor of social work Brené Brown lists four main elements of what she calls shame resilience. These four elements may form a basis of the effort to fight destructive shame, both in contemporary culture and (to some extent) in individual lives:

1 Improving the ability to recognize and accept our own vulnerability, including our own individual shame triggers (in part because this makes us less vulnerable to shame);
2 Developing a critical awareness of the role of external sociocultural factors in shame, including how certain cultural expectations can be involved in activating shame when we fail to live up to them (in part because this awareness places the responsibility for shame outside the self and views shame in a larger context, where we are far from alone with our shame);
3 Improving our ability to establish and engage in reciprocal empathic relationships (cf. the role of empathy as, perhaps, the most potent antidote to shame; see Chapter 7); and
4 Improving our ability to talk about and analyse shame (which pulls shame into the light and, shares it with others and is related to an ability to reflect on shame rather than simply being trapped by it).

Brown's four elements in developing shame resilience could be supplemented with

5 Improving our ability to register the early, often bodily signs of shame (see Section 3.2);
6 Improving our ability to contain and acknowledge our own perceived shame rather than trying to avoid or suppress it;
7 Developing our ability to acknowledge and reflect on our own perfectionism and unrealistic self-expectations (which may be both a basis of and reactions to shame);

and, finally,

8 Improving our ability to recognize and avoid acting our own destructive urge to escape shame by abusing, attacking or shaming others.

To varying degrees, these elements can also be included in the psychotherapeutic work with severely destructive shame in individuals with various forms of mental illness.

At a first glance, Brown's strategy for fighting shame may appear seductively simple, with its concrete directions for what individuals and (marginalized or shamed) social groups can do to fight shame and others' instrumentalization of it as part of an effort to control and suppress the self, certain parts of the self (for example, female sexuality, individuals' striving to be free) or a particular social group (for example, body positivists' fight against cultural shaming of human bodies that do not live up to certain body ideals). Unfortunately, real-life implementation is more complicated; for many reasons. Brown's analyses and strategies seem to be primarily based on – and thus applicable in relation to – what might loosely be called culturally based shame: forms of shame based on general and currently prevailing beliefs or social discourses about how people 'are' and should be and act, which may be grounded in and used as instruments for defending, for example, religious and political and ideological institutions and convictions.

Brown's perspective has fairly obvious advantages in relation to these mainly culturally based forms of shame, and, as mentioned earlier, shame (and anger in reaction to shame) can be a powerful resource in the human struggle for freedom and liberation from external (and, to some extent, internal) limitations on the development of the self. However, it seems to have somewhat less applicability to the severely destructive forms of shame that rest primarily on disturbed early relationships and which are associated with actual mental illness. Even though we can never define a crystal clear distinction between destructive shame that springs from disturbed early relationships versus that springing from social control and oppression, the two forms should not be conflated. We also need to bear in mind that destructive shame stemming from early relationships can sometimes interact with (and intensify) individual feelings of shame in connection with culturally based shaming, including the intensity of the individual's emotional reaction to cultural shame in their current life.

Any legitimate fight against (culturally grounded) shame will have to rest on a balanced and nuanced understanding of shame, in the sense that it must, first of all, acknowledge and respect the existence of constructive forms of shame – related to human sense of shame – which it will hardly be appropriate to fight in nearly the same way as the forms of shame that strictly, and in most people's eyes, lead to unacceptable restrictions on human freedom and well-being. Second, in any fight against shame, it is important to notice when the effort tips over and becomes so radical that it leads to shameless behaviour that violates others' boundaries of intimacy and ordinary and legitimate notions of socially acceptable ways of being and acting in the public space and in interpersonal interactions. Conversely, in any concrete situation, it will naturally be exceedingly complicated to determine exactly where to draw the line between the legitimate expression of human freedom and socially unacceptable and shameless behaviour that might violate others' boundaries and be a threat to the social order and social communities. There are no objective or final answers to the questions, which in any culture and subculture should ideally be the object of ongoing negotiations among the members of the (sub)culture.

Not all forms of culturally based shame should thus be included in the fight against shame and shaming. Far from all forms of shame are oppressive and thus legitimate targets of a common fight against feelings of shame. If we wish to live in well-functioning social communities with a social order, certain ways of being and acting that violate others' boundaries, prevailing social norms and common values should be associated with shame. Exactly where to draw the line between legitimate and illegitimate forms of shame and shaming must always be subject to continual negotiation. Naturally, this also means that the line may differ significantly among (sub)cultures and across time. For example, perceptions of what is socially unacceptable and what is shameful in relation to powerful men's behaviour towards women is currently undergoing significant change in modern Western societies. Similarly, some sections of today's culture is (finally) engaging in an intense debate or struggle about when expressions of sexuality are socially unacceptable or shameful, especially with regard to women's sexuality – a struggle that seems to be redefining women's (and most non-heterosexual individuals') scope for expressing their sexuality (and gender perceptions) without feeling shame or being met with culturally determined shaming.

Ongoing globalization and the development of increasingly multicultural societies may make it considerably more difficult for individual societies to agree what is shameful, what are the boundaries of human intimacy and when violations of certain norms and values (including in relation to religious institutions, public authorities, holy sites and general human honour and dignity) are so unacceptable and perhaps associated with such massive cultural taboos that it is legitimate to subject people who live and act in ways that violate these elevated norms and values to shaming and other forms of severe social sanctions.

Profoundly different ideas about what is shameful and what it is 'natural' to respond to with severe shaming live side by side in multicultural societies. That is a fact and should be addressed in a necessary learning process as we learn to discuss and negotiate with each other about how best to deal with these new challenges, which are part and parcel of living in a multicultural society (Hilgers, 2013, p. 325f.). For example, across (sub)cultures (and generations), we may struggle to agree whether young men's aggressive assertiveness is an expression of shameless and toxic masculinity or should rather be seen as natural and understandable manifestations of healthy masculinity ('boys will be boys') that a real man needs to compete for material wealth and attractive women (to put it in very simplistic and clichéd terms). Similarly, we may not find it easy to agree on such questions as: Does young women's assertive sexual behaviour represent shameless and (from an external perspective) shameful promiscuity ('the whore' in contrast to the far more passive and demure 'Madonna'), or is it rather a natural result of women's liberation in modern Western societies, including women's sexual liberation and their liberation from earlier times' close association between female sexuality and shame? And when does healthy self-esteem and taking pride in oneself and one's own accomplishments and personal qualities tip over into shameless self-conceit and pathetic narcissistic self-promotion at the cost of others? Will we always be able to reach a consensus on these points?

On the other hand, the development of our awareness of cross-cultural differences in the perception of shame and the boundaries of shame should not be allowed to devolve into bottomless moral and ethical relativism, as we give up trying to reach consensus on (or completely abandon the idea of) the existence of certain universal boundaries of shame and notions of shameful behaviour. This issue will not be explored further in the present context, but we need to maintain that there are people whose ways of being and acting are so destructive to social communities and, from an objective perspective, violate others' boundaries and human integrity to such an extent that they should universally be regarded as shameless and met with shaming (and other significant social and legal sanctions) and that their concrete ways of being and acting can never be tolerated. This includes, for example, sexual abuse and paedophilia as well as genocide and societies that violate their citizens' fundamental human rights.

To the extent that we fail to establish the necessary dialogue between different cultural ideas about what is shameful, where the boundaries of shame lie and what constitutes legitimate strategies for dealing with shameful behaviour, these unspoken and perhaps only partially acknowledged disagreements about shame, boundaries of shame, shamelessness and how to deal with shame (articulating and dialogue or hateful attacks on others) will contribute to escalating conflicts between social groups and destructive mutual violations of boundaries of shame across (sub)cultures. Shame and mutual violations of diversely constituted boundaries of shame can thus be causes of destructive interpersonal and social processes, even if we are not necessarily aware what drives increasingly severe internal polarization and escalating social conflicts in modern societies (however, see Kaube & Kieserling, 2022). Thus, we need to develop greater awareness of and capacity for reflection on the way in which many of the taken-for-granted factors that guide our everyday behaviour and mutual interactions may in fact be based on certain cultural beliefs, norms, values and ideals that are not necessarily universal and are therefore not always shared by people from other (sub)cultures. This includes perceived (culturally specific) boundaries of shame, boundaries of intimacy and notions about when a person's ways of being and acting are shameless.

Only a very small part of our interpersonal and social life is regulated by formalized laws and regulations. Much of it is instead regulated by informal norms, expectations and ideas about what is correct, morally acceptable and expectable behaviour in human interactions. In this informal area, constructive shame and destructive shame play a key role as (broadly speaking) moral emotions that help regulate human ways of being and acting. In this sense, shame is an exceptionally important feeling in everyday life and for the necessary maintenance of a common social order that is in everyone's interest. If we are not aware of each other's boundaries of shame and perceptions of what is shameful and why, there is a much higher risk that we might inadvertently violate each other's boundaries as well as a much stronger tendency to meet each other with contempt and intense anger when we find that others overstep our boundaries of shame and we perceive each other as shameless (Hilgers, 2013, p. 326).

This is particularly true in multicultural societies, where the differences in our respective perceptions of shame and boundaries of shame can sometimes be quite dramatic. In the worst case, we may come to see each other as uncivilized, rude, primitive, morally lost or even brute barbarians whom we are fully entitled to dehumanize and treat as inferior, unless we develop a mutual understanding of each other's cultural context and boundaries of shame. From a narrower psychological perspective, we might say that we need to enhance people's capacity for mentalizing; improving people's capacity for seeing the world from another's perspective and having nuanced psychological reflections on why others are and act the way they are and do. In this regard, too, it is important to remember how perceived violations of our own boundaries of shame can be associated with intense feelings of shame, which may activate strong emotional powers in human psychology; powers that might be expressed in aggressive outbursts at others unless we are able to decode how our subjective experiences and urge to attack others in the moment may be associated with shame and inherently different perceptions of reality across (sub)cultures.

Generally, the psychotherapeutic treatment of destructive shame may be based on three core aspects:

1 the decoding and joint articulation of the patient's subjective experience of destructive shame (which is often manifested in indirect ways and behind various masks);
2 a focus on and joint effort to understand the patient's various reactions to and attempts to escape painful destructive shame in the form of social withdrawal, arrogance and excessive pride and anger (*ressentiment*) and aggressive attacks on others; and
3 the common exploration of the possible roots of the destructive shame in recurring maladaptive patterns in past relationships, including how recurring negative experiences in interpersonal relationships may have contributed to the development of an internal saboteur in the patient's psychological dynamic and general destabilization of the patient's self-esteem. As discussed earlier (see Chapter 7), the main foundation of any effective treatment of destructive shame, however, is elements of the therapeutic relationship, including the more personal qualities of the therapist, rather than specific therapeutic techniques.

The primary factor to dampen and heal severely destructive shame in the patient is the therapist's emotional resonance (Jørgensen, 2019, p. 237f.; Rosa, 2016/2019) in the interaction with the patient and the therapist's caring and loving mirroring of the patient's self in the therapeutic space. This interaction enables the patient to achieve corrective emotional experiences to counterbalance the patient's earlier negative and shame-inducing experiences in the contact with others, in which the patient typically felt wrong, overlooked, disparaged, condemned or devalued by important others. The key element in the treatment of destructive shame is thus the establishment of contact between patient and therapist in which interpersonal patterns and psychological destructive forms of contact that caused destructive shame and the development of an unforgiving internal saboteur in the patient are not repeated but are instead contrasted and corrected by very different and much more vitalizing forms of psychological and emotional contact.

We all have dark sides and parts of ourselves that we are far from proud of but may feel ashamed of and try, to varying degrees, to keep hidden from others and perhaps even from ourselves. Nobody is perfect, and everyone is familiar with shame. In my experience, the more we despise or hate parts of ourselves – our history, inner lives, desires and beliefs – and allow shame about them to push us into hiding and withdraw from close contact with others, the more these sides of ourselves and the related destructive shame might come to control our lives, acting as a poison that eats us up from within and keeps us from living, thriving and fully expressing ourselves together with others. On the other hand, if we are able to acknowledge these sides of ourselves, pull them into the light and examine them more closely, perhaps with help from a competent psychotherapist, they will lose much of their toxic power and have far less influence on our self-perceptions and our ways of being in the world. We can be set free to live more fully and engage in the deep emotional and psychological contact that is necessary for us to thrive and develop as human beings.

About the author

Carsten René Jørgensen is an MA Psych, PhD and professor of clinical psychology at Aarhus University, Department of Psychology, trained in group analytic psychotherapy and (since 2001) attached to the Clinic for Personality Disorders at Aarhus University Hospital Risskov/Skejby. He is one of Scandinavia's leading researchers in the field of identity and identity disturbances and borderline personality disorders, and in addition to a large number of scientific papers and chapters on personality disorders, psychotherapy, psychotherapy research and the connections between mental illness and contemporary culture, he is the author of seven significant books on psychology: *Psykologien i Senmoderniteten* [Psychology in Late Modernity] (2002), *Identitet: Psykologiske og Kulturanalytiske Perspektiver* [Identity: Perspectives from Psychology and Cultural Analysis] (2008), *Personlighedsforstyrrelser: Moderne Relationel Forståelse og Behandling af Borderlinelidelser* [Personality Disorders: Modern Relational Understanding and Treatment of Borderline Conditions] (2006, second extensively revised edition 2009), *Danmark på Briksen: Et Psykologisk Perspektiv på Danmark og Danskerne i det Senmoderne* [Denmark on the Couch: A Psychological Perspective on Denmark and the Danes in Late Modernity] (2012), *ADHD: Bidrag til en Kritisk Psykologisk Forståelse* [ADHD: Contributions to a Critical Psychological Understanding] (2014), *The Psychotherapeutic Stance* (2019, Danish edition 2018) and *Identitetskriser: Veje og Vildveje for det Moderne Menneskes Identitet* [Identity Crises: Paths and Detours for the Fragmented Identity of People in Modernity] (2020); all the Danish editions were published by the leading Danish academic publisher Hans Reitzels Forlag, *The Psychotherapeutic Stance* by Springer. In recent years, he has also focused on the psychology of shame, including, especially, how individuals with severe psychological disorders experience and may be controlled by destructive shame.

References

Akhtar, S. (2014). Revenge. In S. Akhtar & H. Parens (Eds.), *Revenge: Narcissistic injury, rage, and retaliation* (pp. 1–19). Jason Aronson.

Akhtar, S. (2015). Shame and shamelessness. In S. Akhtar (Ed.), *Shame: Developmental, cultural, and clinical realms* (pp. 93–113). Routledge.

Albrecht, C. (2011). Anthropologie der Verschiedenheit, Anthropologie der Gemeinsamkeit: Zur Wirkungsgeschichte der Unterscheidung von Scham- und Schuldkulturen [Anthropology of difference, anthropology of similarity: On the reception history of the distinction between shame and guilt cultures]. In M. Bauks & M. F. Meyer (Eds.), *Zur Kulturgeschichte der Scham* (pp. 179–193). Felix Meiner Verlag.

Alix, S., Cosette, L., Cyr, M., Frappier, J.-Y., Caron, P.-O., & Hébert, M. (2020). Self-blame, shame, avoidance, and suicidal ideation in sexually abused adolescent girls: A longitudinal study. *Journal of Sexual Abuse, 29*(4), 432–447.

Al-Mersal, S. (2022). *Min datter var gnisten: Til kvindekamp mod udskamning og ulighed* [My daughter was the spark: A call to female action against shaming and inequality]. Grønningen 1.

Alphen, E.V. (2020). Shame and masculinity in visual culture. In E. V. Alphen (Ed.), *Shame! and masculinity* (pp. 33–63). Valiz.

Améry, J. (1977). *Jenseits von Schuld und Sühne: Bewältigungsversuche eines Überwältigten* [Beyond guilt and atonement: An overwhelmed individual's attempts at coping]. Klett-Cotta.

Anders, G. (1956). *Die Antiquiertheit des Menschen 1: Über die Seele im Zeitalter der zweiten industriellen Revolution* [The antiquatedness of humanity, 1: On the soul in the age of the second industrial revolution]. C.H. Beck.

Andrews, B., Brewin, C. R., Rose, S., & Kirk, M. (2000). Predicting PTSD symptoms in victims of violent crime: The role of shame, anger, and childhood sexual abuse. *Journal of Abnormal Psychology, 109*(1), 69–73.

Andrews, B., Qian, M., & Valentine, J. D. (2002). Predicting depressive symptoms with a new measure of shame: The experience of shame scale. *British Journal of Clinical Psychology, 41*(Pt. 1), 29–42.

Ansell-Pearson, K. (2012). Nietzsche: On the genealogy of morality. In R. Pippin (Ed.), *Introduction to Nietzsche* (pp. 199–215). Cambridge University Press.

APA (2013). *Diagnostic and statistical manual of mental disorders, fifth edition: DSM-5*. American Psychiatric Publishing.

Arbeitskreis OPD (2014). *OPD-2: Operationalisierte psychodynamische Diagnostik: Das Manual für Diagnostik und Therapieplanung* [OPD-2: Operationalized psycho-dynamic diagnostics: The manual for diagnostics and therapy planning]. Huber Verlag.

Aristotle (2013). *Rhetoric* (H. Lawson-Tancred, Trans.). Start Publishing. (Original work published ca. 350 BCE.)

Aristotle (2020). *The Nicomachean ethics* (A. Beresford, Trans.). Penguin Books. (Original work published ca. 350 BCE.)

Aron, L. (2021). *When minds meet: The work of Lewis Aron*. Routledge.

Ayers, M. (2003). *Mother-infant attachment and psychoanalysis: The eyes of shame*. Routledge.

Bach, B., & Farrell, J. M. (2018). Schema modes in borderline personality disorder: The mistrustful, shameful, angry, impulsive, and unhappy child. *Psychiatry Research, 259*, 323–329.

Badour, C. L., Resnick, H. S., & Kilpatrick, D. G. (2017). Associations between specific negative emotions and DSM-5 PTSD among a national sample of interpersonal trauma survivors. *Journal of Interpersonal Violence, 32*(11), 1620–1641.

Bash, H., & Papa, A. (2014). Shame and PTSD symptoms. *Psychological Trauma: Theory, Research, Practice, and Policy, 6*(2), 159–166.

Basran, J., Raven, J., & Plowright, P. (2022). Overview of outcome research on compassion focused therapy. In P. Gilbert & G. Simos (Eds.), *Compassion focused therapy: Clinical practice and applications* (pp. 600–615). Routledge.

Bastian, T. (1998). *Der Blick, die Scham, das Gefühl* [The gaze, the shame, the feeling]. Vandenhoeck & Ruprecht.

Bastian, T., & Hilgers, M. (1990). Kain: Die Trennung von Scham und Schuld am Beispiel der Genesis [Cain: The distinction between shame and guilt as exemplified by the Book of Genesis]. *Psyche, 44*(12), 1100–1112.

Bateman, A., & Fonagy, P. (2004). *Psychotherapy for borderline personality disorder: Mentalization-based treatment*. Oxford University Press.

Bateman, A., & Fonagy, P. (2016). *Mentalization-based treatment for personality disorders*. Oxford University Press.

Benecke, C., & Henkel, M. (2021). Scham, Schuld und Psychopathologie [Shame, guilt and psychopathology]. *Persönlichkeitsstörungen, 25*(1), 18–30.

Benecke, C., & Peham, D. (2007). Scham und Schuld bei Persönlichkeitsstörungen [Shame and guilt in personality disorders]. *Persönlichkeitsstörungen, 11*(1), 21–30.

Benedict, R. (1977). *The chrysanthemum and the sword: Patterns of Japanese culture*. Routledge. (Original work published 1946.)

Benjamin, J. (1996). *Like subjects, love objects: Essays on recognition and sexual difference*. Yale University Press.

Benjamin, J. (2018). *Beyond doer and done to: Recognition theory, intersubjectivity and the third*. Routledge.

Benjamin, J. (2019). *Anerkennung, Zeugenschaft und Moral: Soziale Traumata in psychoanalytischer Perspektive* [Recognition, testimony and morals: Social traumas from a psychoanalytical perspective]. Psychosozial-Verlag.

Bennett, D. S., Sullivan, M. W., & Lewis, M. (2010). Neglected children, shame-proneness and depressive symptoms. *Child Maltreatment, 15*(4), 305–314.

Bernhardt, F. (2021). *Rache: Über einen blinden Fleck der Moderne* [Revenge: On a blind spot in modernity]. Matthes & Seitz.

Bettinghofer, S. (2000). *Übertragung und Gegenübertragung im therapeutischen Prozeß* [Transference and countertransference in the therapeutic process]. Kohlhammer.

Bilevicius, E., Neufeld, D. C., Single, A., Foot, M., Ellery, M., Keough, M. T., & Johnson, E. A. (2019). Vulnerable narcissism and addiction: The mediating role of shame. *Addictive Behaviours, 92*, 115–121.

Bille, J. (2021). *Når mænd forlader mig* [When men leave me]. Politikens Forlag.

Black, R. S. A., Curran, D., & Dyer, K. F. W. (2013). The impact of shame on the therapeutic alliance and intimate relationships. *Journal of Clinical Psychology, 69*(6), 646–654.

Blatt, S. J. (1974). Levels of object representation in anaclitic and introjective depression. *The Psychoanalytic Study of the Child, 29*(1), 107–157.

Blatt, S. J. (2008). *Polarities of experience: Relatedness and self-definition in personality development, psychopathology, and the therapeutic process.* American Psychological Association.

Blatt, S. J., & Zuroff, D. C. (1992). Interpersonal relatedness and self-definition: Two prototypes of depression. *Clinical Psychology Review, 12*(5), 527–562.

Blythin, S. P. M., Nicholson, H., Macintyre, V. G., Dickson, J. M., Fox, J. R. E., & Taylor, P. J. (2020). Experiences of shame and guilt in anorexia and bulimia nervosa: A systematic review. *Psychology and Psychotherapy: Theory, Research and Practice, 93*(1), 134–159.

Bo, I. G. (2017). *Thomas J. Scheff: Skammens mikrosociologi.* In I. G. Bo & M. H. Jacobsen (Eds.), *Følelsernes sociologi* (pp. 173–203). Hans Reitzels Forlag.

Bohleber, W. (2019). Identifizierung, Intersubjektivität und die Anerkennung des Anderen [Identification, intersubjectivity and the recognition of the other]. In J. Benjamin (Ed.), *Anerkennung, Zeugenschaft und Moral: Soziale Traumata in psychoanalytischer Perspektive* (pp. 69–82). Psychosozial-Verlag.

Boiger, M., Uchida, Y., Norasakkunkit, V., & Mesquita, B. (2016). Protecting autonomy, protecting relatedness: Appraisal patterns of daily anger and shame in the United States and Japan. *Japanese Psychological Research, 58*(1), 28–41.

Bollas, C. (1987). *The shadow of the object: Psychoanalysis and the unthought known.* Columbia University Press.

Bollas, C. (2018). *Meaning and melancholia: Life in the age of bewilderment.* Routledge.

Boomgaarden, J. (2011). Das Wissen in der Unwissenheit: Zum Schambegriff bei Søren Kierkegaard [The knowledge of not-knowing: On the concept of shame of Søren Kierkegaard]. In M. Bauks & M. F. Meyer (Eds.), *Zur Kulturgeschichte der Scham* (pp. 137–156). Felix Meiner Verlag.

Brewin, C. R, Cloitre, M., Hyland, P., Shevlin, M., Maercker, A., Bryant, R. A., Humayuna, A., Jones, L. M., Kagee, A., Rousseau, C., Somasundaram, D., Suzuki, Y., Wessely, S., van Ommeren, M., & Reed, G. M. (2017). A review of current evidence regarding the ICD-11 proposals for diagnosing PTSD and complex PTSD. *Clinical Psychology Review, 58*, 1–15.

Bromberg, P. (1998). *Standing in the spaces: Essays on clinical process, trauma and dissociation.* Psychology Press.

Bromberg, P. (2006). *Awakening the dreamer: Clinical journeys.* Analytic Press.

Bromberg, P. (2011). *The shadow of the tsunami and the growth of the relational mind.* Analytic Press.

Broucek, F. J. (1982). Shame and its relationship to early narcissistic developments. *International Journal of Psychoanalysis, 63*(Pt. 3), 369–378.

Broucek, F. J. (1991). *Shame and the self*. Guilford Press.

Broucek, F. J. (1997). Shame: Early developmental issues. In M. R. Lansky & A. P. Morrison (Eds.), *The widening scope of shame* (pp. 41–62). Psychology Press.

Brown, B. (2006). Shame resilience theory: A grounded theory study on women and shame. *Families in Society, 87*(1), 43–52.

Brown, B. (2007). *I thought it was just me: Women reclaiming power and courage in a culture of shame*. Penguin.

Brown, B., Hernandez, V. R., & Villareal, Y. (2011). Connections: A 12–session psychoeducational shame resilience curriculum. In R. L. Dearing & J. P. Tangney (Eds.), *Shame in the therapy hour* (pp. 355–372). American Psychological Association.

Brown, M. Z., Linehan, M. M., Comtois, K. A., Murray, A., & Chapman, A. L. (2009). Shame as a prospective predictor of self-inflicted injury in borderline personality disorder: A multi-modal analysis. *Behavior Research and Therapy, 47*(10), 815–822.

Bruschweiler-Stern, N., Lyons-Ruth, K., Morgan, A. C., Nahum, J. P., Sander, L. W., & Stern, D. N. (The Boston Process Study Group) (2010). *Change in psychotherapy: A unifying paradigm*. W. W. Norton.

Buchman-Wildbaum, T., Unoka, Z., Didas, R., Vizin, G., Demetrovics, Z., & Richman, M. J. (2021). Shame in borderline personality disorder: Meta-analysis. *Journal of Personality Disorders, 35*(suppl. A), 149–161.

Butler, J. (1990). *Gender trouble: Feminism and the subversion of identity*. Routledge.

Butler, J. (1997). *The psychic life of power: Theories in subjection*. Stanford University Press.

Büttner, A. (2020). *Shame*. Koenig Books.

Caligor, E., Kernberg, O. F., Clarkin, J. F., & Yeomans, F. E. (2018). *Psychodynamic therapy for personality pathology: Treating self and interpersonal functioning*. American Psychiatric Publishing.

Cameron, A. Y., Benz, M., & Reed, K. P. (2021). The role of guilt and shame in psychosocial functioning in a sample of women with borderline personality disorder. *Journal of Nervous and Mental Disease, 209*(1), 13–16.

Cameron, A. Y., Erisman, S., & Reed, K. P. (2020). The relationship among shame, nonsuicidal self-injury, and suicidal behaviors in borderline personality disorder. *Psychological Reports, 123*(3), 648–659.

Candea, D.-M., & Szentagotai-Tatar, A. (2018). Shame-proneness, guilt-proneness and anxiety symptoms: A meta-analysis. *Journal of Anxiety Disorders, 58*, 78–106.

Carretta, R. F., & Szymanski, D. M. (2020). Stranger harassment and PTSD symptoms: Roles of self-blame, shame, fear, feminine norms, and feminism. *Sex Roles, 82*, 525–540.

Chasseguet-Smirgel, J. (1985). *The ego ideal: A psychoanalytic essay on the Malady of the Ideal* (P. Barrows, Trans.). Free Association Books. (Original work published 1981.)

Cohen, T. R., Wolf, S. T., Panter, A. T., & Insko, C. A. (2011). Introducing the GASP scale: A new measure of guilt and shame. *Journal of Personality and Social Psychology, 100*(5), 947–966.

Cook, D. R. (1988). Measuring shame: The internalized shame scale. *Alcoholism Treatment Quarterly, 4*(2), 197–215.

Cooley, C. H. (1902). *Human nature and the social order*. Charles Scribner's.

Copjec, J. (2022). Mai '68: Der emotionale Monat. In T. Soiland, M. Frühauf, & A. Hartmann (Eds.), *Postödipale Gesellschaft* (vol. 1, pp. 291–329). Turia + Kant.

Costa, P. T., & McCrae, R. R. (1992). *The NEO personality inventory: Manual, form S and form R*. Psychological Assessment Resources.

Cottee, S. (2021). Incel (e)motives: Resentment, shame and revenge. *Studies in Conflict, & Terrorism, 44*(2), 93–114.

Crowe, M. (2004). Never good enough – Part 1: Shame or borderline personality disorder. *Journal of Psychiatric and Mental Health Nursing, 11*(3), 327–334.

Cunningham, K. C. (2020). Shame and guilt in PTSD. In M. T. Tull & N. A. Kimbel (Eds.), *Emotion in posttraumatic stress disorder: Etiology assessment, neurobiology, and treatment* (pp. 145–171). Academic Press.

Curran, T., & Hill, A. P. (2017). Perfectionism is increasing over time: A meta-analysis of birth cohort differences from 1989 to 2016. *Psychological Bulletin, 145*(4), 410–429.

Currie, C. J., Katz, B. A., & Yovel, I. (2017). Explicit and implicit shame aversion predict symptoms of avoidant and borderline personality disorders. *Journal of Research in Personality, 71*, 13–16.

Curtis, C. (2016). Young women's experiences of self-harm: Commonalities, distinctions and complexities. *Young, 24*(1), 17–35.

Czub, T. (2013). Shame as a self-conscious emotion and its role in identity formation. *Polish Psychological Bulletin, 44*(3), 245–253.

Daas, F. (2021). *The last one* (L. Vergnaud, Trans). Other Press.

Dearing, R. L., Stuewig, J., & Tangney, J. P. (2005). On the importance of distinguishing shame from guilt: Relations to problematic alcohol and drug use. *Addictive Behavior, 30*(7), 1392–1404.

DeCou, C. R., Cole, T. T., Lynch, S. M., Wong, M. M., & Matthews, K. C. (2017). Assault-related shame mediates the association between negative social reactions to disclosure of sexual assault and psychological distress. *Psychological Trauma: Theory, Research, Practice, and Policy, 9*(2), 166–172.

Demmerling, C. (2009). Philosophie der Scham [Philosophy of shame]. In A. Schäfer & C. Thompson (Eds.), *Scham* (pp. 75–102). Ferdinand Schöningh.

Deonna, J., Rodogno, R., & Teroni, F. (2011). *In defence of shame: The many faces of an emotion*. Oxford University Press.

Despentes, V. (2006). *King Kong theory*. Kiepenheuer & Witsch.

DeYoung, P. (2015). *Understanding and treating chronic shame: A relational/neurobiological approach*. Routledge.

DeYoung, P. (2022). *Understanding and treating chronic shame: Healing right brain relational trauma*. Routledge.

Ditlevsen, T. (2020). *Childhood, youth, dependency: The Copenhagen trilogy* (T. Nunnally & M. F. Goldman, Trans.). Penguin Books. (Original works published 1967, 1967, 1971.)

Dost, A., & Yagmurlu, B. (2008). Are constructiveness and destructiveness essential features of guilt and shame feelings respectively? *Journal for the Theory of Social Behavior, 38*(2), 109–129.

Dostoyevsky, F. M. (1996). *Notes from underground* (C. Garnett, Trans.) (pp. 103–219). The Project Gutenberg. www.gutenberg.org/files/600/600-h/600-h.htm. (Original work published 1864.)

Duarte, C., Ferreira, C., & Pinto-Goureia, J. (2016). At the core of eating disorders: Overvaluation, social rank, self-criticism and shame in anorexia, bulimia and binge eating disorder. *Comprehensive Psychiatry, 66*, 123–131.

Duerr, H. P. (1988). *Nacktheit und Scham* [Nakedness and shame]. Suhrkamp.

Duncan, C., & Cacciatore, J. (2015). A systematic review of the peer-reviewed literature on self-blame, guilt and shame. *OMEGA – Journal of Death and Dying, 71*(4),
312–342.

Ehrenberg, A. (2004). *Das erschöpfte Selbst: Depression und Gesellschaft in der
Gegenwart* [The exhausted self: Depression and society today]. Campus Verlag.

Elgat, G. (2017). *Nietzsche's psychology of ressentiment: Revenge and justice in 'On
the genealogy of morals'*. Routledge.

Elias, N. (1939[1969]). *Über den Prozeß der Zivilisation: Soziogenetische und
psychogenetische Untersuchungen* [On the process of civilization: sociogenetic
and psychogenetic studies] (Vols. 1–2). Suhrkamp.

Elison, J., Garafalo, C., & Velotti, P. (2014). Shame and aggression: Theoretical considerations. *Aggression and Violent Behavior, 19*(4), 447–453.

Elison, J., Lennon, R., & Pulos, S. (2006a). Investigating the compass of shame: The
development of the compass of shame scale. *Social Behavior and Personality, 34*(3),
221–238.

Elison, J., Pulos, S., & Lennon, R. (2006b). Shame-focused coping: An empirical study
of the compass of shame. *Social Behavior and Personality, 34*(2), 161–168.

Else-Quest, N. M., Higgins, A., Allison, C., & Morton, L. C. (2012). Gender differences
in self-conscious emotional experience: A meta-analysis. *Psychological Bulletin,
138*(5), 947–981.

Erikson, E. H. (1963). *Childhood and society* (2nd edition). W. W. Norton.

Ernaux, A. (2020). *A girl's story* (A. L. Strayer, Trans.). Seven Stories Press. (Original
work published 2016.)

Ernaux, A. (2023). *Shame*. Fitzcarraldo Editions. (Original work published 1997.)

Fairbairn, W. R. D. (1952). *Psychoanalytic studies of the personality*. Routledge.

Farstad, M. (2016). *Skam: Eksistens, relasjon, profesjon* [Shame: Existence, relationship, profession]. Cappelen Damm Akademisk.

Feiring, C., Taska, L., & Chen, K. (2002). Trying to understand why horrible things
happen: Attribution, shame, and symptom development following sexual abuse.
Child Maltreatment, 7(1), 25–39.

Feiring, C., & Taska, L. S. (2005). The persistence of shame following sexual abuse: A
longitudinal look at risk and recovery. *Child Maltreatment, 10*(4), 337–345.

Fenichel, O. (1945). *The psychoanalytic theory of neurosis*. W. W. Norton.

Ferenczi, S. (1985). *The clinical diary of Sándor Ferenczi*. Harvard University Press.

Ferenczi, S. (1988). Confusion of tongues between adults and the child: The language
of tenderness and of passion. *Contemporary Psychoanalysis*, 24, 196–206. (Original
work published 1933.)

Fessler, D. M. (2007). From appeasement to conformity. Evolutionary and cultural
perspectives on shame, competition, and cooperation. In J. L. Tracy, R. W. Robins,
& J. P. Tangney (Eds.), *The self-conscious emotions: Theory and research* (pp. 174–
193). Guilford Press.

Fischer, S. F. (1985). Identity of two: The phenomenology of shame in borderline
development and treatment. *Psychotherapy, 22*(1), 101–109.

Fjermestad-Noll, J., Ronningstam, E., Bach, B., Rosenbaum, B., & Simonsen, E. (2020).
Perfectionism, shame, and aggression in depressive patients with narcissistic personality disorder. *Journal of Personality Disorder, 34*(suppl.), 25–41.

Flaßpöhler, S. (2021). *Sensibel: Über moderne Empfindlichkeit und die Grenzen des
Zumutbaren* [Sensitive: On modern sensitivity and the limits of what is reasonable].
Klett-Cotta.

Fonagy, P. (2021). Persönlichkeitsstörung und Gewalt – ein psychoanalytisch-bindungstheoretischer Ansatz [Personality disorder and violence – a psychoanalytic-attachment theory approach]. In S. Doering, H. P. Hartmann, & O. F. Kernberg (Eds.), *Narzissmus: Grundlagen – Störungsbilder – Therapie* (pp. 83–128). Schattauer Verlag.

Fonagy, P., & Allison, E. (2014). The role of mentalizing and epistemic trust in the therapeutic relationship. *Psychotherapy, 51*(3), 372–380.

Frankfurt, H. G. (1988). *The importance of what we care about*. Cambridge University Press.

Freud, A. (1993). *The ego and the mechanisms of defence* (C. Baines, Trans.). Routledge. (Original work published 1936.)

Freud, S. (1949). Inhibitions, symptoms and anxiety. In J. Strachey (Ed.), *The standard edition of the complete psychological works of Sigmund Freud* (Vol. 20, pp. 75–176). (Original work published 1926.)

Freud, S. (1958). The dynamics of transference. In J. Strachey (Ed.), *The standard edition of the complete psychological works of Sigmund Freud* (Vol. 12, pp. 99–108). (Original work published 1912.)

Freud, S. (1961). The ego and the id. In J. Strachey (Ed.), *The standard edition of the complete psychological works of Sigmund Freud* (Vol. 19, pp. 1–66). (Original work published 1923.)

Freud, S. (1963). Introductory lectures on psycho-analysis (parts I and II). In J. Strachey (Ed.), *The standard edition of the complete psychological works of Sigmund Freud* (Vol. 15). (Original work published 1933.)

Frevert, U. (2013). *Vergängliche Gefühle* [Transitory feelings]. Wallstein.

Frevert, U. (2020). *The politics of humiliation: A modern history* (A. Bresnahan, Trans.). Oxford University Press. (Original work published 2017.)

Frevert, U. (2023). *The power of emotions: A history of Germany from 1900 to the present*. Cambridge University Press. (Original work published 2020.)

Fuchs, T. (2021). Kränkung, Rache, Vernichtung: Zur Phänomenologie des Hasses [Insult, revenge, destruction: On the phenomenology of hate]. *Psyche, 75*(4), 318–350.

Fukuyama, F. (2018). *Identity: Contemporary politics and the struggle for recognition*. Profile Books.

Gabbard, G. O. (2017). *Psychodynamic psychiatry in clinical practice* (4th edition). CBS Publishers.

Garcia, A. F., Acosta, M., Pirana, S., Edwards, D., & Osman, A. (2017). Factor structure, factorial invariance, and validity of the multidimensional shame-related response inventory-21 (MSRI-21). *Journal of Counseling Psychology, 64*(2), 233–246.

Gelso, C. J. (2018). *The therapeutic relationship in psychotherapy practice: An integrative perspective*. Routledge.

Gelso, C. J., & Hayes, J. A. (1998). *The psychotherapy relationship: Theory, research, and practice*. Wiley.

Gelso, C. J., & Hayes, J. A. (2007). *Countertransference and the therapist's inner experience*. Lawrence Erlbaum Associates.

Gilbert, P. (1998). What is shame? Some core issues and controversies. In P. Gilbert & B. Andrews (Eds.), *Shame: Interpersonal behavior, psychopathology, and culture* (pp. 3–38). Oxford University Press.

Gilbert, P. (2003). Evolution, social roles, and the difference in shame and guilt. *Social Research, 70*(4), 1205–1230.

Gilbert, P. (2007). The evolution of shame as a marker for relationship security. In J. L. Tracy, R. W. Robins, & J. P. Tangney (Eds.), *The self-conscious emotions: Theory and research* (pp. 283–309). Guilford Press.

Gilbert, P. (2009). Introducing compassion-focused therapy. *Advances in Psychiatric Treatment, 15*(3), 199–208.

Gilbert, P. (2011). Shame in psychotherapy and the role of compassion-focused therapy. In R. L. Dearing & J. P. Tangney (Eds.), *Shame in the therapy hour* (pp. 325–355). American Psychological Association.

Gilbert, P., Pehl, J., & Allan, S. (1994). The phenomenology of shame and guilt: An empirical investigation. *British Journal of Medical Psychology, 67*(1), 23–36.

Gilligan, J. (1996). *Violence: Reflections on our deadliest epidemic.* James Kingsley.

Gilligan, J. (2003). Shame, guilt and violence. *Social Research, 70*(4), 1149–1180.

Gilligan, J. (2011). *Why some politicians are more dangerous than others.* Polity Press.

Gilligan, J. (2016). Can psychoanalysis help us to understand the causes and prevention of violence? *Psychoanalytic Psychology, 30*(2), 125–137.

Goffman, E. (1963). *Stigma: Notes on the management of spoiled identity.* Penguin.

Goffman, E. (2004). *Social samhandling og mikrosociologi* [Social interaction and microsociology]. Hans Reitzels Forlag.

Goodhart, D. (2017). *The road to somewhere: The new tribes shaping British politics.* Penguin.

Goss, K., & Allan, S. (2009). Shame, pride and eating disorders. *Clinical Psychology and Psychotherapy, 16*(4), 303–316.

Goss, K., & Gilbert, P. (2002). Eating disorders, shame and pride: A cognitive-behavioral functional analysis. In P. Gilbert & J. Miles (Eds.), *Body shame: Conceptualisation, research and treatment* (pp. 219–255). Brunner-Routledge.

Göttlich, M., Westermair, A. L., Beyer, F., Bußmann, M. L., Schweiger, U., & Krämer, U. M. (2020). Neural basis of shame and guilt experience in women with borderline personality disorder. *European Archives of Psychiatry and Clinical Neuroscience, 270*(8), 979–992.

Gramzow, R., & Tangney, J. P. (1992). Proneness to shame and the narcissistic personality. *Personality and Social Psychology Bulletin, 18*(3), 369–376.

Gratz, K. L., Rosenthal, M. Z., Tull, M. T., Lejuez, C. W., & Gunderson, J. G. (2010). An experimental investigation of emotional reactivity and delayed emotional recovery in borderline personality disorder: The role of shame. *Comprehensive Psychiatry, 51*(3), 275–285.

Greenberg, J. A., & Mitchell, S. A. (1983). *Object relations in psychoanalytic theory.* Harvard University Press.

Greenson, R. R. (1967). *The technique and practice of psychoanalysis.* Hogarth Press.

Greiner, U. (2014). *Schamverlust: Vom Wandel der Gefühlskultur* [Loss of shame: On the transformation of the culture of emotions]. Rowohlt Verlag.

Grinker, R. R. (1955). Growth inertia and shame: Their therapeutic implications and dangers. *International Journal of Psychoanalysis, 36*(4–5), 242–253.

Gullestad, S. (2020). Blikket utenfra [The outside gaze]. *Tidsskrift for Norsk psykologforening, 57*(6), 435–439.

Gupta, S., Rosenthal, M. Z., Mancini, A. D., Cheavens, J. S., & Lynch, T. R. (2008). Emotion regulation skills mediate the effects of shame on eating disorder symptoms in women. *Eating Disorders, 16*(5), 405–417.

Han, B.-C. (2012). *Transparenzgesellschaft* [Transparency society]. Matthes & Seitz.

Hartmann, H. (1958). *Ego psychology and the problem of adaptation* (D. Rapaport, Trans.). International Universities Press. (Original work published 1939.)

Hartmann, H. (1972). *Ich-Psychologie: Studien zur psychoanalytischen Theorie* [Ego psychology: Studies of psychoanalytical theory]. Klett-Cotta Verlag. (Original work published 1964.)

Haslett, A. (2016, 4 October). Donald Trump, shamer in chief. *The Nation.*

Hawes, D. J., Helyer, R., Herlianto, E. C., & Willing, J. (2013). Borderline personality features and implicit shame-prone self-concept in middle childhood and early adolescence. *Journal of Clinical, & Adolescent Psychology, 42*(3), 302–308.

Hegel, G. W. F. (2019). *The phenomenology of spirit.* University of Notre Dame. (Original work published 1807.)

Heigl-Evers, A., & Nitzschke, B. (1994). Das analytische Prinzip Deutung und das interaktionelle Prinzip Antwort [The analytical principle of "interpretation" and the interactional principle of "answer"]. In A. Heigl-Evers & J. Ott (Eds.), *Die psychoanalytisch-interaktionelle Methode. Theorie und Praxis* (pp. 53–109). Vandenhoeck & Ruprecht.

Hejdenberg, J., & Andrews, B. (2011). The relationship between shame and different types of anger: A theory-based investigation. *Personality and Individual Differences, 50*(8), 1278–1282.

Hell, D. (2007). Die beschämte Scham [The ashamed shame]. In G. Schönbächler (Ed.), *Die Scham in Philosophie, Kulturanthropologie und Psychoanalyse* (pp. 23–28). Collegium Helveticum.

Hell, D. (2018). *Lob der Scham: Nur wer sich achtet, kann sich schämen* [Praise of shame: Only someone with self-respect can be ashamed]. Psychosozial-Verlag.

Heller, A. (1985). *The power of shame: A rational perspective.* Routledge.

Heller, A. (2003). Five approaches to the phenomenon of shame. *Social Research, 70*(4), 1015–1030.

Henriksen, J.-O., & Mesel, T. (2021). *Shame's unwelcome interruptions and responsive movements: Body, morality – an interdisciplinary study.* Cappelen Damm Akademisk.

Herman, J. L. (2011). Posttraumatic stress disorder as a shame disorder. In R. L. Dearing & J. P. Tangney (Eds.), *Shame in the therapy hour* (pp. 261–275). American Psychological Association.

Hilgers, M. (2013). *Scham: Gesichter eines Affekts* [Shame: Faces of an affect]. Vandenhoeck & Ruprecht.

Hill, C. E., Thompson, B. J., Cogar, M. C., & Debnan, D. W. (1993). Beneath the surface of long-term therapy: Therapist and client report on their own and each other's covert processes. *Journal of Counseling Psychology, 40*(3), 278–287.

Hirsch, M. (2017). *Schuld und Schuldgefühle: Zur Psychoanalyse von Trauma und Introjekt* [Guilt and feelings of guilt: On the psychoanalysis of trauma and introject]. Vandenhoeck & Ruprecht.

Hirsch, M. (2022). *Traumatische Realität und psychische Struktur: Zur Psychodynamik schwerer Persönlichkeitsstörungen* [Traumatic reality and psychological structure: On the psychodynamics of severe personality disorders]. Psychosozial-Verlag.

Hitler, A. (1939). *My struggle* (J. Murphy, Trans.). Hurst and Blackett. (Original work published 1925.) https://gutenberg.net.au/ebooks02/0200601h.html

Hjort, V. (2020). *Er mor død* [Is mother dead]. Turbine.

Hjortkjær, C. (2020). *Utilstrækkelig: Hvorfor den nye moral gør de unge psykisk syge* [Inadequate: Why the new morality makes young people mentally ill]. Klim.

Hochschild, A. R. (2003). Let them eat war. *European Journal of Psychotherapy & Counseling, 6*(3), 175–185.

Hochschild, A. R. (2016). *Strangers in their own land: Anger and mourning on the American right.* New Press.

Hofstadler, B. (2019). Einige psychoanalytische Aspekte der Scham [Some psychoanalytic aspects of shame]. *Forum Psychoanalyse, 35*(4), 329–339.

Hoggett, P. (2017). Shame and performativity: Thoughts on the psychology of neoliberalism. *Psychoanalysis, Culture & Society, 22*(4), 364–382.

Hollan, D. (2012). Cultures and their discontents: On the cultural mediation of shame and guilt. *Psychoanalytic Inquiry, 32*(6), 570–581.

The Holy Bible: English Standard Version. (2001). Crossway Bibles.

Holzhey-Kunz, A. (2007). Unter dem Blick des Anderen: Die Scham als Objekt und Subjekt der Philosophie [Under the gaze of the other: Shame as an object and subject of philosophy]. In G. Schönbächler (Ed.), *Die Scham in Philosophie, Kulturanthropologie und Psychoanalyse* (pp. 15–22). Collegium Helveticum.

Honneth, A. (1996). *The struggle for recognition: On the moral grammar of social conflicts* (J. Anderson, Trans.). MIT Press. (Original work published 1992.)

Hook, A., & Andrews, B. (2005). The relationship of non-disclosure in therapy to shame and depression. *British Journal of Clinical Psychology, 44*(Pt. 3), 425–438.

Horney, K. (1945). *Our inner conflicts.* W. W. Norton.

Horney, K. (1950). *Neurosis and human growth: The struggle toward self-realization.* W. W. Norton.

Horvath, A., & Greenberg, L. S. (1994). *The working alliance. Theory, research, and practice.* Wiley.

Hosser, D., Windzio, M., & Greve, W. (2008). Guilt and shame as predictors of recidivism. A longitudinal study with young prisoners. *Criminal Justice and Behavior, 35*(1), 138–152.

Isenberg, N. (2016). *White trash: The 400–year untold story of class in America.* Atlantic Books.

Jacobsen, M. H., & Kristiansen, S. (2002). *Erving Goffman: Sociologien om det elementære livs sociale former* [Erving Goffman: The sociology of the social forms of elementary life]. Hans Reitzels Forlag.

Jacquet, J. (2015). *Scham: Die politische Kraft eines unterschätzten Gefühls* [Shame: The political power of an underappreciated emotion]. Fischer Verlag.

Jaksic, N., Marcinko, D., Hanzek, M. S., Rebernjak, B., & Ogrodniczuk, J. S. (2017). Experience of shame mediates relationship between pathological narcissism and suicidal ideation in psychiatric outpatients. *Journal of Clinical Psychology, 73*(12), 1670–1681.

James, A. (2012). *Assholes: A theory.* Doubleday.

James, A. (2016). *Assholes: A theory of Donald Trump.* Doubleday.

Janin, C. (2015). Shame, hatred, and pornography: Variations on an aspect of current times. *International Journal of Psychoanalysis, 96*(6), 1603–1614.

Jones, O. (2011). *Chavs: The demonization of the working class.* Verso.

Jørgensen, C. R. (2006). Disturbed sense of identity in borderline personality disorder. *Journal of Personality Disorders, 20*(6), 618–644.

Jørgensen, C. R. (2008). *Identitet: Psykologiske og kulturanalytiske perspektiver* [Identity: Perspectives from psychology and cultural analysis]. Hans Reitzels Forlag.

Jørgensen, C. R. (2009). *Personlighedsforstyrrelser. Moderne relationel forståelse og behandling af borderlinelidelser* [Personality disorders: Modern relational understanding and treatment of borderline conditions]. Hans Reitzels Forlag.

Jørgensen, C. R. (2010). Invited essay: Identity and borderline personality disorder. *Journal of Personality Disorder, 24*(3), 344–364.

Jørgensen, C. R. (2018a). Identity. In J. Livesley & R. Larstone (Eds.), *Handbook of personality disorders* (pp. 107–123). Guilford Press.

Jørgensen, C. R. (2018b). *Den psykoterapeutiske holdning.* Hans Reitzels Forlag. (Published in English as Jørgensen, 2019.)

Jørgensen, C. R. (2019). *The psychotherapeutic stance.* Springer.

Jørgensen, C. R. (2020). *Identitetskriser: Veje og vildveje for det fragmenterede moderne menneskes identitet* [Identity crises: Paths and detours for the fragmented identity of people in modernity]. Hans Reitzels Forlag.

Jørgensen, C. R. (Forthcoming). *Narcissisme: Fra samtidskultur til personlighedspatologi* [Narcissism: From contemporary culture to personality pathology]. Manuscript in preparation. Hans Reitzels Forlag.

Jørgensen, C. R., & Bøye, R. (2022). How does it feel to have a disturbed identity? The phenomenology of identity diffusion in patients with borderline personality disorder. A qualitative study. *Journal of Personality Disorders, 36*(1), 40–69.

Jørgensen, C. R., & Bøye, R. (2024). 'I am ashamed that I exist. I feel like apologizing for existing': The phenomenology of shame in patients with borderline personality disorder. A qualitative study. *Personality Disorder: Theory, Research, and Treatment, 15*(3), 181–192.

Josephsen, M. (2021). *De andre* [The others]. Gyldendal.

Jurist, E. (2019). *Minding emotions: Cultivating mentalization in psychotherapy.* Guilford Press.

Kafka, F. (1971). The metamorphosis (W. & E. Muir, Trans.). In F. Kafka, *The complete stories* (N. N. Glatzer, Ed.) (pp. 89–139). Schocken Books. (Original work published 1915.)

Kaiser, S. (2020). *Politische Männlichkeit: Wie Incels, Fundamentalisten und Autoritäre für das Patriarchat mobilmachen* [Political masculinity: How incels, fundamentalists, and authoritarians mobilize for patriarchy]. Suhrkamp.

Kant, I. (1992). An answer to the question: What is enlightenment? (T. Humphrey, Trans.). Hackett. (Original work published 1783.) www.nypl.org/sites/default/files/kant_whatisenlightenment.pdf

Kant, I. (2018). *Groundwork for the metaphysics of morals:* Yale University Press. (Original work published 1785.)

Karan, E., Niesten, I. J. M., Frankenberg, F. R., Fitzmaurice, M., & Zanarini, M. C. (2014). The 16-year course of shame and its risk factors in patients with borderline personality disorder. *Personality and Mental Health, 8,* 169–177.

Karterud, S. (1995). *Fra narcissisme til selvpsykologi: En innføring i Heinz Kohuts forfatterskap* [From narcissism to self-psychology: An introduction to Heinz Kohut's writings]. Ad Notam Gyldendal.

Karterud, S. (2018). *Personlighed* [Personality]. Hans Reitzels Forlag.

Kaube, J., & Kieserling, A. (2022). *Die Gespaltene Gesellschaft* [The divided society]. Rowohlt Berlin.

Kaufman, G. (1985). *Shame: The power of caring.* Shenkman.

Kaufman, G. (1992). *The psychology of shame: Theory and treatment of shame-based syndromes* (3rd edition). Springer.

Kealy, D., Spidel, A., & Ogrodniczuk, J.S. (2017). Self-conscious emotions and suicidal ideation among women with and without history of childhood sexual abuse. *Counselling and Psychotherapy Research, 17,* 269–275.

Kealy, D., Treeby, M. S., & Rice, S. M. (2021). Shame, guilt, and suicidal thoughts: The interaction matters. *British Journal of Clinical Psychology, 60*, 414–423.

Keith, L., Gillanders, D., & Simpson, S. (2009). An exploration of the main sources of shame in an eating-disordered population. *Clinical Psychology and Psychotherapy, 16*, 317–327.

Kelly, A. C., & Carter, J. C. (2013). Why self-critical patients present with more severe eating disorder pathology: The mediating role of shame. *British Journal of Clinical Psychology, 52*, 148–161.

Kelly, A. C., & Tasca, G. A. (2016). Within-persons predictors of change during eating disorders treatment: An examination of self-compassion, self-criticism, shame, and eating disorder symptoms. *International Journal of Eating Disorders, 49*, 716–722.

Kelly, A. E. (2000). Helping construct desirable identities: A self-representational view of psychotherapy. *Psychological Inquiry, 126*, 475–494.

Kelly, V. C., & Lamia, M. C. (2018). *The upside of shame. Therapeutic interventions using positive aspects of a 'negative' emotion.* W.W. Norton.

Kernberg, O. F. (1993). *Severe personality disorders: Psychotherapeutic strategies.* Yale University Press.

Kilborne, B. (1999). The disappearing who: Kierkegaard, shame, and the self. In J. Adamson & H. Clark (Eds.), *Scenes of shame: Psychoanalysis, shame, and writing.* State University of New York Press.

Kilborne, B. (2002). *Disappearing persons: Shame and appearance.* State University of New York Press.

Kilborne, B. (2005). Shame conflicts and tragedy in The Scarlet Letter. *Journal of the American Psychoanalytic Association, 53*, 465–483.

Killingmo, B. (1989). Conflict and deficit: Implications for technique. *International Journal of Psychoanalysis, 70*, 65–79.

Kim, S., Thibodeau, R., & Jorgensen, R. S. (2011). Shame, guilt, and depressive symptoms: A meta-analytic review. *Psychological Bulletin, 137*, 68–96.

Kimmel, M. (2013). *Angry white men. American masculinity and the end of an era.* Nation Books.

King, V. (2016). 'If you show your real face, you'll lose 10 000 followers': The gaze of the other and transformations of shame in digitalized relationships. *CM: Communication and Media, 38*, 71–90.

Kinston, W. (1987). The shame of narcissism. In D. L. Nathanson (Ed.), *The many faces of shame* (pp. 214–245). Guilford Press.

Kirby, J. N., Tellegen, C. L., & Steindl, S. R. (2017). A meta-analysis of compassion-based interventions: Current state of knowledge and future directions. *Behavior Therapy, 48*, 778–792.

Kjellqvist, E.-B. (1996). *Rødt og hvidt: Om skam og skamløshed* [Red and white: on shame and shamelessness] (A. M. Kalsbøll, Trans.). Gyldendal. (Original work published 1993.)

Kleindienst, N., Bohus, M., Ludäscher, P., Limberger, M. F., Kuenkele, K., Ebner-Priemer, U. W., Chapman, A. L., Reicherzer, M., Stieglitz, R.-D., & Schmahl, C. (2008). Motives for nonsuicidal self-injury among women with borderline personality disorder. *Journal of Nervous and Mental Disease, 196*, 230–236.

Köhler, A. (2017). *Scham. Vom Paradies zum Dschungelcamp.* Zu Klampen Verlag.

Kohut, H. (1971). *The analysis of the self: A systematic approach to the psychoanalytic treatment of narcissistic personality disorders.* International Universities Press.

Kohut, H. (1975). *Die Zukunft der Psychoanalyse.* Suhrkamp Verlag.

Kohut, H. (1985). *Self psychology and the humanities: Reflections on a new psychoanalytic approach*. W. W. Norton.

Kohut, H. (1996). *The Chicago lectures*. Analytic Press.

Konstan, D. (2003). Shame in ancient Greece. *Social Research, 70*, 1031–1060.

Korneliussen, N. (2020). *Blomsterdalen* [The Flower Valley]. Gyldendal.

Kramer, U., Pascual-Leone, A., Rohde, K. B., & Sachse, R. (2018). The role of shame and self-compassion in psychotherapy for narcissistic personality disorder: An exploratory study. *Clinical Psychology and Psychotherapy, 25*, 272–282.

Krischer, M., & Drust, M. (2021). Scham und Schuld bei der Behandlung von Jugendlichen mit Borderline-Persönlichkeits-Organisation [Shame and guilt in treating adolescents with Borderline Personality Organization]. *Persönlichkeitsstörungen, 25*, 64–75.

Krizan, Z., & Johar, O. (2015). Narcissistic rage revisited. *Journal of Personality and Social Psychology, 108*, 784–801.

Küchenhoff, J. (2007). Sehen und Gesehen werden: Identität und Beziehung im Blick [Seeing and being seen: Identity and relationship]. *Psyche, 61*, 445–462.

Küchenhoff, J. (2018). Scham und Beschämung – auch in psychoanalytischen Institutionen [Shame and embarrassment – Also in psychoanalytic institutions]. *Forum Psychoanalyse, 34*, 329–342.

Lacan, J. (1985). *Det symbolske: Skrifter i udvalg* [The symbolic: Selected writings] (K. R. Soleim, Trans.). Gyldendal. (Original work published 1966.)

Lachmann, F. M. (2016). Some reflections on Shame, the film. *Psychoanalytic Psychology, 33*, 371–377.

Ladany, N., Klinger, R., & Kulp, L. (2011). Therapist shame: Implications for therapy and supervision. In R. L. Dearing & J. P. Tangney (Eds.), *Shame in the therapy hour* (pp. 307–322). American Psychological Association.

Lammers, C.-H., Röpke, S., & Dulz, B. (2007). Selbstwert und Borderline Persönlichkeitsstörung [Self-esteem and borderline personality disorder]. *Persönlichkeitsstörungen, 11*, 31–40.

Lammers, M. (2016). *Emotionsbezogene Psychotherapie von Scham und Schuld*. Schattauer Verlag.

Lampe, L. (2016). Avoidant personality disorder as a social anxiety phenotype: Risk factors, associations and treatment. *Current Opinion Psychiatry, 29*, 64–69.

Landmark, A. (2018). Skam: Psykoterapi og frihet [Shame: Psychotherapy and freedom]. *Tidsskrift for Norsk psykologforening, 56*, 796–805.

Landweer, H. (1999). *Scham und Macht: Phänomenologische Untersuchungen zur Sozialität eines Gefühls* [Shame and power: Phenomenological investigations into the sociality of an emotion]. Mohr Siebeck.

Lansky, M. R. (1994). Shame: Contemporary psychoanalytic perspectives. *Journal of the American Academy of Psychoanalysis, 22*, 433–441.

Lansky, M. R. (1999). Shame and the idea of a central affect. *Psychoanalytic Inquiry, 19*, 347–361.

Lansky, M. R. (2005). Hidden shame. *Journal of the American Psychoanalytic Association, 53*, 865–890.

Lansky, M. R. (2008). Beobachtungen zur Dynamik der Einschüchterung: Spaltung und projektive Identifizierung als Abwehrmanöver gegen Scham [Observations on the dynamics of intimidation: Division and projective identification as defensive maneuvers against shame]. *Psyche, 62*, 929–961.

Lasch, C. (1993). *Eliternes oprør og forræderiet mod demokratiet* [The rebellion of the elites and the betrayal of democracy]. Forlaget Hovedland.

Lee, D. A., Scragg, P., & Turner, S. (2001). The role of shame and guilt in traumatic events: A clinical model of shame-based and guilt-based PTSD. *British Journal of Medical Psychology, 74*, 451–466.

Leeming, D., & Boyle, M. (2004). Shame as a social phenomenon: A critical analysis of the concept of dispositional shame. *Psychology and Psychotherapy: Theory, Research and Practice, 77*, 375–396.

Lepold, K. (2021). *Ambivalente Anerkennung* [Ambivalent recognition]. Campus Verlag.

Lesmeister, R. (2009). *Selbst und Individuation: Facetten von Subjektivität und Intersubjektivität in der Psychoanalyse* [Self and individuation: Facets of subjectivity and intersubjectivity in psychoanalysis]. Brandes & Apsel.

Lesmeister, R. (2021). *Selbst-Schicksale: Psychoanalytische Studien zum beschädigten, leeren und tragischen Selbst* [Self-fates: Psychoanalytic studies of the damaged, empty and tragic self]. Psychosozial-Verlag.

Lessen, P. A. (2005). *Self psychology: An introduction.* Jason Aronson.

Levin, S. (1971). The psychoanalysis of shame. *International Journal of Psychoanalysis, 52*, 355–362.

Levinas, E. (1969). *Totality and infinity: An essay on exteriority* (A. Lingis, Trans.). Duquesne University Press. (Original work published 1961.)

Lewis, H. B. (1971). *Shame and guilt in neurosis.* International Universities Press.

Lewis, H. B. (1987a). Shame and the narcissistic personality. In D. L. Nathanson (Ed.), *The many faces of shame* (pp. 93–132). Guilford Press.

Lewis, H. B. (1987b). Shame – The sleeper in psychopathology. In H. B. Lewis (Ed.), *The role of shame in symptom formation.* Lawrence Erlbaum Associates.

Lewis, M. (1992). *Shame: The exposed self.* Free Press.

Lewis, M. (1998). Shame and stigma. In P. Gilbert & B. Andrews (Eds.), *Shame. Interpersonal behavior, psychopathology, and culture* (pp. 126–140). Oxford University Press.

Lewis, M. (2003). The role of the self in shame. *Social Research, 70*, 1181–1204.

Lewis, M. D., Sullivan, M., Stanger, C., & Weiss, M. (1989). Self development and self-conscious emotions. *Child Development, 60*, 146–156.

Lietzmann, A. (2007). *Theorie der Scham: Eine anthropologische Perspektive auf ein menschliches Characteristikum* [Theory of shame: An anthropological perspective on a human characteristic]. Verlag Dr. Kovac.

Limburg, K., Watson, H. J., Hagger, M. S., & Egan, S. J. (2017). The relationship between perfectionism and psychopathology: A meta-analysis. *Journal of Clinical Psychology, 73*, 1301–1326.

Lind, C. (2022). *Pigedyr* [Girl animal]. Gyldendal.

Lindsay-Hartz, J. (1984). Contrasting experiences of shame and guilt. *American Behavioral Scientist, 27*, 689–704.

Linehan, M. (1993). *Cognitive-behavioral treatment of borderline personality disorder.* Guilford Press.

Löchel, E. (2019). Scham und Beschämung im Zeitalter der Social Media [Shame and embarrassment in the age of social media]. *Psychosozial, 42*(157), 31–43.

Löchel, E. (2021). Human enhancement und promotheische Scham: Eine psychoanalytische Betrachtung [Human enhancement and promotional shame: A psychoanalytic view]. In S. Elsner (Ed.), *Enhancement: Kritische Theorie und Psychoanalytische Praxis* (pp. 87–110). Psychosozial-Verlag.

Loevinger, J. (1976). *Ego development.* Jossey-Bass.

Lopez-Castro, T., Saraiya, T., Zumberg-Smith, K., & Dambreville, N. (2019). Association between shame and posttraumatic stress disorder: A meta-analysis. *Journal of Traumatic Stress, 32*, 484–495.

Lotter, M.-S. (2012). *Scham, Schuld, Verantwortung: Über die kulturellen Grundlagen der Moral* [Shame, guilt, responsibility: On the cultural foundations of morality]. Suhrkamp Verlag.

Lowenfeld, H. (1976). Notes on shamelessness. *Psychoanalytic Quarterly, 45*, 62–72.

Lowenfeld, H., & Lowenfeld, Y. (1970). Our permissive society and the superego. Some current thoughts about Freud's cultural concepts. *Psychoanalytic Quarterly, 39*, 590–608.

Löwenthal, L. (2021). *Falsche Propheten: Studien zur faschistischen Agitation* [False prophets: Studies in fascist agitation]. Suhrkamp Verlag. (Original work published 1949.)

Luoma, J. B., Chwyl, C., & Kaplan, J. (2019). Substance use and shame: A systematic and meta-analytic review. *Clinical Psychology Review, 70*, 1–12.

Luyten, P., Fontaine, J. R. J., & Corveleyn, J. (2002). Does the test of self-conscious affect (TOSCA) measure maladaptive aspects of guilt and adaptive aspects of shame? An empirical investigation. *Personality and Individual Differences, 33*, 1373–1387.

Lynd, H. M. (1958). *On shame and the search for identity.* Science Editions.

Lyons-Ruth, K., Bruschweiler-Stern, N., Morgan, A. C., Nahum, J. P., & Reis, B. (2018). Engagement and the emergence of a charged other: Boston Change Study Group. *Contemporary Psychoanalysis, 54*, 540–559.

Macdonald, J. (1998). Disclosing shame. In P. Gilbert & B. Andrews (Eds.), *Shame: Interpersonal behavior, psychopathology, and culture* (pp. 141–157). Oxford University Press.

Macdonald, J., & Morley, I. (2001). Shame and non-disclosure: A study of the emotional isolation of people refereed for psychotherapy. *British Journal of Medical Psychology, 74*, 1–21.

Majer, R. (2013). *Scham, Schuld und Anerkennung: Zur Fragwürdigkeit moralischer Gefühle* [Shame, guilt and recognition: On the questionability of moral feelings]. De Gruyter Verlag.

Manne, A. (2014). *The life of I: The new culture of narcissism.* Melbourne University Press.

Marcus, M. (1974). *Den frygtelige sandhed: En brugsbog om kvinder og masokisme* [The awful truth: A workbook on women and masochism]. Tiderne skifter.

Margalit, A. (1996). *The decent society.* Harvard University Press.

Marks, S. (2021). *Scham: Die tabuisierte Emotion* [Shame: The taboo emotion]. Patmos Verlag.

Marks, S., & Mönnich-Marks, S. (2008). Nationalismus und Schamabwehr. *Psyche, 62*, 1015–1038.

Maroda, K. J. (2012). *Psychodynamic techniques: Working with emotions in the therapeutic relationship.* Guilford Press.

Matos, M., Pinto-Gouveia, J., & Duarte, C. (2013). Internalizing early memories of safeness and warmth: The mediating role of shame on depression. *Behavioral and Cognitive Therapy, 41*, 479–493.

Matos, M., Pinto-Gouveia, J. P., & Duarte, C. (2015). Constructing a self protected against shame: The importance of warmth and safeness memories and feelings on the association between shame memories and depression. *International Journal of Psychology and Psychological Therapy, 15*, 317–335.

Matos, M., & Steindl, S. R. (2020). You are already all you need to be: A case illustration of compassion-focused therapy for shame and perfectionism. *Journal of Clinical Psychology, 76*, 2079–2096.

McElvaney, R., Lateef, R., Collin-Vezina, Alaggia, R., & Simpson, M. (2021). Bringing shame out of the shadows: Identifying shame in child sexual abuse disclosure processes and implications for psychotherapy. *Journal of Interpersonal Violence, 37*(19–20), NP18738–NP18760.

Mead, G. H. (1934). *Mind, self, and society*. University of Chicago Press.

Meier-Carlsen, E. (2000). *De overflødiges oprør: En trussel mod demokratiet?* [Revolt of the superfluous: A threat to democracy]. Centrum.

Meyer, M. F. (2011). Scham im klassischen griechischen Denken [Shame in classical Greek thinking]. In M. Bauks & M. F. Meyer (Eds.), *Zur Kulturgeschichte der Scham* (pp. 35–54). Felix Meiner Verlag.

Meyer-Drawe, K. (2009). Am Ursprung des Selbstbewusstseins: Scham [At the origin of self-confidence: shame]. In A. Schäfer & C. Thompson (Eds.), *Scham* (pp. 37–51). Ferdinand Schöningh.

Michaelsen, S. (2022, 3 June). Wer sich für seinen Körper schämt, organisiert keinen Aufstand [Someone who is ashamed about their body is not going to organize a rebellion]. *Süddeutsche Zeitung Magasin*.

Mishra, P. (2017). *Age of anger: A history of the present*. S. Fischer Verlag.

Mitchell, S. A. (1993). *Hope and dread in psychoanalysis*. Basic Books.

Mneimne, M., Fleeson, W., Arnold, E. M., & Furr, R. M. (2018). Differentiating the everyday emotion dynamics of borderline personality disorder from major depressive disorder and bipolar disorder. *Personality Disorders: Theory, Research, and Treatment, 9*, 192–196.

Mollon, P. (2002). *Shame and jealousy: The hidden turmoils*. Routledge.

Morrison, A. P. (1986). Shame, ideal self, and narcissism. In A. P. Morrison (Ed.), *Essential papers on narcissism* (pp. 348–371). New York University Press.

Morrison, A. P. (1989). *Shame: The underside of narcissism*. Analytic Press.

Morrison, A. P. (2011). The psychodynamics of shame. In R. L. Dearing & J. P. Tangney (Eds.), *Shame in the therapy hour* (pp. 23–43). American Psychological Association.

Morrison, A. P., & Stolorow, R. D. (1997). Shame, narcissism, and intersubjectivity. In M. R. Lansky & A. P. Morrison (Eds.), *The widening scope of shame* (pp. 63–87). Psychology Press.

Mosquera, P. M. R. (2018). Honor and harmed social-image: Muslims' anger and shame about the cartoon controversy. *Cognition and Emotion, 32*, 1205–1219.

Müller, J. W. (2016). *Was ist Populismus? Ein Essay* [What is populism? An essay]. Suhrkamp Verlag.

Muran, J. C., & Barber, J. P. (2010). *The therapeutic alliance: An evidence-based guide to practice*. Guilford Press.

Murphy, S. A., & Kiffin-Petersen, S. (2017). The exposed self: A multilevel model of shame and ethical behavior. *Journal of Business Ethics, 141*, 657–675.

Nathanson, D. L. (1987a). A timetable for shame. In D. L. Nathanson (Ed.), *The many faces of shame*. Guilford Press.

Nathanson, D. L. (1987b). The shame/pride axis. In H. B. Lewis (Ed.), *The role of shame in symptom formation* (pp. 183–205). Lawrence Erlbaum Associates.

Nathanson, D. L. (1992). *Shame and pride: Affect, sex, and the birth of the self*. W. W. Norton.

Nathanson, D. L. (1994). Shame, compassion, and the borderline personality. *Psychiatric Clinics of North America, 17*, 785–810.

Nathanson, D. L. (1997). Shame and the affect theory of Silvan Tomkins. In M. R. Lansky & A. P. Morrison (Eds.), *The widening scope of shame* (pp. 107–138). Psychology Press.

Nechita, D.-M., Bud, S., & David, D. (2021). Shame and eating disorders symptoms: A meta-analysis. *International Journal of Eating Disorders, 54*(11), 1899–1945.

Neckel, S. (1991). *Status und Scham: Zur symbolischen Reproduktion sozialer Ungleichheit* [Status and shame: On the symbolic reproduction of social inequality]. Campus Verlag.

Neckel, S. (2009). Soziologie der Scham [Sociology of shame]. In A. Schäfer & C. Thompson (Eds.), *Scham* (pp. 103–118). Ferdinand Schöningh.

Nichols, R. (2016). A sense of shame among the virtues. *Journal of Moral Education, 45*, 166–178.

Nielsen, N. Å. (1989). *Dansk etymologisk ordbog* [Danish eytmological dictionary]. Gyldendal.

Nietzsche, F. (1882[1997]). *Den muntre videnskab*. Det lille forlag.

Nietzsche, F. (1886[1919]). *Jenseits von Gut und Böse*. Kröner Verlag.

Nietzsche, F. W. (1969). *On the genealogy of morals* (W. Kaufmann, Trans.). Vintage Books. (Original work published 1887.)

Nissen-Lie, H. A. (2016). Jaget av skammen: Et essay om filmen Shame av Steve McQueen [Hunted by shame: An essay on the film Shame by Steve McQueen]. *Matrix, 32*, 98–106.

Nussbaum, M. (2004). *Hiding from humanity: Disgust, 'shame' and the law*. Princeton University Press.

Nussbaum, M. (2011). Objectification and internet misogyny. In S. Levmore & M. Craven (Eds.), *The offensive internet: Speech, privacy, and reputation*. Harvard University Press.

Nussbaum, M. (2021). *Citadels of pride: Sexual assault, accountability, and reconciliation*. W. W. Norton.

Ofstad, H. (1971). *Vår foragt for svaghet: En analyse af nazismens former og vurderinger* [Our contempt for weakness: An analysis of the forms and appraisals of Nazism]. Pax.

Ogden, T (1979). On projective identification. *International Journal of Psychoanalysis, 60*, 357–373.

Øktedalen, T., Hagtved, K. A., Hoffart, A., Langkass, T. F., & Smucker, M. (2014). The trauma related shame inventory: Measuring trauma-related shame among patients with PTSD. *Journal of Psychopathology and Behavioral Assessment, 36*, 600–615.

Olsen, L., Caspersen, S., Andersen, J. G., Andersen, L., & Ploug, N. (2021). *Rige børn have more fun: Et portræt af det danske klassesamfund* [Rich children play best: A portrait of Danish class society]. Gyldendal.

Oluyori, T. (2013). A systematic review of qualitative studies on shame, guilt and eating disorders. *Counselling Psychology Review, 28*, 47–59.

Orange, D. (1995). *Emotional understanding: Studies in psychoanalytic epistemology*. Guilford Press.

Orange, D. (2008). Whose shame is it anyway? Lifeworlds of humiliation and systems of restoration. *Contemporary Psychoanalysis, 44*, 83–100.

Ordbog over the danske sprog [Dictionary of the Danish language] (1919). Det Danske Sprog-og Litteraturselskab. https://ordnet.dk/ods

Ortony, A. (2022). Are all 'basic emotions' emotions? A problem for the (basic) emotions construct. *Perspectives on Social Science, 17*, 41–61.

Panksepp, J. (2005). Affective consciousness: Core emotional feelings in animals and humans. *Consciousness and Cognition, 14*, 30–80.

Panksepp, J., & Biven, L. (2012). *The archaeology of mind: Neuroevolutionary origins of human emotions.* W. W. Norton.

Paul, A. T. (2011). Die Gewalt der Scham. Elias, Duerr und das problem der historizität menschlicher Gefühle. In M. Bauks & M. F. Meyer (Eds.), *Zur Kulturgeschichte der Scham* (pp. 195–216). Felix Meiner Verlag.

Peters, J. R., & Geiger, P. J. (2016). Borderline personality disorder and self-conscious affect: Too much shame but not enough guilt. *Personality Research: Theory, Research, and Treatment, 7*, 303–308.

Peters, J. R., Geiger, P. J., Smart, L. M., & Baer, R. A. (2014). Shame and borderline personality features: The potential mediating role of anger and anger rumination. *Personality Disorders: Theory, Research, and Treatment, 5*, 1–9.

Pettersen, K. T. (2013). A study of shame from sexual abuse within the context of Norwegian incest center. *Journal of Child Sexual Abuse, 22*, 677–694.

Pfaller, R. (2022). *Zwei Enthüllungen über Scham* [Two revelations about shame]. S. Fischer Verlag.

Piers, G., & Singer, M. B. (1953). *Shame and guilt: A psychoanalytic and cultural study.* Charles C. Thomas.

Pines, M. (1995). The universality of shame: A psychoanalytic approach. *British Journal of Psychotherapy, 11*, 346–357.

Plassmann, R. (2019). *Psychotherapie der Emotionen: Die Bedeutung von Emotionen für die Entstehung und Behandlung von Krankheiten* [Psychotherapy of emotions: The importance of emotions in the development and treatment of illness]. Psychosozial-Verlag.

Plassmann, R. (2021). *Das gefühlte Selbst: Emotionen und seelisches Wachstum in der Psychotherapie* [The felt self: Emotions and mental growth in psychotherapy]. Psychosozial-Verlag.

Plato (1956). *Protagoras and Meno* (A. Beresford, Trans.). The Library of Liberal Arts / The Bobbs-Merrill. (Original work published ca. 380 BCE.)

Plessner, H. (2003). *Macht und menschliche Natur: Gesammelte Schriften* (Bd. V) [Power and human nature: Collected writings (vol. V)]. Suhrkamp Verlag.

Plessner, H. (2019). *Philosophische Antropologie* [Philosophical anthropology]. Suhrkamp Verlag.

Potthoff, P. (2014). Abriss der relationalen Psychonalyse [Outline of relational psychoanalysis]. In P. Potthoff & S. Wollnik (Eds.), *Die Begegnung der Subjekte: Die intersubjektiv-relationelle Perspektive in Psychoanalyse und Psychotherapie* (pp. 43–63). Psychosozial-Verlag.

Pugh, L. R., Taylor, P. J., & Berry, K. (2015). The role of guilt in the development of post-traumatic stress disorder: A systematic review. *Journal of Affective Disorders, 182*, 138–150.

Rance, N., Clarke, V., & Moller, N. (2017). The anorexia nervosa experience: Shame, solitude and salvation. *Counselling and Psychotherapy Research, 17*, 127–136.

Reckwitz, A. (2020). *Society of singularities* (V. A. Pakis, Trans.). Polity Press. (Original work published 2017.)

Reckwitz, A., & Rosa, H. (2021). *Spätmoderne in der Krise: Was leistet die Gesellschaftstheorie?* [Late modernity in crisis: What does social theory achieve?] Suhrkamp Verlag.

Retzinger, S. M. (1991). *Violent emotions: Shame and rage in marital quarrels.* Sage.

Retzinger, S. M. (1998). Shame in the therapeutic relationship. In P. Gilbert & B. Andrews (Eds.), *Shame: Interpersonal behavior, psychopathology, and culture* (pp. 206–222). Oxford University Press.

Rinofner-Kreidl, S. (2009). Scham und Schuld: Zur Phänomenologie selbstbezüglicher Gefühle [Shame and guilt: On the phenomenology of self-referential feelings]. *Phänomenologische Forschungen, 2009,* 137–173.

Rinofner-Kreidl, S. (2012). Scham und Autonomie [Shame and autonomy]. *Phänomenologische Forschungen, 2012,* 163–191.

Ritter, K., Vater, A., Rüsch, N., Schröder-Abé, M., Schütz, A., Fydrich, T., Lammers, C.-H., & Roepke, S. (2014). Shame in patients with narcissistic personality disorder. *Psychiatry Research, 215,* 429–437.

Rizvi, S. L. (2010). Development and preliminary validation of a new measure to assess shame: The shame inventory. *Journal of Psychopathology and Behavioral Assessment, 32,* 438–447.

Rizvi, S. L., Brown, M. Z., Bohus, M., & Linehan, M. M. (2011). The role of shame in the development and treatment of borderline personality disorder. In R. L. Dearing & J. P. Tangney (Eds.), *Shame in the therapy hour* (pp. 237–259). American Psychological Association.

Rizvi, S. L., & Linehan, M. M. (2005). The treatment of maladaptive shame in borderline personality disorder: A pilot study of opposite action. *Cognitive and Behavioral Practice, 12,* 437–447.

Rogers, C. R. (1957). The necessary and sufficient conditions of therapeutic personality change. *Journal of Consulting Psychology, 21,* 95–103.

Rohde-Dachser, C. (2020). *Spuren des Verlorenen: Beiträge zur klinischen Psychoanalyse und zur Geschlechterdifferenz* [Traces of what was lost: Contributions to clinical psychoanalysis and gender differences]. Psychosozial-Verlag.

Rohde-Dachser, C. (2021). *Was sich verändert und was bleibt: Psychoanalytische Beiträge über Vergänglichkeit, den Wunsch nach Unsterblichkeit und das Leben im Augenblick* [What changes and what remains: Psychoanalytic contributions on transience, the desire for immortality and living in the moment]. Psychosozial-Verlag.

Roitmann, N. C. (2021). KAT ved skyld og skam [CBT in relation to guilt and shame] In M. Arendt & N. K. Rosenberg (Eds.), *Kognitiv adfærdsterapi på tværs: Transdiagnostiske problemer og metoder* (pp. 357–382). Hans Reitzels Forlag.

Römer, I. (2017). Scham: Phänomenologische Überlegungen zu einem sozialtheoretischen Begriff [Shame: Phenomenological reflections on a social theoretical term]. *Gestalt Theory, 39,* 313–330.

Rosa, H. (2019). *Resonance: A sociology of our relationship to the world* (J. Wagner, Trans.). Wiley. (Original work published 2016.)

Rosa, H. (2022). *Demokratie braucht Religion* [Democracy needs religion]. Kösel.

Röst, R. (2021). *Grundvold* [Foundations]. Gyldendal.

Rüsch, N., Corrigan, P. W., Bohus, M., Jacob, G. A., Brueck, R., & Lieb, K. (2007). Measuring shame and guilt by self-report questionnaires: A validation study. *Psychiatry Research, 150,* 313–325.

Rüsch, N., Corrigan, P. W., Bohus, M., Kühler, T., Jacob, G. A., & Lieb, K. (2007). The impact of posttraumatic stress disorder on dysfunctional implicit and explicit emotions among women with borderline personality disorder. *Journal of Nervous and Mental Disease, 195*, 537–539.

Rüsch, N., Lieb, K., Göttler, I., Hermann, C., Schramm, E., Richter, H., Jacob, G. A., Corrigan, P. W., & Bohus, M. D. (2007). Shame and implicit self-concept in women with borderline personality disorder. *American Journal of Psychiatry, 164*, 500–508.

Rutishauser, B. (1969). *Max Schelers Phänomenologie des Fühlens: Einer kritische Analyse seiner Analyse von Scham und Schamgefühl* [Max Scheler's Phenomenology of Feeling: A critical analysis of his analysis of shame and the feeling of shame]. Francke Verlag .

Sadek, N. (2017). Islamophobia, shame, and the collapse of Muslim identities. *International Journal of Applied Psychoanalytic Studies, 14*, 200–221.

Safran, J. D., & Muran, J. C. (2000). *Negotiating the therapeutic alliance: A relational treatment guide*. Guilford Press.

Sandel, M. (2020). *The tyranny of merit: What's become of the common good?* Allen Lane.

Sanders, O. (2009). In die Schamlosigkeit pendeln – ein durch Adorno inspirierter Versuch über Entwicklungen in Nahverkehr und Universität [Commuting into shamelessness – an Adorno-inspired attempt at developments in local transport and universities]. In A. Schäfer & C. Thompson (Eds.), *Scham* (pp. 119–141). Ferdinand Schöningh.

Sanftner, J. L., & Tantillo, M. (2011). Body image and eating disorders: A compelling source of shame for women. In R. L. Dearing & J. P. Tangney (Eds.), *Shame in the therapy hour* (pp. 277–304). American Psychological Association.

Saraiya, T., & Lopez-Castro, T. (2016). Ashamed and afraid: A scoping review of the role of shame in post-traumatic stress disorder (PTSD). *Journal of Clinical Medicine, 5*, 94.

Sartre, J.-P. (2018). *Being and nothingness: An essay on phenomenological ontology* (S. Richmond, Trans.). Simon and Schuster. (Original work published 1943.)

Sassenfeld, A. (2015). *Relationale Psychotherapie: Grundlagen und klinische Prinzipien* [Relational psychotherapy: Basics and clinical principles]. Psychosozial-Verlag.

Schäfer, A., & Thompson, C. (2009). Scham – eine Einführung [Shame – an introduction]. In A. Schäfer & C. Thompson (Eds.), *Scham* (pp. 7–36). Ferdinand Schöningh.

Schafer, R. (1997). *Tradition and change in psychoanalysis*. New International Universities Press.

Scheel, C. N., Bender, C., Tuschen-Caffier, B., Brodführer, A., Matthies, S., Hermann, C., Geisse, E. K., Svaldi, J., Brakemeier, E.-L., Philipsen, A., & Jacob, G. A. (2014). Do patients with different mental disorders show specific aspects of shame. *Psychiatry Research, 220*, 490–495.

Scheel, C. N., Bender, C., Tuschen-Caffier, B., & Jacob, G. A. (2013). SHAME: Entwicklung eines Fragebogens zur Erfassung positiver und negativer Aspekte von Scham [SHAME: Development of a questionnaire to record positive and negative aspects of shame]. *Zeitschrift für Klinische Psychologie und Psychotherapie, 42*, 280–290.

Scheel, C. N., Eisenbarth, H., & Rentzsch, K. (2020). Assessment of different dimensions of shame proneness: Validation of the SHAME. *Assessment, 27*, 1699–1717.

Scheel, C. N., Schneid, E.-M., Tuescher, O., Lieb, K., Tuschen-Caffier, B., & Jacob, G. A. (2013). Effect of shame induction in borderline personality disorder. *Cognitive Therapy Research, 37*, 1160–1168.

Scheff, T. J. (1994). *Bloody revenge: Emotions, nationalism, and war*. Westview Press.

Scheff, T. J. (2003). Shame in self and society. *Symbolic Interaction, 26*, 239–262.

Scheff, T. J. (2007). Runaway nationalism: Alienation, shame, and anger. In J. L. Tracy, R. W. Robins, & J. P. Tangney (Eds.), *The self-conscious emotions: Theory and research* (pp. 426–440). Guilford Press.

Scheff, T. J. (2011). The ubiquity of hidden shame in modernity. *Cultural Sociology, 8*, 129–141.

Scheff, T. J., Daniel, G. R., & Sterphone, J. (2018). Shame and the theory of war and violence. *Aggression and Violent Behavior, 39*, 109–115.

Scheff, T. J., & Retzinger, S. M. (1991). *Emotions and violence: Shame and rage in destructive conflicts*. Lexington Books.

Scheler, M. (1957). Über Scham und Schamgefühle [Shame and feelings of shame]. In *Schriften aus dem Nachlass* (Vol.1, pp. 65–155). Francke Verlag.

Scheler, M. (1994). *Ressentiment*. Marquette University Press. (Original work published 1912.)

Schlander, C. (2020). *Compassion-fokuseret terapi i praksis* [Compassion-focused therapy in practice]. Hans Reitzels Forlag.

Schlander, C. (2021). Udfordringer med selvomsorg [Challenges with self-care]. In M. Arendt & N. K. Rosenberg (Eds.), *Kognitiv adfærdsterapi på tværs: Transdiagnostiske problemer og metoder* (pp. 403–420). Hans Reitzels Forlag.

Schlossberger, M. (2000). Philosophie der Scham [Philosophy of shame]. *Deutsche Zeitschrift für Philosophie, 48*, 807–829.

Schmetkamp, S. (2012). *Respekt und Anerkennung* [Respect and recognition]. Mentis.

Schmidt, L.-H. (2006). *Om vreden* [On anger]. Danmarks Pædagogiske Universitetsforlag.

Schneider, C. D. (1987). A mature sense of shame. In D. L. Nathanson (Ed.), *The many faces of shame* (pp. 194–213). Guilford Press.

Schoenleber, M., & Berenbaum, H. (2010). Shame aversion and shame-proneness in cluster C personality disorders. *Journal of Abnormal Psychology, 119*, 197–205.

Schoenleber, S., & Berenbaum, H. (2012a). Shame regulation in personality pathology. *Journal of Abnormal Psychology, 121*, 433–446.

Schoenleber, S., & Berenbaum, H. (2012b). Aversion and proneness to shame in self- and informant-reported personality disorder symptoms. *Personality Disorders: Theory, Research, and Treatment, 3*, 294–304.

Schoenleber, M., Berenbaum, H., & Motl, R. (2014). Shame-related functions and motivations for self-injurious behavior. *Personality Disorders: Theory, Research, and Treatment, 5*, 204–211.

Schreiber, J. M. (2022). *Ich möchte lieber nicht: Eine rebellion gegen den terror des Positiven* [I'd rather not: A rebellion against the terror of positivity]. Piper Verlag.

Schultz-Venrath, U. (2022). Mentalizing shame, shamelessness and Fremdscham (shame by proxy) in groups. In O. R. Epstein (Ed.), *Shame matters: Attachment and relational perspectives for psychotherapists* (pp. 90–114). Routledge.

Schüttauf, K. (2008). Die zwei Gesichter der Scham [The two faces of shame]. *Psyche, 62*, 840–865.

Scott, L. N., Stepp, S. D., Hallquist, M. N., Whalen, D. J., Wright, A. G. C., & Pilkonis, P. A. (2015). Daily shame and hostile irritability in adolescent girls with borderline personality disorder symptoms. *Personality Disorders: Theory, Research, and Treatment, 6*, 53–63.

Scott, L. N., Wright, A. G. C., Beeney, J. E., Lazarus, S. A., Pilkonis, P. A., & Stepp, S. D. (2017). Borderline personality disorder symptoms and aggression: A within-person process model. *Journal of Abnormal Psychology, 126*, 429–440.

Seidler, G. H. (2000). *In Others' Eyes: An Analysis of Shame* (A. Jenkins, Trans.). Verlag International Universities Press. (Original work published 1995.)

Sekowski, M., Gambin, M., Cudo, A., Wozniak-Prus, M., Penner, F., Fonagy, P., & Sharp, C. (2020). The relations between childhood maltreatment, sham, guilt, depression and suicidal ideation in inpatient adolescents. *Journal of Affective Disorders, 276,* 667–677.

Sennett, R. (1974). *Verfall und Ende des öffentlichen Lebens: Die Tyrannei der Intimität* [Decay and end of public life: The tyranny of intimacy]. Fischer Verlag.

Sennett, R. (2002). *Respekt im Zeitalter der Ungleichheit* [Respect in the age of inequality]. Berlin Verlag.

Shah, A. (2015). The cultural faces of shame. In S. Akhtar (Ed.), *Shame: Developmental, cultural, and clinical realms* (pp. 49–70). Routledge.

Shanahan, S., Jones, J., & Thomas-Peter, B. (2011). Are you looking at me, or am I? Anger, aggression, shame and self-worth in violent individuals. *Journal of Rational-Emotive, & Cognitive-Behavior Therapy, 29*(2), 77–91.

Sheehy, K., Noureen, A., Khaliq, A., Dhingra, K., Husain, N., Pontin, E. E., Cawley, R., & Taylor, P. J. (2019). An examination of the relationship between shame, guilt and self-harm: A systematic review and meta-analysis. *Clinical Psychology Review, 73,* 1–13.

Skårderud, F. (1998). *Uro: En reise i det moderne selvet* [Unrest: A journey in the modern self]. Aschehoug.

Skårderud, F. (2001a). Tapte ansigter [Lost faces]. In T. Wyller (Ed.), *Skam: Perspektiver på skam, ære og skamløshet i det moderne* (pp. 37–52). Fagbokforlaget.

Skårderud, F. (2001b). Det tragiske mennesket [The tragic human being]. In T. Wyller (Ed.), *Skam: Perspektiver på skam, ære og skamløshet i det moderne* (pp. 53–67). Fagbokforlaget.

Skårderud, F. (2001c). Skammens stemmer – om taushet, veltalenhet og raseri i behandlingsrommet [The voices of shame – about silence, eloquence and rage in the treatment room]. *Tidsskriftet for Den norske legeforening, 121,* 1613–1617.

Skårderud, F. (2003). Shame in cyberspace: Relationships without faces: The e-media and eating disorders. *European Eating Disorders Review, 11,* 155–169.

Skårderud, F. (2007). Shame and pride in anorexia nervosa: A qualitative descriptive study. *European Eating Disorders Review, 15,* 81–97.

Skårderud, F., Sommerfeldt, B., & Robinson, P. (2018). *Hunger: Mentalization-based treatments for eating disorders.* Springer.

Slimani, L. (2018). *Sex und Lügen: Gespräche mit Frauen aus der islamischen Welt* [Sex and lies: Conversations with women from the Islamic world]. Btb Verlag.

Smarsh, S. (2018). *Heartland: A memoir of working hard and being broke in the richest country on earth.* Scribner.

Soiland, T. (2022). Geniessen als Faktor des Politischen: Psychoanalytische Zugänge zur Gegenwart: Eine Einleitung [Enjoyment as a political factor: Psychoanalytic approaches to the present: An introduction]. In T. Soiland, M. Frühauf, & A. Hartmann. *Postödipale Gesellschaft, bd.1* (pp. 9–51). Turia + Kant.

Solomon, J. (2022). Shame as a behavioral system: Its links to attachment, defence and dysregulation. In O. R. Epstein (Ed.), *Shame matters: Attachment and relational perspectives for psychotherapists* (pp. 6–21). Routledge.

Sørensen, L. J. (2013). *Skam: Medfødt og tillært: Når skam fører til sjælemord* [Shame: Innate and learned: When shame leads to soul murder]. Hans Reitzels Forlag.

Spitzen, T. L., Tull, M. T., Baer, M. M., Dixon-Gordon, K. L., Champman, A. L., & Gratz, K. L. (2020). Predicting engagement in nonsuicidal self-injury (NSS) over the course of 12 months: The roles of borderline personality disorder pathology and emotional consequences of NSSI. *Journal of affective disorders, 277*, 631–639.

Stadter, M. (2011). The inner world of shaming: An object relations perspective and therapeutic approach. In R. L. Dearing & J. P. Tangney (Eds.), *Shame in the therapy hour* (pp. 45–68). American Psychological Association.

Stanghellini, G., & Mancini, M. (2018). The life-world of persons with borderline personality disorder. In G. Stanghellini, M. Broome, A. Raballo, A. V. Fernandez, P. Fusar-Poli, & R. Rosfort (Eds.), *The Oxford handbook of phenomenological psychopathology* (pp. 665–681). Oxford University Press.

Starck, A., & Weiß, H. (2021). Scham und Schuld in der psychoanalytischen Theorieentwicklung – ihre Rolle beim Zwang [Shame and guilt in psychoanalytic theory development – their role in coercion]. *Persönlichkeitsstörungen, 25*, 3–17.

Stearns, P. N. (2016). Shame, and the challenge for emotions history. *Emotion Review, 8*, 197–206.

Steinberg, B. S. (1991). Psychoanalytic concepts in international politics: The role of shame and humiliation. *International Review of Psychoanalysis, 18*, 65–85.

Steiner, J. (2006). *Narzisstische Einbrüche: Sehen und Gesehenwerden: Scham und Verlegenheit bei pathologischen Persönlichkeitsorganisationen* [Narcissistic collapses: seeing and being seen: Shame and embarrassment in pathological personality organizations]. Klett-Cotta Verlag.

Stern, D. N. (1985). *The interpersonal world of the infant*. Karnac.

Stern, D. N. (2004). *The present moment in psychotherapy and everyday life*. W. W. Norton.

Streeck, U., & Leichsenring, F. (2015). *Handbuch psychoanalytisch-interaktionelle Therapie: Behandlung von strukturellen Störungen und schweren Persönlichkeitsstörungen* [Handbook of psychoanalytic-interactional therapy: Treatment of structural disorders and severe personality disorders]. Vandenhoeck & Ruprecht.

Streeck-Fischer, A. (2021). *Jugendliche zwischen Krise und Störung: Herausforderungen für die psychodynamische Psychotherapie* [Adolescents between crisis and disorder: Challenges for psychodynamic psychotherapy]. Schattauer Verlag.

Strenger, C. (1989). The classic and the romantic vision of psychoanalysis. *International Journal of Psychoanalysis, 70*, 593–610.

Stuewig, J., & McCloskey, L. A. (2005). The relation of child maltreatment to shame and guilt among adolescents: Psychological routes to depression and delinquency. *Child Maltreatment, 10*, 324–336.

Stuewig, J., Tangney, J. P., Heigel, C., Harty, L., & McCloskey, L. (2010). Shaming, blaming, and maiming: Functional links among moral emotions, externalization of blame, and aggression. *Journal of Research in Personality, 44*, 91–102.

Stuewig, J., Tangney, J. P., Kendall, S., Folk, C. R., & Dearing, R. L. (2015). Children's proneness to shame and guilt predict risky and illegal behaviors in young adulthood. *Child Psychiatry and Human Development, 46*, 217–227.

Sundhedsstyrelsen (2022). *Den nationale sundhedsprofil 2021* [The national health profile 2021]. Statens Institut for Folkesundhed.

Szentagotai-Tatar, A., & Miu, A. C. (2016). Individual differences in emotion regulation, childhood trauma and proneness to shame and guilt in adolescence. *PLoS ONE, 11*, e0167299.

Tangney, J. P., & Dearing, R. L. (2002). *Shame and guilt*. Guilford Press.

Tangney, J. P., & Dearing, R. L. (2011). Working with shame in the therapy hour. In R. L. Dearing & J. P. Tangney (Eds.), *Shame in the therapy hour* (pp. 375–404). American Psychological Association.

Tangney, J. P., Dearing, R. L., Wagner, P. E., & Gramzow, R. (2000). *The test of self-conscious affect-3*. George Mason University.

Tangney, J. P., Stuewig, J., & Mashek, D. J. (2007). What's moral about the self-conscious emotions? In J. L. Tracy, R. W. Robins & J. P. Tangney (Eds.), *The self-conscious emotions: Theory and research* (pp. 21–37). Guilford Press.

Tangney, J. P., Wagner, P., Fletcher, C., & Gramzow, R. (1992). Shame into anger? The relation of shame and guilt to anger and self-reported aggression. *Journal of Personality and Social Psychology, 62,* 669–675.

Tangney, J. P., Wagner, P., & Gramzow, R. (1992). Proneness to shame, proneness to guilt, and psychopathology. *Journal of Abnormal Psychology, 101,* 469–478.

Tangney, J. P., Wagner, P. E., Hill-Barlow, D., Marschall, D. E., & Gramzow, R. (1996). Relation of shame and guilt to constructive versus destructive responses to anger across the lifespan. *Journal of Personality and Social Psychology, 70,* 797–809.

Tangney, J. P., Wagner, P. E., Hill-Barlow, D., Marschall, D. E., & Gramzow, R. (2006). Relation of shame and guilt to constructive versus destructive responses to anger across the lifespan. *Journal of Personality and Social Psychology, 70,* 797–809.

Taylor, T. F. (2015). The influence of shame on posttrauma disorders: Have we failed to see the obvious? *European Journal of Psychotraumatology, 6,* 28847.

Thater, D. (Artist) (1998). The best animals are the flat animals – the best space is the deep space. Solo show, Mak Center for Art + Architecture, Los Angeles, CA, 28 October–17 January, 1999.

Theweleit, K. (2019). *Männerphantasien* [Male fantasies]. Matthes, & Seitz Verlag.

Tiedemann, J. L. (2010). *Die Scham, das Selbst und der Andere: Psychodynamik und Therapie von Schamkonflikten* [Shame, the self and the other: Psychodynamics and therapy of shame conflicts]. Psychosozial-Verlag.

Tiedemann, J. L. (2013). *Scham* [Shame]. Psychosozial-Verlag .

Tignor, S. M., & Colvin, C. R. (2017). The interpersonal adaptiveness of dispositional guilt and shame: A meta-analytic investigation. *Journal of Personality, 85,* 341–363.

Tisseron, S. (2000). *Phänomen Scham: Psychoanalyse eines sozialen Affektes* (R. Tiffert, Trans.). Ernst Reinhardt Verlag. (Original work published 1992.)

Tolstoy, L. (2002). *Anna Karenina* (R. Pevear and L. Volkohonsky, Trans.). Penguin Books. (Original work published 1878.)

Tomkins, S. S. (1963). *Affect, imagery, consciousness: Vol. II: The negative affects.* Springer.

Tomkins, S. S. (1987). Shame. In D. L. Nathanson (Ed.), *The many faces of shame* (pp. 133–161). Guilford Press.

Tracy, J. L., & Robins, R.W. (2007). The self-conscious emotions. A cognitive appraisal approach. In J. L. Tracy, R. W. Robins, & J. P. Tangney (Eds.), *The self-conscious emotions: Theory and research* (pp. 3–20). Guilford Press.

Treurniet, N. (1996). Über eine Ethik der psychoanalytischen Technik [On an ethics of psychoanalytic technique]. *Psyche, 50,* 1–31.

Troop, N. A., Allan, S., Serpell, L., & Treasure, J. L. (2008). Shame in women with a history of eating disorders. *European Eating Disorders Review, 16,* 480–488.

Troop, N. A., & Redshaw, C. (2012). General shame and bodily shame in eating disorders: A 2.5 year longitudinal study. *European Eating Disorder Review, 20,* 373–378.

Trump, M. (2020). *Too much and never enough: How my family created the world's most dangerous man.* Simon & Schuster.

Tugendhat, E. (1993). *Vorlesungen über Ethik* [Lectures on ethics]. Suhrkamp Verlag.

Tyler, I. (2020). *Stigma: The machinery of inequality.* Zed Books.

Unoka, Z., & Vizin, G. (2017). To see in a mirror dimly: The looking glass self is self-shaming in borderline personality disorder. *Psychiatry Research, 258,* 322–329.

Vaillant, G. E. (1993). *The wisdom of the ego.* Harvard University Press.

VanDerhei, S., Rojahn, J., Stuewig, J., & McKnight, P. E. (2013). The effect of shame-proneness, guilt-proneness, and internalizing tendencies on nonsuicidal self-injury. *Suicide and Life-Threatening Behavior, 44,* 317–330.

Velotti, P., Elison, J., & Garofalo, C. (2014). Shame and aggression: Different trajectories and implications. *Aggression and Violent Behavior, 19,* 454–461.

Velotti, P., Garofalo, C., Bottazzi, F., & Caretti, V. (2017). Faces of shame: Implications for self-esteem, emotion regulation, aggression, and well-being. *Journal of Psychology, 151,* 171–184.

Velotti, P., Rogier, G., & Sarlo, A. (2020). Pathological narcissism and aggression: The mediating role of difficulties in the regulation of negative emotions. *Personality and Individual Differences, 155,* 109757.

Vescio, T. K., Schermerhorn, N. E. C, Gallagos, J. M., & Laubach, M. L. (2021). The affective consequences of threats to masculinity. *Journal of Experimental Social Psychology, 97,* 104195.

Vizin, G., Urban, R., & Unoka, Z. (2016). Shame, trauma, temperament and psychopathology: Construct validity of the experience of shame scale. *Psychiatry Research, 246,* 62–69.

Walser, M. (1998). *Dankesrede von Martin Walser zur Verleihung des Friedenspreises des Deutschen Buchhandels in der Frankfurter Paulskirche am 11. Oktober 1998* [Martin Walser's acceptance speech for the Peace Prize of the German Book Trade in the Paulskirche in Frankfurt on October 11, 1998]. https://hdms.bsz-bw.de/frontd oor/deliver/index/docId/440/file/walserRede.pdf

Watkins, M. (2018). The social and political life of shame: The U.S. 2016 presidential election. *Psychoanalytic Perspectives, 15,* 25–37.

Watson, S., Gomez, R., & Gullone, E. (2017). The shame and guilt scales of the test of self-conscious affect-adolescent (TOSCA-A): Factor structure, concurrent and discriminant validity, and measurement and structural invariance across ratings of males and females. *Assessment, 24,* 517–527.

Weiß, H. (2008). Groll, Scham und Zorn: Überlegungen zur Differenzierung Narzisstischer Zustände [Resentment, shame and anger: Considerations for differentiating narcissistic states]. *Psyche, 62,* 866–886.

Weiß, H. (2017). *Trauma, Schuldgefühl und Wiedergutmachung: Wie Affekte innere Entwicklung ermöglichen* [Trauma, guilt and reparation: How affects enable inner development]. Klett-Cotta Verlag.

Weiß, H. (2019). Sehen und Gesehenwerden: Zur Dialektik des Schamerlebens [Seeing and being seen: On the dialectics of the experience of shame]. *Psychosozial, 157,* 20–30.

Weston, M. C. (2008). *Fra skam til selvrespekt* [From shame to self-respect]. Dansk Psykologisk Forlag.

Wicker, F. W., Payne, G. C., & Morgan, R. D. (1983). Participant descriptions of guilt and shame. *Motivation and Emotion, 7,* 25–39.

Widmer, P. (2009). Vom Mysterium zum Sprachversagen: Lacans Beiträge zur Scham [From mystery to language failure: Lacan's contributions to shame]. In A. Schäfer & C. Thompson (Eds.), *Scham* (pp. 51–75). Ferdinand Schöningh.

Wiklander, M., Samuelson, M., Jokinen, J., Nilsonne, Å., Wilchek, A., Rylander, G., & Åsberg, M. (2012). Shame-proneness in attempted suicide patients. *BMC Psychiatry, 12*, 50.

Wilde, O. (1891). *The picture of Dorian Gray*. Penguin Classics.

Wilden, A. (1968). Lacan and the discourse of the other. In J. Lacan (1968). *Speech and language in psychoanalysis* (pp. 157–313). Johns Hopkins University Press.

Wilkinson, R., & Pickett, K. (2009). *The spirit level: Why more equal societies almost always do better*. Allen Lane.

Williams, B. (2008). *Shame and necessity*. University of California Press.

Wilson, E. (1987). Shame and the other: Reflections on the theme of shame in French psychoanalysis. In D. L. Nathanson (Ed.), *The many faces of shame* (pp. 162–193). Guilford Press.

Winnicott, D. W. (1949). Hate in the countertransference. *International Journal of Psychoanalysis, 30*, 69–74.

Winnicott, D. W. (1971). *Playing and reality*. Routledge.

Winter, D., Koplin, K., & Lis, S. (2015). Can't stand the look in the mirror? Self-awareness avoidance in borderline personality disorder. *Borderline Personality Disorder and Emotion Dysregulation, 2*, 13.

Wirth, H-J. (2002). *Narzissmus und Macht: Zur Psychoanalyse seelischer Störungen in der Politik* [Narcissism and power: On the psychoanalysis of mental disorders in politics]. Psychosozial-Verlag.

Wong, V. Z., Christian, C., Hunt, R. A., & Levinson, C. A. (2020). Network investigation of eating disorder symptoms and positive and negative affect in clinical eating disorder sample. *International Journal of Eating Disorders, 54*, 1202–1212.

Wong, Y., & Tsai, J. (2007). Cultural models of shame and guilt. In J. L. Tracy, R. W. Robins, & J. P. Tangney (Eds.), *The self-conscious emotions: Theory and research* (pp. 209–223). Guilford Press.

Wurmser, L. (1981a). Das Problem der Scham [The problem of shame]. *Psyche, 13*, 11–35.

Wurmser, L. (1981b). *The mask of shame*. Johns Hopkins University Press.

Wurmser, L. (1986). Die innere Grenze – das Schamgefühl: Ein Beitrag zur Überich-Analyse [The inner boundary: The feeling of shame – a contribution to superego analysis]. *Psyche, 18*, 16–41.

Wurmser, L. (1987). Shame: The veiled companion of narcissism. In D. L. Nathansons (Ed.), *The many faces of shame* (pp. 64–92). Guilford Press.

Wurmser, L. (1993). *Das Rätsel des Masochismus: Psychoanalytische Untersuchungen von Über-Ich-Konflikten und Masochismus* [The mystery of masochism: Psychoanalytical studies of superego conflicts and masochism]. Springer Verlag.

Wurmser, L. (1994). Die doppelte Wirklichkeit: Die Phänomene von Spaltung und Sexualisierung bei schwerer Traumatisierung [Dual reality: The phenomena of splitting and sexualization in severe traumatization]. *Psychoanalyse im Widerspruch, 12*, 25–43.

Wurmser, L. (1997). The shame about existing: A comment about the analysis of moral masochism. In M. R. Lansky & A. P. Morrison (Eds.), *The widening scope of shame* (pp. 367–382). Psychology Press.

Wurmser, L. (1999). Man of the most dangerous curiosity: Nietzsche's fruitful and frightful vision and his war against shame. In J. Adamson & H. Clarke (Eds.), *Scenes of shame: Psychoanalysis, shame and writing* (pp. 111–146). SUNY.

Wurmser, L. (2008). Scham, Rache, Ressentiment und Verzeihung [Shame, revenge, ressentiment and forgiveness]. *Psyche, 62*, 962–989.

Wurmser, L. (2015). Primary shame, mortal wound and tragic circularity: Some new reflections on shame and shame conflicts. *International Journal of Psychoanalysis, 96*, 1615–1634.

Wurmser, L. (2019). *Scham und der böse Blick: Verstehen der negativen therapeutischen Reaktion* [Shame and the evil eye: Understanding the negative therapeutic response]. Kohlhammer Verlag.

Yeomans, F. E., Clarkin, J. F., & Kernberg, O. F. (2015). *Transference-focused psychotherapy for borderline personality disorder*. American Psychiatric Publishing.

You, S., Talbot, N. L., & Conner, K. R. (2012). Emotions and suicidal ideation among depressed women with childhood sexual abuse histories. *Suicide and Life-Threatening Behavior, 42*, 244–254.

Young, J., Klosko, J. S., & Weishaar, M. E. (2003). *Schema therapy: A practitioner's guide*. Guilford Press.

Zabel, L. (2019). *Narzisstische Depression. Theorie und Konzepte in Psychiatrie und Psychoanalyse* [Narcissistic depression. Theory and concepts in psychiatry and psychoanalysis]. Psychosozial-Verlag.

Zahavi, D. (2013). Scham als soziales Gefühl [Shame as social feeling]. *Phenomenologische Forschungen, 2013*, 319–337.

Zahavi, D. (2014). *Self and other: Exploring subjectivity, empathy, and shame*. Oxford University Press.

Zweig, S. (2016). *Impatience of the heart*. Penguin Press. (Original work published 1939.)

Index

Note: Entries in **bold** refer to tables.

For Product Safety Concerns and Information please contact our EU
representative GPSR@taylorandfrancis.com
Taylor & Francis Verlag GmbH, Kaufingerstraße 24, 80331 München, Germany

Young People, Social Capital and Ethnic Identity

Edited by
Tracey Reynolds

Routledge
Taylor & Francis Group

LONDON AND NEW YORK

First published 2011
by Routledge
2 Park Square, Milton Park, Abingdon, Oxfordshire OX14 4RN

Simultaneously published in the USA and Canada
by Routledge
711 Third Avenue, New York, NY 10017

First issued in paperback 2016

Routledge is an imprint of the Taylor & Francis Group, an informa business

This book is a reproduction of *Ethnic and Racial Studies*, vol. 33, issue 5. The Publisher requests to those authors who may be citing this book to state, also, the bibliographical details of the special issue on which the book was based.

Typeset in Times New Roman by Taylor & Francis Books

British Library Cataloguing in Publication Data
A catalogue record for this book is available from the British Library

ISBN 13: 978-1-138-98742-5 (pbk)
ISBN 13: 978-0-415-55211-0 (hbk)

Disclaimer
The publisher would like to make readers aware that the chapters in this book are referred to as articles as they had been in the special issue. The publisher accepts responsibility for any inconsistencies that may have arisen in the course of preparing this volume for print.